Man t
Control
in
Nonprofit
Organizations

MW01628615

Ninth Edition

David W. Young, D.B.A.
Professor Emeritus
Health Sector Management Program
Public and Nonprofit Management Program
School of Management
Boston University

The Crimson Press
Cambridge, Massachusetts

The Crimson Press

A Division of The Crimson Group, Inc.

MANAGEMENT CONTROL IN NONPROFIT ORGANIZATIONS
Ninth Edition

Published by The Crimson Press, a division of The Crimson Group, Inc.,
1770 Massachusetts Avenue, Suite 323, Cambridge, Massachusetts 02140.

Copyright © 2012 by The Crimson Group, Inc.

All rights reserved. No part of this publication may be reproduced or distributed in any form or by any means, or stored in a database or retrieval system, including but not limited to, network or other electronic storage or transmission, or broadcast for distance learning, without the prior written consent of The Crimson Group, Inc.

ISBN 978-0-578-09943-9
Library of Congress Control Number: 2011946258

Preface

The first edition of this book was published in 1975 by Robert N. Anthony and Regina Herzlinger, both of whom were on the faculty of the Harvard Business School. It was a text-only book, although there was a supplement that contained readings and suggested cases for instructors to use in the classroom. The text was 355 pages long, and won the 1977 James A. Hamilton Award from the American College of Healthcare Executives, an award given annually to the author(s) of a management or healthcare book judged outstanding by ACHE's Book of the Year Committee.

The revised edition (by the same two authors) was published in 1980. Unlike the first edition, it had several cases following each chapter and was 600 pages long. Shortly after it was published, Regina Herzlinger decided to pursue other activities, and Bob Anthony asked me to assume the role of second author. I thus became involved with the third edition, which was published in 1984. I remained the second author through 2003, when the seventh edition was published. In 2007, one year after Bob's death (at the age of 90), I prepared the eighth edition, which was published in 2008.

EVOLUTION FROM THE THIRD TO THE NINTH EDITION

Many changes have been to the book during the almost 30 years that have transpired between the third edition and this one. New chapters have been introduced, others have had their content expanded. New concepts and techniques (such as activity-based costing) have been included as they emerged in the literature and seemed applicable to nonprofit organizations.

The second through the seventh edition contained many cases that were designed to be used in the classroom. For the eighth edition, due to the book's growing length (and cost!), all cases were eliminated except the practice cases at the end of several technical chapters. This edition continues with that policy. Instructors may design a customized set of cases for their courses, and order them from The Crimson Press Curriculum Center, or from other sources if they wish.

Curriculum Center Cases at No Charge. Instructors who adopt the book for a university course or an executive education program may obtain cases published by The Crimson Press Curriculum Center at no charge. This arrangement applies only to cases contained in the collection of The Crimson Press Curriculum Center. It does not apply to the Center's background notes, nor to cases ordered from other sources.

Cases ordered from The Crimson Press Curriculum Center will be sent to the instructor as an E-Packet. This is a PDF file that may be uploaded to a course Web site for use by students, or printed out and distributed to them in hard copy format.

Obtaining Cases. An Appendix at the end of the book lists the cases that were in prior editions, plus others that have been written during the past several years. The cases are organized by chapter, with the level of difficulty and sector focus shown. All of these cases can be ordered from The Crimson Press Curriculum Center: *www.thecrimsongroup.org* (click on *Curriculum Center).* Other sources for cases include:

> **The John F. Kennedy School's Case Program.** Here, instructors can find cases on government and nonprofit organizations.
>
> **Harvard Business School Publishing.** Cases on nonprofit organizations also can be found at Harvard Business School Publishing, Go to:
> *http://harvardbusinessonline.hbsp.harvard.edu*

Case Books. There also are several case books that instructors may wish to consider. These can be found most easily by going to *www.Amazon.com* and searching on the topic "nonprofit organizations."

USE OF THE BOOK

Courses for which this text has been designed have existed for over 40 years in many universities. As the field of management control in nonprofit organizations has developed, ideas about the material in this book have evolved. In addition, in the four years that have passed since the eighth edition was published, a great deal of literature has emerged relating to both the management of nonprofit organizations in general, and management control in those organizations in particular. At the same time, many changes have taken place in the environments of most nonprofit organizations, forcing many of them to rethink the way they conduct their operations.

As a result of these developments, several substantive changes have been made to the book's content. Organizationally, the book remains structured into three parts—introduction, management control principles, and management control systems. Most chapters have been rewritten, however, some more than others, and some appendices have been added or updated. Several of the chapters introduce some new concepts being developed in both the management field in general, and management accounting and control in particular. The book looks at how these emerging concepts relate to the management control effort in nonprofit organizations.

Not Just Accounting

As instructors who have used earlier editions know, this is not primarily a book on accounting. Rather, its focus is much broader, dealing with accounting matters only as they relate to more general management issues in nonprofit organizations. Such a course, usually titled something close to the title of the book, is often offered by an accounting department, but the book also has been used in courses offered by economics and finance departments, and by management departments in schools of education, medicine, public health, social work, theology, and public administration.

Although written to apply to all types of nonprofit organizations, including governmental entities, the book can easily be adapted to a course that focuses on a single type, such as education or health care. This can be accomplished by the selection of cases appropriate to that type. The book also may be used in short programs designed for nonprofit organization managers. The selection of chapters and cases for such programs depends on the nature of the short program. In one type of program, the principal topics of the whole book may be discussed; in another type, the focus might be on a specific area of management control, such as programming, budgeting, or program evaluation. Finally, the book also has been used by individual managers in nonprofit organizations as background reading or for reference purposes.

ACKNOWLEDGMENTS

Much of the content of the text was originally written by Bob Anthony. Over the years, the material has been amended, tweaked, and updated, but the essence of many chapters is still his. Regina Herzlinger made significant contributions to the first two editions, and much of what remains in several chapters no doubt was prepared by her. I am thankful to both of them, not only for the content of theirs that remains, but also for the contributions they made to my knowledge about nonprofit organizations, and my general intellectual development.

Professor Leslie Breitner, of the Desautels Faculty of Management at McGill University, provided many suggestions on how the book's content could be improved. Professor Emanuele Padovani, of the Forlí campus of the University of Bologna, also made some valuable contributions to my thinking about, among other matters, issues of outsourcing and the managerial use of social indicators.

Several physicians who used previous editions of the book in conjunction with executive education programs at Harvard's School of Public Health, made suggestions that allowed me to either correct errors or (I hope!) improve the readability of the text. And, as is always the case, many students, through their case analysis and in-class discussions, contributed to my thinking about the material in several chapters.

I am most grateful for all of this assistance, although clearly responsibility for all errors, omissions, and turgidity remains mine.

Comments on the book are welcomed. Please send them to *DavidYoung204@cs.com*. To avoid having your E-mail deleted as spam, please use *Management Control Systems* as the subject.

David W. Young
Lexington, Massachusetts
December 2011

Brief Contents

Table of Contents

Part I

Introduction

Management control in nonprofit organizations—as an academic subject—has been taught in schools of business, public administration, social work, public health, education, and others for many years. Nevertheless, its concepts and techniques are not widely used, or, where used, are not always used appropriately.

Many nonprofit organizations continue to believe they can survive on the strength of their missions and their ability to attract increasing amounts of public and private support for their activities. Unfortunately, many are finding that the support they once enjoyed is waning, and that they must put a greater focus on management in general, and management control in particular.

This change in focus has been facilitated by a change in the prevailing attitude toward nonprofit management on the part of both the professionals who work in nonprofit organizations (such as physicians, nurses, educators, social workers, curators, and others) and the managers of these organizations (who frequently are professionals themselves). Most of these individuals now recognize the need for strong management skills, including skills in the area of management control.

This introductory part discusses the scope of the material covered in the book and the nature of the organizations to which it can be applied. Chapter 1 outlines the territory of the field of management control, indicating what it includes and, equally important, what it does not. Chapter 2 discusses the nature and size of nonprofit organizations, as well as the types of services they offer.

Chapter 1
The Management Control Function

All organizations, even the tiniest, engage in some form of management control. In large organizations, management control tends to be formal, whereas in smaller ones it often is quite informal. Management control has existed as long as organizations have been in existence. One of the earliest works on the subject was Chester Barnard's *The Functions of the Executive*.[1] Originally published in 1938, this landmark book dealt with management control as well as other management activities. Since then, managers and academics have contributed to the evolution and definition of principles for designing management control systems and carrying out the management control activity.

As with most principles of management, management control principles are incomplete, inconclusive, tentative, vague, contradictory, and inadequately supported by experimental or other evidence. Some initial "truths" have been proven wrong. Other principles, however, have shown considerable validity in terms of managerial and organizational performance, leading managers to take them into account at an increasing rate.

Most studies of management control have been conducted in for-profit businesses. Consequently, descriptions of management control tend to assume a profit orientation. This book, by contrast, looks at management control in nonprofit organizations. The underlying thesis is that the basic concepts of management control are the same in both for-profit and nonprofit organizations, but that, because of the special characteristics of nonprofit organizations, the way managers apply these concepts will differ in some important respects.

PLANNING AND CONTROL ACTIVITIES

Managers engage in a wide variety of activities. They lead, teach, organize, influence, plan, and control. This book focuses on the latter two activities. In the planning activity, managers decide what should be done and how to do it. In the control activity, they attempt to obtain the desired results.

There are three different types of planning and control activities: strategic planning, management control, and task control. Since the focus here is on management control, the other two types of activities are described only briefly. The purpose in doing so is to clarify the boundaries of management control.[2]

Strategic Planning

Senior management generally determines an organization's goals and the general nature of the activities needed to achieve them, or what Michael Porter calls the organization's strategy.[3] *Strategic*

[1] Chester I. Barnard, *The Functions of the Executive,* 30th anniversary ed. Cambridge, Mass.: Harvard University Press, 1968.

[2] For a more thorough description of these activities, see Robert N. Anthony, *The Management Control Function* Boston: Harvard Business School Press, 1988

[3] Michael E. Porter, "What is Strategy," *Harvard Business Review,* Nov-Dec, 1996.

planning is the process of deciding on these goals and activities. While goals tend to change slowly, the activities needed to attain them may change more frequently, generally whenever senior management perceives a threat to the organization's success, new programmatic opportunities, or a better way to achieve the goals. Since threats and opportunities do not arise in orderly, predictable ways, strategic planning decisions are not made according to a prescribed timetable. The strategic planning process therefore is essentially irregular and in many respects unsystematic.

Task Control

At the other extreme are the activities used in carrying out the day-to-day operations of the organization, in particular the performance of specific tasks. *Task control* is the process of assuring that these operations are carried out effectively and efficiently.

Task control activities vary with the nature of the organization's operations. In a hospital, for example, maintaining an adequate inventory in the pharmacy is task control. So is assuring adequate housekeeping on the wards, and the timely preparation of paychecks.

Many task control activities do not involve managers. If they are automated, they do not even involve human beings, except to assure that the task control activity is functioning properly and to deal with matters not included in the automated process. For example, many organizations with sizable inventories, such as hospitals, have a computer place a replacement order directly with the appropriate vendor whenever the quantity of an item on hand decreases to a preset limit.

Management Control

Management control sits between strategic planning and task control. It accepts the goals and activities determined in the strategic planning process as given, and focuses on the activities needed to attain them. As such, it attempts to assure that the organization's programs are effective and efficient. An effective program is one that moves the organization toward its goals. An efficient program is one that accomplishes its purposes at the lowest possible cost.

Unlike strategic planning, management control is regular and systematic, with steps repeated in a predictable way. And, unlike task control, which may not involve human beings, management control is fundamentally behavioral. It involves managers interacting with people in the organization, particularly other managers. In many nonprofit organizations, it involves managers interacting with the organization's professional staff.

In part, management control assists managers in deciding on the optimum allocation of resources. In this respect, it is governed by *economic* principles. Management control also looks at the influence of measurement and reporting systems on the behavior of managers, professionals, and others; in this respect, it is governed by *social psychology* principles. Clearly, the principles found in these two disciplines are quite different. Moreover, their relative importance to the management control activity varies greatly in different situations. One of the goals of this book is to help readers develop a critical eye, and an ability to ask the questions that will enable them to incorporate the optimal mix of economic and behavioral factors into their management control efforts.

THE CONTEXT FOR MANAGEMENT CONTROL

The way the management control activity is carried out in a given organization is influenced by that organization's external and internal environments. The external environment is important because management control must be concerned with matters such as the actions of customers or clients, the constraints imposed by funding providers and legislative bodies, and the customs and norms of the society in which the organization exists. The internal environment is important because management control affects, and is affected by, the organization's structure, its members' behavior, its information systems, and its cultural norms. Some of these internal aspects are discussed briefly here. They are discussed more fully in Part III.

Organizational Structure

Organizations can be structured in a variety of ways, generally determined by the tasks that managers and employees need to perform. Some organizations have a *functional* structure, in which employees and managers are grouped according to common tasks such as production, marketing, or finance. Other organizations have a *program* structure, in which employees and managers who perform different functions or tasks are grouped according to common programs or services. Still others have a *matrix* structure in which programs and functional responsibilities have equal or reasonably equal weight.[4]

The management control activity takes the existing organizational structure as given, and overlays it with a network of *responsibility centers*. A responsibility center is a group of people working toward some financial objective, and, with increasing frequency, toward some non-financial objectives as well. It is headed by a manager who is responsible for the actions of its members. The network of responsibility centers is called the *management control structure*. The management control structure is discussed briefly later in this chapter and in considerable detail in Chapter 6.

Organizational Relationships and Members' Behavior

Organizational units can be classified as either line or staff units. Line units are directly responsible for carrying out the work of the organization. Staff units provide advice and assistance to the line units. Line managers are the focal points in management control. Their judgment is incorporated into the approved plans, they must work with others to accomplish their objectives, and their performance is measured, in large part, by their responsibility center's performance.

Staff people collect, summarize, and present information that is useful in the management control activity. They also make calculations that translate management judgments into the format of the management control system. A staff unit may consist of many people; indeed, the control department may be one of the largest staff departments in an organization. However, the significant program and control decisions are made by line managers, not by staff people.

The person responsible for the design and operation of the management control system is the controller.[5] In practice, the controller may have other titles, such as chief financial officer or vice president of fiscal affairs.

The idea that the controller has a broader responsibility than merely keeping the books is widely accepted in for-profit organizations and in many nonprofit organizations as well. Not too long ago, controllers were called *chief accountants* and were expected to confine their activities to collecting and reporting financial information. With the development of formal management control systems, and the increased emphasis on information needed for planning and decision making, the controller's function broadened considerably.

Despite this broadened function, the controller is still a staff person. His or her job is to work with line managers to determine their information needs, and to provide them with the information

---

[4] For additional discussion, see Robert L. Burns, Elisabeth H. Bradley, and Bryan J. Weiner, *Shortell and Kaluzny's Health Care Management: Organization, Design, and Behavior*, 6th edition, Clifton Park, NY, Delmar Cengage Learning, 2012.

[5] This is the preferred term. However, in some organizations, the word is spelled *comptroller*. In any event, the term is always pronounced as if it were spelled controller. Pronouncing it "*compt* roller" is archaic.

they find helpful. Sometimes a line manager with a problem of inadequate resources is told to "see the controller." In making such a statement, senior management effectively has put the controller into a line capacity. The controller then becomes a *de facto* manager, with a corresponding diminution in the responsibility of the organization's regular line managers. This usually leads to less than optimal management of the whole organization.[6]

Information

As the above discussion suggests, an important part of management control is information. As with any resource, the information resource involves both costs and benefits. An important task for the controller working with responsibility center managers is to assure that the value of the information provided by the management control system exceeds the cost of collecting and disseminating it.

Information may be either quantitative or qualitative; a report that "Louise is doing a good job" is qualitative information. A report that "Louise delivered 25 hours of client service" is quantitative information. Quantitative information may be either monetary or nonmonetary. A report that "Thelma earned $200" is monetary, while a report that "Thelma worked 15 hours" is nonmonetary. Although many organizations collect and disseminate nonmonetary information, much of the information used in management control is monetary. The system that collects, summarizes, analyzes, and reports such information is the *accounting system.*

Accounting Information. An accounting system provides historical information: the organization's actual revenues and costs. This information typically has three purposes: management control, reporting to outside parties, and special analyses.

Management control. Information for management control purposes usually is classified in two ways: by responsibility centers and by programs. As discussed later, the accounting system must have an ability to integrate these two.

Reporting to outside parties. Some accounting information is contained in general-purpose financial reports. Other information is prepared for outside entities according to reporting requirements that they specify. State and local government agencies that accept funds from the federal government, for example, must prepare reports on their use of these funds. The content of these reports is specified by the agency that grants the funds.

Ideally, the information contained in these special-purpose reports simply summarizes information already contained in the accounting system. This is because the information needs of outside entities presumably do not vary greatly from those of management. The ideal is not always the case, however. The appropriation structure specified by Congress for federal agencies, for example, rarely results in reporting configurations that are useful for the information and control needs of managers in those organizations.

Special analyses. Special analyses include reports used in connection with litigation or one-time studies. In many organizations, for example, the accounting system collects information that is useful for strategic planning. Strategic decisions are made only occasionally, however, and each decision requires tailor-made information. This information cannot ordinarily be collected in any routine, recurring fashion. Rather, it must be assembled when the need arises and in the form required for the specific decision being made.

---

[6] Senior management may decide to assign responsibility for certain detailed decisions, such as approval of travel vouchers, to the controller. This is different from assigning line responsibility to the controller.

Although the management control system includes information found in the accounting system, it also provides two types of monetary information not found in the accounting system: estimates of what will happen in the future and estimates of what should happen. The former are called *forecasts;* the latter are called *standards* or *budgets*. Budgets are discussed in more detail later in this chapter and in Chapter 8.

Cost Information. The accounting system ordinarily collects information on both nonmonetary and monetary inputs to an organization's activities. Nonmonetary inputs are expressed as physical quantities, such as hours of labor, reams of paper, or kilowatt-hours of electricity. When this nonmonetary information is converted to monetary information, the result is called *costs*. Monetary information in this form provides a common denominator that permits the quantities of individual resources to be combined. For example, labor cost can be combined with material cost.

Cost is a measure of the amount of resources used for a purpose. In accounting terms, this purpose is called a *cost object*. The education of a student, the care of a patient, the completion of a research project, and the development of a museum exhibit are all examples of cost objects. Ordinarily, responsibility centers work on cost objects.

Inputs are resources used by a responsibility center in working on a cost object. Thus, the patients in a hospital or the students in a school are not the inputs of a responsibility center. Rather, a responsibility center's inputs are the resources it uses to treat patients or educate students.

Input information consists of three basic types of cost construction: full costs, differential costs, and responsibility costs. Each is used for a different purpose, and considerable misunderstanding can arise if the cost construction for one purpose is used inappropriately for another. Full costs and responsibility costs are ordinarily collected in the accounts. For reasons discussed below, differential costs are not collected in the accounts.

Full costs. These costs represent the total amount of resources used to produce a cost object. Since cost objects often are programs, full costs sometimes are called program costs. The full cost of a cost object is the sum of its direct costs plus a fair share of the organization's indirect (or overhead) costs. *Direct costs* can be traced to a single cost object. For example, the salaries and fringe benefits of persons who work exclusively on a single cost object (such as a research project) are direct costs of that cost object. *Indirect costs,* by contrast are incurred jointly for two or more cost objects, and a fair share of them must be allocated to each cost object to obtain full cost. They are discussed in greater detail in Chapter 3.

Differential costs. These costs vary under one set of conditions from what they would be under another. They are useful in many decisions involving a choice among two or more alternative courses of action. Typically, the decision requires estimating how costs will change under two or more proposed alternatives. Since the costs that are relevant for a given decision depend on the nature of the situation, there is no general way of labeling a given item of cost as differential or nondifferential, and therefore no way of recording differential costs in the formal accounts. An analyst assessing differential costs would use information from the program structure and/or the responsibility structure to estimate the costs that were relevant for each of the proposed alternatives, and thus how costs would differ from one alternative to the next.

In many alternative choice decisions, an important classification of costs is whether they are variable or fixed. *Variable costs* are those that change proportionally with changes in the volume of activity. Since twice as many workbooks are required in teaching two fifth-grade students than in teaching one, the cost of books used in education is a variable cost. By contrast, the salary of the school's principal does not change with the number of students, so it is a *fixed cost*. Other costs, such as teachers' salaries, share features of both, changing as volume increases or decreases but not in direct proportion. Differential costs are the subject of Chapter 4.

Responsibility costs. These costs are incurred by or on behalf of a responsibility center. They provide managers with information on the cost of the responsibility center as an organizational unit, rather than on the programs with which the responsibility center is involved.

Responsibility costs are classified as either controllable or non-controllable. An item of cost is controllable if it is influenced in a significant way by the actions of the manager of the responsibility center in which it was incurred. Since all items of cost are ultimately controllable by someone in the organization, the term "controllable" always refers to a specific responsibility center. Moreover, the definition refers to a significant amount of influence, rather than complete influence. Few managers have complete influence over any item of cost.

Output Information. Inputs almost always can be measured in terms of cost, but outputs are much more difficult to measure. In many responsibility centers, outputs cannot be measured at all. In a for-profit organization, revenue is often an important surrogate for output, but even there it rarely is a complete expression of output, since it does not encompass everything that the organization does. For example, it excludes such activities as pollution control and environmental protection, which may be important outputs from a societal perspective. Nor does it include activities that enhance customer loyalty, which are important from a strategic perspective.

Many nonprofit organizations do not have good quantitative measures of output. A school can easily measure the number of students graduated, but it is much more difficult—usually impossible—to measure how much education each of them acquired. Nevertheless, although a nonprofit's outputs may not be completely measurable, it is a fact that it *has* outputs; that is, it does something.

The degree to which outputs can be measured quantitatively varies greatly with circumstances. If the quantity of output is relatively homogeneous, such as membership certificates in an association, it often can be measured precisely. If, however, the outputs are heterogeneous, such as different types of healthcare services, an organization has problems in summarizing the separate outputs into a meaningful measure of total output.

Converting dissimilar goods and services to monetary equivalents —by computing revenue—is one way of solving this problem. Indeed, if fees are structured properly, the total quantity of output of a client-serving organization can be measured by its revenues. This is true even though the services consist of dissimilar activities such as the use of beds, nursing care, operating rooms, and various laboratory, x-ray, and other procedures in a hospital.

At best, revenue measures the *quantity* of output. Measurement of the *quality* of output is much more difficult, and often cannot be made at all. In many situations, quality is determined strictly on a judgmental basis. In some, there is a go-no-go measurement—either the output is of satisfactory quality or it is not. For example, it is always difficult, and often not even feasible, to measure, or even estimate, the outputs of a school. Instead, graduates, courses completed successfully, and similar measures are used as surrogates. Measuring the outputs of government agencies, symphony orchestras, or churches is similarly problematic.

Part of the measurement difficulty arises because, in addition to producing goods and services, responsibility centers produce *intangible* effects—some intentionally and some unintentionally. They may prepare employees for advancement, for example, or instill attitudes of loyalty and pride of accomplishment or, alternatively, attitudes of disloyalty and indolence. They may also affect the image of the organization as perceived by the outside world. Some of these outputs, such as better trained employees, are created to benefit operations in future periods, such that they will become inputs at some future time. These kinds of outputs are therefore *investments* in the broadest sense of the term. Because of inherent obstacles to measurement, however, investments in intangibles are rarely recorded in the formal accounting system. Output measures are discussed more fully in Chapter 10.

Efficiency and Effectiveness

Efficiency and effectiveness are the two criteria used to judge the performance of a responsibility center. They are almost always used in a relative, rather than absolute, sense. One does not ordinarily say that Unit A is 80 percent efficient, for example. Rather, one says that Unit A is more or less efficient than Unit B, or that it is more or less efficient now than it was in the past, or that it was more or less efficient than planned or budgeted.

Efficiency. Efficiency is the ratio of a responsibility center's outputs to its inputs. For example, Unit A is more efficient than Unit B if it uses either (a) fewer resources than Unit B but has the same output or (b) the same resources as Unit B but has more output. Note that the first measure of efficiency does not require output to be quantified; it only requires a reasonable judgment that the outputs of the two units are approximately equal. If management is satisfied that Units A and B are both doing a satisfactory job, and if their jobs are of comparable magnitude, then the unit with fewer inputs (that is, lower costs) is more efficient. For example, if two elementary schools are judged to be furnishing adequate education, the one with lower costs is more efficient.

The second type of efficiency measure, which contrasts different levels of output given approximately equal levels of input, requires some quantitative indication of output. It therefore is more difficult to use in many situations. If two elementary schools have the same costs, for example, one can be said to be more efficient than the other only if it provides more education, but this is extremely difficult to measure.

In many responsibility centers, measures of efficiency can be developed that relate actual costs to some standard. The standard expresses the costs that management has determined *should be* incurred for a given level of output. Such measures often are useful efficiency indicators.

Effectiveness. The relationship between a responsibility center's outputs and its objectives is an indication of its effectiveness. That is, the more a responsibility center's outputs contribute to its objectives, the more effective it is. Since outputs (and success in meeting them) may be difficult to quantify, however, measures of effectiveness often are difficult to obtain. Effectiveness, therefore, is usually expressed in qualitative, judgmental terms, such as "College A is doing a first-rate job;" or "College B has slipped somewhat in recent years."

An organizational unit should attempt to be both efficient and effective; it is not a matter of being one or the other. A manager who uses fewer resources than specified in the budget may be efficient; but if the center's output is an inadequate contribution to the organization's goals, the manager is ineffective.

Example The employees in a welfare office may process claims and applications with little wasted motion, making the office efficient. If the personnel have the attitude that their function is to ensure the perfect completion of every form, however, rather to help clients obtain welfare services, the office is ineffective.

The Role of Profit. One important goal in a for-profit organization is to earn a satisfactory profit, and the amount of profit therefore is an important measure of effectiveness. Since profit is the difference between revenue, which is a measure of output, and expense,[7] which is a measure of input, it also is a measure of efficiency. Thus, in a for-profit organization, profit measures both effectiveness and efficiency. Since, by definition, a nonprofit organization does not have a goal to earn a profit, the difference between revenue and expense says nothing about effectiveness.

THE MANAGEMENT CONTROL STRUCTURE

The management control structure is an organization's network of responsibility centers. Large organizations usually have complicated hierarchies of responsibility centers: units, sections, departments, branches, and divisions. With the exception of those at the bottom of the organization, each responsibility center consists of aggregations of smaller responsibility centers, and the entire organization is itself a responsibility center. One function of senior management is to plan and control the work of these responsibility centers.

Example A university consists of a number of responsibility centers, such as its schools of law and medicine and its college of arts and sciences. Each school or college, in turn, comprises separate responsibility centers, such as a language department or a physics department. These departments may, in turn, be divided into separate responsibility centers; the language department may, for example, be composed of sections for each language. The management control activity is to plan and coordinate the work of all these responsibility centers.

As discussed above, a responsibility center exists to accomplish one or more purposes; these are its objectives, and they should help the organization to achieve its overall goals, which were determined in the strategic planning process. A responsibility center also has inputs of labor, material, and services. The language department in the above example has inputs of faculty, staff, educational materials, and maintenance services. It uses these inputs to produce its outputs. If the responsibility center is effective, its outputs will be closely related to its objectives. One output of the language department is the knowledge and skill that its students acquire in language; another might be instructional recordings or tapes for use outside the university. These outputs are related to the language department's objectives and presumably help satisfy one or more of the university's goals.

Types of Responsibility Centers

There are five principal types of responsibility centers: revenue centers, discretionary expense centers, standard expense centers, profit centers, and investment centers. The principal factor in the selection of one type over another is control. That is, senior management's objective in choosing a given type of responsibility center is to hold the center's manager accountable for those inputs and outputs over which he or she can exercise a reasonable amount of control.

Revenue Centers. A revenue center is a responsibility center where the manager is charged primarily with attaining some predetermined amount of revenue. Of course, a revenue center incurs expenses, and these are agreed upon between the manager and his or her superiors. However, the

[7] The term *expense* is not synonymous with *cost*. Cost is a measure of resources consumed for any specified purpose, whereas expense always refers to resources that are consumed in operations of a specified time period. Outlays to manufacture a product are costs in the period in which the product is manufactured, but they become expenses only in the period in which the product is sold and the related revenue is earned.

manager's *performance* is measured in terms of the amount of revenue earned by the responsibility center. A university's development office frequently is treated as a revenue center.

Example In one university, the school of management was treated as a revenue center. The school was expected to generate approximately $50 million a year in revenues for the university. The university gave the school an operating budget of about $20 million. If revenues exceeded $50 million, the school did not automatically receive an increase in its operating budget.

Discretionary and Standard Expense Centers. An expense center's manager is held responsible for the expenses incurred during a specified time period. This means that the management control system focuses on the center's inputs. Although every responsibility center has outputs—that is, it does something—in many cases it is neither feasible nor necessary to measure them in monetary terms. It would be extremely difficult to measure the monetary value that the accounting department contributes to the whole organization, for example.

A *discretionary expense center* ordinarily is used when there is no easy way to measure the center's outputs, such as in an accounting or legal department. If this is the case, the manager is held responsible for a fixed amount of expenses for the month or other reporting period, and is not permitted to exceed this amount unless there are compelling reasons to do so, and approval by his or her superiors.

A *standard expense center* is used when the units of output can be rather easily identified and measured, such as in a hospital's laundry or radiology department. With a standard expense center, the manager is not responsible for a fixed amount of expenses, but for a predetermined expense (input) for each unit of output. A standard expense center ordinarily is used when the manager cannot control the amount of output that his or her department is required to produce, which happens when, the amount of output is determined by requests from other responsibility centers. In this case, the manager's budget for each reporting period is determined by multiplying the actual output produced by the standard expense per unit. His or her department's financial performance is measured against this figure.

Example During a particular month, a department of radiology received requests from the department of pediatrics for 500 chest x-rays and 200 neck x-rays. The agreed-upon expenses were $100 per chest x-ray and $150 per neck x-ray. The expense budget against which the radiology manager's performance is measured was $50,000 (500 x $100) for chest x-rays and $30,000 (200 x $150) for neck x-rays, for a total of $80,000.[8]

In a business enterprise, most manufacturing departments are standard expense centers, and most staff units are discretionary expense centers. In many nonprofit organizations, both types of departments are discretionary expense centers. As a result, managers of departments whose outputs are dictated by requests from other departments frequently have a difficult time staying within their budgets. Such an arrangement is sub-optimal.

Profit Centers. In a profit center, the manager is responsible for both revenues (a monetary measure of outputs) and expenses (a monetary measure of inputs). Profit is the difference between the two. Thus, a profit center manager's performance is measured in terms of both the revenue his or her center earns and the expenses it incurs.

---

[8] The computations are somewhat more complicated than this. This issue is taken up in detail in Part III.

Many nonprofit organizations have responsibility centers that charge fees for their services and incur expenses in delivering them. This is the case with many hospital departments; with the housing, dining, and other auxiliary services of a university; and with utilities, waste collection, and similar enterprises of a municipality. In these instances, the responsibility center can be thought of as a profit center, even though use of the term may seem contradictory in a nonprofit organization.

Investment Centers. In an investment center, a manager is responsible for both profit and the assets used in generating it. This responsibility frequently is measured in terms of a return on assets (ROA), which is a ratio of profit to assets employed, usually expressed as a percentage.

An investment center adds more to a manager's scope of responsibility than does a profit center, just as a profit center involves greater scope than an expense center. Although investment centers are quite appropriate for situations in which a manager is responsible for a clearly identified set of assets, they are rarely used in nonprofit organizations.

Mission Centers and Support Centers

Regardless of type, responsibility centers can be classified as either mission centers or support centers. The output of a *mission center* contributes directly to the objectives of the organization. The output of a *support center* contributes to the work of other responsibility centers, which may be either mission centers or support centers; its output is thus one of the inputs of these responsibility centers. A support center is often called a *service center*.

Example In a museum, the curatorial and education departments ordinarily are designated as mission centers—they contribute directly to the objectives of the museum. Finance and human resources departments usually are designated as support centers—they contribute to the work of other responsibility centers but do not contribute *directly* to the objectives of the museum.

Many mission centers are also profit centers, although some are designated as revenue or expense centers. A support center may be a discretionary expense center, a standard expense center, or a profit center. If the latter, it "sells" its services to other units within the organization, and its output is measured by the revenue generated from its sales. However, its objective usually is not to make a profit—that is, an excess of revenue over expenses—but rather to break even. The extension of the profit center concept to support centers, although prevalent in industry, is rare in nonprofit organizations. When properly designed, however, support centers functioning as profit centers can provide a powerful instrument for management control.

Responsibility Centers and Programs

Many organizations distinguish between responsibility centers and programs. These organizations have both program structures and responsibility center structures in their management control systems. The responsibility center structure, which contains information classified by responsibility center, is used for planning each responsibility center's activities, coordinating its work with other responsibility centers, and measuring the performance of its manager. The program structure, by contrast, contains information about the organization's programs or planned programs. Managers use this information for three principal purposes:

1. To make decisions about the kinds and amounts of resources that should be devoted to each program.

2. To provide a basis for setting fees charged to clients, or for requesting reimbursement of the program's costs.
3. To permit comparisons with similar programs in other organizations. For example, managers in a hospital with an open heart surgery program might wish to compare its costs or revenues with those of similar programs in other hospitals.

When there is both a responsibility center structure and a program structure, the management control system must identify their interactions. In some instances, a responsibility center may work solely on one program, and it may be the only responsibility center working on that program. If so, the program structure corresponds to the responsibility center structure. This is the case in most municipal governments, for example. One organization unit is responsible for providing police protection, another for education, another for solid waste disposal, and so on.

One-to-one correspondence between programs and responsibility centers does not always exist, however. For example, a regional office of the U.S. Department of Transportation (DOT), which is a responsibility center, may work on several DOT programs. When this happens, the management control system must identify the relationships between the organization's responsibility centers and its programs.

Exhibit 1-1 uses a hospital to depict the relationship between responsibility centers and programs. Here, responsibility centers are divided between mission centers and support centers. A given mission center, such as the Outpatient department, can work for several programs. Here, it provides 12,500 visits for the Sports Medicine Program, 10,000 visits for the Alcohol Detoxification Program, and 8,500 visits for the Drug Rehabilitation Program.

Exhibit 1-1 Relationship Between Responsibility Centers and Programs

	Programs			
Responsibility Centers	**Sports Medicine**	**Alcohol Detoxification**	**Drug Rehabilitation**	**Open-Heart Surgery**
Mission centers:				
Routine care	3,800 days	1,200 days	300 days	8,000 days
Surgery	1,000 operations	--	--	500 operations
Laboratory	2,000 tests	500 tests	300 tests	2,000 tests
Radiology	8,000 procedures	--	--	1,500 procedures
Outpatient care	12,500 visits	10,000 visits	8,500 visits	--
Support centers:				
Housekeeping				
Dietary				
Laundry				
Administration				
Social service				

Support center costs are allocated to mission centers in order to determine the full cost of each mission center. The full cost of each program can then be determined by measuring its use of the services provided by the various mission centers.

At the same time, a given program, such as the Drug Rehabilitation Program, can receive services from several mission and support centers. Here, it receives 300 days of care from the Routine Care mission center, 300 tests from the Laboratory, and 8,500 visits from the Outpatient department. It also receives housekeeping, dietary, laundry, and administrative services from the hospital's support centers. If these departments were established as profit centers, they might sell their services to both mission centers and programs; otherwise, their costs would be allocated to mission centers and programs.

THE MANAGEMENT CONTROL PROCESS

The formal management control process has four principal phases:

1. Programming
2. Budgeting
3. Measuring
4. Reporting and evaluating

These phases occur in a regular cycle, and together they constitute a closed loop, as indicated in Exhibit 1-2.

Exhibit 1-2 **Phases of the Management Control Process**

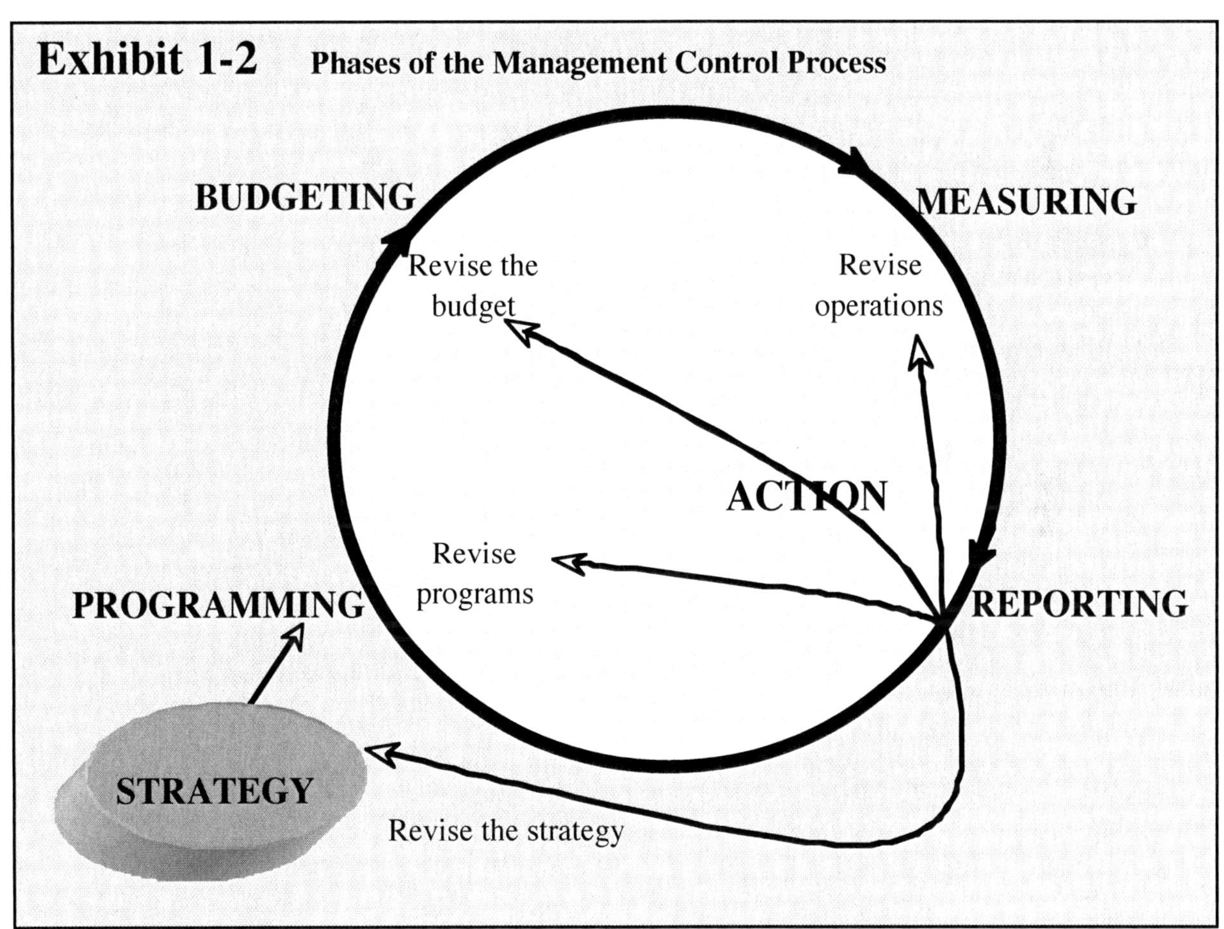

Programming

In the programming phase, senior management determines the major programs the organization will initiate during the coming period and the approximate revenues and expenses associated with each. These decisions are made within the context of the goals and activities that emerged from the strategic planning activity. If a new program represents a change in strategy, the decision to initiate it effectively is part of the strategic planning process, rather than the management control process. Strategic planning and management control merge in the programming phase.

Some organizations state their programs in the form of a *long-range plan* that projects outputs and inputs for several years ahead—usually five years, but possibly as few as three, or in the case of public utilities as many as 20. Other organizations do not have a formal mechanism for describing their future programs. They rely instead on annual proposals for new programs or amounts to be invested in new fixed assets.

Programs in industrial companies are usually products or product lines, plus activities such as research that cannot be related to specific products. The company's long-range plan states the amount and character of the resources that are to be devoted to each program, and the planned uses of these resources. In a nonprofit organization, programs define the types of services the organization has decided to provide.

To the extent feasible, decisions about new programs are based on economic analyses, which compare estimated revenues or other benefits from a proposed program with the program's estimated costs. In many for-profit companies, as well as in most nonprofit organizations, reliable estimates of a program's benefits cannot be made. Decisions about these programs tend to rest on senior management's ability to exercise sound judgment in the face of some persuasive program advocates, political considerations, and the frequently parochial interests of external constituencies.

Budgeting

A budget is a plan, expressed in quantitative (usually monetary) terms, that covers a specified period, usually a year. In the budgeting phase of the management control process, each program's objectives are translated into terms that correspond to the spheres of responsibility of the managers charged with implementing them. Thus, during the budgeting phase, plans made in program terms are converted into responsibility terms.

Example In a university, a program on medieval art may have several objectives: train a certain number of students, provide some cross-cultural experiences, raise a designated amount of support from alumni, and so forth. During the budgeting phase, the university determines the faculty and staff resources that are to be committed to the program, the necessary operating expenses (such as travel) for the program, and, perhaps, some program objectives (for example, to admit a certain number of international students to the program). The manager of the program assumes responsibility for accomplishing these objectives within some specified amount of resources (the budget), and the department chairs assume responsibility for providing the requisite faculty to teach in the program. The program manager also may obtain commitments from his or her subordinates to achieve certain objectives (such as to send three newsletters to 90 percent of alumni or to initiate a fundraising campaign).

The process of arriving at the budget is essentially one of negotiation between responsibility center managers and their superiors. The end product of these negotiations is a statement of the outputs expected during the budget year and the resources (inputs) that will be used to achieve these outputs. As such, the agreed-upon budget is a *bilateral commitment*. Responsibility center managers commit to producing the planned output with the agreed amount of resources, and their superiors commit to agreeing that such performance is satisfactory. Both commitments are subject to the qualification "unless circumstances change significantly."

Measuring

During the period of actual operations, managers supervise what is going on and the accounting staff keeps records of actual resources consumed and actual output achieved. In many organizations, the records of resources consumed (costs) are maintained in such a way to reflect the costs incurred by both programs and responsibility centers. Program cost records are used as a basis for future programming; responsibility cost records are used to measure the performance of responsibility center managers.

Reporting and Evaluating

Accounting information, along with a variety of other information, is summarized, analyzed, and reported to those individuals who are responsible for knowing what is happening in the organization, as well as those charged with attaining agreed-upon levels of performance. The reports enable managers to compare planned outputs and inputs with actual ones. The information in these reports is used for three purposes: operational control, performance assessment, and program evaluation.

Operational Control. The reports help managers to coordinate and control the organization's current operations. Using this information, together with information obtained from conversations or other informal sources, managers attempt to (a) identify situations that may be "out of control," (b) investigate them, and (c) initiate corrective action where necessary and feasible.

Performance Assessment. The reports also are used by senior management to assess operating performance. Such assessments lead to actions related to responsibility center managers: praise for a job well done, constructive criticism, promotion, reassignment, or, in extreme cases, termination. Such information is also used to guide managers of responsibility centers in the development of improved methods of operating.

Program Evaluation. For a variety of reasons, the plan for a program may be sub-optimal. If so, a program evaluation may reveal that the program needs to be revised or perhaps discontinued.

The reporting and evaluating phase thus closes the loop of the management control process. Evaluation of actual performance can lead back to the first phase, a revision of the program, or to the second phase, a revision of the budget, or to the third phase, a modification in operations. It can also lead to senior management reconsidering the organization's approaches to achieving its goals, or even to a revision of the organization's goals.

CHARACTERISTICS OF A GOOD MANAGEMENT CONTROL SYSTEM

Management control systems differ considerably from one organization to the next. In some organizations they work well; in others, they are in need of considerable redesign if they are to help the organization achieve its goals. In assessing the quality of a management control system, analysts tend to focus on several criteria. The absence of one or more of these criteria is an indication that the system is in need of redesign.

A Total System

Properly designed, a management control system is a total system—it embraces all aspects of an organization's operations. It needs to be a total system because an important management function is to assure that all parts of the organization are in balance with one another. To monitor and maintain this balance, senior management must have information about all parts of operations. By contrast, information collected for strategic planning usually is specific to the matters under consideration, which rarely encompass the whole organization. Similarly, information used in task control is usually tailor-made for the requirements of each activity, and therefore limited in its scope.

Goal Congruence

A basic principle of social psychology is that persons act according to their perceived best interests. Because of this, one characteristic of a good management control system is that it encourages managers to act in accordance with *both* their own best interests *and* the best interests of the organization as a whole. In the language of social psychology, the system should encourage *goal congruence*—it should be structured so that the goals of individual managers are consistent with the goals of the organization as a whole.

Perfect congruence between individual and organizational goals rarely exists. As a minimum, however, the system should not include evaluation and reward criteria that make an individual manager's best interests inconsistent with the best interests of the organization. For example, a lack of goal congruence exists if the management control system emphasizes reduced costs and, in so doing, encourages managers to sacrifice quality, provide inadequate service, or engage in activities that reduce costs in one department but cause more than an offsetting increase in another.

Financial Framework

With rare exceptions, a management control system should be built around a financial structure—that is, with estimates and measures stated in monetary amounts. This does not mean that accounting information is the sole, or even the most important, part of the control system; it means only that the accounting system provides a unifying core to which managers can relate other types of information. Although the financial structure is usually the central focus, nonmonetary measures, such as minutes per visit (or procedure, or operation), number of persons served, percent of applicants admitted, and reject and spoilage rates are also important parts of the system.

Rhythm

The management control process usually is rhythmic, following a defined pattern and timetable, month after month, year after year. In budget preparation, certain steps are taken in a prescribed sequence and at certain dates each year: dissemination of guidelines, preparation of estimates, transmission of these estimates up through the several echelons of the organization, review of these estimates, final approval by senior management, and dissemination back through the organization.

Integration

A management control system should be a coordinated, integrated system. Although data collected for one purpose may differ from those collected for another, these data should be reconcilable. The management control system is a single system, but it is perhaps more useful to think of it as two interlocking subsystems—one focused on programs and the other on responsibility centers. Furthermore, much of the data used in the management control system are also used in preparing a variety of other reports and analyses used by both line managers and professional staff.

BOUNDARIES OF MANAGEMENT CONTROL

Management control is an important activity, but it is by no means the whole of management. Managers also must make judgments about people: their integrity, their ability, their potential, their fitness for a given job, or their compatibility with colleagues. Senior management is responsible for building an effective organization and for motivating the people who comprise that organization to work toward its goals. Of course, managers also have functions that are not "management" as such. John Kotter has discussed the external activities of a manager by describing the external agencies and persons on which the head of a large municipal, urban teaching hospital must depend.[9] These are shown in Exhibit 1-3.

Exhibit 1-3 External Agencies and Persons Related to a Large Urban Teaching Hospital

- The mayor's office, which must approve the hospital's budget, support the hospital publicly, and avoid employing everyone to whom the mayor owes a favor.
- Other parts of the city's bureaucracy, which provide services such as construction.
- A dozen unions or employee associations that could call a strike or work stoppage.
- The civil service, which could make it easy or difficult to get competent employees.
- The city council, which could call hearings that could take up a hospital manager's time and be a source of embarrassment.
- Accreditation agencies, which could put the hospital out of business.
- The state government, which could constrain the hospital's activities in a variety of ways.
- Its medical school affiliate, which supplies the hospital with interns and residents.
- The local press, which could embarrass the hospital and upset the mayor.
- The federal government, which supplies the hospital with funds and regulates certain activities.
- Other hospitals in the city, whose major actions could have a positive or negative impact on the hospital.
- The local community, which, if organized, could constrain the hospital's actions through the press, the mayor, or the city council.

BOUNDARIES OF THE BOOK

The management control activity helps an organization to reach its goals, but management control does not have anything to do directly with the existence of the organization or the formulation of its goals. This book therefore is not concerned with whether there *should be* an organization, or with whether it *should have* its existing goals—be they good or bad. Management control occurs in both the UNICEF and the Mafia. Our focus thus precludes criticism of the goals

9 John P. Kotter, "Power, Success and Organizational Effectiveness," *Organizational Dynamics*, Winter 1978.

themselves, on moral, public policy, or other grounds. We do not, for example, debate the question of the extent to which the government should be responsible for health care. We accept the fact that Congress has assigned certain healthcare responsibilities to the department of Health and Human Services, and start our analysis with this as a given.

Exclusion of Systems Approach

The focus on management control in an existing organization means that some exciting topics are not given the attention that their importance might otherwise warrant. Of these, perhaps the most important is the systems approach. Health care, for example, should be viewed as a system, comprising all the individuals, organizations, and policies that are intended to provide an optimal level of health care. When viewed in this way, it is apparent that the U.S. healthcare system is deficient. Its morbidity rates, infant mortality rates, and other indicators of health status rank nowhere near the top of the list of developed countries, despite the fact it spends more on health care per capita than most other nations. Healthcare facilities are poorly distributed. Many ill people who could be treated inexpensively in a clinic are sent unnecessarily to a hospital. Many people cannot afford adequate health insurance.

All these facts are indications that it should be possible to provide better health care at substantially lower cost by emphasizing new organizational arrangements, such as more ambulatory care facilities; a new mix of personnel, such as more nurse practitioners and physician extenders; more emphasis on preventive medicine; and so on. In short, a focus on health care as a system is fascinating, and an analysis of the healthcare system can lead to major improvements in its functioning. Similarly, governmental organizations, higher educational facilities, and volunteer organizations are all best understood when viewed from a systemic perspective.[10]

This book takes a narrower focus, however, addressing the activities of individual organizations. Within the healthcare system, the focus will be limited to a hospital, a clinic, or a nursing home, for example. Within the educational system, the focus will be on individual schools, colleges, or universities. This perspective accepts the role of an organization and its goals essentially as givens, and concentrates on how improvements in the management control system might help the organization to perform more efficiently and effectively.

Such a focus tends to be less than satisfying to many people because it rules out discussion of certain current, sometimes glamorous, high-payoff topics. These topics should, of course be discussed, but in another context. Thus, in the chapters that follow, there is relatively low emphasis placed on the systems in which nonprofit organizations exist, but instead on the individual organizations that comprise those systems. It is tempting to focus on global systems' problems and to neglect the problems of individual organizations, but this book tries to resist that temptation.

[10] A similar argument could be made about secondary education in the U.S. For an example, see Gordon MacInnes, *In Plain Sight: Simple, Difficult Lessons from New Jersey's Expensive Effort to Close the Achievement Gap*, New York, The Century Foundation Press, 2009.

Suggested Cases for Classroom Use with this Chapter

See the Appendix at the end of the book for a more complete description of each case and ordering information.

Hamilton Hospital	Distinguishing among strategic planning, management control, and task control in a physician group practice.
Boulder Public Schools	Assessing structure and process in a highly bureaucratic context, and the appropriate balance between centralization and decentralization in a management control system.
South Kingston Health Center	Determining a viable strategy in a neighborhood health center.
Commonwealth Business School	Attaining a balance between departments and programs in a university.

Suggested Additional Readings

Michael Allison and Jude Kaye, *Strategic Planning for Nonprofit Organizations,* Second Edition, 2003.

Helmut Anheier, *Nonprofit Organizations: Theory, Management, Policy*, 2005.

Evan M. Berman, *Performance and Productivity in Public And Nonprofit Organizations*, 2006.

John M. Bryson, *Strategic Planning for Public and Nonprofit Organizations: A Guide to Strengthening and Sustaining Organizational Achievement,* Jossey Bass Public Administration Series, 2004.

Peter F. Drucker, *Managing the Nonprofit Organization,* 2006.

James A. Phills, *Integrating Mission and Strategy for Nonprofit Organizations*, 2005.

John A. Yankey and Richard L. Edwards, *Effectively Managing Nonprofit Organizations*, 2006.

John Zietlow, Jo Ann Hankin, and Alan G. Seidner, *Financial Management for Nonprofit Organizations: Policies and Practices*, 2007.

Chapter 2

Characteristics of Nonprofit Organizations

Although the precise line between a for-profit and a nonprofit organization occasionally is fuzzy, the following definition is adequate for this book: "A nonprofit organization is an entity whose goal is something other than earning a profit for its owners; usually it is to provide services." This definition corresponds approximately to that in most state statutes.[1]

The definition also emphasizes a basic distinction between the two types of organizations—a distinction that is the cause of many management control problems in nonprofit organizations. In a for-profit company, decisions made by management are intended to increase or at least maintain profits. Success is measured, to a significant degree, by the amount of profit the organization earns, usually in relation to the assets it used to generate the profit, or its return on its assets.

In contrast, decisions made by management in a nonprofit organization ordinarily are intended to produce the best possible services with the available resources. Success is measured primarily by how much service the organization provides and by the quality of its services. More generally, the success of a nonprofit organization is measured by how much it contributes to the public well-being.

Since service is a vaguer, less measurable concept than profit, it is more difficult to measure performance in nonprofit organizations than in for-profit ones. It is also more difficult to make clear-cut choices among alternative courses of action, to establish relationships between service costs and benefits, and even to quantify the amount of benefits. Despite these difficulties, management must do what it can to assure that the organization's resources are used efficiently and effectively. Thus, the central problem is to find out which management control policies and practices that have proven successful in the for-profit world also can be useful in nonprofit organizations.

The distinction between for-profit and nonprofit organizations is not black and white. A for-profit company must render services that its customers find adequate if it is to earn a profit. A nonprofit organization must receive funds from operating revenues or other sources that are at least equal to its expenses if it is to remain viable.[2] Thus, the distinction is not based on the need for funds, per se, but on the predominant attitude toward the uses of those funds.

Nor does the distinction relate solely to the types of services provided. Some hospitals, medical clinics, schools, and even religious organizations operate as for-profit entities, even though the serv-

[1] Some people prefer the term *not-for-profit* on the grounds that a business enterprise with a net loss is literally a *nonprofit* organization. Practice varies widely among states and occasionally is not uniform for the statutes of any given state. In federal statutes the usual term is "nonprofit." In income tax regulations, not-for-profit refers to a corporation or other entity that is operated as a hobby of the owners. For additional discussion, go to www.learningtogive.org/papers/paper41.html, or www.investorwords.com/3331/non_profit_organization.html

[2] Indeed, to remain viable over the long term, a nonprofit organization usually must earn an *excess* of revenue over expenses, sometimes called a "surplus" or an "increase in net assets." This issue is discussed in some detail in Appendix 2A.

ices they provide are comparable to those provided by nonprofit organizations. Also, in addition to proprietary (for-profit) organizations, many nonprofit organizations are managed by for-profit companies.

NATURE OF THE NONPROFIT SECTOR

Any categorization of nonprofit organizations is certain to have gray areas. Nevertheless, the categories shown in Exhibit 2-1 will serve as a useful frame of reference for this book. As this exhibit indicates, an important distinction exists between public (governmental) and private (tax-exempt) organizations. Within the public category, the division among federal, state, and local government entities provides a useful organizing scheme; any of these entities can have agencies, commissions, or authorities.[3]

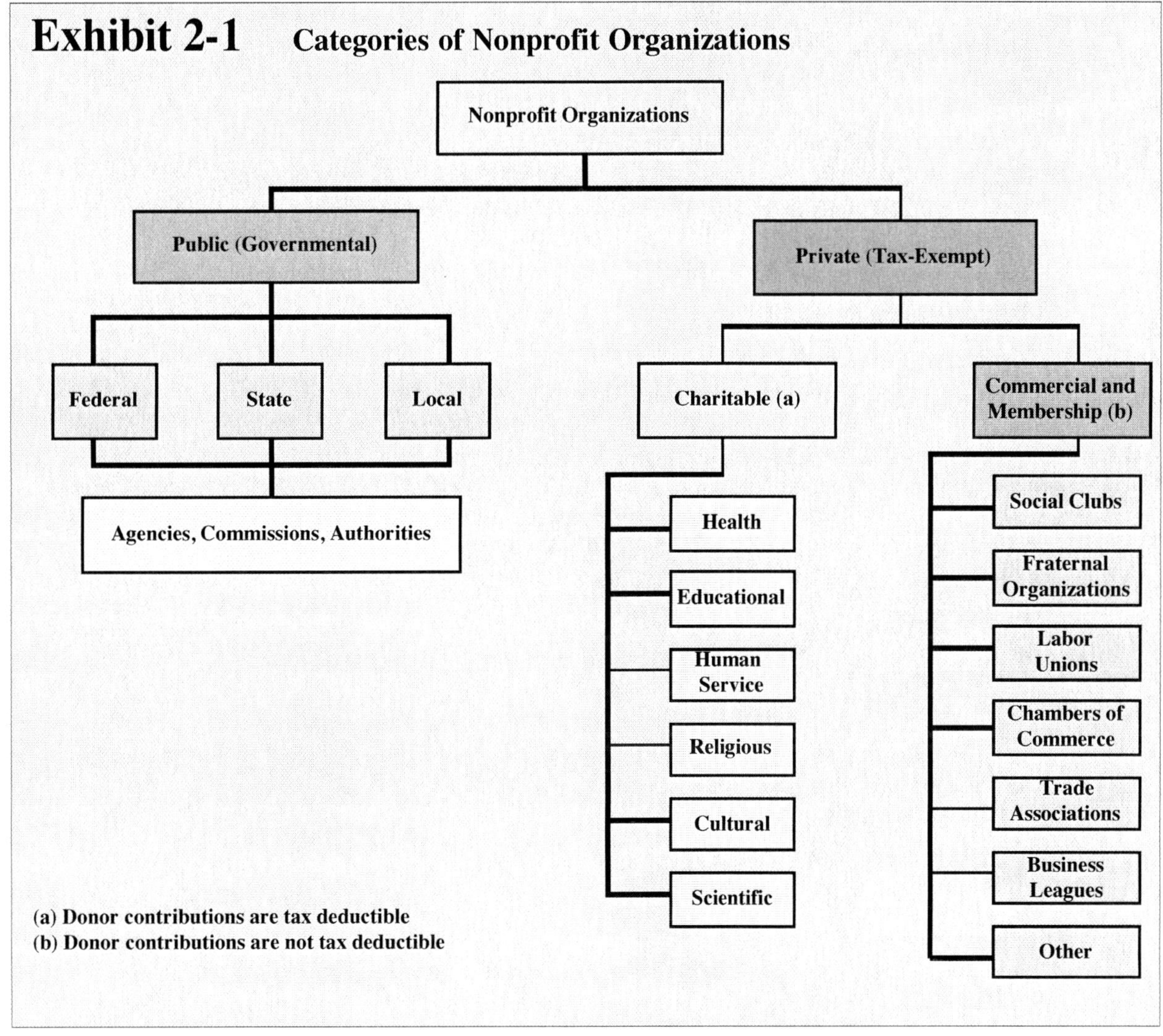

3 The details of several different sectors of the nonprofit world are discussed in Appendix 2-B.

Within the private category, an important distinction is between charitable organizations, for which donor contributions are tax deductible, and commercial and membership organizations, for which they ordinarily are not. The former category includes health, educational, human service, religious, cultural, and scientific organizations. The latter category comprises social clubs, fraternal organizations, labor unions, and similar entities.

Diversity of Demands on Managers

In summary, the nonprofit sector comprises many different types of entities, with diverse activities, clientele, technology requirements, and funding sources. Because of these and many other differences, any discussion of management control in nonprofit organizations must be viewed as highly contingent: a management control system that works for one nonprofit organization quite likely will not work for another. Nevertheless, there are certain management control principles that are applicable to almost all nonprofit organizations, and certain issues that all nonprofit managers inevitably confront as they attempt to improve the effectiveness and efficiency of their organizations. These are the focus of this book.

Size and Composition of the Private Nonprofit Sector

Exhibit 2-2 gives an idea of the number and magnitude of nonprofit organizations in the U.S. The data are from the Internal Revenue Service's Form 990, a document that all nonprofits must submit annually; they are for 2008, the most recent year for which IRS summaries are available.

As the exhibit indicates, organizations classified as 501(c)(3)—what are called "charitable" in Exhibit 2-1—comprise about 77 percent of all 501(c) organizations (148,821 of 192,968). These are the major focus of this text. In 2008, they had total assets of slightly under $2.5 billion, annual revenue of about $1.35 billion, and operating deficits totaling just under $19 million.[4]

The averages in Exhibit 2-2 are a bit misleading given the wide diversity in the size of these organizations. Exhibit 2-3 corrects for this somewhat, by dividing them into six categories based on the amount of their total assets. As it shows, 5,932 of the 148,821 501(c)(3) organizations owned $2 billion of the $2.5 billion total assets. Stated somewhat differently, about 4 percent of all 501(c)(3) organizations have about 80 percent of all 501(c)(3) assets. These same 4 percent have about 71 percent of all revenue but their deficits were almost $19.9 million (versus total deficits of $18.6 million for all 501(c)(3) organizations).[5]

[4] It is worth noting that the comparable figures for 2004 (contained in the 8th edition of this text) were 218,851 501(c)(3) organizations. Even though the number of 501(c)(3) organizations declined by about 70,000, their total assets grew by about $500 million (from just over $2 billion in 2004 to just under $2.5 billion in 2008. Their total revenue between those two years grew from about $1.15 billion to about 1.35 billion, but their surpluses fell from a positive $94.3 million to a negative $18.6 million. In short, in the four years between the 8th and 9th editions of this text, 501(c)(3) organizations as a whole became smaller in number, larger in size, less efficient (in terms of surplus as a percent of revenue) , and, overall, less financially viable.

[5] In 2004, these large nonprofits had $75 million in surpluses out of a total of $94 million in 501(c)(3) surpluses. In addition, between 2004 and 2008, the number of very small nonprofits (under $100,000 in assets) declined from over 60,000 to just under 33,000, almost a 50 percent fall. Similarly, the number of nonprofits with assets between $100,000 and $499,999 fell from just over 60,000 to just under 30,000 (more than 50 percent). The number of small to medium nonprofits ($500,000 to $999,999 in assets) fell from just over $26,000 to just over 15,000. The remaining categories changed very little.

Exhibit 2-2 Number and Magnitude of 501(c) Organizations in 2008

IRS Code	Description	Number (a)	Total Assets (millions)	Average Assets (000)	Total Revenue (millions)	Average Revenue (000)	Total Surplus (millions)	Average Surplus
501(c)(3)	Religious, educational, charitable, scientific, or literary organizations; testing for public safety organizations. Also, organizations preventing cruelty to children or animals, or fostering national or international amateur sports competition (b)	148,821	$2,484.4	$16.7	$1,352.3	$9.1	$(18.6)	$(125)
501(c)(4)	Civic leagues, social welfare organizations, and local associations of employees	9,316	90.2	9.7	83.8	9.0	2.0	216
501(c)(5)	Labor, agriculture, and horticultural organizations	6,618	28.1	4.2	19.7	3.0	(0.1)	(15)
501(c)(6)	Business leagues, chambers of commerce, and real estate boards	13,078	7.3	0.6	35.1	2.7	(2.0)	(155)
501(c)(7)	Social and recreational clubs	7,851	22.2	2.8	10.9	1.4	0.1	14
501(c)(8)	Fraternal beneficiary societies and associations	2,471	98.6	39.9	14.1	5.7	(.6)	(229)
501(c)(9)	Voluntary employee beneficiary associations	4,813	125.3	26.1	130.3	27.1	(7.9)	(1,641)
	Totals and overall averages	192,968	$2,856.2	$14.8	$1,646.2	$8.5	$(27.1)	$(140)

Notes: a. Based on number of Form 990 returns filed with the IRS. All figures are estimates based on a small number of sample returns.

b. Excludes private foundations, most churches, certain other types of religious organizations, and most organizations with receipts of less than $25,000

Source: IRS Statistics of Income Division, July 2011

Exhibit 2-3 Magnitude of 501(c)(3) Organizations Shown in Exhibit 2-2

	Amount of Total Assets (in 000)						
Item	Under $100 (a)	$100 to $499.9	$500 to $999.9	$1,000 to $9,999.9	$10,000 to $49,999.9	$50,000 or More	Total
Number of returns	32,965	29,921	15,553	51,163	13,287	5,932	148,821
Total assets (000)	$1,172	$7,684	$11,398	$182,048	$282,486	$1,999,638	$2,484,426
Total revenue (000)	13,657	16,297	13,812	158,557	194,034	955,909	1,352,266
Total surplus (000)	(503)	133	(999)	1,925	736	(19,900)	(18,608)

Note: a. Includes returns with zero assets or assets not reported

Source: IRS Statistics of Income Division, July 2011

Employment in the Nonprofit Sector

Another way to look at the size of the nonprofit sector is in terms of employment. Exhibit 2-4 breaks down non-farm employees working in nonprofit organizations into several categories. The figures are not exact because the census categories do not quite conform to the definition of nonprofit that is used here, and the numbers in several categories include for-profit organizations. They are, however, satisfactory as a basis for some general impressions.

Exhibit 2-4 Number of Employees in Nonprofit Organizations

	Number of Employees (000)			Percent Change	
Entity	March 2004	March 2008	November 2011	2004-08	2008-11
Government					
Federal	2,713	2,726	2,817	0.5%	3.3%
State	5,116	5,169	5,073	1.0%	-1.9%
Local	14,163	14,492	14,099	2.3%	-2.7%
Health Services					
Ambulatory services	4,890	5,604	6,223	14.6%	11.0%
Hospitals	4,268	4,609	4,791	8.0%	3.9%
Nursing and residential care facilities	2,799	2,982	3,203	6.5%	7.4%
Education	2,904	3,014	3,250	3.8%	7.8%
Social Assistance	2,127	2,490	2,684	17.1%	7.8%
Performing arts and spectator sports	353	430	411	21.8%	-4.4%
Museums, historical sites, zoos, and parks	110	134	133	21.8%	-0.7%
Membership associations	2,908	2,955	3,013	1.6%	2.0%
Total	42,351	44 ,605	45,697	5.3%	2.4%
Total non-farm employees	130,773	137,846	131,708		
Nonprofit as a percent of total non-farm	32.4%	32.4%	34.7%		

Source: U.S. Department of Labor, Bureau of Labor Statistics, Table B-1. Employees on non-farm payrolls by industry sector

As the exhibit shows, in 2011, nonprofit organizations employed just under 35 percent of the nation's non-farm workforce. As it also indicates, local governments are the largest employer, and health services the largest non-governmental employer. In addition, health services, especially ambulatory services, showed the greatest percentage growth in employees.

Although their number of employees is comparatively small, nonprofits in the performing arts, spectator sports, museums, historical sites, zoos, and parks saw a percentage decline in the last four years. This followed a large percentage increase between 2004 and 2008.

Many nonprofits make extensive use of volunteer labor. Because of this, looking only at paid employees would understate the amount of effort expended on behalf of these organizations' clientele. For example, in 2010 there were almost 63,000 people who provided volunteer services to nonprofits. Exhibit 2-5 shows where they spent their time. As it indicates, over a third volunteered for religious organizations, with another quarter devoting their time to educational or youth services.

Exhibit 2-5 Percentage Distribution of Volunteers in the U.S., by Industry For 2010

Civic, political, professional, international	5.3%
Educational or youth services	26.5
Environmental or animal care	2.4
Hospital or other health	7.9
Public safety	1.3
Religious	33.8
Social or community service	13.6
Sport, hobby, culture, arts	3.3
Other	3.7
Not available	2.2
Total	100.0%

Source: United States Department of Labor, Bureau of Labor Statistics, Volunteering in the U.S., Table 4, Volunteers by type of main organization for which volunteer activities were performed and selected characteristics, September 2010.

The Federal Government

The federal government is by far the largest single nonprofit organization. Its immensity can be difficult to comprehend. In 2011 it owned 650 million acres of land, almost 30 percent of the land area of the United States. Federally owned and managed lands included national parks, forests, and wildlife refuges.[6] As of the end of 2011 the U.S. General Services Administration (GSA) managed approximately 95.6 million rentable square feet of space in 190 federally-owned buildings, including 70 historic buildings (seven are national landmarks), and 500 leased buildings in the Washington D.C. area alone.[7] The landlord for the civilian federal government, the Public Buildings Service (PBS), a division of the GSA, acquires space on behalf of the federal government, and acts as a caretaker for federal properties across the country. PBS owns or leases 9,624 properties, maintains an inventory of more than 370.2 million square feet of workspace, and preserves more than 481 historic properties.[8]

In 2010, the executive branch of the federal government employed over 2.1 million civilians,[9] of which over 36 percent worked for the Department of Defense (DOD). The next largest entity was Veterans' Affairs, with 14.4 percent of the total. Data for all executive branches and independent agencies are shown in Exhibit 2-6.[10]

The proposed federal expenditure budget for fiscal year 2012 was $3.6 trillion. A breakdown of the totals is shown in Exhibit 2-7, which indicates that over 65 percent of the budget is for

6 http://www.nationalatlas.gov/printable/fedlands.html

7 http://www.gsa.gov/portal/category/21530

8 http://www.gsa.gov/portal/content/104444

9 This is below the number in Exhibit 2-4 because it excludes government employees who work outside the executive branch (e.g., judicial and legislative branch employees and postal service employees). It also excludes non-civilian employees, such as members of the armed services.

10 In the 8th edition of this text, published in 2008, the federal government employed about 1.8 million civilians. Therefore, in the four years between the two editions, the number of federal civilian employees grew by about 17 percent, or roughly 4 percent a year.

spending that is legislatively mandated, such as Social Security and Medicare. These often are called “entitlement funds.”

Exhibit 2-6 Federal Government Executive Branch Civilian Employment (As of September 2010, in thousands)

Entity	Number	% of Total
Executive departments		
Defense	772.6	36.5%
Veterans Affairs	304.7	14.4
Homeland Security	183.5	8.7
Justice	117.9	5.6
Treasury	110.1	5.2
Agriculture	106.9	5.0
Interior	70.2	3.3
Health and Human Services	69.8	3.3
Transportation	58.0	2.7
Commerce	56.9	2.7
State	39.0	1.8
Labor	17.6	0.8
Energy	16.1	0.8
Housing and Urban Development	9.6	0.5
Education	4.5	0.2
Total: Executive departments	**1,937.4**	**91.5%**
Independent agencies		
Social Security Administration	70.0	3.3.%
National Aeronautics and Space Administration	18.7	0.9
Environmental Protection Agency	18.7	0.9
General Services Administration	12.8	0.6
Tennessee Valley Authority	12.5	0.6
Federal Deposit Insurance Corporation	6.4	0.3
Office of Personnel Management	5.9	0.3
Smithsonian Institution	5.0	0.2
Nuclear Regulatory Commission	4.2	0.2
Small Business Administration	4.0	0.2
Other	21.9	21.0
Total Independent Agencies	**180.1**	**8.5%**
Total Executive Branch	**2117.5**	**100.0%**

Excludes: Central Intelligence Agency, National Security Agency, Defense Intelligence Agency, National Imagery and Mapping Agency, and U.S. Postal Service

Source: U.S. Office of Personnel Management

Exhibit 2-7 2012 Federal Budget by Item

Item	Billions of $	Percent of Total
Mandatory spending		
Social Security	761.0	21.1%
Medicare	468.0	13.0
Medicaid and the State Children's Health Insurance Program (SCHIP)	269.0	7.5
Unemployment/Welfare/Other mandatory spending	598.0	16.6
Interest on National Debt	240.0	6.7
Troubled Asset Relief Program	13.0	0.4
Total Mandatory Spending	**2349.0**	**65.3%**
Discretionary spending		
Department of Defense (a)	553.0	15.4%
Overseas Contingency Operations (b)	126.5	3.5
Department of Health and Human Services	82.2	2.3
Department of Education	77.4	2.2
Department of Veterans Affairs	58.8	1.6
Department of State and Other International Programs	52.8	1.5
Department of Homeland Security	43.2	1.2
Department of Housing and Urban Development	41.7	1.2
Department of Energy	29.5	0.8
Department of Agriculture	22.0	0.6
Department of Justice	20.9	0.6
National Aeronautics and Space Administration	18.7	0.5
Department of Treasury	14.0	0.4
Department of Transportation	13.4	0.4
Department of Labor	12.8	0.4
Department of the Interior	12.1	0.3
Social Security Administration	10.2	0.3
Department of Commerce	9.8	0.3
Environmental Protection Agency	9.0	0.3
National Science Foundation	7.8	0.2
Disaster costs	6.0	0.2
Army Corps of Engineers	4.6	0.1
Corporation for National and Community Service	1.3	0.0
Small Business Administration	1.0	0.0
General Services Administration	0.6	0.0
Other Agencies	20.3	0.6
Total Discretionary Spending	**$1,249.6**	**34.7%**
Total Spending	**$3,598.6**	**100.0%**

Notes (a). The Iraq War and the War in Afghanistan are not included in the Department of Defense regular budget. They are included instead in Overseas Contingency Operations.

(b) Called the "Global Ware on Terror" in some previous budgets

Source: Source: www.gpo.gov/fdsys/browse/collectionGPO.action?collectionCode=budget

CHARACTERISTICS OF NONPROFIT ORGANIZATIONS

The remainder of this chapter discusses nine characteristics of nonprofit organizations that affect the management control process:

1. The absence of a profit measure
2. Different tax and legal considerations
3. A tendency to be service organizations
4. Greater constraints on goals and strategies
5. Less dependence on clients for financial support
6. The dominance of professionals
7. Differences in governance
8. Importance of political influence
9. A tradition of inadequate management controls

Of these, the absence of a profit measure is the most important characteristic. Since it affects all nonprofit organizations, it will be discussed at length. The other characteristics affect many, but not all, nonprofit organizations. They do so to varying degrees and are not unique to nonprofit organizations; they therefore are tendencies rather than pervasive characteristics.

ABSENCE OF A PROFIT MEASURE

All organizations use resources to produce goods and services; that is, they use inputs to produce outputs. As discussed in Chapter 1, an organization's effectiveness is measured by the extent to which its outputs accomplish its goals, and its efficiency is measured by the relationship between its outputs and the inputs needed to produce them. In a for-profit organization, profit provides an overall measure of both effectiveness and efficiency. The absence of a single, satisfactory, overall measure of performance comparable to the profit measure is the most serious problem nonprofit managers face in developing effective management control systems. To appreciate the significance of this statement, one needs to consider the usefulness and the limitations of the profit measure in for-profit organizations.

The profit measure has the following advantages: It (1) provides a single criterion that can be used to evaluate proposed courses of action, (2) permits a quantitative analysis of those proposals in which benefits (usually revenues) can be directly compared with costs, (3) provides a single, broad measure of performance, (4) facilitates decentralization, and (5) permits comparisons of performance among entities that carry out dissimilar functions. Each of these points is discussed below, and contrasted with the situation in a nonprofit organization.

Single Criterion

In a for-profit business, profit provides a way of focusing the considerations involved in choosing among alternative courses of action. The analyst and the decision maker can address such questions as: Is the proposal likely to produce a satisfactory level of profits? Is Alternative A likely to add more to profits than Alternative B?

Of course, the decision maker's analysis is rarely as simple and straightforward as this. Most proposals cannot be analyzed exclusively in terms of their effect on profits, since almost all proposals involve considerations that cannot be measured in monetary terms. Nevertheless, these qualifications do not invalidate the general point that profit provides a focus for decision making.

In a nonprofit organization, there often is no clear-cut objective criterion that can be used in analyzing proposed alternative courses of action. Members of the management team of a nonprofit organization often will not agree on the relative importance of various objectives. In a municipality, for example, all members of the management team may agree that the addition of a new firehouse would add to the effectiveness of the fire department. But some will likely disagree on the importance of an expenditure to increase the effectiveness of the fire department versus a comparable expenditure on parks, streets, or welfare.

Quantitative Analysis

The easiest type of proposal to analyze is one in which estimated costs can be compared directly with estimated benefits (or revenue). Such an analysis is possible when the objective is profitability. However, for most important decisions in a nonprofit organization, managers have no accurate way of estimating the relationship between costs and benefits; that is, they have difficulty judging what effect a given expenditure will have on achieving the goals of the organization. Would the addition of another professor increase the value of the education that a college provides by an amount that exceeds his or her salary? How much should be spent on a program to retrain unemployed persons? Issues of this type are difficult to analyze in quantitative terms because there is no good way to estimate the benefits of a given increment in spending.

Performance Measurement

Profit provides a measure that incorporates a great many separate aspects of performance. The best manager is not the one who generates the most sales volume, considered by itself; nor the one who uses labor, material, or capital most efficiently; nor who has the best control of overhead costs. Rather, the best manager is the one who, on balance, does the best job of combining of all these separate activities. Profit incorporates all of these elements. The key consideration is not who improved different items on the operating statement, but who improved the organization's return on assets. This measure provides managers with an easily understood signal as to how well they are doing, and it provides others with an objective basis for judging a given manager's performance.

Although the principal goal of a nonprofit organization is to render service, the amount and quality of services rendered cannot be quantified easily. As a result, the organization's performance with respect to its goals is difficult and sometimes impossible to measure. For example, the success of an educational institution depends more on the ability and diligence of its faculty, which is difficult to measure, than on such measurable characteristics as the number of courses offered or the ratio of faculty to students.

Decentralization

For-profit organizations have a well-understood goal. The performance of many individual managers can be measured in terms of their contribution toward that goal. Because of this, senior management can safely decentralize, or delegate, many decisions to lower levels in the organization.

If an organization has multiple goals and no good way of measuring performance in attaining them, it has difficulty in delegating important decisions to lower level managers. For this reason, many problems in government organizations must be resolved in Washington or in state capitals, rather than in local offices. The paperwork and related procedures involved in sending problems to senior management, and in transmitting the resulting decisions back to the field, can be quite elaborate, giving rise to part of the criticism that is levied against the *bureaucracy*. Such criticism frequently is often unwarranted because, in the absence of something corresponding to the profit measure, there is no easy way for governmental organizations to decentralize.

Comparison of Unlike Units

The profit measure (usually ROA) permits performance comparisons among heterogeneous For example, the performance of a department store can be compared with that of a paper mill in terms of a single criterion: which had the higher return on assets?

Profitability therefore provides a way of combining heterogeneous elements of performance within a company, and is a way of making valid comparisons among organizations. For-profit entities can be compared, at least roughly, even though their size, technology, products, and markets are quite different from one another.

Nonprofit organizations can be compared with one another only if they have similar functions. A fire department can be compared with other fire departments, and a general hospital with other general hospitals. There is no way of comparing the effectiveness of a fire department with that of a hospital, however.

TAX AND LEGAL CONSIDERATIONS

Most nonprofit organizations benefit from certain provisions of tax legislation. The general nature of these benefits is summarized below. This section also briefly discusses some of the legal implications of nonprofit status, particularly with regard to the generation and distribution of a financial surplus and the creation of for-profit subsidiaries.[11]

Tax Considerations

Nonprofit organizations ordinarily are exempt from income, property, and sales taxes. In some instances, individuals who lend money to nonprofits do not pay taxes on the interest income they receive. Contributions and gifts to nonprofit organizations also may be tax deductible, depending on the nonprofit's 501(c) status.

Income Taxes. Most nonprofit organizations are exempt from paying federal, state, and municipal taxes on income related to their nonprofit activities. They are required to report their revenues and expenses to the Internal Revenue Service on Form 990, and they pay taxes on income generated from activities that fall outside their nonprofit charters. Such activities are known as unrelated business activities.

A nonprofit organization can lose its tax-exempt status if it engages in activities that are not considered appropriate to its mission, such as substantial lobbying or participation in political campaigns. A nonprofit organization also can lose its tax exempt status if a significant part of its income results from activities that are unrelated to its charter.

The line between unrelated and tax-exempt activities frequently is tricky to define. For example, most YMCAs do not pay taxes on the income from their gymnasiums and swimming pools, even though these facilities compete directly with for-profit physical fitness centers that offer similar services.

[11] This information is a broad brush approach only, and it is not a substitute for a legal or tax opinion.

There are essentially two ways a nonprofit organization can engage in for-profit activities and maintain its tax-exempt status: it can pursue a venture that is either (a) related to its tax-exempt purpose or (b) unrelated, but insubstantial. If the organization's for-profit activity falls into the first category, it will preserve its tax-exempt status and pay no federal income taxes. If the activity falls into the second category, it will pay unrelated business income taxes on the portion of its activity that is unrelated, but will maintain its tax-exempt status for everything else.

Many nonprofit organizations that engage in for-profit activities organize in such a way that these activities are carried out in separate, wholly owned subsidiaries. The key advantage of a separate subsidiary is that, for income tax purposes, it minimizes the risk to the parent organization's tax-exempt status.

A nonprofit's venture into unrelated business activities can have implications that extend beyond the tax consequences. Some observers, for instance, have expressed concern about potential conflicts of interest.

Example In an effort to earn money from the test-preparation field, the College Board launched a Web site to compete with such firms as Kaplan, Inc. and Princeton Review. The Board's company was set up as a for-profit subsidiary, with 70 percent ownership by the Board. Competitors argued that the Web site was a conflict of interest since it was 70 percent owned by the nonprofit entity that prepared the tests. The Board argued that it needed the capital and stock options to compete for top talent.

The College Board is not alone in setting up for-profit subsidiaries that engender conflict-of-interest concerns. The American Association of Retired Persons (through its for-profit subsidiary, AARP Services) sells insurance, credit cards, and other services to its members. Until 2009, the American Medical Association (via an entity called "Medem") linked doctors with patients for a profit.[12] The National Geographic Society (via National Geographic Ventures) has wholly owned for-profit television and film production, mapping, and retail store subsidiaries.[13]

State and Municipal Taxes. Governmental and charitable organizations are exempt from local property taxes. In many states and municipalities, they are also exempt from sales taxes on the goods and services they sell. In addition, some are exempt from social security contributions and enjoy reduced postal rates. In comparing the costs of a nonprofit organization with those of a for-profit one in the same industry, therefore, the nonprofit's costs will be inherently lower for these reasons. However, some nonprofit organizations make contributions in lieu of taxes to their local municipalities. The purpose of these contributions is to pay for the services provided to the nonprofit organization by its municipality, such as trash collection, snow removal, and police and fire protection. Not all nonprofits make these payments.

Examples Harvard University purchased a 30-acre site in Watertown, Massachusetts, a small suburb just outside of Cambridge, for which it paid a private developer $162 million. More than $100 million in state and federal money had gone into cleaning up the site and getting it ready for development and inclusion on Watertown's tax roles. Had it been purchased by a for-profit entity, it would have constituted one-third of the town's real estate tax base. As a nonprofit organization,

---

[12] In 2009, Medem sold its health platform to Medfusion, which it said would allow it to "refocus its energies on the physician notification market with its HCNN initiative." For details, see http://chilmarkresearch.com/2009/07/21/medem-folds

[13] Lisa Rein, "Fairfax Closes Door on Nonprofit Tax Breaks," *The Washington Post,* October 8, 2002.

> Harvard was not obligated to pay any real estate taxes. Although Harvard was discussing with Watertown how much it would pay "in lieu of taxes," Watertown's town manager was quoted as saying that the university's proposal was "confusing and unworkable. They are asking for rights no other taxpayer in the country would be granted."[14]
>
> In 2002, supervisors for Fairfax County, Virginia voted to indefinitely suspend granting any new property tax exemptions to nonprofit organizations. The supervisors argued that, because of budget constraints, the county could not afford to forego any additional tax revenue for the foreseeable future. The county estimated that it forfeited $20,000 to $50,000 of tax revenue each year from newly granted exemptions.[15]

Tax-Exempt Bonds. Individuals who purchase bonds issued by states and municipalities do not pay federal or state taxes on the bond interest income they receive. Some states issue bonds whose proceeds are used by nonprofit hospitals and educational institutions, and the income on these bonds usually is tax exempt as well. Because holders of these bonds do not pay taxes on the interest income they receive, they are willing to accept a lower interest rate than they would on a bond of similar grade whose interest is taxable.

Contributions. Individuals and corporations that make contributions to charitable organizations can itemize and deduct these contributions in calculating their taxable income. The organizations that qualify for these deductions are spelled out in detail in Sections 170 and 501(c)(3) of the Internal Revenue Code (which is why charitable organizations frequently are termed 501(c)(3) organizations). In addition to the entities shown in Exhibit 2-1, they include nonprofit veterans' groups, cemeteries, and day-care centers. States, municipalities, and fraternal organizations also are included if the contributions they receive are designated for charitable purposes.

Legal Considerations

Three legal issues are of great concern to managers of nonprofit organizations: (a) ownership of the entity, (b) generation and distribution of a profit or surplus, and (c) legal obligations under a nonprofit charter.

Ownership of the Entity. A for-profit organization is owned by its shareholders, who expect to receive dividends and/or stock price appreciation as a return on the equity capital they furnish. By contrast, nonprofits cannot obtain equity capital from outside investors. Instead, their equity capital must be from donations and contributions. Moreover, a nonprofit organization cannot distribute its assets or income to, or otherwise operate for the benefit of, any individual. Indeed, trustees usually serve without monetary compensation. A nonprofit has nothing comparable to stock options, for example, which constitute an important employee incentive in many for-profit organizations. However, under the current tax code, neither high salaries nor large cash reserves are necessarily a violation of 501(c)(3) requirements. Considerable judgment is required, of course, in determining what is a "high salary" or a "large cash reserve."

When a nonprofit organization is dissolved, the entity's value ordinarily is transferred to another nonprofit organization, such as a foundation, or to the state or municipality where it operates, but never to private individuals. In the case of a conversion from nonprofit to for-profit status, the

[14] Joan Vennochi, "Rich Old Harvard is Jeopardizing Watertown's Security," *Boston Globe*, July 13, 2001.

[15] Diane Brady, "When Nonprofits Go After Profits," *Business Week*, June 26, 2000.

determination of the amount of value is an important concern for the state agency charged with regulating nonprofit organizations. This is because the entity's market value may be much greater than the difference between its recorded assets and liabilities. When this is the case, the determination of the appropriate "value" of the nonprofit organization becomes a matter of judgment and frequently considerable contention.[16]

Mergers. Partly because of declining philanthropy, and partly because of corporate individuals serving on their boards, some nonprofit organizations also have begun to merge. As with corporate mergers, there can be difficulties.

Example Second Harvest and Foodchain, two nonprofits concerned with fighting hunger, were, in the view of many, a perfect merger. Second Harvest distributed mainly canned goods, while Foodchain specialized in handling hot foods. Second Harvest was facing declines in contributions of canned goods, with many of its donors preferring to shift to prepared meals. Their clients were asking for more hot meals rather than ingredients that had to be mixed and prepared. Foodchain was facing a growing demand for its services but did not have enough staff or funding to meet the demand. Although the two organizations had contrasting cultures and financial stability, they were being strongly encouraged to merge by their donors and board members. The merger was announced in April 2000.[17]

Surplus Generation and Distribution. Legally, a nonprofit organization is allowed to earn an excess of revenues over expenses, sometimes called a surplus. This is its principal means of accumulating the equity capital that it may need for expansion, the replacement of fixed assets, or a buffer in the case of hard times. The organization is, of course, prohibited from paying out any of its surplus as cash dividends. A methodology to determine the appropriate size of the surplus is discussed in Appendix 2A.

Under certain circumstances, nonprofit organizations can create for-profit subsidiaries, which are permitted to pay dividends. For example, a nonprofit research laboratory may have a subsidiary that holds patents developed by its employees. It gives these employees ownership shares in the subsidiary, and thereby rewards them with a share of license fees for the patents they develop.

Since 1983, the Internal Revenue Service has allowed nonprofit organizations to establish profit-sharing plans under certain conditions.[18] In making this determination, the IRS reasoned that profit-sharing plans could have a favorable effect on employee performance, and thus could further the organization's charitable purposes. However, the IRS prohibits the organization from distributing a portion of its surplus to its managers "after the fact." There must be a profit-sharing plan in place prior to any sort of distribution.

The need for a preexisting plan arises because, under federal tax codes, no earnings of a tax-exempt organization may benefit a private individual. In this regard, the *Taxpayer Bill of Rights,* which became effective in September 1996, greatly expands public access to the annual federal tax filings of all tax-exempt organizations, and gives the IRS authority to take legal action against tax-exempt organizations that engage in prohibited "private inurement" activities.

---

[16] For a discussion of this point, see David W. Young, "Ownership Conversions in Health Care Organizations: Who Should Benefit?" *Journal of Health Politics, Policy, and Law,* 10, no. 4, Winter 1986.

[17] Jonathan Eig, "The Urge to Merge Hits Charities," *The Wall Street Journal,* April 18, 2000.

[18] IRS Revenue Procedure 83-36. For a discussion of some of the issues involved in establishing such a plan, see Charlotte P. Armstrong and Rylee Routh, "Profit-Sharing Choice for Non-profit organizations," *Pension World,* April 1984.

Legal Obligations Under a Nonprofit Charter. In exchange for their tax exempt status, nonprofit organizations are required to provide benefits to their communities. A subject of some considerable debate among nonprofits concerns the nature and extent of these benefits. In a December 2006 report, the Congressional Budget Office estimated that nonprofit hospitals receive $12.6 billion in annual tax exemptions, on top of the $32 billion in federal, state, and local subsidies that the hospital industry as a whole receives each year. It is not clear that all of this is being returned to their communities. Under new standards that the IRS implemented in 2009, hospitals need to account for their community benefits more specifically than at present.[19]

Example Some cities require hospitals to meet community care standards before being exempted from property taxes. Hospitals wishing to retain their tax-exempt status are required to contribute to their communities in a variety of ways, such as by accepting uninsured patients or running a 24-hour emergency room. Some hospitals have been accused of violating the spirit of this agreement, however.[20] For example, at one time, one nonprofit system, St. Louis-based BJC HealthCare, was counting the salaries of its employees as a community benefit (a practice that it agreed to discontinue).[21]

SERVICE ORGANIZATIONS

Most nonprofit organizations are service organizations and thus do not have the same management control advantages as companies that manufacture and sell tangible goods. There are several important differences between the two types of organizations:

- Services cannot be stored, whereas goods can be stored in inventory, awaiting a customer order. If the facilities and personnel available to provide a service today are not used today, the potential revenue from their sale is lost forever.

- Service organizations tend to be labor intensive. Although they require relatively little capital per unit of output, controlling their output requires managing the people who deliver the services. This generally is more difficult than managing an operation whose work flow is paced or dominated by machines.

- It is not always easy to measure the quantity of services. Keeping track of tangible goods, both during the production process or when the goods are sold, is usually easy. By contrast, a medical group practice can measure the number of patients a physician treats in a day, and even classify patient visits by type. However, this by no means measures the amount of service the physician provides to each of these patients.

- The quality of a service cannot be inspected in advance. The quality of tangible goods can be inspected in most cases before the goods are delivered to customers, and any defects

19 To see the IRS's final report, go to www.irs.gov/pub/irs-tege/execsum_hospprojrept.pdf

20 For details, see United States Government Accountability Office, Report to the Ranking Member, Committee on Finance, U.S. Senate: *Nonprofit Hospitals: Variation in Standards and Guidance Limits Comparison of How Hospitals Meet Community Benefit Requirements,* September 2008. Available at www.gao.gov/new.items/d08880.pdf

21 John Carreyrou and Barbard Martinez, "Nonprofit Hospitals, Once for the Poor, Strike it Rich," *The Wall Street Journal,* April 4, 2008.

are usually physically evident. At best, the quality of a service can be inspected during the time it is rendered to the client. Judgments as to the quality of most services are subjective, however, since for the most part, objective measurement instruments and unambiguous quality standards do not exist.

CONSTRAINTS ON GOALS AND STRATEGIES

Within wide limits, a for-profit organization can select the industry or industries in which it will do business. It can choose any of a number of different ways of competing in its industry, and it can change these strategies fairly easily should its management choose to do so. Most nonprofit organizations have much less latitude, and therefore tend to change strategies slowly, if at all. Universities add or close professional schools less frequently than large corporations add or divest operating divisions. A municipality is expected to provide certain services for its residents, such as education, public safety, or welfare. It usually can make decisions about the amounts of these services it will provide, but it cannot easily decide to discontinue them.

Example The Minneapolis Minnesota Library Board approved a plan in 2007 that called for permanently closing three of the city's branch libraries.[22] They are not alone. In 2008, the U.S. Environmental Protection Agency, as part of then-President Bush's planned reduction of $100 million in federal spending, closed some of its regional libraries despite protests by federal employees. Libraries in Chicago, Illinois; Dallas, Texas; and Kansas City, Missouri also closed in 2008.[23]

Many nonprofit organizations also must provide services as directed by an outside agency, rather than as decided by their own management or governing board. Private social service organizations must conform to state or municipal guidelines, for example, and organizations that receive funding support from the government must conform to the terms of the contract or grant. Moreover, the charters of many nonprofit organizations specify in fairly explicit terms the types of services they can provide.

Finally, federal and state legislatures may limit total spending on certain programs, or they may dictate spending limits for certain cost objects, such as travel. Similarly, donors to nonprofit organizations may restrict management's options on the uses of their contributions.

Diversification Through New Ventures

Despite the various constraints they face, many nonprofit organizations have grown and diversified considerably during the past two decades, some through the formation of for-profit subsidiaries. The process a nonprofit follows in its decision to undertake a new venture is complex, involving legal, strategic, and managerial concerns. Some of these issues are introduced here, and are discussed further in Chapter 7.

In many instances, new ventures have made financial contributions that have helped the parent organization to subsidize activities that were not financially feasible on their own. Indeed, during the 1980s, and again in the late 1990s and early 2000s, many nonprofits saw substantial reductions in federal assistance. Some of them used diversification strategies to ensure their survival, and, in so doing, entered into direct competition with for-profit organizations, particularly small ones. One survey placed unfair competition from nonprofit organizations as third among the top concerns of

[22] Brandt Williams, "Library Closings May be Just the Beginning," Minnesota Public Radio, October 26, 2006.

[23] American Library Association. Go to http://www.ala.org/ala/alonline/currentnews/newsarchive/2006abc/september2006a/epaclosings.cfm

small business people. The argument was that, since nonprofit organizations pay no taxes, they can compete unfairly with many small businesses.

Examples The Higher Education Reconciliation Act of 2006 contained a provision repealing the "50-percent rule," a statute limiting the number of Internet courses that nonprofit universities could offer. With its repeal, many nonprofits began to use aggressive marketing tactics to lure prospective students.[24]

Some years ago, the nonprofit Metro Washington Park Zoo in Oregon began to sell cans of Zoo-Doo—elephant manure that could be used as fertilizer. Washington D.C.'s National Zoo began to host champagne breakfasts in its reptile house. And the Minnesota Zoo began to charge cross country skiers $4 to traverse its grounds.[25]

Some nonprofit organizations have aligned their efforts with for profit firms. In many instances, a nonprofit will license its name to a corporation and earn royalties from the corporation's sales.

Example In 1996, the New York Parks Commission announced a $2 million alliance with Coca Cola Co., whose products became the official soft drink of the state's park system. The Commission also persuaded Saturn dealerships to donate $250,000 of playground equipment for three parks in return for small signs at each facility advertising their donation.[26] Similarly, portions of highways and roadways across the country now are being maintained by for-profit companies in exchange for small signs noting their contributions to the area's beautification.

The issue of competition between nonprofit and for-profit organizations is complicated by the presence of for-profit companies in activities traditionally conducted by nonprofit organizations. This is particularly true in health care, where considerable debate has raged over the merits of such a shift and its impact on the cost and quality of care.

Example The authors of a survey concluded that ownership of healthcare organizations is important to the American public. Half of the respondents saw the spread of investor ownership as a "bad thing" for the healthcare system. Roughly two-thirds saw nonprofit healthcare organizations as more trustworthy and less likely to charge high prices for treatment. Between a third and half of the public saw nonprofit health care as being more humane.[27]

Competition of nonprofits with small businesses is further muddied because analysts attempting to address the financial consequences have not distinguished clearly among three types of growth by nonprofits: (1) expanded sales of goods and services that do not compete with small businesses (e.g., hospital care), (2) expanded sales of goods and services that already were competing with small businesses (e.g. Girl Scout cookies), and (3) sales of goods and services that are relatively new to the nonprofit arena (e.g., tanning salons at a YMCA). Until a distinction of this sort is made, analysts will not be able to address the issue fully or appropriately.

---

[24] Betsy Vereckey, "For-profits battle competition in 2006," *Boston Globe*, December 26, 2006.

[25] Michael Allen, "Let's Hope Pythons Don't Enjoy a Sip of Veuve Clicquot," *The Wall Street Journal*, February 12, 1990.

[26] Terzah Ewing, "Meet the New Entrepreneurs: State Parks," *The Wall Street Journal*, February 11, 1997.

[27] Mark Schlesinger, Shannon Mitchell and Bradford H. Gray, "Public Expectations Of Nonprofit And For-Profit Ownership In American Medicine: Clarifications And Implications," *Health Affairs*, 23, no. 6 (2004): 181-191.

Regardless of the category, these sorts of activities are suggestive of a new focus of nonprofit organizations: entrepreneurial behavior.

Examples Ashoka: Innovators for the Public, a nonprofit, international venture-capital foundation, based in Arlington, Virginia, has provided financial and professional backing for more than 1,000 social entrepreneurs in 34 countries. These individuals use business techniques and expertise to help people help themselves. In the view of William Drayton, Ashoka's founder and chairman, there is no difference between those who use their skills in business and those who use them in the pursuit of social goals. In addition, many U.S. business schools now have courses on social entrepreneurship, and graduates are engaging in such diverse activities as assisting with small nonprofit startups, improving the efficiency of city government, and developing innovative new product lines in shelters for the homeless.[28]

The Social Innovation Forum, part of Root Cause, a nonprofit, creates partnerships between the nonprofit and private sectors. Through a competitive selection process, it identifies promising Boston-area nonprofits, gives them free services like management consulting and executive coaching, and introduces them to potential donors.[29]

SOURCES OF FINANCIAL SUPPORT

A for-profit company obtains financial resources from the sales of its goods and services. If the flow of this revenue is inadequate—if, for example, the company makes a product that the market does not want—the company does not survive. Moreover, a company cannot sell products unless their quality is acceptable, and their selling prices are in line with what the market is willing to pay. Thus, the market dictates the limits of a for-profit company's operations.

Some nonprofit organizations also obtain all (or substantially all) of their financial resources from sales revenue. This is the case with most community hospitals as contrasted with teaching hospitals, private schools and colleges that depend entirely on tuition from students, and research organizations whose resources come from contracts for specific projects. These client-supported nonprofit organizations are subject to essentially the same forces as their for-profit counterparts, such as, proprietary hospitals and for-profit research organizations.

Other nonprofit organizations receive significant financial support from sources other than revenue for services rendered. In these public-supported organizations, there is no direct connection between the amount of resources provided to the organization and the amount of services received by clients. Individuals receive essentially the same services from a government unit (such as mail delivery, street lighting, or public parks) whether they pay high taxes or no taxes. Unrestricted grants by a foundation are not made because of services the nonprofit provides to the grantor. Appropriations made by a state legislature to a university or hospital are not related directly to the services received by the people who pay state taxes.

Contrast Between Client-Supported and Public-Supported Organizations

In almost all instances, client-supported organizations want more clients. More clients imply more revenues, and more revenues imply greater success. In public-supported organizations there is no such relationship. Indeed, additional clients may place a strain on resources. This is especially

[28] Emily Mitchell, "Getting Better at Doing Good," *Time*, February 21, 2000.

[29] Sacha Pfeiffer, "Bottom-Line Philanthropy: Nonprofits Find Help Developing Pitches Aimed at Donors Used to Seeing Results," *The Boston Globe*, April 30, 2008.

true when a nonprofit's available resources are fixed by appropriations as in the case of government agencies. Or, if they are limited to the income from endowment or annual giving, as in the case of many educational, religious, and cultural organizations. Thus, in a public-supported organization, a new client may be only a burden—someone to be accepted with misgivings. In most for-profit or client-supported nonprofit organizations, by contrast, a new client is an opportunity to be pursued vigorously.

This negative or ambivalent attitude toward clients gives rise to complaints about the poor service and surly attitude of some public employees. Clients of client-supported organizations tend to hear "please" and "thank you" more often than clients of public-supported organizations.

Example A study conducted some years ago by the Comptroller of New York found that 63.9 percent of the time, individuals calling food stamp dispensing centers could not get through to a staff person because of busy signals or a failure to answer within 15 rings. Moreover, 84.4 percent of the callers who reached a staff person were given incorrect and incomplete information.[30]

In some public-supported organizations, this contrast is even stronger. A welfare organization should be motivated to decrease its clientele, rather than increase it; that is, it should seek ways to rehabilitate clients and remove them from the welfare rolls. The Small Business Administration (SBA) should work to change high-risk businesses into low-risk businesses that will no longer need the special services of the SBA. The idea that an organization should deliberately set out to reduce its clientele is foreign to the thinking of for-profit managers.

Competition provides a powerful incentive to use resources wisely. Profits decline if a for-profit firm permits its costs to get out of control, its product line to become obsolete, or its quality to decrease. A public-supported organization has no such automatic danger signal. As a substitute for the market mechanism for allocating resources, managers of public-supported organizations compete with one another for available resources. The sanitation department, the parks department, and the road maintenance department all try to get as large a slice as possible of a municipality's budget pie. In responding to their requests, senior management tries to judge what services clients should have, or what best serves the public interest, rather than what the market wants. The U.S. Postal Service maintains rural post offices, for example, even though they are not profitable.

Just as the success of a client-supported organization depends on its ability to satisfy its clients, the success of a public-supported organization depends on its ability to satisfy its resource providers. Thus, a state university maintains close contact with the state legislature, and a private university may place somewhat more emphasis on athletics than the faculty thinks is warranted in order to satisfy contributors to the alumni fund. Similarly, a sanitation department is likely to place considerable emphasis on removing the mayor's garbage in a timely way. Furthermore, acceptance of support from the public frequently carries with it a responsibility for accounting to the public which, in many instances, must be done in greater detail than exists in a client-supported organization.

PROFESSIONALS

In many nonprofit organizations, the individuals who are the keys to success are professionals: physicians, scientists, combat commanders, teachers, social workers, artists, ministers, and so forth. Professionals often have motivations that are inconsistent with good resource utilization. This creates a dilemma that has important implications for senior management.

Professionals are motivated by at least two sets of standards: those of their organizations and those of their colleagues. The former are related to organizational objectives; the latter may be in-

[30] Comptroller's Report, *The City of New York*, Vol. 12, No. 6, February 1988.

consistent with organizational objectives. In fact, the rewards for achieving organizational objectives may be much less potent than those for achieving professional objectives. The reluctance of university faculty to serve on school or department committees, or to place priority on teaching rather than research, is a direct reflection of this reward structure.

In addition, many professionals, by nature, prefer to work independently. Examples are academicians, researchers, and physicians. Because the essence of management is getting things done through people, professionals with such a temperament are not naturally suited to the role of manager. This is one reason managers in nonprofit and other professional organizations are less likely to have come up through the ranks than those in for-profit organizations.

Although leadership in a nonprofit organization may require more management skills than professional skills, custom often requires that the manager be a professional. A military support unit is usually managed by a military officer, even though a civilian might be a better qualified manager. Traditionally, the head of a research organization is a scientist; the president of a university, a professor; the head of a hospital, a physician. This tradition is diminishing, however.

In many nonprofit organizations, the professional quality of the people is of primary importance and other considerations are secondary. Promotion is often geared to the criteria established by the profession rather than those of the organization, per se. To the extent that these criteria reflect an individual's worth to the profession but not to the organization, they may run counter to the efficiency and effectiveness of the organization as a whole. Moreover, professionals tend to need a longer time to prove their worth to the profession than managers need to prove their worth to the organization.

Traditionally, a professional's education has not included a managerial component. Most educators believe that training in the skills of the profession is far more important than training in the skills needed to manage organizations employing members of the profession. Consequently, sheer ignorance has often led professionals to underestimate the importance of the management function. While education and external pressures for better organizational performance are working to change this perception, the culture of many nonprofit organizations has reinforced the tendency to disparage managers.

Financial incentives tend to be less important to professional people. This is both because professionals usually consider their current compensation to be adequate and because their primary satisfaction ordinarily comes from their work. Professionals also tend to give inadequate weight to the financial implication of their decisions. Many physicians, for example, feel that no limit should be placed on the amount spent to save a human life. Unfortunately, in a world of limited resources, such an attitude is unrealistic.

GOVERNANCE

Although the statement that shareholders control a corporation is an oversimplification, particularly in the post-Great-Depression era, shareholders do have the ultimate authority. They may exercise this authority only in a crisis, but it nevertheless is there. The movement of stock prices is an immediate and influential indication of what shareholders think of management. In for-profit organizations, policy and management responsibilities are vested in the board of directors, which derives its power from the shareholders. In turn, the board delegates power to the chief executive officer (CEO), who serves at the board's pleasure, and acts as the board's agent in the management of the organization. He or she is replaced if there are serious differences of interest or opinion, or if there are problems in performance.

Governing Boards in Nonprofit Organizations

In many nonprofit organizations, the line of responsibility is often not clear. There are no shareholders, members of the governing body are seldom paid for their services, and many are chosen for political or financial reasons rather than for their ability to exercise sound judgment about the organization's management.

More importantly, a nonprofit's governing body often is insufficiently informed about major issues facing the organization, and its decisions therefore are not always optimal. Thus, governing boards tend to be less influential in nonprofit organizations than in for-profit ones.

At an absolute minimum, a governing board has the responsibility to take action when the organization is in trouble. Since there is no profit measure to provide a warning, the personal appraisal by board members of the health of the organization is much more important in a nonprofit organization than in a for-profit one. In order to have a sound basis for such an appraisal, board members need to spend a considerable amount of time learning about the organization, and they need to have enough expertise to understand the significance of what they learn. This often is not the case.

The juxtaposition of the above two paragraphs points to one of the most serious governance problems faced by many nonprofit organizations. For reasons indicated in the first paragraph, many governing boards do an inadequate job of fulfilling the responsibilities outlined in the second. Frequently, there is not even a general recognition of the board's responsibility.

In universities, for example, a widely quoted maxim is "The function of a Board is to hire a president and then back him, period."[31] Similarly, many hospital boards are dominated by physicians who are qualified to oversee the quality of care but who have neither the expertise nor the willingness to assess the effectiveness and efficiency of hospital management.

In government organizations at all levels, auditors verify compliance with statutory rules on spending, but few oversight agencies pay attention to how well management performs its functions. Although legislative committees look for headline-making sins, many such committees do not have the inclination to arrive at an informed judgment on management performance.

Government Organizations

In government organizations, external influences tend to come from a number of sources, leading to a diffusion of power. In federal and state governments, for example, there is a division of authority among executive, legislative, and judicial branches. Consequently, there are often conflicting judgments about objectives and the appropriate means to attain them. In a for-profit company, the board of directors and the chief executive officer usually have similar objectives, and there is nothing comparable to a "legislative branch."

There may also be a vertical division of authority among the federal, state, and local levels of government, with each level responsible for different facets of the same problem. For example, the federal government finances major and many minor highways, whereas local governments construct and maintain other highways and roads.

Agencies (or units within agencies) may have their own special-interest clienteles (such as the Maritime Administration and shipping interests) with political power that is stronger than that of the

---

[31] Perhaps because the academic environment encourages writing, more has been written about college and university trustees than about other types of governing boards. Publications of the Association of Governing Boards of Colleges and Universities, One Dupont Circle, Washington, D.C., contain much material about the governance of colleges and universities. The classic book is still Beardsley Ruml and Donald M. Morrison, *Memo to a College Trustee,* New York: McGraw-Hill, 1959.

chief executive of the agency. Similarly, senior-management authority may be divided, especially in states where expenditure authority is vested in committees of independently elected officials. The same problem occurs in localities governed by commissions, each of whose members administers a particular segment of the organization, such as streets or health. By contrast, elected officials, such as the attorney general, the treasurer, the secretary of state, or the director of education may manage their organizations fairly independently.

A manager's latitude also may be determined by political boundaries that are structural in nature. For example, the mayor of Los Angeles has much narrower responsibility than the mayor of New York because county governments in California are responsible for many services that in New York fall under the city organization.

Often, too, government bureaucracy is insulated from senior management by virtue of job security and rules. Career civil servants may know that they will outlast the term of office of the elected or appointed chief executive. If a particular project cannot be sold to the current boss, the project's sponsors may bide their time and hope to sell it to the next one. Conversely, if they dislike a new policy, they may drag their heels long enough to allow new management to take over and possibly rescind the policy.

This fragmentation of authority complicates management control. A particularly significant consequence is that the public administrator comes to depend on political power to influence those who cannot be controlled directly. Consequently, managers must focus on their political credit as well as their financial credit; they must measure the political costs and benefits of alternatives, as well as their financial costs and benefits.

POLITICAL INFLUENCES

As the above description suggests, many nonprofit organizations are political in nature—they are responsible to the electorate or to a legislative body that presumably represents the electorate. There are several consequences of this status.

Necessity for Reelection

In government organizations, decisions result from multiple, often conflicting, pressures. In part, these political pressures are inevitable, and, up to a point, desirable. In effect, since elected officials are accountable to voters, the pressures presumably represent the forces of the marketplace. Elected officials cannot function if they are not reelected. In order to be reelected, they must advocate the perceived needs of their constituents. To gain support for programs important to their constituents, however, they often must support the programs of some of their colleagues, even though they personally do not favor them. This logrolling phenomenon is also present in for-profit organizations, but to a lesser extent.

Public Visibility

In some instances, the need for improved management arises not because a nonprofit organization is large and complex, but because it is highly visible.

Example KERA/Channel 13 is one of two television stations that broadcast programs prepared by North Texas Public Broadcasting (NTPB). In the words of Gerry Ferral, president and CEO of NTPB: "KERA has about 150 employees and a budget of slightly under $20 million, which is not very

> big in terms of major companies. And if our products were widgets or thingamajigs no one would ever notice us. But because PBS is very public, we must deal with many of the same workplace issues and public relations needs that very, very large companies must deal with."[32]

More generally, in a democratic society, the press and the public feel they have a right to know everything about a government organization. In the federal government and some state governments, this feeling is codified by freedom of information statutes, but the channels for distributing this information are not always unbiased. Although some media stories describing mismanagement are fully justified, others tend to be exaggerated or give inadequate recognition to the inevitability of mistakes by managers in any organization. To reduce the potential for unfavorable media stories, government managers may take steps to reduce the amount of sensitive information that flows through the formal management control system. Unfortunately, this also lessens the usefulness of the system.

Multiple External Pressures

The electoral process, with institutionalized public review through the media and opposing political parties, results in a wider variety of pressures on managers of public organizations than on managers of private ones, whether nonprofit or for-profit. In general, elected public officials generate more controversy about their decisions than do business managers. In the absence of profit as a clear-cut measure of performance, these pressures may be erratic, illogical, or even influenced by momentary fads. Frequently, these pressures lead to an emphasis on short-term goals, or on program decisions devoid of careful analysis. Shareholders demand satisfactory earnings, whereas the public and governing bodies of nonprofit organizations do not always channel their pressures toward good resource utilization.

Legislative Restrictions

Government organizations must operate within statutes enacted by the legislative branch, which are much more restrictive than the charter and bylaws of corporations, and which often prescribe detailed practices. In many instances it is relatively difficult to change these statutes.

Management Turnover

In some public organizations senior management tends to turnover rapidly because of administration changes, political shifts, military orders, and the hiring of managers who only dabble in government jobs. Each change requires learning lead time and frequently a change in priorities. This rapid turnover results in short-run plans and programs that quickly produce visible results, rather than in substantive long-range programs.

Civil Service

There is widespread belief that Civil Service regulations operate to inhibit good management control. It is by no means clear, though, that Civil Service regulations are different in any important respect from personnel regulations in some large companies. One important difference in many state and municipal governments is that Civil Service laws effectively inhibit the use of both the carrot and the stick. As a result, a Civil Service Syndrome may develop: You need not produce success;

---

[32] Judy Corwin, "Managing a Nonprofit—The Case of Public Broadcasting," *Baylor Business Review*, Spring 2000.

you need merely to avoid making major mistakes. This attitude is a major barrier to employees and managers who wish to improve organizational effectiveness.

Nevertheless, Civil Service regulations in many government organizations may be no more inhibiting than union regulations and norms in for-profit organizations. Example are restrictive and inefficient union rules regarding work assignments, such as the number of engineers and other personnel aboard trains, or the division between electricians and plumbers on a construction project. An important difference, however, is that union rules generally affect individuals near the bottom of the organization, whereas Civil Service rules affect individuals throughout the organization, including many managers.

TRADITION

In the 19th century, accounting was primarily fiduciary in nature; that is, its purpose was to keep track of funds entrusted to an organization to ensure that they were spent honestly. In the 21st century, accounting in business organizations has assumed much broader functions. It furnishes useful information to interested outside parties as well as to management. Nonprofit organizations have been slow to adopt 21st century (or even 20th century!) accounting and management control concepts and practices, including, in some instances, the use of accrual accounting.[33]

Barriers to Progress

Since nonprofit organizations lack the semiautomatic control provided by the profit mechanism, they need good management control systems even more than businesses. Yet, many such organizations, particularly government organizations, have lagged behind. For government, there seem to be three principal explanations.

First, for many years, there was a prevalent attitude that the differences between government and business were so great that government could not use management control techniques developed by business. This attitude continues to be implicit in some texts on government accounting. Second, at the federal level, Congress, particularly the House Committee on Appropriations, has been reluctant to shift to a new budget format. Because of the importance of the budget, this reluctance affects the whole management control system. A similar problem exists in many states. In part, the reluctance is based on simple inertia, but it also reflects a suspicion—generally unwarranted—that the change is an attempt by the executive branch to conceal something from the legislative branch. Third, many career officials recognize that a good management control system is two edged: it provides information for management, but it also provides information for outside agencies, such as the Office of Management and Budget, Congress, special interest groups, and the media. Some of these officials are not anxious for outside agencies to have access to new and better information.

It is important to note that the first reason is based on the premise that good management control systems cannot be developed in the public sector. The second reason is based on the premise that the proposed new formats provide poorer information. The third reason is based on the premise that a revised management control system will provide better information. All three reasons cannot be correct.

---

33 The absence of accrual accounting is not confined to the U.S. For details, see E. Caperchioni and R. Mussari (eds), *Comparative Issues in Local Government Accounting*. Norwell, Massachusetts: Kluwer Academic Publishers, 2000. For a brief history of the accounting function and its development in the last century, see William Steinberg, "Cooked Books," *The Atlantic*, January 1992.

SUMMARY

The characteristics of nonprofit organizations described in this chapter can be grouped into two categories—technical and behavioral. Both are important to the material in this book. Technical characteristics relate to the difficulty of measuring outputs and assessing the relationship between inputs and outputs. This difficulty is unique to a nonprofit organization. Improvements in output measurement are possible, however, and managers need to spend considerable efforts to make them. Nevertheless, it must be recognized at the outset that the resulting system will never provide as good a basis for planning or measuring performance as the profit measure does in for-profit organizations.

Behavioral characteristics encompass all the other topics in this book. The significance of these characteristics is twofold. First, most behavioral factors that impede good management control can be overcome by improved understanding and education. Second, unless these problems are overcome, any improvement in the technical area is likely to have little real impact on the management control function.

Suggested Cases for Classroom Use with this Chapter

See the Appendix at the end of the book for a more complete description of each case and ordering information.

Granville Symphony Orchestra	Uncovering some misleading results in the financial statements in an annual report.
New England Trust	Using ratios and some other information to identify different nonprofit organizations with contrasting financial structures.
South Central Mental Health Association	Resolving some organizational issues in a mental health agency.
Office of Community Development	Resolving some organizational design issues in an antipoverty agency.
Usuluteca (A)	Formulating a national drug policy in a developing country.
Usuluteca (B)	Assessing further issues and tradeoffs in the national drug policy.

Suggested Additional Readings

Carol L. Barbeito, *Human Resource Policies and Procedures for Nonprofit Organizations*, 2006.

Tracy Daniel Connors (ed.), *The Nonprofit Handbook: Management*, New York, John Wiley & Sons, 2001.

James J. Fishman and Stephen Schwarz, *Nonprofit Organizations: Statutes, Regulations, And Forms*, University Casebook, 2006.

Gary M. Grobman, *The Nonprofit Handbook: Everything You Need to Know to Start and Run Your Nonprofit Organization*, 2008.

Robert D. Herman and Associates, *The Jossey-Bass Handbook of Nonprofit Leadership and Management*, Second edition, San Francisco, Jossey Bass, 2005.

Bruce R. Hopkins, *Starting and Managing a Nonprofit Organization: A Legal Guide*, 2004.

Bruce R. Hopkins and David Middlebrook, *Nonprofit Law for Religious Organizations: Essential Questions & Answers*, 2008.

Steven J. Ott, *Understanding Nonprofit Organizations: Governance, Leadership, and Management*, 2001.

Emanuele Padovani and David W. Young, *Managing Local Governments: Designing Management Control Systems that Deliver Value*. London, Routledge, 2012.

Dennis D. Pointer and James E. Orlikoff, *The High-Performance Board: Principles of Nonprofit Organization Governance* (The Jossey-Bass Nonprofit and Public Management Series), 2002.

www.mapnp.org/library A free management library for nonprofits

www.nonprofit.gov A network of links to federal government information and services

www.nccs.urban.org Statistics on the nonprofit sector

www.guidestar.org A national data base of nonprofit organizations; contains copies of Form 990 for several thousand nonprofits

Appendix 2-A

Determining an Appropriate Surplus for a Nonprofit Organization

The accounting and financial management literature on nonprofit organizations is in considerable agreement that these organizations need adequate financial surpluses for four reasons.

1. To assist the organization to obtain the funds necessary to replace assets that wear out or become obsolete
2. To finance the cash needs associated with a growth in revenues in conjunction with the expansion of its charitable or nonprofit activities
3. To provide the funds necessary to grow and diversify fixed assets as the organization expands its charitable activities
4. To protect the organization from fluctuations in revenues from year to year, and from general economic and other uncertainties surrounding its ongoing operations.

As a result, a nonprofit organization, especially one that has significant plant, equipment, and other fixed assets (such as a hospital, a museum, a university, or a port authority), or one that is growing rapidly, needs to earn a surplus.[34]

These requirements are not unique to nonprofit organizations. Rather, what distinguishes a nonprofit from a for-profit organization is the absence of "owners" or "investors." As a result, a nonprofit organization does not need a surplus to provide a return to its owners. Apart from this distinction, however, any organization that wishes to remain in business, or that is called upon to expand its operations, needs a surplus for one or more of the above four requirements.

Failure to understand these requirements and their implications has led many observers to suggest that the term "nonprofit" implies there should be a zero surplus. Nothing could be further from the truth. Rather, the important question is whether the surplus of a given nonprofit organization is "appropriate." This question can be addressed from the perspective of each of the above four requirements.

Requirement #1. Fixed Asset Replacement

The surplus requirements associated with replacing fixed assets (principally plant and equipment) arise because, at some point, all fixed assets wear out or become technologically obsolete. Because of inflation, their replacement cost usually is more than their initial cost.

---

[34] For discussion on the need for a surplus, see Herzlinger, Regina E., and Denise Nitterhouse, *Financial Accounting and Managerial Control for Nonprofit Organizations,* Cincinnati, Ohio, South-Western Publishing Co., 1994; Suver, James D., Bruce R. Neumann, and Keith E. Boles, *Management Accounting for Healthcare Organizations, 3rd edition,* Chicago, Healthcare Financial Management Association and Pluribus Press, Inc., 1992. Ziebell, Mary T., and Don T. DeCoster, *Management Control Systems in Nonprofit Organizations,* San Diego, Harcourt Brace Jovanovich, Publishers, 1991; and Young, David W., "Nonprofits Need Surplus Too," *Harvard Business Review,* January-February 1982.

Some have argued that sufficient funds would be available for fixed asset replacement if their depreciation were "funded," i.e., if an equivalent amount of cash were sequestered each year in a special fund dedicated to fixed asset replacement. However, funded depreciation would be sufficient only if there were no inflation. In an inflationary economy, the inflation base is the asset's purchase price, whereas the earnings on the funded depreciation come from a base that is only a small fraction of the asset's purchase price. This phenomenon is illustrated in Exhibit 1.

Exhibit 1. Funded Depreciation and Asset Replacement Under Inflation

Assumptions:
Purchase Price of Asset = $50,000
Economic Life of Asset = 5 years
Depreciation = $10,000 per year ($50,000 ÷ 5 years)
Rate of inflation and return on invested depreciation funds = 10 percent

Earnings from funded depreciation:

Year	Beginning Balance	Depreciation Amount	New Balance	Investment Earnings	Ending Balance
1	$ 0	$10,000	$10,000	$1,000	$11,000
2	11,000	10,000	21,000	2,100	23,100
3	23,100	10,000	33,100	3,310	36,410
4	36,410	10,000	46,410	4,641	51,051
5	51,051	10,000	61,051	6,105	67,156

Inflation in purchase price of asset:

Year	Beginning Balance	Amount of Inflation	Ending Balance
1	$50,000	$5,000	$55,000
2	55,000	5,500	60,500
3	60,500	6,050	66,550
4	66,550	6,655	73,205
5	73,205	7,320	80,525

Difference between funds available and replacement cost = $67,156 - $80,525 = ($13,369)

As this exhibit illustrates, with inflation, there is a gap between available funds and the asset's replacement cost. This is true even if the rate of inflation is below the return on invested funds. Indeed, since the return on invested funds has a base (the amount of accumulated depreciation plus investment earnings) that is much smaller that the original cost of the asset, but inflation is affecting the full cost of the asset, the spread between the return on invested funds and the inflation rate must be quite large if funded depreciation is to provide for asset replacement.[35]

[35] Of course, the replacement cost of some assets, such as personal computers, is less than their original cost. However, these situations are rare. Far more common are technological advances that render an asset obsolete, and that require its replacement before the end of its estimated economic life (i.e., its depreciation period). Because the obsolete asset has not been fully depreciated, its "depreciation fund" be less than initially forecast. Yet, the purchase price for the new asset likely will be much greater than the cost of the obsolete one. This phenomenon has been particularly prevalent in the healthcare field.

How Large a Surplus?

To determine whether a nonprofit organization's surplus is appropriate in light of Requirement #1, the surplus must be considered in comparison to the organization's assets. That is, we must compute the organization's return on assets (ROA), which is the ratio between surplus and total assets. ROA also is used to measure the financial performance of for-profit organizations, although analysts frequently will also focus on a company's return on equity (ROE).[36]

For purposes of assessing the appropriateness of a nonprofit organization's surplus, ROA is a more useful measure than ROE. This is because ROE is influenced by the amount of an organization's debt, whereas ROA is not. Thus, ROE is concerned not only with the organization's *financial performance,* but also with its *financing strategy*. This phenomenon is illustrated in Exhibit 2.

Exhibit 2. Ratios Related to ROA and ROE

Computation of ROA

$$\frac{\text{Surplus}}{\text{Revenue}} \times \frac{\text{Revenue}}{\text{Assets}} = \frac{\text{Surplus}}{\text{Assets}}$$

Profit margin *Asset turnover* *ROA*

Impact of Leverage

$$\frac{\text{Surplus}}{\text{Assets}} \times \frac{\text{Assets}}{\text{Equity}} = \frac{\text{Surplus}}{\text{Equity}}$$

ROA *Leverage* *ROE*

As Exhibit 2 indicates, surplus must be looked at in conjunction with revenues and assets. Thus, the profit margin can be multiplied by the asset turnover ratio to determine the return on assets. Note that when an organization has debt, it can have more assets on its balance sheet than otherwise would be possible. This phenomenon, called *leverage,* can be measured by a ratio of total assets to equity. ROA, multiplied by leverage, determines ROE. Thus, other things equal, debt allows an organization to have an ROE that exceeds its ROA.

Because nonprofit organizations do not have the ability to raise capital through equity offerings, as do their for-profit counterparts, they must rely to a greater extent on surpluses to generate the funds to replace their assets. Otherwise, their only options are capital campaigns, donations, or continual increases in their debt levels. However, (a) capital campaigns are highly infrequent events, (b) donations for the replacement of fixed assets are rare in most nonprofits, and, (c) as discussed below, increases in debt levels often are imprudent.

Profit Margin: A Mistaken Focus. In determining the appropriateness of a surplus, many analysts focus only on a nonprofit organization's *profit margin*. This is a mistaken notion. To understand why, note that an organization with a low profit margin can achieve a appropriate ROA by having a high asset turnover. A good example might be a day care center, which might have a low profit margin but could turn its assets (mainly inventory) over more than once a month. By contrast, an organization with a high base of fixed assets, such as a port authority, would not be able to turn its assets over as fast as a day care center. It thus needs a higher profit margin if it is to earn a appropriate ROA. To illustrate the above point, consider the following two sets of ratios:

[36] This is sometimes referred to as return on investment (ROI)

	Profit margin x	*Asset turnover* =	*ROA*
Day Care Center	.01	15.0	.15
Port Authority	.10	1.5	.15

Note that in both instances, the ROA is 15 percent. Thus, having a high profit margin is not necessarily good or bad. Rather, the key issue is the *combination* of profit margin and asset turnover. ROA measures how well an organization is performing overall in earning a return on its invested assets.

Making the Computations. Assume that we wish to compute a appropriate surplus for both the day care center and the port authority. We first would need to agree on two assumptions: (1) an appropriate ROA, given the entity's fixed assets and their rate of inflation[37] and (2) a target asset turnover ratio.

Assume we agree that the port authority's fixed assets are inflating at a rate of 9 percent and the day care center's at a rate of 3 percent. Assume further that we think the port authority (with a high proportion of fixed assets relative to total assets) should have an asset turnover ratio of 1.5, and the day care center (with a low proportion of fixed assets) a ratio of 15. We now can compute the relevant profit margins as follows:

	ROA ÷	*Asset turnover* =	*Profit margin*
Day Care Center	.03	15.0	.002
Port Authority	.09	1.5	.06

Once we know the revenue figures for the two organizations, we can compute the absolute amount of the surplus. Assume that the day care center had revenues of $200,000 and the port authority had revenues of $200 million. Appropriate surpluses for Requirement #1 then could be computed as follows:

	appropriate Profit Margin x	*Revenue* =	*Surplus*
Day Care Center	.002	$200,000	$400
Port Authority	.06	$2,000,000	$120,000

The Impact of Leverage

As Exhibit 2 indicates, leverage, i.e., the use of debt, can allow an organization to purchase more assets than otherwise would be possible. To understand the role of leverage, you should note that, if an organization had no debt whatsoever, its assets and equity would be equal. Its leverage ratio, therefore, would be one. As it begins to rely on debt to finance its assets, the ratio increases. Exhibit 3 illustrates this phenomenon with a simple example, beginning with a balance sheet in which assets and equity are equal, and moving to a situation in which assets are twice as large as equity. As can be seen, the leverage ratio increases to a level of 2.0 under these circumstances.

Advantages of Leverage. As Exhibit 3 shows, leverage allows an organization to own more assets than it could if it relied only on its own equity. Note that equity has remained unchanged in this example while assets have doubled. In effect, the organization is using debt as a "lever" to expand its asset base. This, in turn, allows it to deliver more services than otherwise would be possible, and therefore to earn more revenue.

[37] While it may be difficult to ascertain the precise rate of inflation affecting an organization's assets, the use of one or more inflation indices usually is sufficient to determine an approximate ROA standard.

Exhibit 3. Examples of Leverage

	Assets	=	*Liabilities*	+	*Equity*
Situation 1: No debt	1,000		0		1,000
Leverage = 1,000 ÷ 1,000 = 1.0					
Situation 2: Debt of $500	*Assets*	=	*Liabilities*	+	*Equity*
	1,500		500		1,000
Leverage = 1,500 ÷ 1,000 = 1.5					
Situation 3: Debt of $1,000	*Assets*	=	*Liabilities*	+	*Equity*
	2,000		1,000		1,000
Leverage = 2,000 ÷ 1,000 = 2.0					

In short, two organizations with identical ROA ratios could have quite different ROE ratios, as the following example illustrates:

	ROA	x	Leverage	=	ROE
Organization #1	15%		1.5		22.5%
Organization #2	15%		2.0		30.0%

Note that Organization #1 has leverage of 1.5, i.e., debt that is 50 percent of its equity. This transforms its 15% ROA into a 22.5% ROE. Organization #2, by contrast, has leverage of 2.0, i.e., debt that is 100 percent of its equity, thereby allowing it to transform its 15% ROA into a 30% ROE.

Drawbacks to Leverage. Leverage does not come without some drawbacks. Borrowings must be repaid, and generally there is an interest charge. Organizations that rely heavily on borrowed funds spend considerable time and effort predicting and managing their cash flows so as to assure themselves of sufficient cash on hand to meet their debt service obligations.

Financial Risk versus Business Risk. One way to think about leverage is in terms of the *financial risk* it creates as compared with the organization's overall *business risk*. Financial risk and leverage are synonymous. That is, other things equal, the higher an organization's leverage, the higher its debt service obligation, and the greater the risk that it will be unable to meet this obligation, i.e.., the greater its financial risk.

Business risk, by contrast, refers to the certainty of an organization's annual cash flows. Specifically, organizations that have a relatively high business risk have a high degree of *uncertainty* about their cash flows. A good example of an organization with a high business risk is a farming cooperative, where product availability and cost are greatly influenced by unpredictable climactic conditions. A good example of an organization with a low business risk is a day care center in a wealthy suburban neighborhood. The farming cooperative quite likely would face a great deal of uncertainty from one year to the next about its annual cash flows, whereas the day care center would be almost completely certain of its.

The relationship between financial and business risk is illustrated in Exhibit 4. As it suggests, other things equal, an organization with low business risk can have a fairly high financial risk. Assuming the organization structures its debt properly, the relative certainty of its annual cash flows gives it some appropriate assurance that it will be able to meet its debt service obligations each year.

Exhibit 4. Business Risk vs. Financial Risk

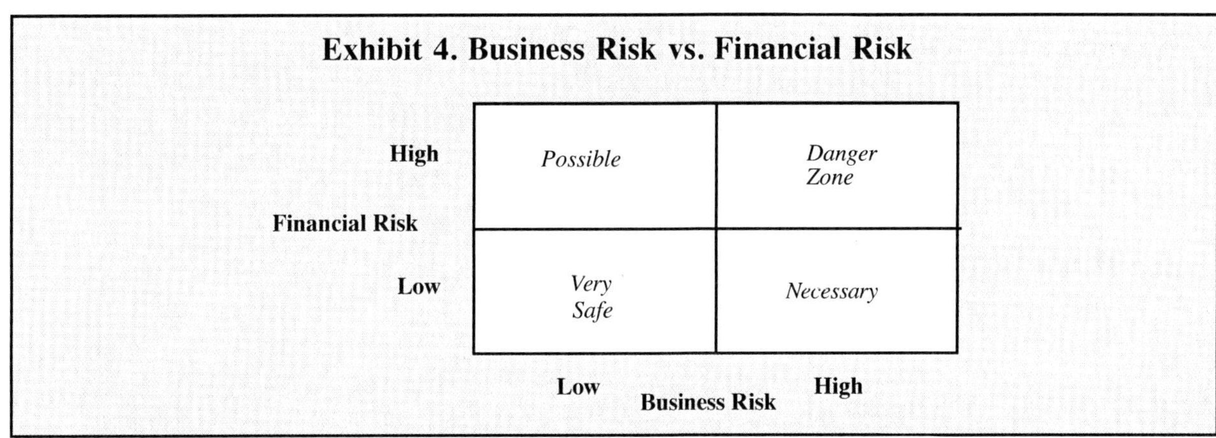

By contrast, an organization with a high business risk generally would find it unwise to have high financial risk. Since debt service obligations remain constant each year, the organization could quite easily find itself in a situation where, because of events beyond its control, its cash flows were not sufficient to meet these obligations. The result could be detrimental to the organization's financial viability.

Returning to the above example of Organization #1 and Organization #2, the important point to notice is that the *financial performance* of the two organizations was the same, i.e., the surplus of each was 15 percent of its assets. By adopting a different *financing strategy*, however, Organization #2 was able to earn a higher ROE. This is why it is important to focus on ROA and not ROE when assessing the appropriateness of a nonprofit organization's surplus.

In short, ROA is a more appropriate measure of financial performance than ROE because it measures an organization's ability to generate sufficient surpluses to replace its assets as they wear out or become obsolete. Computed over a period of several years, ROA effectively measures the ability of a nonprofit organization to remain financially viable. Indeed, if ROA does not approximate the rate of inflation for the fixed assets an organization must replace, and if the organization is unable to obtain contributions from donors to replace its assets, it will atrophy.

Requirement #2. Cash Needs

When an organization is both growing and selling its goods and services on credit—a common situation for many nonprofit organizations—this requirement translates into a need to have sufficient cash on hand to meet financial obligations. That is, nonprofit organizations that are expanding their operations, and that have cash tied up in accounts receivable and inventory, must earn surpluses to finance the cash needs associated with their growth.

If an organization without a surplus uses debt to supply these cash needs, it will be unable to repay the debt until its growth rate slows or other measures are taken (such as accelerating the collection of accounts receivable or delaying the payment of accounts payable). Therefore, under these circumstances, debt generally is considered to be an undesirable alternative.

The impact of growth on cash is illustrated in Exhibit 5. The exhibit shows a growing organization that (a) has a 2-month collection lag in its accounts receivable, (b) pays its expenses immediately, and (c) earns a zero surplus. Under these circumstances, the organization will constantly be short of cash. For example, the $100 in revenue earned in month 1 is received in month 3 (two months later), when the accounts receivable are collected. However, with growth, the expenses, and hence cash outflows, in month 3 are $104, causing a $4 decline in cash. This cash shortage accumulates from month to month, resulting in a negative $24 at the end of six months.

Exhibit 5. Cash Needs Associated with Growth

Assumptions:

1. Growth in revenue and expenses of approximately 2 percent a month.
2. Accounts receivable collection lag of two months.
3. All expenses paid immediately.
4. No growth in inventory or other current items.

	MONTH					
	1	2	3	4	5	6
Operating statement						
Revenue	100	102	104	106	108	110
Expenses	100	102	104	106	108	110
Surplus	0	0	0	0	0	0
Cash flows:						
Cash collections (1)	96	98	100	102	104	106
Less: cash payments (2)	100	102	104	106	108	110
Change in cash	(4)	(4)	(4)	(4)	(4)	(4)
Cumulative cash change	(4)	(8)	(12)	(16)	(20)	(24)

1. From revenue earned two months ago that went into accounts receivable.
2. Same as expenses due to assumptions #3 and #4 above.

How Large a Surplus?

In the simplified example in Exhibit 5, a surplus equivalent to the "Change in cash" line would avoid the cash shortages. This is shown in Exhibit 6. Note that, with a net income of $4 per month, there is no change in cash. Of course, the cash problem also could be averted by slowing growth or accelerating the collection of accounts receivable, but many nonprofit managers and their boards see growth as highly desirable, and usually find it difficult to collect receivables much faster than the norm in their organization's industry (which for many nonprofits is far longer than 2 months). Thus, profit margin (or an increased profit margin) is sometimes the only feasible option. It can be attained by increasing revenue or decreasing expenses. Here, we did it by decreasing expenses.

Exhibit 6. Using Surplus to Finance Growth-Related Cash Needs

Assumptions:

1. Expenses $4 per month less than in Exhibit 5.
2. All other assumptions unchanged

	MONTH					
	1	2	3	4	5	6
Operating statement:						
Revenue	100	102	104	106	108	110
Expenses	96	98	100	102	104	106
Surplus	4	4	4	4	4	4
Cash flows:						
Cash collections	96	98	100	102	104	106
Cash payments	96	98	100	102	104	106
Change in cash	(0)	(0)	(0)	(0)	(0)	(0)
Cumulative change	(0)	(0)	(0)	(0)	(0)	(0)

Requirements #3 and #4. Expand and Diversity Assets, and Provide for Economic Uncertainties

These requirements relate to planned expansion activities of a nonprofit organization and the economic uncertainties in the environment where it operates. As such, they are inherently more difficult to measure and quantify than Requirements #1 and #2.

Requirement #3 involves an examination of an organization's growth strategy and the potential sources of financing the corresponding asset expansion (e.g., whether contributions are available or debt financing is appropriate). The surplus needed for meeting Requirement #4 involves an analysis of the organization's financial history, including the stability of its prices and its mixture of operating surpluses and deficits over time. Wide swings in prices for the organization's goods or services, for example, or the occasional occurrence of an operating deficit, usually indicate that a surplus is necessary whenever feasible. These surpluses, in turn, can help to fund future deficits.

Summary

Of the four requirements for a surplus, this appendix has focused mainly on the first two. These are the most easily quantified measures, and ones that generally can be determined by focusing on a nonprofit's financial statements for several years, including *pro forma* financial statements. Although the latter two measures are more strategic and environmental in nature, they nevertheless are important, and should be considered in assessing the appropriateness of a nonprofit organization's surplus.

Not all nonprofits will need a surplus for each of the four requirements. Others will base a portion of their desired surplus on each. Few nonprofits will have *none* of the requirements present, however. In this regard, a key job for a nonprofit's senior management is to determine which of the four requirements are appropriate, and to sum the associated surplus requirements for each as part of the organization's annual budgetary process. To do otherwise is to jeopardize the organization's long-run financial viability.

Appendix 2-B
Differences Among Nonprofit Organizations

The description of nonprofit organizations in this chapter is intended to apply to these organizations in general. Clearly, the characteristics discussed in the chapter do not fit all such organizations equally well. This appendix attempts to relate the broad description of nonprofit organizations contained in the text to each of the principal nonprofit sectors. Of course, these too are broad-brush generalizations to which many exceptions can be found in individual organizations.

Healthcare Organizations

Nonprofit hospitals, nursing homes, health maintenance organizations, clinics, and similar healthcare organizations closely resemble their for-profit counterparts. Indeed, other than the presence of owners expecting a return on their investments, there are few differences between a voluntary hospital and a proprietary hospital. The healthcare environment is changing dramatically, and competition among healthcare organizations of all kinds has become much more intense in the past few years than ever before.

Nevertheless, most healthcare organizations still have fewer competitive pressures than a typical for-profit business. Much revenue is still received from third-party payers, such as Blue Cross, managed care plans, other insurance companies, and the government, rather than directly from clients. Additionally, they are dominated by professionals, and have no clear-cut line of responsibility to a defined group of owners. Spurred on by public concern about the rising cost of health care and by the necessity of justifying their fees on the basis of a plausible measurement of cost, many hospitals have made dramatic improvements in their cost accounting systems in recent years. Others lag far behind the advances that have taken place in the healthcare sector as well as in other industries.

With passage of the Affordable Care Act, healthcare organizations will feel even greater pressure to develop improved management control systems. There is not yet a great deal of evidence of progress, however.[38]

Educational Organizations

Private colleges and universities whose tuition approximates the cost of education also resemble for-profit educational entities. To the extent they are supported by contributions and endowment earnings, however, the relationship between tuition revenues and the cost of services is less direct. Like hospitals, they are dominated by professionals, and their governing boards tend to have relatively little influence. They are also subject to competitive pressures. In recent years, under the leadership of the National Association of College and University Business Officers NACUBO, many have made substantial improvements in their management control systems.

State colleges and universities are supported primarily by appropriations from state legislatures. Although these funds may be based on a formula that takes into account the number of students or

---

[38] For a discussion of some of the challenges that confront healthcare entities attempting to develop "accountable care organizations" (ACOs), see David W. Young "Bumps along the ACO Road," *Healthcare Financial Management*, December 2011. This article can be obtained by going to www.DavidYoung.org, clicking on publications, and clicking on the article name.

credit hours, they are not the same as fees charged to clients because the individual student or parent ordinarily does not make the decision that the education received is worth the amount charged. In other respects, state institutions are similar to private colleges and universities. In recent years, the legislative oversight bodies of some states have paid much attention to the financial management of their colleges and universities, and this has led to great improvements in their management control systems. Public elementary and secondary schools generally use an accounting system developed under the auspices of the U.S. Office of Education, which is urged as a condition of federal support. A few communities have developed excellent systems on their own initiative.

Membership Organizations

The purpose of membership organizations is to render services to their members. They include religious organizations, labor unions, trade associations, professional associations, fraternal organizations, social and country clubs, cemetery societies, and political organizations. To the extent that they are supported by membership dues, fluctuations in the amount of such dues is an indication of the perceived value of services rendered by the organization. This is true even though there is rarely a direct connection between an individual's dues and the services he or she receives.

Many membership organizations are dominated by professionals and have weak governing boards. Some, such as religious organizations and labor organizations, face strong competitive pressures. Others, such as professional associations, have no effective competition.

Historically, religious organizations have had notoriously weak management control systems. In recent years, however, several denominations have developed good systems and have encouraged their use at local levels. Religious organizations have a particularly difficult problem in deciding on the programs to be undertaken and in measuring the value of services rendered. Souls saved per pew hour preached is not a feasible measurement.

Human Service and Arts Organizations

Human service organizations include family and child service agencies, the Red Cross, scouting and similar youth organizations, and various charitable organizations. Arts organizations include museums, public broadcasting stations, symphony orchestras, theaters, and ballet companies. Although they have quite different missions, human service and arts organizations share a characteristic that unites them from a management control perspective. Specifically, with some notable exceptions, these organizations rely heavily on public support, either from the government or from contributions by individuals, companies, and foundations. Their revenues therefore do not directly measure the value of services provided to clients. Those who provide support tend to exercise an increasing amount of influence over the financial affairs of these organizations.

In recent years, considerable improvements have been made in the management control systems of these organizations. These improvements are primarily a result of the influence of such organizations as the United Way of America and professional associations of museums and broadcasting stations. Significant opportunities for further improvement remain, however.

The Federal Government

Except for certain businesslike activities, such as the U.S. Postal Service, the federal government does not receive fees from clients. Its goals are multiple and fuzzy, and the value of its services is especially difficult to measure. In addition, the federal government is subject to more external power and political influence than other nonprofit organizations. These forces make management control especially difficult. Furthermore, many federal agencies are unique. There is only one State Department, for example, so there is no basis for comparing their performance with that of other units. Some improvements have occurred in recent years, but much remains to be done.

State and Local Governments

Collectively, state and local governments are by far the largest category of nonprofit organizations. Like the federal government, they are subject to a variety of external power and political influences, and therefore have difficult management control problems.

Generally, their revenue is not directly related to services provided to clients. Although the person whose house is on fire is a client in one sense, the main function of the fire department is to protect the whole community. Proposals for specific programs are often political in nature, and frequently are not subject to economic analysis. The objectives of these organizations are difficult to define in ways that permit measurements of attainment. What is adequate fire or police protection?

Although management control in state and local government is inherently difficult, good systems are especially necessary. With a few notable exceptions, such systems do not now exist in most government units. Tradition has greatly hampered development of adequate systems. Many government units keep their accounts solely on a cash receipts and disbursements basis, a practice that has been obsolete since the 19th century. Only recently has pressure for change begun to emerge—driven in large part by public dissatisfaction with rising taxes and revelations of poor management.[39]

[39] For a discussion of the challenges faced by local governments in developing improved management control systems, see, Emanuele Padovani and David W. Young, *Managing Local Governments: Designing Management Control Systems that Deliver Value*, London, Routledge, 2012

Part II

Management Control Principles

Before discussing management control systems and their implementation, we need to understand some of the principles on which these systems are based. Because management control systems are focused internally, this text does not discuss general purpose financial statements—the vehicles by which nonprofit organizations report their financial activities and results to outside parties. Instead, we look at internal matters, mainly at costs and cost behavior.

Chapter 3 looks at full-cost accounting in terms of the decisions that managers must make to establish a full-cost system. Chapter 4 takes up the topic of differential costs, discussing different types of costs and how they are calculated. Finally, Chapter 5 examines one of the more important aspects of management control in nonprofit organizations: pricing decisions. The chapter looks at some considerations for managers who make these decisions.

A common theme in Chapters 3, 4, and 5 is cost (and expense) measurement. Cost information plays a central role in many management decisions in nonprofit organizations. These decisions include:

- Determining the financial viability of programs or products, which requires full-cost information.
- Choosing among alternative courses of action, which relies on differential costs.
- Setting prices, which often uses a combination of full costs and differential costs.

Cost information also is important in decisions about the management control system. In setting up the management control system, senior management structures costs in terms of the managers who are responsible for incurring them. Costs structured in this way are called *responsibility costs*. They are discussed in Part III.

Full costs and responsibility costs are incorporated into an organization's accounts so they can be collected on a regular basis. By contrast, a differential cost analysis is specific to the issue under consideration; therefore, differential costs, as such, are not included in the accounts.

Chapter 3
Full-Cost Accounting

Answering the question "What did it cost?" is important in many organizations, but arriving at an answer can be much more difficult than it might first appear. Obviously, it is rather easily answered if we are discussing the purchase of inputs (supplies, labor, and so on) for the service-delivery process. Even calculating the full cost of a "unit" produced—whether it is a dialysis procedure or 50 minutes of psychotherapy—is relatively easy as long as the organization provides completely homogeneous goods or services. Complications arise when an organization provides multiple goods and services, and uses different kinds and amounts of resources to provide each of them. This chapter discusses some of these complications.

USES OF FULL-COST INFORMATION

Information on the full cost of carrying out a particular endeavor has four basic uses: pricing, profitability assessment, comparative analyses, and external reporting. Most managers use cost information for one or all of these purposes at different times and under varying decision-making scenarios.

Pricing

One of the basic functions of cost information is to assist management in setting prices. Clearly, cost information is not the only information that is used for this purpose, but it is an important ingredient. In a similar vein, some nonprofit organizations are paid on the basis of their full costs, thereby creating the need for a full-cost analysis that effectively establishes the "price." In some other situations, an organization is a price-taker, and a full-cost analysis is not used in setting prices.

Profitability Assessments

Even if an organization is a price taker, it must calculate full costs if management is to know whether a particular program or product is financially viable.[1] If a product is not covering its full costs, it is, by definition, a "loss leader." Since an organization cannot have all its products be loss leaders, full-cost accounting serves to highlight where cross subsidization is taking place.

Comparative Analyses

Many organizations can benefit from comparing their costs with those of similar organizations that deliver the same sorts of products. Although full-cost information can assist in this effort, comparative analyses can be complicated. For example, before undertaking such an analysis, we would need to know whether the organizations used for comparison measure their costs in the same way as we do. As the discussion in this chapter demonstrates, there can be a variety of complexities in undertaking comparative analyses

[1] Technically, the term *product* refers to either a good or a service. It could refer to a lab test, a museum exhibit, an opera, a served client, or a discharged client. This is not meant to suggest that a client or a patient is a "product," but rather to clarify a shorthand that will make it easier to discuss the concepts without excessive verbiage.

Examples Northern College, a small private liberal arts college, is interested in comparing its cost per student with the cost per student in some similar colleges. In making this comparison, the college must consider issues such as average class size, the existence of specialized programs in athletics, art, music or other subjects, special services (such as career counseling), whether it wishes to include room and board and/or the library costs in the comparison, and the method used to calculate the cost (e.g., whether it amortizes its library collections and, if so, over what time period), and a variety of similar matters.

Concord Health Network, an integrated delivery system (IDS), is interested in comparing its cost per patient with the cost per patient in similar IDSs. In making this comparison, Concord must consider issues such as average occupancy rate of its hospitals, the existence of specialized programs in, say, cardiology or oncology, the provision of services (such as social work or discharge planning), whether it wishes to include outpatient costs in the comparison, and so on.

As these examples suggest, the definition of what is to be included in a full-cost calculation requires a managerial decision. Indeed, because there is such a wide range of choices embedded in an organization's cost accounting system, many managers simply make comparisons over time for their own organization, knowing that the methodology has remained consistent from one year to the next.

External Reporting

In situations where a third-party pays on the basis of cost, an organization usually must calculate its full costs according to certain guidelines. It then must submit the resulting cost report to the third-party before receiving payment. Similarly, some grant-making organizations, such as foundations, require the grantee to compute the full cost of each project or program they supported.

THE FULL-COST ACCOUNTING METHODOLOGY

Conceptually, the goal of full-cost accounting is quite basic: to measure as accurately as possible the resources consumed in producing a particular product. In some instances, the measurement process is quite easy. For example, an organization that produces a single good or service usually has little difficulty in calculating the full cost of each unit. All costs associated with the organization, and hence the good or service, can be added together and divided by the number of units produced during a particular accounting period to arrive at a full cost per unit.

Example In a freestanding dialysis clinic, computing the full cost of a dialysis procedure is relatively easy. The clinic can add together all of its costs for an accounting period, such as a month, and divide by the number of procedures provided during the month. Since all procedures are more or less identical, this average cost figure is quite accurate.

By contrast, organizations that produce a variety of goods or services, each requiring different amounts of resources, will have a more difficult time determining the cost for each unit sold.

Example In a freestanding ambulatory surgery center that performs several different types of surgical interventions, computing the full cost of an operation is considerably more complicated than it was for a procedure in the dialysis clinic. Since each operation consumes different kinds and amounts of resources, an average cost per operation would quite likely be misleading.

For organizations with a heterogeneous mix of outputs, such as the above ambulatory surgery center, the full-cost accounting effort typically goes through two stages, which are discussed below. In Stage 1, the accounting staff undertakes several steps, at the end of which all costs reside in the organization's mission centers. During Stage 2, each mission center's costs are *attached* to its outputs (or products). Combined, the two stages constitute the full cost accounting methodology.

Sometimes, the decisions for each stage are made by the organization's accounting staff, rather than its managers. This is not optimal. Senior managers, including professional leaders, such as physician or social workers, must take an active role in the various cost accounting decisions if they are to assure themselves of having a cost accounting system that meets their needs.

THE STAGE 1 PROCESS

Stage 1 entails four activities: (a) defining the organization's cost objects, (b) selecting the cost centers that will be used to collect costs, and dividing them between service centers and mission centers, (c) assigning all costs to one or more cost centers, and (d) allocating service center costs into mission centers.

Defining Cost Objects

A final cost object is the unit of output for which we wish to know the full cost. In a hospital, for example, the final cost object might be an all inclusive day of care. As such, it would include all surgical procedures, laboratory tests, radiology exams, pharmaceutical usage, and so on. When this is the case, calculating the full cost of a day of care is as simple as calculating the cost of a dialysis procedure in the above example: total costs divided by total days of care provided.

In most hospitals, the final cost objects are more complicated than an all-inclusive day of care. In some instances, for example, one cost object is a day of "routine" care (e.g., room, dietary, housekeeping, laundry, and nursing costs), with separate cost objects for other activities, such as a day of intensive care, a laboratory test, a radiological procedure, and so on. In other hospitals, the final cost object is something broader than a day, such as a discharge. If a discharge is the cost object, the hospital includes all costs associated with the patient's entire stay (i.e., for all days of care, rather than just an average single day). Here, too, however, computing the average cost per discharge would be quite easy: total costs divided by total discharges.

Complications arise only when we decide that different cost objects use resources differently, such as when we want to know the cost of a discharge according to the patient's diagnosis, or DRG.[2] In this case, the *final cost object*, the DRG, is computed by summing a variety of *intermediate cost objects*. The final cost object is used for billing payers (or for a comparison with the payment the hospital receives from its payers), and the intermediate cost objects are smaller units needed to produce the final cost object.

Example If a hospital wants to know the cost of a patient with DRG 200 (the final cost object), it must add the costs of all resources provided to the patient during his or her stay (the intermediate cost objects). These include operative procedures, laboratory tests, radiological procedures, pharmaceuticals, intensive care days, routine care days, and so forth. This means that it needs to determine the cost of each intermediate cost object.

When the final cost object becomes more heterogeneous than a single procedure (such as a dialysis) or an all-inclusive day, our focus shifts to the intermediate cost objects that were used to produce it. Different combinations of these intermediate cost objects will affect the cost of the final

[2] A DRG (Diagnosis-Related Group) is a single diagnosis, or a collection of several similar diagnoses.

cost object, even though the final result (or "product")—the discharge of a patient—is the same. Thus, our real interest is in the cost of the intermediate cost objects, or the intermediate "products," as they sometimes are called. We will return to this idea later in the chapter.

Selecting Cost Centers

To calculate the cost of the intermediate products, we first assign all costs to cost centers. Cost centers can be thought of as "buckets" in which an organization's costs are accumulated for conducting the Stage 1 analysis. Frequently, an organization's cost centers are identical to its departments. For example, in a hospital, the department of radiology might be one cost center, the social work department another, the housekeeping department a third, and so on. However, some departments are a collection of several cost centers. For example, a department of radiology might be divided into the cost centers of CT scanning, angiography, magnetic resonance imaging, and so on. If this is done, radiology's intermediate cost objects will be produced in several different cost centers.

Mission Centers versus Service Centers. An organization's cost centers are divided between mission centers and service centers. Mission centers are associated with the organization's main focus (or mission). In a hospital, mission centers provide care to patients and usually charge (or are paid by third parties) for their services. Because of this, they often are called "revenue centers."

Service centers, by contrast, accumulate the costs of activities the organization carries out to support its mission centers. In a hospital, housekeeping, laundry, dietary, administration, and the like would be considered service centers, while inpatient care, radiology, pathology, the pharmacy, and so forth would be classified as mission centers.

In some instances, a service center may charge both mission centers and other service centers for their support activities, but they do not charge clients directly.[3]

Example The annual cost of caring for a child in the Western Home for Children (the final cost object) depends on the services the child receives (intermediate products). There are four basic types of services: foster home care, psychological testing, social work counseling, and psychotherapy. Each of these services is also a mission center, where a variety of costs are accumulated. The psychological testing center, for example, includes the costs of part-time psychologists, testing materials, and the fee the agency pays to an outside organization to have the tests processed and scored. The costs in the psychological testing mission center are accumulated for the year, and are divided by the number of children tested to give a cost per child tested. Each child who was tested has this cost added to his or her other costs to arrive at the total cost of caring for him or her for the year.

Assigning Costs to Cost Centers

After an organization's cost centers have been determined, all costs then must be *assigned* to either a service center or a mission center. This usually is not difficult, although it can become somewhat complicated at times. For example, if a radiology department has several separate costs centers, as described above, it must find a way to assign the salary of, say, its scheduler to each center. The scheduler is easily assigned to the overall radiology cost center, but not so easily assigned to individual cost centers within radiology. The assignment can be carried out by either developing techniques that measure cost usage in considerable detail, or establishing a distribution formula.

---

[3] This internal charge is called a *transfer price*. It is discussed in greater detail in Chapter 6.

Example A social worker in the foster home department of Western Home for Children is supervised by a person who also supervises the psychologists in the testing department. The supervisor's salary must be distributed between the two departments. To do so, the accountants might develop a formula, using, say, relative hours of service or number of personnel in each cost center as the distribution mechanism. Alternatively, the supervisor might be asked to maintain careful records of time spent in each cost center, which the accountants then could use to distribute the salary. In this latter case, the cost accounting effort would be more precise since the cost (time) would be directly traceable to each cost center. Obviously, doing so is more costly than using a formula.

Allocating Service Center Costs

The full cost of a mission center includes its *fair share* of the organization's service center costs. To allocate service center costs to mission centers, we must choose a basis of allocation for each service center that measures its use by the other cost centers as accurately as possible. For example, the allocation basis for the housekeeping service center might be square feet. We can measure the number of square feet in each cost center and divide total housekeeping costs by total square feet to get a housekeeping cost per square foot. We then multiply that rate by the number of square feet in each cost center to determine its fair share of the housekeeping center's costs.

Assignment versus Allocation. It is important to distinguish between "assignment" and "allocation." Assignment precedes allocation, and serves to place costs into service and mission centers. By contrast, *allocation* distributes service center costs among mission centers.[4]

Precision of Allocation Bases. When selecting allocation bases, it is important to keep in mind that increased precision generally requires greater measurement efforts, giving rise to higher accounting costs. For example, not all square feet in an organization are equally easy to clean. Therefore, rather than using number of square feet to allocate housekeeping costs, we might allocate them on the basis of hours spent. While hours spent is a more accurate basis, and would give us a more accurate cost figure, its use requires an ongoing compilation of the necessary data.

In summary, the more precise an allocation basis, the more accurately one captures true resource consumption. Exact measurement of resource consumption can be a time-consuming and complicated process, however, and less accurate approaches occasionally are adopted in response to time, staffing, and technical constraints.

Allocation Methodology. Once we have selected an appropriate allocation basis for each service center, we then can allocate the service center costs to the mission centers. Three methods of varying complexity and accuracy are available for doing this: *direct*, *stepdown*, and *reciprocal.*

With the *direct* method, service center costs are allocated to mission centers only, and not to other service centers. This is the simplest method, and is used by many organizations. It is the least precise of the three, however, in that it excludes the cost effects associated with one service center's use of another service center.

The *stepdown* method allocates service center costs into both other service centers and mission centers. Because it allocates service centers to other service centers as well as to mission centers, the

---

[4] This terminology can be confusing. *Allocation* is sometimes called *apportionment*, and vice versa. Moreover, the terms *assignment, distribution, allocation,* and *apportionment* occasionally are used interchangeably. In addition to these terminology differences, service center costs that are allocated to production centers often are called *indirect* or *overhead costs*. The context usually clarifies the meaning, but because of these terminology differences, it is important to understand the activities taking place rather than to memorize definitions of the terms.

stepdown method is more complicated than the direct method. It also is more accurate in that it includes the cost effects associated with one service center's use of another. However, once a service center's costs have been allocated, it cannot receive an allocation. Thus, for a given service center, the stepdown method includes only the cost effects of its use of the service centers that precede it in the allocation sequence, and not those that follow it.

With the *reciprocal* method, all service centers make and receive allocations to and from each other, as well as to mission centers. The allocation amounts are determined by a set of simultaneous equations, which are solved on a computer. Because all service centers both make and receive allocations, the reciprocal method is the most accurate of the three, but also the most complicated to use.

An Example Using the Stepdown Method. Despite the greater accuracy of the reciprocal method, many organizations find that the stepdown method strikes about the right balance between accuracy and ease of use. Thus, we will use it here for illustrative purposes.

Choosing a Service Center Sequence. When the stepdown method is used, the sequence followed in allocating the service centers can have an impact on the costs in each mission center. Because the analysis is of costs already incurred, however, the sequence will not affect total costs, which will remain the same under all sequences.

Conceptually, the approach to choosing a sequence is to rank service centers in order of their use by other service centers. That is, the service center that uses other service centers the *least* is allocated *first,* and the service center that uses other service centers the *most* is allocated *last*. Clearly, considerable judgment is required to determine this sequence, and, even then, there is no such thing as the "right" sequence.

Conducting the Allocations. After we have chosen the sequence for service centers, the allocation effort can begin. To illustrate, assume that a small social service agency has the three service centers and two mission centers, shown in Exhibit 3-1 (the amounts are shown in thousands and rounded). The service centers are Administration (assigned costs of $100), Housekeeping (assigned costs of $20), and Client Records (assigned costs of $30). The mission centers are Foster Home Care (assigned costs of $1,000) and Group Home Care (assigned costs of $500). The agency's total costs are thus $1,650, as shown at the bottom of the Assigned Costs column.

The allocation process begins with the first service center in the sequence (here, we have chosen Administration), which, as the note in parentheses under its *column* indicates, is allocated on the basis of number of employees. Each remaining cost center will receive its share of Administration costs based on its proportion of employees.

The next service center to be allocated is Housekeeping. The amount to be allocated is its assigned costs of $20 *plus* the $25 that was allocated to it from Administration. As a result a total of $45 must be allocated. As the parentheses under the Housekeeping column indicate, it is allocated to the remaining centers on the basis of square feet, such that the more space a receiving cost center has, the greater its share of Housekeeping costs.

The final service center to be allocated is Client Records, which, as the exhibit indicates, has a total of $50 to be allocated: $30 of assigned costs, plus $10 allocated from Administration, and $10 allocated from Housekeeping. It is allocated to the remaining cost centers on the basis of the number of client records.

We now can add up the costs of the two mission centers. Foster Home Care has $1,000 of assigned costs, plus $40 of allocated Administration, $20 of allocated Housekeeping, and $30 of allocated Client Records, for a total of $1,090. Group Home Care has $500 of assigned costs, plus $25 of Administration, $15 of Housekeeping, and $20 of Client Records, for a total of $560.

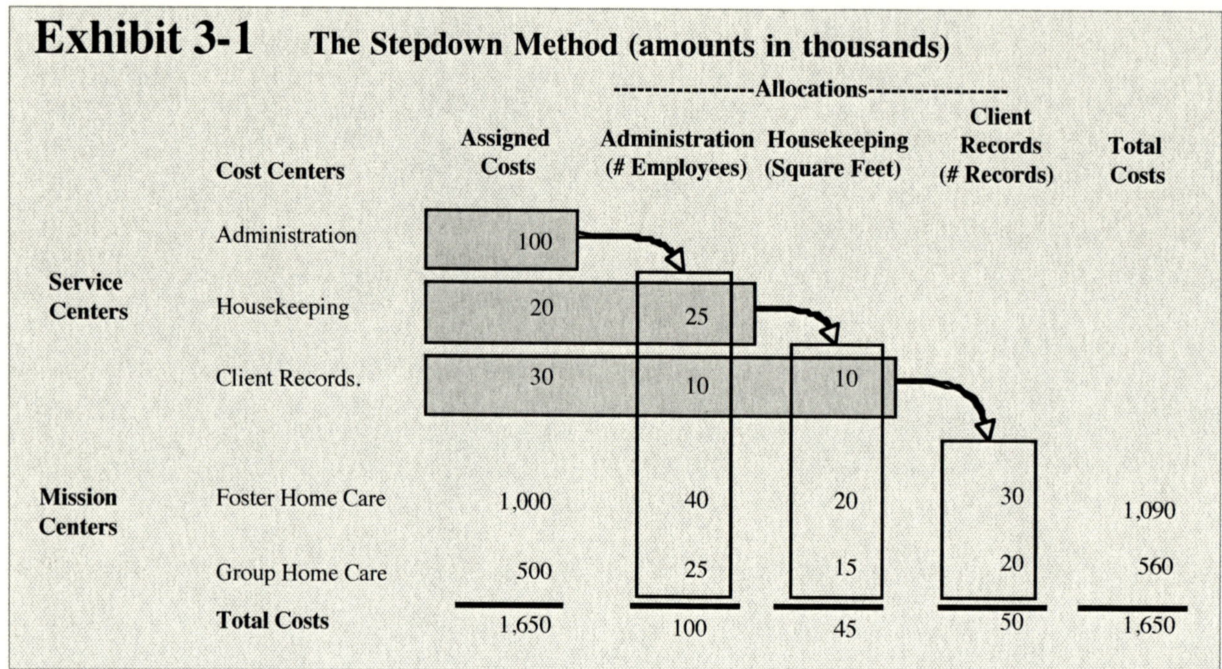

Exhibit 3-1 The Stepdown Method (amounts in thousands)

	Cost Centers	Assigned Costs	Allocations: Administration (# Employees)	Allocations: Housekeeping (Square Feet)	Allocations: Client Records (# Records)	Total Costs
Service Centers	Administration	100				
	Housekeeping	20	25			
	Client Records.	30	10	10		
Mission Centers	Foster Home Care	1,000	40	20	30	1,090
	Group Home Care	500	25	15	20	560
	Total Costs	1,650	100	45	50	1,650

Note that our total costs of $1,650 remained the same as they were prior to allocating service center costs. However, we now have fully allocated the service center costs to the two mission centers. We did so by first allocating the Administration service center costs to the Housekeeping and Client Record service centers, as well as to the two mission centers, then allocating the Housekeeping service center costs (with its Administration allocation included) to Client Records and the two mission centers, and finally allocating Client Records to the two mission centers.

In summary, the full cost of a mission center includes its assigned costs, plus the costs allocated to it from the organization's service centers. The stepdown method shown in Exhibit 3-1 is one of the formal techniques used to carry out the process.

Key Aspects of the Stepdown Method. There are several important points to keep in mind about the stepdown method.

1. Only service center costs are allocated. Mission center costs are not. Mission centers receive costs from service centers, but once a cost has been allocated to a mission center it stays there.

2. The *allocation basis* chosen for a service center attempts to measure the use of that center's resources by the other cost centers—both service centers and mission centers. For example, in a hospital's laundry, "pounds washed" frequently is used as the allocation basis. Each cost center receives a portion of the laundry center's costs in accordance with its proportion of the total pounds of laundry washed. If a particular cost center sent no laundry to be washed, it would not receive an allocation.

3. The amount of a service center's allocation to other cost centers depends, in part, on its position in the sequence. If it is allocated late in the sequence, it will contain some costs from service centers allocated earlier in the sequence. If it is allocated early, it will not.

4. Total costs do not change. Different allocation bases and stepdown sequences only change the distribution of total costs among the mission centers. Thus, the effect of any change in methodology is solely one of making shifts among cost centers. Sometimes these cost shifts can be quite significant, however.

STAGE 2. ATTACHING A MISSION CENTER'S COSTS TO ITS COST OBJECTS

At the end of Stage 1, all costs reside in mission centers. Stage 1 can have some flaws, but with minimal effort, it usually can provide a reasonably accurate depiction of mission center costs. It is during Stage 2, when a mission center's costs are attached to its cost objects, that complications can arise.

There are two approaches used to attach mission center costs to cost objects. The first is a *process system,* which typically is used when all units of output are roughly identical. All mission center costs for a given accounting period are simply divided by the total number of units produced to give an average cost per unit. This approach would be appropriate for the dialysis clinic discussed earlier, and for many other situations where all output units are roughly identical, such as with a meals-on-wheels program.

By contrast, a *job order system* is used when the units of output are quite different. Consider, for example, a repair garage for a municipality's waste disposal vehicles. Adding all costs for a given accounting period, such as a day, and dividing by the number of vehicles repaired to determine an average cost per repaired vehicle, would provide quite misleading information. Instead, the garage would use a job ticket, on which the time and parts associated with each repair effort would be recorded separately. These items then would be costed out by means of hourly wage rates, unit prices, and so on. Many nonprofits face similar situations with heterogeneous output units.

Examples The research department at a university may work on several different research projects, and each project must be costed out individually.

The counseling department of a social service agency comes into contact with many clients, and wishes to know the cost associated with each.

The special education department of a middle school provides services to many students, and wishes to know the cost for each student.

The internal medicine department of a rural group practice sees many patients each day and wants to know the cost of each patient's visit.

As the above examples illustrate, the mission centers of many nonprofit organizations have units of output whose diversity requires a job order system. Implementing such a system requires understanding the nature of a mission center's costs. These are shown in Exhibit 3-2.

As this exhibit indicates, a mission center's costs fall into two categories: *direct* and *indirect*. Direct costs are those that can be attached to a cost object unambiguously; they typically comprise direct labor and direct materials. There is no big problem here. A job ticket (or its equivalent) can be used to record their use, and unit rates can be used to cost them out.

Exhibit 3-2 Elements of Full Production Cost

TYPE OF COST	DESCRIPTION	EXAMPLES
Direct	Costs that are unambiguously associated with the mission center where the cost objects are produced, and that can be attached rather easily to any given cost object by using . . .	
Direct Labor	. . . time and motion studies.	Technicians in a radiology department; nurses on an inpatient ward
Direct Materials	. . . material usage studies.	Reagents in a laboratory; medical supplies on an inpatient ward
Other Direct	. . . machine and/or equipment studies.	Depreciation on a piece of equipment that is used for a single cost object
Indirect		
Indirect Labor	Costs that also are unambiguously associated with the mission center where the cost objects are produced, but that cannot be attached directly to a given cost object.	Quality inspectors, supervisors
Indirect Materials		Cleaning solvents for machines, record-keeping supplies
Other Indirect		Depreciation on the mission center's computers
Allocated service center costs	Service center costs that are allocated to the mission center during Stage 1. They also cannot be attached directly to a given cost object.	Laundry, housekeeping, and general administration costs

The problem arises with a mission center's *indirect costs,* i.e., those costs that cannot be unambiguously associated with a cost object. As shown in Exhibit 3-2, these costs fall into four categories: (a) indirect labor, such as supervisory time, (b) indirect materials, i.e., materials that cannot be directly associated with a cost object, such as cleaning solvents for machines, (c) other indirect costs, such as depreciation on administrative computers, and (d) service center costs that were allocated to the mission center during Stage 1.

In a typical job order context, indirect costs are "attached" to products through the use of one or more "overhead rates." The *absorption process*, as this effort is called, can be a little tricky, and can give misleading results on occasion. For example, when only one overhead rate is used, as frequently happens, the implicit assumption is that the unit used in that rate (e.g., machine hours or direct labor hours), drives the use of all indirect costs. However, indirect costs generally arise from a more complex array of forces, such that an absorption process using a single overhead rate can give management misleading information about the full cost of a cost object. This can lead to poorly informed pricing decisions and profitability analyses.

Enter Activity-Based Costing

Activity-based costing, or ABC, is now used in many settings (both manufacturing and service) to correct for this deficiency. Designers of ABC systems use multiple "indirect cost pools," and try to design each pool so that the resources in it are as homogeneous as possible. They then identify an activity that drives the use of each pool's resources, and use it to compute the pool's overhead rate. For example, an indirect cost pool in a laboratory might be the labor and supervisory time needed to set up the machines for processing a batch of tests (such as blood samples). In this case, the appropriate cost pool would be everything associated with setting up the machines (such as cleaning and adjusting tolerances), and the appropriate unit of activity for the pool would be one machine setup. As a result, a unit of output (a test in this case) in a small batch would get a higher share of the setup costs than a unit in a large batch.

Many nonprofit organizations, especially hospitals, have developed fairly sophisticated Stage 1 accounting systems, but few have developed ABC systems for the Stage 2 effort. As a result, they have limited or—perhaps worse—incorrect, information about the cost of their intermediate cost objects (such as laboratory tests and radiological procedures).[5] If the costs of their intermediate cost objects are wrong, then so too are the costs of their final cost objects.

Developing an ABC System

To use ABC, an organization begins by identifying the activities that cause the indirect costs for one product or batch of products to differ from those of another. The details of this process are discussed in many cost accounting texts, and are beyond the scope of this chapter.[6] In general, however, there are four categories of activities that can influence the use of manufacturing overhead.[7]

- *Facility-Sustaining Activities*. These activities include facility management, building repair and maintenance, security, and grounds maintenance.
- *Product-Sustaining Activities*. Activities that are needed to assure that products are produced according to specifications. They include process engineering, product specifications, engineering, and product enhancements.
- *Batch-Related Activities*. Activities that are performed each time a batch of products is produced, such as set up time for machines, material movements, and inspections.
- *Unit-Level Activities*. Activities that relate directly to the number of units produced, such as utility usage or machine hours. (Unit-level activities also include direct costs; the three other categories include only indirect costs.)

These categories form the building blocks of an ABC system. Once they have been identified, the accounting staff first needs to create one or more "cost pools" within each category, and then define and measure the unit that causes a product to use each pool's resources. Here, the search is for a "cost driver"—a unit that reflects the demand for a pool's resources. For some activities, this is relatively easy; for others, it can be tricky.

To see the how an ABC system can improve Stage 2 of a full-cost analysis, let's use a relatively simple example. An abbreviated Stage 1 stepdown cost report for Owens Hospital is shown in Exhibit 3-3.

---

[5] Some hospitals argue that they can determine the cost of their intermediate cost objects by using ratios of costs to charges (RCCs) or relative value units (RVUs). However, both of these methods are flawed. For a discussion of the flaws, see David W. Young, "The Folly of Using RCCs and RVUs for Intermediate Product Costing," *Healthcare Financial Management*, April 2007. A PDF version of this article may be obtained by going to the "publications" section of www.DavidYoung.org, and clicking on the article title.

[6] A particularly good source for additional information is R. Cooper and R. S. Kaplan, *The Design of Cost Management Systems*, Englewood Cliffs, New Jersey, Prentice Hall, 1991.

[7] For a full discussion of these activities, see Cooper and Kaplan, *The Design of Cost Management Systems*, pp. 269-272.

Exhibit 3-3 Abbreviated Full-Cost Report for Owens Hospital (Stage 1)

	Assigned Costs	Allocated Costs	Costs to be Allocated	Depre-ciation (Sq Ft)	Main-tenance (Hours)	House-keeping (Sq Ft)	Adminis-tration (Salary $)	Full Cost
				----------Allocations	----------			
	1	2=4+5+6+7	3=1+2	4	5	6	7	8=1+2
Service Centers								
Building depreciation	1,200,000	0	1,200,000					
Building maintenance	950,000	105,000	1,055,000	105,000				
Housekeeping services	300,000	154,555	454,555	95,000	59,555			
Admin & General	1,300,000	381,605	1,681,605	156,000	158,250	67,355		
Mission Center								
Radiology	*1,750,000*	*688,321*		140,000	147,700	64,300	336,321	*2,438,321*
Laboratory	2,000,000	788,814		160,000	172,545	69,500	386,769	2,788,814
Dialysis Unit	*1,250,000*	*423,930*		50,000	116,050	22,455	235,425	*1,673,930*
Inpatient Care	7,000,000	959,723		350,000	158,250	165,600	285,873	7,959,723
Outpatient	2,250,000	889,212		144,000	242,650	65,345	437,217	3,139,212
Total cost	18,000,000			1,200,000	1,055,000	454,555	1,681,605	18,000,000

Assume that during the period covered by the cost report, the dialysis unit did 8,000 procedures, and radiology did 30,000 procedures. Thus, the average cost of a dialysis procedure was $209.24 ($1,673,930 ÷ 8,000), and the average cost of a radiological procedure was $81.28 ($2,438,321 ÷ 30,000). If the hospital wanted to know the cost of treating two patients, each of whom received 2 radiology procedures and 3 dialysis procedures, and if neither department had an ABC system, it might conclude that the costs for the two patients were identical, as shown below.

	Patient A			**Patient B**		
	Radiology	Dialysis	Total	Radiology	Dialysis	Total
Number of procedures	2	3	--	2	3	--
Cost per procedure	$81.28	$209.24	--	$81.28	$209.24	--
Total cost	$162.55	$627.72	$790.28	$162.55	$627.72	$790.28

For dialysis, this analysis would be reasonably accurate. As discussed earlier, cost centers that produce a single product do not need an ABC system. In the dialysis unit, for example, the only product is a dialysis procedure, and since all dialysis procedures are roughly identical, the average cost per procedure is a relatively accurate number.

By contrast, the radiology department conducts a wide variety of procedures: chest x-rays, limb x-rays, CT scans, magnetic resonance imaging, and so forth. Each procedure requires some technician time, and some procedures require supplies, such as a contrast medium. These are all contained in the $1,750,000 assigned cost figure, and are also direct costs of the procedures. That is, it is relatively easy to use time and motion studies to determine the portion of the cost for any given procedure that results from technician time, contrast-media, and other supplies.

But what about the supervisor in the department who doesn't work on procedures? Or the department's scheduling personnel? Or any of a variety of other people in the department who don't work directly on procedures? These are all assigned costs of the radiology department, and are contained in the $1,750,000 figure. But they are *indirect* with regard to any given procedure. And yet, if we are to know the full cost of a particular procedure, we must find a way to attach some portion of these costs to it.

And then there are the $688,321 in service center costs that were allocated to the radiology department during Stage 1. They also are *indirect* with regard to any given procedure, but we also must find a way to attach a portion of these costs to each procedure.

ABC in the Radiology Department

To apply ABC to the department of radiology, we first must determine cost pools for homogeneous collections of indirect cost activities, and then identify a driver for each pool. One possibility is shown in Exhibit 3-4. There are several important aspects that should be noted about this exhibit. First, labor and material costs (column 3) are direct, and therefore can be distributed easily between radiology's two cost centers: the Chest X-Ray Unit and the CT Scan Unit.

Second, in this example, we have five indirect cost pools (listed across the top). Four of these (columns 7, 8, 10, and 12) are the hospital service centers whose costs were allocated to radiology in Exhibit 3-3, and the total amounts shown are the same as the allocations. The fifth indirect cost pool is the radiology department's administrative costs (column 5), which are direct costs of the department but cannot be unambiguously associated with any given unit (intermediate cost object) carried out in the department. As Note 5 in the exhibit indicates, these costs are assigned to the two units in radiology that we are using as examples (the Chest X-Ray Unit and the CT Scan Unit). The assignments are based on the direct salary dollars associated with each unit.

Third, we must identify a cost driver for each indirect cost pool so we can assign its costs to the department's two units. For the hospital service centers, this example uses the same bases that were used to allocate the costs into the department (such as square feet for depreciation and housekeeping). It then computes the amount of space, maintenance hours, and salary dollars associated with each of the two units (or intermediate cost centers) where procedures are conducted, and uses the resulting percentages to distribute the costs between them.

Although the specific results would differ depending on the chosen indirect cost pools and cost drivers, as well as on the inclusion of additional radiology units, this exhibit makes it clear that the average cost of $81.28 per procedure is quite misleading. Using the results from Exhibit 3-4, the per-patient comparisons between an average cost and an ABC-based cost are as follows.

	Patient A (Two Chest X-Rays)			**Patient B (Two CT Scans)**		
	Average	ABC	Difference	Average	ABC	Difference
Number of units	2	2	--	2	2	--
Cost per unit	$81.28	$65.07	--	$81.28	$162.33	--
Total cost	$162.55	$130.14	($32.41)	$162.55	$324.66	$162.11

Summary of Stage 2

Nonprofit organizations that wish to measure the costs of their intermediate cost objects more accurately can benefit considerably from activity-based costing. Clearly, there are situations where a single overhead rate is adequate (such as in the dialysis unit), and, therefore, there is no need for ABC. But there are many other situations where a more sophisticated approach is needed

Outside of health care, the use of ABC has led many managers to change their thinking about the full cost of their products. It is likely that similar conclusions would be reached in a nonprofit organization that undertook an ABC effort. Indeed, in an era of intense pressures for cost control, a nonprofit that does not have an ABC system may lack essential information for decision-making. If nothing else, as the Owens Hospital example suggests, ABC can help senior management to identify more clearly the nature and extent of cross-subsidization taking place among their organization's programs and services.

Exhibit 3-4. Computing Full Cost Per Unit in Radiology, Using an ABC Approach

							Allocations from Stage 1							
	Labor & Material Cost/Unit	Number of Units	Directly Attachable Direct Cost	% of Salary Dollars	Dept. Admin Cost	% of Space	Depre-ciation Cost	House-keeping Cost	% of Maint. Hours	Main-tenance Cost	% of Salary Dollars	Adminis-tration Cost	Total Cost	Cost per Unit
Reference Number	1	2	3	4	5	6	7	8	9	10	11	12	13	14
Cost Center														
Chest X-ray Unit	40.00	25,000	$1,000,000	0.70	$280,000	0.40	$56,000	$25,720	0.20	$29,540	0.70	$235,425	$1,626,685	$65.07
CT Scan Unit	70.00	5,000	350,000	0.30	120,000	0.60	84,000	38,580	0.80	118,160	0.30	100,896	811,636	$162.33
Total		30,000	$1,350,000		$400,000		$140,000	$64,300		$147,700		$336,321	$2,438,321	

Explanation of columns (see reference number above):

1 Computed based on a time, motion, and material usage study for each procedure.
2 Obtained from department records
3 Equals column 1 * column 2.
4 Obtained from department records (department salaries only)
5 Total obtained from department records. Assigned to units based on percent of salary $
6 Obtained from department records
7 Total from Stage 1 (Exhibit 3-3). Assigned to units based on percent of space occupied.
8 Same as 7
9 Obtained from department records
10 Total from Stage 1. Assigned to units based on percent of maintenance hours
11 Same as 4
12 Total from Stage 1. Assigned to units based on percent of salary $
13 Sum of columns 3, 5, 7, 8, 10, and 12
14 Column 13 divided by column 2

COMPLICATING FACTORS

In practice, the full-cost accounting effort in both Stages 1 and 2 has many variations and nuances. Most of these "complicating factors," are dealt with more appropriately in a cost accounting textbook. There are a few worth noting, however.

Defining Direct Costs

There are differences in the ways that different organizations draw the line between direct and indirect costs. For example, in calculating the cost of university research projects, one university may count pensions and other fringe benefits of researchers as direct costs, while another may count these items as indirect costs; one may charge secretarial assistance directly to a project, but another may charge all secretarial help to a common pool (a service center), allocate it to different mission center, and then attach it to each project using a cost driver, much as we did with administration costs at Owens Hospital. Similarly, if electricity, heat, and other utilities are metered for each mission center, they are direct costs; if not, they must be allocated to mission centers. Because of these differences in accounting practices, comparisons of indirect costs among different universities (or other nonprofits) are likely of little use.

Appropriateness of Indirect Costs

Frequently, the issue is not one of distinguishing between direct and indirect costs, but of the appropriateness of the cost item itself. For example, some people claim that university indirect costs have been rising unchecked for years, and now total over 50 percent of direct costs for most major research institutions. University officials contend that such costs are needed to run the university. At issue are several questions: (1) What kinds of costs should be allowed? (2) Which projects should help to pay for these costs? (3) What kinds of efficiency standards should be used (such as how many librarians are needed to run the library)?

Example Much university research is supported by the federal government through contracts and grants. If the support comes in the form of a contract, the university is paid in accordance with the principles contained in the Office of Management and Budget (OMB) Circular A-21, *Cost Principles for Educational Institutions*. These principles provide for direct costs plus an equitable share of indirect costs, including a use allowance for depreciation of buildings and equipment, operations and maintenance of plant, general administration and general expenses, departmental administration, student administration and services, and library.[8]

Despite the OMB's principles, university overhead costs have presented an ongoing problem, and claims of overcharging for indirect costs are frequent. In some instances, the debate has reached the faculty ranks, with faculty expressing concern that high indirect rates impede a university's ability to obtain research funding.

Similar claims have surfaced in other nonprofit organizations, as well. In health care, for example, concerns have been voiced about the costs that teaching hospitals charge Medicare for graduate medical education. Teaching hospital administrators claim that these costs are appropriate in that, over the long-term, they benefit Medicare's beneficiaries. This, of course, is not a debate that will be resolved by improved cost accounting alone.

[8] For details, see http://www.whitehouse.gov/omb/circulars_a021_2004/

Imputed Costs

In certain situations, imputed costs need to be incorporated into the cost accounting system. The cost of polluting water is such a cost, but U.S. companies have not been charged for the social cost of the rivers they pollute. By contrast, in the Ruhr Valley in Germany, polluters pay a charge based on the effect of the effluent on the river's biochemical oxygen demand. The revenue derived from this charge is used to provide for water treatment.

Example The Dutch government developed a system of national accounting to reflect the damage done to the air, water, soil, and animal and plant life, and to account for the cost of maintaining or restoring them. Sweden, France, and Norway also have engaged in similar efforts, or what is now called "green accounting."[9]

SUMMARY

A calculation of full cost is necessary if the result is to be used as a basis for pricing an organization's products. Many nonprofits engage in such an effort. A full-cost calculation also is useful if judgments are to be made about the extent to which a program is paying for itself, subsidizing other programs, or is a "loss leader." Full-cost information also may facilitate comparisons among the costs of two or more nonprofit organizations that are delivering similar services. However, as this chapter has indicated, such comparisons should be made with caution, as there can be many differences—all quite legitimate—in how different organizations go about the cost accounting effort.

Suggested Cases for Classroom Use with this Chapter

See the Appendix at the end of the book for a more complete description of each case and ordering information.

Croswell University Hospital	Determining the cost of different procedures in a department of Ob-Gyn
Jefferson High School	Determining the cost of different students in a high school
Harbor City Community Center	Preparing a stepdown analysis to compute full cost
Lincoln Dietary Department	Assessing the potential for ABC in a dietary department
Neighborhood Servings	Using ABC for costing meals to the homebound
Owen Hospital (B)	Builds on the example in the text to incorporate the laboratory and inpatient care
South Bristol Hospital	Determining DRG "winners" and "losers" in a hospital
University of Miami Medical Center	Determining the cost of graduate medical education
Atherton Medical Education Programs	Determining the cost of graduate medical education

[9] Marlise Simons, 'Europeans Begin to Calculate the Price of Pollution," *New York Times*, December 9, 1990.

Practice Case (A): Mossey Bog Transportation Agency

The Mossy Bog Transportation Agency (MBTA) had two service departments (maintenance and administration) and two mission departments (rapid transit and slow transit). Rapid Transit used high-speed trains and was highly equipment-intensive, while Slow Transit, using rickshaws, was highly labor-intensive. Management had decided to allocate maintenance costs on the basis of depreciation dollars in each department, and administration costs on the basis of labor hours worked by the employees in each department.

The following data (dollar amounts in thousands) appeared in the agency's records for the current period:

	Service Centers		**Production Centers**		
	Maintenance	**Administration**	**Rapid Transit**	**Slow Transit**	**Total Costs**
Direct plus distributed costs	$1,160	$2,400	$8,000	$4,000	$15,560
Depreciation dollars (1)	$200	$2,000	$3,000	$ 800	$6,000
Labor hours	20,000	10,000	10,000	40,000	

Note (1) Depreciation dollars are included in "Direct plus distributed costs" figures. For example: $1,160,000 in the maintenance department includes $200,000 of depreciation. The depreciation figures are only for cost allocation purposes.

Assignment

1. Allocate the service center costs to the production centers using the stepdown method, and determine the relevant total costs. Begin with the maintenance department.

2. To what use would you put this information? Please be specific: what are the next steps you would take as a manager based on this information?

Practice Case (B): Museum of Frozen History

The Museum of Frozen History was a nonprofit organization dedicated to educating the public about the history of ice cream. Instead of charging an admission fee, the museum actually sold ice cream, using the revenue to fund its operating expenses. It produced 15 different flavors that it offered to its visitors in one-pint cartons. The museum bought special ingredients from around the world, and then blended them with cream from its cows, and packaged them for sale.

The museum's major cost was raw materials (the special flavors and the cream). However, there was a substantial amount of manufacturing overhead in the process of turning cream into ice cream, blending the flavors, and packaging the resulting product into the cartons. Most of these activities were highly automated, and the museum used very little direct labor. In fact, one of its displays showed how the manufacture of ice cream had been transformed from a highly labor-intensive activity into one that was almost completely automated.

Some of the flavors were very popular and sold in large volumes; however, a few of the new or esoteric blends produced very low volumes. The museum priced its ice cream at full production cost, plus a markup of 20 percent.

The museum's budget included manufacturing overhead of $3 million, which was allocated on the basis of each product's direct-labor cost. The budgeted direct-labor cost for the year was $600,000. Based on the sales budget and the raw materials budget, the museum's controller estimated that purchases and use of raw materials would total $6 million.

Exhibit 1 shows the expected direct manufacturing cost for a one-pint carton of two of the museum's ice creams. On reviewing this, the controller believed the traditional product-costing system was providing misleading cost information. She developed an analysis of the budgeted manufacturing overhead costs, shown in Exhibit 2. Data for the production of Colombian Cocoa and Miami Mango are shown in Exhibit 3.

Assignment

1. Compute the museum's overhead rate under the current system, and use it to determine the full product cost and selling price of one pint of Colombian Cocoa ice cream and one pint of Miami Mango.

2. Make the same computations using an ABC approach.

3. What are the pros and cons of adopting the ABC system? Should the museum adopt it?

MUSEUM OF FROZEN HISTORY

Exhibit 1. Direct Manufacturing Costs for a One-Pint Carton of Ice Cream

	Colombian Cocoa	Miami Mango
Direct material	$3.20	$4.20
Direct labor	.30	.30

Exhibit 2. Analysis of Budgeted Manufacturing Overhead Costs

Activity	Cost Driver	Budgeted Units	Budgeted Cost
Purchasing	Purchase orders	1,158	$ 579,000
Material handling	Setups	1,800	720,000
Quality control	Batches	720	144,000
Cream Freezing	Machine hours	96,100	961,000
Flavor Blending	Blending hours	33,600	336,000
Packaging	Packaging hours	26,000	260,000
Total manufacturing overhead costs			$3,000,000

Exhibit 3. Production Data

	Colombian Cocoa	Miami Mango
Budgeted production and sales	100,000 pints	2,000 pints
Batch size	10,000 pints	500 pints
Setups	3 per batch	3 per batch
Purchase order size	25,000 pints	500 pints
Cream Freezing time	1 hour per 100 pints	1 hour per 100 pints
Flavor Blending time	1/2 hour per 100 pints	1/2 hour per 100 pints
Packaging time	1/10 hour per 100 pints	1/10 hour per 100 pints

Solution to Practice Case (A)

This is a relatively simple case in calculating full costs. It requires you to assign costs to cost centers and to determine appropriate bases of allocation for service center costs. Most of the information is provided in the case itself.

Question 1 (Amounts in thousands)

				Service Centers		
Department	**Initial Costs**	**Allocated Costs**	**Total to Allocate**	**Maintenance**	**Administration**	**Total**
Maintenance (1)	$1,160	0	$1,160			
Administration (2)	2,400	400	2,800	$ 400		
Rapid Transit	8,000			600	$ 560	$9,160
Slow Transit	4,000			160	2,240	6,400
Total	$15,560			$1,160	$2,800	$15,560

Notes: 1. $1,160,000 maintenance costs ÷ $5,800,000 depreciation dollars (excludes depreciation dollars in the maintenance department) = $.20 per depreciation dollar.

2. $2,800,000 (2,400,000 + 400,000) administration costs ÷ 50,000 labor hours (only uses labor hours in Rapid Transit and Slow Transit departments) = $56.00 per labor hour.

Question 2

The next step is to use this information to set prices (or to compare existing revenue with full costs). Specifically, we would need to estimate total number of rides on each form of transit, and divide total costs by that figure to get a cost per ride. This would then need to be marked up by a percentage to give us the surplus we required.

Solution to Practice Case (B)

This case entails working through the basics of activity-based costing. ABC was discussed in the chapter but can be tricky to apply in practice. This case provides an opportunity to experience the nitty gritty of ABC.

Question 1. Overhead rate = total manufacturing overhead cost ÷ budgeted direct labor dollars = $3,000,000 ÷ $600,000 = $5 per DL$

	Colombian Cocoa	Miami Mango
Direct materials	$3.20	$4.20
Direct labor	.30	.30
Overhead (.30 x $5.00)	1.50	1.50
Full production cost	$5.00	$6.00
Markup (30%)	1.50	1.80
Selling price	$6.50	$7.80

Question 2

Activity	Cost Driver	Budgeted Activity	Budgeted Cost	Unit Cost
Purchasing	Purchase orders	1,158	$ 579,000	$500
Material handling	Setups	1,800	720,000	400
Quality control	Batches	720	144,000	200
Cream freezing	Machine hours	96,100	961,000	10
Flavor blending	Blending hours	33,600	336,000	10
Packaging	Packaging hours	26,000	260,000	10

Formulas:

Purchasing	# purchase orders x $500 ÷ number of pints of output
Material handling:	#setups x $400 ÷ number of pints of output
Quality control	# batches x $200 ÷ number of pints of output
Cream freezing	# hours x $10 ÷ number of pints of output
Flavor blending	# hours x $10 ÷ number of pints of output
Packaging	# hours x $10 ÷ number of pints of output

Cost of Colombian Cocoa

1. Direct material	3.20
2. Direct labor	.30
3. Purchasing (4 orders x $500 ÷ 100,000 pounds)	.02
4. Material handling (30 setups x $400 ÷ 100,000 pounds)	.12
5. Quality control (10 batches x $200 ÷ 100,000 pounds)	.02
6. Cream freezing (1,000 hours x $10 ÷ 100,000 pounds)	.10
7. Blending (500 hours x $10 ÷ 100,000 pounds)	.05
8. Packaging (100 hours x $10 ÷ 100,000 pounds)	.01
Total	$3.82

Cost of Miami Mango

1. Direct material	4.20
2. Direct labor	.30
3. Purchasing (4 orders x \$500 ÷ 2,000 pounds)	1.00
4. Material handling (12 setups x \$400 ÷ 2,000 pounds)	2.40
5. Quality control (4 batches x \$200 ÷ 2,000 pounds)	.40
6. Cream freezing (20 hours x \$10 ÷ 2,000 pounds)	.10
7. Blending (10 hours x \$10 ÷ 2,000 pounds)	.05
8. Packaging (2 hours x \$10 ÷ 2,000 pounds)	.01
Total	\$8.46

Question 3

The museum's strategy appears to be to sell both popular blends of ice cream (high volume, produced in large batches) and esoteric blends (low volume, produced in small batches). In this case, direct labor hours may not be a good cost driver for absorbing manufacturing overhead into a pint of ice cream. Rather, the ABC analysis seems more appropriate, given that small batches of ice cream require more manufacturing overhead.

The differences are not trivial, as the following comparison shows:

	Colombian Cocoa	Miami Mango
Current System:		
Price per pint	\$6.50	\$7.80
Cost per pint	5.00	6.00
Contribution per pint to profits	\$1.50	\$1.80
Number of pints	100,000	2,000
Total contribution to profits	\$150,000	\$3,600
ABC System:		
Price per pint	\$6.50	\$7.80
Cost per pint	3.82	8.46
Contribution per pint to profits	\$2.68	\$(0.66)
Number of pints	100,000	2,000
Total contribution to profits	\$268,000	\$(1,320)

While the museum may wish to continue to sell Miami Mango as a small loss leader, it can at least evaluate it as such, rather than as a small winner. Moreover, the museum may be able to price the flavor more appropriately, reflecting its premium nature.

Chapter 4

Differential-Cost Accounting

A significant concept in management accounting is that *different costs are used for different purposes*. The full-cost accounting principles discussed in Chapter 3 are useful for activities such as pricing, profitability analysis, and cost-based reimbursement. They are inappropriate, however, for a variety of decisions—called alternative choice decisions—made regularly in both for-profit and nonprofit organizations. The contrast between full- and differential-cost accounting, as well as between these two and responsibility-cost accounting, is shown in Exhibit 4-1. As this exhibit indicates, the principal kinds of alternative choice decisions are (a) retaining or discontinuing a program or service that is unprofitable on a full-cost basis, (b) performing an activity in-house or outsourcing it, (c) offering a special price for one of the organization's products in exchange for, say, a large volume of business, and (d) selling or disposing of an obsolete asset.

Exhibit 4-1 Different Costs for Different Purposes

	Full-Cost	Differential-Cost	Responsibility-Cost
Costs Used	Direct versus Indirect	Fixed versus Variable	Controllable versus Non-controllable
Activities	Assignment of costs to	Analysis of cost	Programming
	Choice of allocation bases	Cost-volume-profit analysis	Budgeting
	Allocation of service center costs to mission centers	Contribution analysis	Variance analysis
			Reporting and evaluation
	Attachment of mission center costs to cost objects		
Management Uses/Decisions	Pricing	Retain or discontinue an unprofitable program	Program additions and modifications
	Product line profitability	Outsource an activity	Cost control
	Strategic decisions concerning which products to offer	Offer a special price	Performance measurement
		Sell an obsolete asset	

There is nothing illegal or unethical about looking at costs differently for different purposes. Rather, as managers' decision-making needs change, so too do the costs that are relevant for the decision. With full-cost accounting, for example, the goal is to determine each client's or program's direct costs and its fair share of the organization's overhead (or indirect) costs, thereby helping to inform pricing decisions and profitability analyses.

With *responsibility accounting*, the focus is on the individuals who exert control over an organization's costs. Relatively few nonprofit organizations have developed high quality responsibility accounting systems. Yet, without such a system, it is difficult to operate effectively and efficiently. Responsibility accounting is the subject of Part III

Differential-cost accounting is the subject of this chapter. We begin with an assessment of the kinds of cost analyses that are needed for an alternative choice decision, and then move to a discussion of cost behavior, addressing the distinction between costs used for a full-cost analysis and those used for a differential-cost analysis. We then take up the subject of cost-volume-profit (CVP) analysis. We look at CVP analysis (sometimes called *breakeven* analysis) in its most basic form, and then examine a variety of special considerations that can serve to complicate it.

Finally, we look at some of the issues that managers must consider in undertaking a differential-cost analysis, concluding with a discussion of some of the complications inherent in an outsourcing (sometimes called *make-or-buy*) decision—a type of alternative choice decision that most organizations make frequently. This final section of the chapter highlights some recent developments in *privatization*—an outsourcing strategy being used increasingly by many nonprofits, especially government entities.

THE NATURE OF COST ANALYSIS FOR ALTERNATIVE CHOICE DECISIONS

A key question in an alternative choice analysis is: "How will costs (and sometimes revenues) change under the proposed set of circumstances?" That is, which costs (and revenues) will be *different?* For example, if an organization outsources an activity, some existing costs will be eliminated but some new costs will be incurred. If a product or service line is discontinued, some costs will be eliminated, but so (usually) will be some revenues. In the special-price and obsolete-asset situations, some revenue will be received but costs will change only minimally or not at all.

Assessing differential revenues ordinarily is easy, but determining how costs will change can be quite tricky. Indeed, using full-cost information as a basis for assessing cost behavior can lead managers to make decisions that are financially detrimental to their organizations.

Example The full cost of educating a child in a certain public school system is $7,500 a year. This figure includes teachers' salaries, curriculum supplies and materials, a fair share of individual school overhead expenses (such as the principal's salary) and a fair share of the school system's overhead expenses (such as the school system superintendent's salary). The decision to reduce enrollment by 10 students clearly would not save $75,000 ($10 x $7,500), since it is unlikely that teacher salaries, individual school overhead, or school system overhead would change with a reduction of 10 students.

Even the decision to close an entire school would not save $7,500 per student since it is unlikely that the school system's overhead expenses would be reduced. Moreover, if closing a given school resulted in shifting some tax revenues that had been assigned to the school system to some other use, and these revenues amounted to $7,500 per student, the school system would be worse off as a result of the closing—its revenues would have declined by more than its costs.

COST BEHAVIOR

Chapter 3 described the distinction between direct and indirect costs. This chapter uses a different distinction—dividing costs between those that are relatively fixed and those that vary with changes in volume. This fixed/variable distinction lets us see more clearly how a change in the volume of activity of a particular program or service line will affect its costs. These different types of costs, as well as the refinements of step-function and semi-variable costs, are shown schematically in Exhibit 4-2.

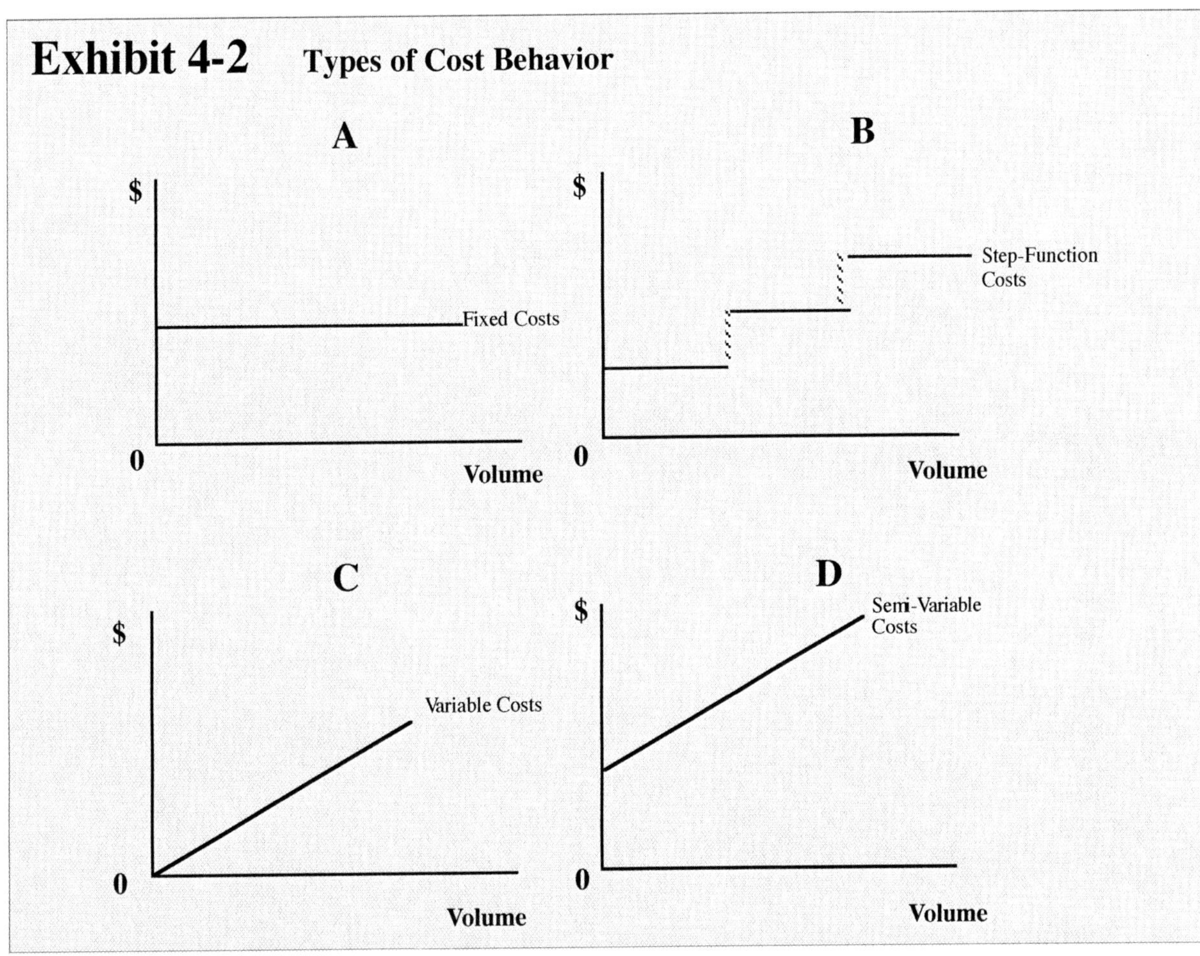

Fixed Costs

Fixed costs are independent of the number of units that are produced. While no costs are fixed if the time period is long enough, the relevant range for fixed costs (i.e., the span of units over which they remain unchanged) generally is quite large, so they can be viewed graphically as shown in Segment A of Exhibit 4-2. An example of a fixed cost in most organizations is rent. Regardless of the number of units produced, the amount of rent remains the same.

Step-Function Costs

Step-function costs are similar to fixed costs except they have a much narrower relevant range. As such, they do not change in a smooth fashion, but are added in "lumps," or "steps." The result is that, graphically, they take the form shown in Segment B, where the dotted lines represent discontinuous jumps. A good example of a step-function cost in many organizations is supervision. In a hospital or social service agency, for instance, as the number of nurses, social workers, and other professionals increases, supervisory personnel must be added. Since it is difficult for most organizations to add part-time supervisory help, supervisory costs will tend to behave in a step-like fashion. Similarly, in a school system or university, new faculty are added in step-like increments when the number of students (either in the school or in a given course) reaches a certain level.

Variable Costs

Variable costs, shown in Segment C, change in a roughly linear fashion with changes in volume, such that, as volume increases, total variable costs increase in constant proportion. The result is a straight line whose slope is determined by the amount of variable costs associated with each unit of output. In a hospital laboratory, for example, reagents would be a variable cost, increasing in direct proportion to increases in the number of tests processed. Some organizations will have relatively high variable costs per unit, resulting in a line that slopes upward quite steeply; others will have relatively low variable costs for each unit of output, resulting in a line with a more gradual slope.

Semi-Variable Costs

Semi-variable costs (sometimes called mixed costs) share features of both fixed and variable costs. There is a minimum level that is fixed, and the cost line then rises linearly with increases in volume. The result is a line that begins at some level above zero, and slopes upward, as shown in Segment D. A good example of a semi-variable cost is electricity. Typically, there is some base cost each month for electrical service that an organization must incur even if it uses no electricity at all. Costs then increase in accordance with the number of kilowatt hours used. Similar cost patterns exist for other utilities such as telephone, gas, and water.

Total Costs

Total costs are the sum of the fixed, step-function, variable, and semi-variable components. Because cost analyses combining all four types of costs are quite complex, however, most analysts generally classify all costs as either fixed or variable. For semi-variable costs, this can be accomplished by incorporating the fixed element into total fixed costs and adding the variable element to the variable costs. For step-function costs, the width of the relevant range typically dictates whether the cost is added to fixed costs or incorporated into the unit-variable amount.

Example The Abbington Youth Center has annual rent and other fixed costs of $100,000, and variable supply and material costs of $100 per student. Its annual meal costs are semi-variable. They have a fixed element (a part-time dietitian) of $14,000, and a variable component (food and beverage) of $500 per student.

In computing Abbington's costs, we can divide the fixed and variable components of the semi-variable cost into its separate components. The result is the following breakdown of costs:

Cost Element	Fixed Amount	Variable Amount (per student)
Rent and other fixed	$100,000	$ 0
Supplies and materials	0	100
Meals	$14,000	500
Total	$114,000	$600

Abbington also has student-teacher ratios of 3:1 for its Infants and Toddlers Program and 15:1 to its Adolescent After-School Program. Faculty salaries (all part-time) are $30,000 per year. The step function relationships for these two programs are shown below:

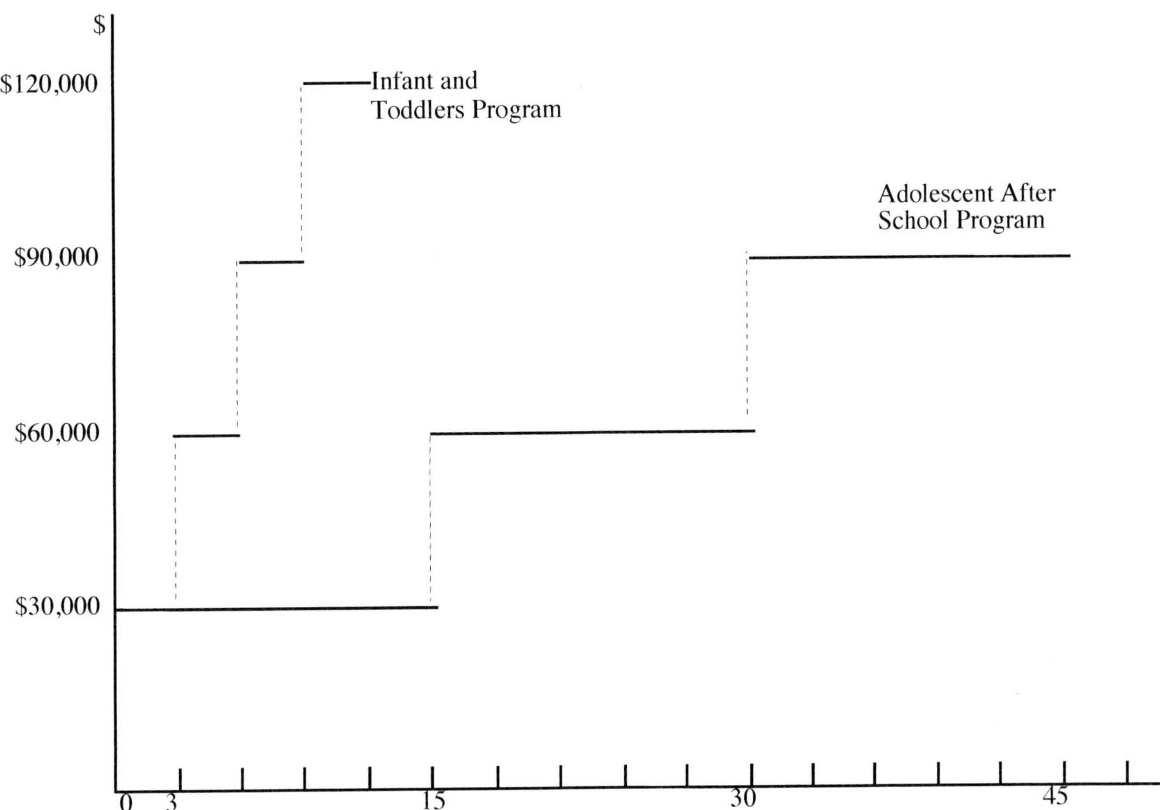

Once teacher salaries have been simplified in this manner, they can be added to either the variable or the fixed cost totals. Since the Infant and Toddlers Program cost function is nearly linear, we might decide to treat it as a variable cost at $10,000 per student. In contrast, because salaries for the Adolescent After-School Program have a larger relevant range (15 students versus 3 students in the Infant and Toddlers Program), we might treat them as fixed. With these simplifications, total costs are as follows:

Cost Element	Fixed Amount	Variable Amount(per student)
Rent and other fixed	$100,000	$ 0
Supplies and materials	0	100
Meals	$14,000	500
Teachers:		
Infant and Toddlers	0	10,000
Adolescent After-School (30 to 45 students)	90,000	0
Total	$204,000	$10,600

Note that the fixed costs of the Adolescent After-School Program are only valid within a range of 30 to 45 students. Above 45 students, they jump to a higher step. Also, the variable cost of $10,600 per student is not quite accurate since $10,000 of it is actually a portion of a step-function change. Nevertheless, because the steps in the Infants and Toddlers Program are so small, the amount is a reasonable representation of the pattern of cost changes that are associated with volume. Of course, we also must be concerned with the mix of students since the cost impact of, say, three more students will depend on which program they enter. We will discuss output mix complication later in the chapter.

COST-VOLUME-PROFIT ANALYSIS

Once costs have been classified as either fixed or variable, we can analyze how they will vary with changes in the volume of activity. A technique used in such situations is *cost-volume-profit (CVP) analysis*. The intent of CVP analysis is to determine either (a) the volume of activity needed for an organization to achieve its profit (or financial surplus) goal, (b) the price that it needs to charge to achieve its profit goal, or (c) the cost limits (fixed and/or variable) it needs to adhere to if it is to achieve its profit goal.

A CVP analysis usually is conducted for a particular activity within an organization—such as a product line or program. It begins with the basic equation for profit:

$$\textit{Profit} = \textit{Total revenue (TR)} - \textit{Total costs (TC)}$$

Total revenue for many activities is quite easy to calculate. If we assume that price is represented by the letter p and volume by the letter x, then total revenue is price times volume, or:

$$TR = px$$

Total costs are somewhat more complicated. CVP analysis requires a recognition of the different types of cost behavior: fixed, step-function, variable, and semi-variable. Let's begin with the simplest of cases, where there are no step-function or semi-variable costs. In this instance, the formula would be quite simple:

$$\textit{Total costs} = \textit{Fixed costs} + \textit{Variable costs}$$

Fixed costs can be represented by the letter a, and variable costs per unit by the letter b. Thus, total variable costs is bx, where, as before, x represents volume. The resulting cost equation is:

$$TC = a + bx$$

This means that the basic profit equation can be shown as: Profit = px - (a + bx), which can be represented graphically as shown on the next page. On this graph, point x1 is the *breakeven volume*—it is the point at which total revenue, px, equals total costs, a + bx. With volume in excess of x1, the organization earns a surplus; below x1, it incurs a loss.

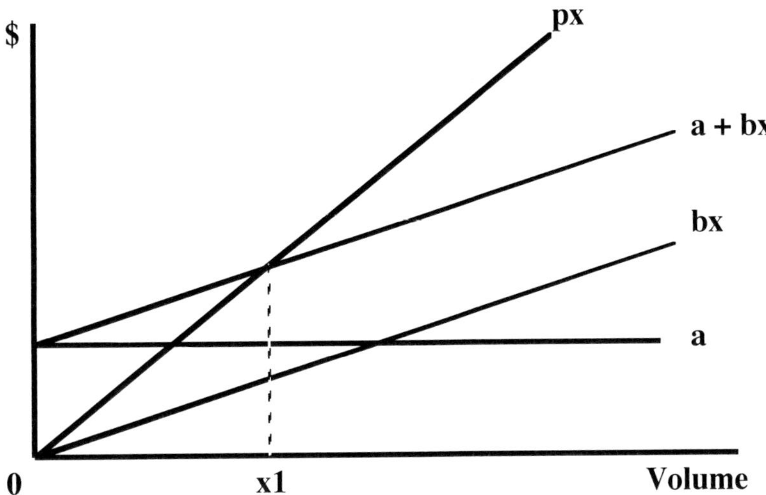

Example The Alberta Chamber of Commerce (ACOC) publishes a monthly magazine for its members. The publication department has fixed costs of $100,000 a month, variable costs per magazine of $.80, and charges $1.80 per magazine. To determine breakeven volume (number of magazines per month), we can begin with the CVP formula, and substitute the known elements. We then solve for the unknown, which in this case is volume, or x.

$$\text{Profit} = px - (a + bx)$$

At breakeven, Profit = 0, and px = a + bx, or

$$\begin{aligned} 1.80x &= 100{,}000 + .80x \\ 1.00x &= 100{,}000 \\ x &= 100{,}000 \end{aligned}$$

Breakeven therefore is 100,000 magazines. To confirm:

Revenue: $1.80 (100,000)	=		$180,000
Less: costs:			
Variable: $0.80 (100,000)	=	80,000	
Fixed:		100,000	180,000
Profit			$ 0

Unit Contribution Margin

An important aspect of CVP analysis is unit contribution margin. This is the contribution to fixed costs that comes about as a result of each additional unit sold, or the difference between price and unit-variable cost. By rearranging the terms of the CVP formula, we can see that breakeven volume is simply fixed costs divided by unit contribution margin, as follows:

$$\begin{aligned} px &= a + bx \\ px - bx &= a \\ x(p - b) &= a \\ x &= \frac{a}{(p - b)} \end{aligned}$$

Stated somewhat differently, price minus unit-variable cost tells us how much each unit sold *contributes* to the recovery of fixed costs. When this amount is divided into fixed costs, the result is the volume needed to recover all fixed costs, i.e., breakeven volume.

Example The ACOC publication department has a unit contribution margin of $1.00 ($1.80 - $.80). When we divide this amount into its fixed costs of $100,000, we arrive at its breakeven volume of 100,000 magazines.

Incorporating Other Variables into a CVP Analysis

Thus far, we have been using CVP analysis to solve only for breakeven volume. Clearly, if we knew (a) how many units of our product we were likely to sell, (b) our fixed costs, and (c) our unit-variable costs, we then could determine the price needed to break even. Similarly, if we were in an environment where price was given, and we knew approximately how many units we could sell at that price, we could set up either fixed costs or unit-variable costs as the unknown and solve for it.

We also could incorporate a need for a financial surplus into a CVP analysis simply by adding the amount of desired surplus to our fixed costs. We then could calculate a "breakeven point" with the new level of "fixed costs."

CVP Analysis with Semi-Variable Costs

As discussed earlier, incorporating semi-variable costs into a CVP analysis is relatively easy. Since semi-variable costs have fixed and variable components, we simply need to add the fixed component to the fixed cost total, and the variable component to the unit-variable cost amount.

Example In addition to its other costs, the ACOC's publication department has electricity costs of $2,000 a month regardless of usage, plus an additional amount per kilowatt hour of use. Electricity usage is tied directly to the number of magazines produced, and the association's accountants have calculated the rate to be about $.04 per magazine. To determine the monthly number of magazines needed to breakeven, we again can begin with the basic formula, insert the known elements, and solve for the unknown.

$$\begin{aligned} px &= a + bx \\ 1.80x &= (100{,}000 + 2{,}000) + (.80x + .04x) \\ .96x &= 102{,}000 \\ x &= 106{,}250 \end{aligned}$$

Breakeven now is 106,250 magazines.

CVP Analysis with Step-Function Costs

As discussed in the example of Abbington Youth Center, the analysis of step-function costs can be a little tricky. Ideally, we would like to be able to assume that, for any given volume level, we could simply add together the step-function costs and the fixed costs to give us the total applicable fixed costs. We then could use the CVP formula. Unfortunately, since volume is the unknown in the equation, the process is not quite that simple, as the following example illustrates.

Example Return to the first situation for the ACOC (i.e., ignore the electricity costs). Assume that, in addition to the $100,000 in fixed costs stipulated there, the publication department has some supervisory costs. These costs behave as follows:

Volume	Costs
0 - 50,000	$ 10,000
50,001 - 100,000	20,000
100,001 - 150,000	30,000
150,001 - 200,000	40,000

If we use the first level of step-function costs in the breakeven formula, we have the following equation:

$$1.80x = (100{,}000 + 10{,}000) + .80x$$
$$1.00x = 110{,}000$$
$$x = 110{,}000$$

The problem with this solution is that, while the breakeven volume is 110,000 magazines, the relevant range for the step-function costs was only 0 - 50,000 magazines. Thus, a breakeven of greater than 50,000 magazines is invalid, and we must move to the next step on the step function, which gives us the following equation:

$$1.80x = (100{,}000 + 20{,}000) + .80x$$
$$1.00x = 120{,}000$$
$$x = 120{,}000$$

This solution is also invalid. Only when we get to the third level do we encounter a valid solution, as follows.

$$1.80x = (100{,}000 + 30{,}000) + .80x$$
$$1.00x = 130{,}000$$
$$x = 130{,}000$$

The conclusion we can draw from this analysis is that the incorporation of step-function costs into the CVP formula requires a trial-and-error process to reach the breakeven volume.

COMPLICATING FACTORS

In addition to the complications with step-function costs, there are several other factors that can complicate a CVP analysis. Some of these relate to the occasional need to use full-cost reports as the source of cost information. Others relate to the fact that a fixed cost also can be differential under certain circumstances. Still others relate to the difficulty of associating some of an organization's fixed costs with its programs.

Multiple Products or Services

Thus far, we made all of CVP calculations with only one product. When there are two or more products, the analysis becomes more complicated. Consider the following situation:

Example The outpatient department (OPD) at Tsing Tao Hospital has three types of visits: simple, regular, and complex. Monthly fixed costs are $25,650. Other information is as follows:

	Simple	Regular	Complex	Total
Fee per visit	$30	$40	$50	
Variable costs	18	22	25	
Unit contribution margin	$12	$18	$25	
Visits per month	1,000	400	600	2,000

To determine the OPD's breakeven under these circumstances, we can calculate a weighted average unit contribution margin, and divide it into fixed costs. The easiest way to calculate a weighted average unit contribution margin is to begin by calculating total contribution for all visit types, as follows:

	Simple	Regular	Complex	Total
Unit contribution margin	$12	$18	$25	
Visits per month	1,000	400	600	
Total contribution	12,000	$7,200	$15,000	$34,200

The weighted average unit contribution margin is calculated by dividing total contribution by total visits, as follows:

$$\$34{,}200 \div 2{,}000 = \$17.10$$

We now can calculate the breakeven point by dividing fixed costs by the weighted average unit contribution margin, or $25,650 ÷ $17.10 = 1,500. Thus, we must provide 1,500 visits a month to break even.

The problem with this approach is that a change in product mix (visit types in the above example) will change the breakeven point. It is relatively easy to observe this phenomenon in the above example since we can see that changing the mix of visits (but keeping the total number at 2,000) will change total contribution. This, in turn, will change the weighted average unit contribution margin. The result is that fixed costs will be divided by a different number than before, resulting in a different breakeven figure.

Example Assume that the OPD at Tsing Tao Hospital provided the anticipated 2,000 visits during a month, and that the cost and fee figures given in the above example remained the same, but that the mix of visits was as follows:

Simple	500
Regular	200
Complex	1,300

The computations for breakeven now are as follows:

	Simple	Regular	Complex	Total
Contribution margin	$12	$18	$25	
Visits per month	500	200	1,300	2,000
Total contribution	$6,000	$3,600	$32,500	$42,100

The weighted average unit contribution margin now is $21.05, calculated as follows:

$$\$42{,}100 \div 2{,}000 = \$21.05$$

As a result, breakeven becomes 1,219 visits (rounded) ($25,650 ÷ $21.05)

The breakeven has changed because the mix of visits has changed. This will happen any time an organization's products have different individual unit contribution margins. In this case, the mix has changed to a greater number of high unit-contribution-margin visits. All else being equal, a higher unit contribution margin means a lower breakeven point. That is why the breakeven number of visits fell from 1,500 to 1,219 with the change in mix.

An important conclusion to be drawn here is that a breakeven figure with multiple products or services can be unstable—as mix changes, so will the breakeven figure. It is important to bear in mind, however, that an unstable breakeven figure comes about only when the individual contribution margins vary. If they are roughly similar, changes in mix, even if they are large, will have relatively little impact on the breakeven volume.

Because of this instability, CVP analysis tends to be used relatively little on an ongoing basis in organizations with multiple products or services. It frequently is used, however, in conjunction with an analysis of the possible introduction of a new product. Indeed, it is an essential aspect of a good marketing analysis.

Use of Information from Full-Cost Reports

Two potential problems arise when information for a differential-cost analysis is obtained from a full-cost report: cost distinctions and the behavior of allocated costs. Each of these potential problems calls for the analyst to exercise caution in obtaining and working with full-cost data.

Cost Distinctions. The analysis of differential costs would be simplified if, as occasionally is assumed, all indirect costs are fixed and all direct costs are variable. But this is rarely the case. Exhibit 4-3 contains examples of four different cost types and their fixed/variable, direct/indirect distinctions. Note that each of the four cells in the matrix contains a possible cost, leading to the conclusion that the direct and indirect costs in a full-cost accounting system must be analyzed individually to determine how they can be expected to behave as volume changes.

Exhibit 4-3 **Cost Examples: Fixed/Variable versus Direct/Indirect in the Foster Home Program of a Social Service Agency**

	Fixed	Variable
Direct	Supervisor's salary in the foster home care program	Payments to foster parents for room and board
Indirect	A portion of the executive director's salary, which is a fixed cost, and is part of administration—a service center whose costs are allocated to the foster home program	Electric bills, which are mainly variable costs, and are part of administration—a service center whose costs are allocated to the foster home program

Behavior of Allocated Costs. Additional complexities are introduced into a cost analysis when overhead costs are included. There are two such complexities: allocation bases and the step-down sequence.

Misleading Allocation Bases. Although an organization may be attempting to measure the use of service center resources as precisely as possible in its Stage 1 full cost analysis, there nevertheless can be many instances where a given service center's basis of allocation does not accurately reflect the actual use of its services by receiving cost centers. If, for example, a product line is discontinued, the organization may be able to reduce some of the service center costs that were allocated to the mission center in question. In most instances, however, only the variable costs in the service center (plus, perhaps, some step-function costs) will be reduced. The remaining costs will be allocated to other cost centers.

Example Consider the administration and general (A&G) service center. A reduction of staff in a given mission center will lead to a reduction in total salaries in that mission center. If A&G costs are allocated on the basis of salaries, there will be a reduction in the amount of A&G allocated to this mission center. It is highly unlikely, however, that there will be a reduction in the staff or other costs in the A&G cost center. Thus, more A&G costs will be allocated to those cost centers that did not reduce their salaries.

The reverse may happen as well. That is, a reduction in a mission center's activity may lead to a decrease in a service center's costs, but the mission center may not realize the full effect.

Example Consider a housekeeping service center whose costs are allocated on the basis of square feet. A change in the activities in a given mission center may reduce the center's need for housekeeping services, which may permit the manager of the housekeeping service center to reduce some costs. Yet, unless the space used by the mission center is reduced, the cost report (that allocates housekeeping on a square-footage basis) will not show an equivalent reduction in the housekeeping costs allocated to the mission center. The costs allocated to the mission center will fall slightly as a result of the lower housekeeping costs *overall,* but the reduced allocation will be much less than the actual cost savings that took place in the housekeeping service center. The rest of the savings will accrue to those cost centers that continue to receive the same amount of housekeeping as before.

Effects of the Stepdown Sequence. Costs of those service centers lowest in the stepdown sequence will include allocations from the service centers above them. This is because the total cost allocated from each service center includes both its assigned costs plus the costs that were allocated to it from previous service centers (or "steps") in the stepdown.

Example In a hospital, if the social work service center is far down in the stepdown sequence, the social service costs allocated to a particular mission center will have a significant allocated component (e.g., administration, housekeeping, laundry, and so on). It may be possible to reduce the use of social workers in a mission center by reducing the number of patients receiving social services, or by changing the nature of the treatment plans. However, the full impact of that change on the costs in the social services cost center will be overstated if one uses the fully allocated social service amount. This is because the costs in the social services cost center that have been allocated to it from a variety of other service centers will not be affected at all by the change in the mission center's use of social workers.

DIFFERENTIAL COSTS VERSUS FIXED AND VARIABLE COSTS

With an understanding of costs according to the nature of their behavior, and with some background in the elements of CVP analysis, we are in a position to undertake a differential-cost analysis. Effectively, a differential-cost analysis attempts to identify the behavior of an organization's costs under one or more alternative scenarios. These scenarios are related to the decision under consideration. To illustrate this point, consider the following:

Example Clearwater Transportation Service operates two mini-vans that transport senior citizens on errands and shopping trips. It charges $2.00 a mile for each service mile driven. Last year, Van 1 drove 60,000 service miles, and Van 2 drove 30,000 service miles. The variable cost per mile (gasoline, tires, wear and tear) for each van was 80 cents. Each driver (both were part-time) was paid a salary of $20,000 per year. Rent and administration totaled $60,000, and were allocated to each van on the basis of the number of service miles driven. As a result, total revenues and expenses for the year were as follows:

Item	Van 1		Van 2		Total
Revenue	2.00 x 60,000 =	$120,000	2.00 x 30,000 =	$60,000	$180,000
Expenses:					
Variable costs	.80 x 60,000 =	48,000	.80 x 30,000 =	24,000	72,000
Drivers		20,000		20,000	40,000
Overhead costs (rent and admin.)		40,000		20,000	60,000
Total expenses		$108,000		$64,000	$172,000
Surplus (Deficit)		$ 12,000		($4,000)	$ 8,000

To answer the question of whether Clearwater's financial performance would have improved if Van 2 (which lost money) had been discontinued at the beginning of the year, we must structure the data in terms of differential costs. The question is not whether Van 2 lost money on a *full-cost* basis (as it did), but rather the nature of its differential costs and revenues; that is, how would Clearwater's revenues and costs have changed if Van 2 had been discontinued?

Although the data are not as good as we might like, we nevertheless can see that discontinuing Van 2 would have eliminated its revenue and its variable costs, as well as the fixed cost of the driver. From all indications, however, the overhead costs (rent and administration) would have continued (i.e., they were not differential). The result would have been a shift from an $8,000 surplus to an $8,000 deficit, as the analysis below indicates:

Item		Van 1
Revenue	2.00 x 60,000 =	$120,000
Expenses:		
Variable costs	.80 x 60,000 =	48,000
Driver		20,000
Overhead costs (rent and administration)		60,000
Total expenses		128,000
Surplus (Deficit)		($8,000)

This example illustrates several important principles.

Principle #1. Full-Cost Information can be Misleading

The kind of information available from a full-cost system can produce highly misleading results if used for differential-cost decisions. This is due mainly to the apparent behavior of overhead costs when they are allocated, as contrasted with their true behavior. Note that the overhead allocated to Van 2 did not go away when we eliminated the vehicle; it simply was reallocated to Van 1.

Principle #2. Differential Costs can Include both Fixed and Variable Costs

Although initially counterintuitive, differential costs can include both fixed and variable costs. In the Clearwater case, the driver's salary, while a fixed cost of Van 2, was eliminated when we eliminated the van. However, as long as we operate the van, we have the fixed cost of the salary; it does not fluctuate in accordance with the number of miles driven (within the relevant range). But when we eliminate the van, we also eliminate this cost in its entirety; thus, it is differential in terms of a decision to eliminate or retain the van.

Principle #3. Assumptions are Needed

Differential-cost analyses focus on the future. As such, they require the analyst to make assumptions about many factors, from unit prices to staff efficiency. For example, inflation will affect an organization's costs, and perhaps its prices. The general state of the economy along with a wide variety of other matters will affect volume. For many managers, these factors raise concerns about the reliability of a differential-cost analysis. Despite these concerns, however, since we do not have perfect knowledge of the future, we must speculate as best we can about how costs and revenues will behave.

Principle #4. Sensitivity Analysis is Essential

Because assumptions play such a crucial role in a differential analysis, we must attempt to identify and document them as completely as possible, and to explore how changes in them would affect the conclusions of the analysis. This activity is called *sensitivity analysis*.

If we were doing a sensitivity analysis for the Clearwater scenario, we might try to determine how many more miles Van 1 would need to drive for the organization to maintain its $8,000 surplus. Or, if we thought we might be able to reduce our rent and administrative costs with an elimination of Van 2, we might ask by how much they would need to fall to maintain the $8,000 surplus. For example, if we could reduce them by $16,000 by eliminating Van 2, we would be indifferent. That is, with administrative costs reduced to $44,000 ($60,000-$16,000), Van 1 would earn a surplus of $8,000—the same as we were earning with both vans. As a result, any reduction in overhead beyond $16,000 that resulted from the elimination of Van 2 would favor the decision to eliminate it.

Principle #5. Causality Must be Present

A key aspect of differential analysis is causality—for an item to be included in a differential analysis, it must be *caused* by the alternative under consideration. For example, if we assume there will be an increase in the miles driven by Van 1, we would need to be certain that it was *caused* by the elimination of Van 2. If Van 1 would have driven more miles anyway, the increased mileage is irrelevant for the differential analysis. If, on the other hand, we assume that the elimination of Van 2 means that some people who would have used it now would use Van 1 instead, then the increased mileage is relevant for the differential analysis. We would need to include that additional mileage in computing Van1's revenue and variable expenses under the alternative scenario.

The same is true for cost items such as rent and administration. If we were planning to decrease our administrative costs with or without Van 2, then the change is irrelevant for the differential analysis. If, by contrast, the elimination of Van 2 would allow us to decrease administrative costs (such as to eliminate a portion of the dispatcher wage expenses), then we would need to include this decrease in the differential analysis.

Principle #6. Information Must be Structured Appropriately

An analysis of differential costs is most easily performed when the fixed and variable costs of the particular activity are analyzed separately from the allocated overhead costs. An analysis that separates costs in this way usually is structured in terms of *contribution to overhead.* The difference between a unit's revenue and its variable, semi-variable, fixed, and step-function costs is its contribution to the organization's overhead costs.

A *contribution income statement,* which is the term given to this analysis, has a different format from a more traditional income statement. One typical construction is as follows:

Total Revenue (net)
Less: total variable costs
Equals: margin (for fixed and overhead costs)
Less: the product's or program's fixed costs
Equals: product's or program's contribution to the organization's overhead costs
Less: allocated overhead costs
Equals: surplus (deficit) on a full-cost basis

Exhibit 4-4 shows how a contribution income statement would look for Clearwater. As it illustrates, while Van 2 was losing money on a full-cost basis, it was contributing $16,000 to overhead.

Exhibit 4-4 Example of a Contribution Income Statement

Item	Van 1		Van 2		Total
Revenue	2.00 x 60,000 =	$120,000	2.00 x 30,000 =	$60,000	$180,000
Less: Variable expenses	.80 x 60,000 =	48,000	.80 x 30,000 =	24,000	72,000
Contribution to fixed expenses		$72,000		$36,000	$108,000
Less: Fixed expenses (Drivers)		20,000		20,000	40,000
Contribution to overhead		$52,000		$16,000	$ 68,000
Overhead (rent and admin.)		40,000		20,000	60,000
Surplus (deficit)		$ 12,000		($ 4,000)	$ 8,000

The general principle is that, in the short-run, it is unwise to eliminate an activity that is contributing to the coverage of overhead, even if it is losing money on a full-cost basis. This is because eliminating the activity will reduce the total contribution to overhead costs and thus will either reduce the organization's surplus or increase its deficit. Indeed, it was the elimination of the $16,000 contribution from Van 2 that led to a change from an $8,000 surplus to an $8,000 deficit.

THE OUTSOURCING DECISION

Until now, the discussion of differential costs has been in situations where an alternative choice decision involved a change in volume. This is the characteristic of most keep/drop and special price situations. Many other types of alternative choice decisions do not involve a change in volume, however. Perhaps the most common of these is an outsourcing (sometimes called "make/buy" or "contract out") decision. In many government entities, but elsewhere as well, the outsourcing decision involves *privatizing* the service (i.e., contracting with a private, for-profit entity to provide it).

In federal, state, and local governments, outsourcing has become increasingly popular. It has touched on a wide variety of services that previously were seen as the exclusive domain of government, and in almost all instances, the principal driving force has been cost savings. The diversity of privatization initiatives has been impressive, ranging from prison operations to animal control.

Examples In Indianapolis, outsourcing reduced public employment by 40 percent over three years in fields outside of police and fire services. Sunnyvale, California, relied on a temporary employment company for 25 percent of its workforce.

Butte, Montana, saved $600,000 a year by contracting with a private firm to run its municipal hospital. Newark, New Jersey, used a private firm to collect about one-third of its refuse, at a reported annual savings of over $200,000. It also hired private contractors to provide services such as tree trimming, building demolition, snow plowing, and street cleaning. Farmington, New Mexico, contracted with an independent firm to run its airport control tower at a cost savings of almost $200,000 a year. Scottsdale, Arizona,—the first U.S. city to use a private company for fire protection—boasted better than average fire response times, at less than half the cost to cities of comparable size.[1]

Some municipalities have privatized the management of their zoos. According to the American Zoo and Aquarium Association, of the nation's 100 zoos, one-third are privatized. Since a zoo is a freestanding programmatic entity, the computation of cost savings is quite easy.

Maywood, California, exemplifies what is perhaps the most dramatic illustration of outsourcing seen to date anywhere. The city outsourced everything! [2]

Outsourcing Principles

Each outsourcing opportunity is unique, and must be analyzed separately to decide on the relevant costs and other matters. However, there are a few general principles that are pertinent to almost all such decisions.

Time Period. The longer the time period involved, the more costs are differential. For example, if the alternative being considered is to outsource a single printing job rather than use in-house facilities, the only reduction in costs might be the savings in paper and ink; the printing presses remain, payment to employees probably would not be reduced, and no overhead costs would be affected. If, however, the proposal is to discontinue the in-house print shop permanently, all the direct costs associated with operating it would be saved, as well as, perhaps, some of the overhead costs that are associated with it.

Role of Depreciation. A common error in calculating differential costs for outsourcing decisions (and other alternative choice decisions) is to include depreciation on plant and equipment as a cost that would be saved if the organization used an outside contractor to provide the service. This is because depreciation is not a differential cost. Once assets have been acquired, the costs incurred to purchase them are *sunk costs*. Depreciation is simply the accounting mechanism that assigns each period with the expense associated with "using up" the asset. Since the past cannot be undone, and money spent cannot be recovered, there are no cash effects associated with depreciation.

Of course, if the asset can be sold, the amount realized is a differential cash inflow associated with the outsourcing decision, but this amount is based on the asset's market value, not its book value (purchase price less accumulated depreciation). Moreover, it is a one-time cash inflow only, and thus is relevant only for the first year of outsourcing.

1 Neil A. Martin, "When Public Services Go Private," *World*, May-June 1986, pp. 26-28.

2 For details, see D. Streitfeld, "A City Outsources Everything. Sky Doesn't Fall," *International Herald Tribune*, 19 July 2010.

If the outsourcing time frame is sufficiently long, such that the acquisition of new assets would be required under the "make" option, but not under the "buy" option, then depreciation might be used as a surrogate for the costs associated with replacing the assets as they wear out. However, the replacement cost rarely will correspond to the original purchase cost. It might be lower in the case of assets whose replacement cost is falling (such as computers), or higher if the replacement cost is increasing (such as medical technology).[3]

Non-Quantifiable Factors. In any outsourcing decision (in fact, in any *alternative choice decision*) there are a variety of factors that cannot be quantified easily, if at all, and that can easily tip the balance in one direction or another, frequently overriding the financial analysis. This is especially true if the financial analysis indicates that all options under consideration have roughly similar cost and revenue implications.

Non-quantitative considerations typically include factors such as quality, service, delivery, and reputation of the vendor. They also may include market considerations, such as the difficulty and/or cost of switching from one vendor to another if a particular relationship does not work out to management's satisfaction.

Examples A university that contracts for snow plowing services for its exterior parking lots typically has an easy time switching from one vendor to another. There are many people with pickup trucks and snow plowing blades who can provide the service. By contrast, a hospital that outsources its laundry services, may have a difficult time switching vendors since the number of such vendors may be quite small.

A related consideration is the cost of switching back to internal service provision. After outsourcing a service, an organization will likely eliminate the facilities, equipment, and trained personnel needed to provide it. Obtaining replacement facilities and equipment, and training new personnel may be quite costly. If the market for vendors is not very competitive, such that the organization will have a difficult time finding a replacement vendor, it may find itself at the mercy of its vendor.

Finally, non-quantitative factors can include stakeholder sensitivity. If a municipality outsources a service, such as waste collection and disposal, and the service is not performed according to expectations, the citizenry generally looks to the municipality, not to the private contractor, as the responsible party. Depending on the service and its importance to the community, this can have an impact on how the citizenry votes in the next election.

Example If a municipality outsources the printing of a brochure for a summer youth program and the vendor performs badly, the mistakes can be corrected before the citizenry is aware of them. By contrast, if the municipality outsources snow removal, and the streets are not plowed within a reasonable time after a heavy snowstorm, the citizenry will be acutely aware of the problem, even if corrective measures are taken later.

The combination of the three issues of stakeholder sensitivity, the nature of the market for vendors, and the difficulty of either switching vendors or returning to internal service provision are shown schematically in Exhibit 4-5.

---

[3] If asset acquisition is a significant aspect of the decision, that is, if assets must be acquired in order to pursue the *make* option, then depreciation alone is insufficient. Instead, a technique known as *net present value* is required. This technique is discussed in Chapter 7.

As this exhibit indicates, if stakeholder sensitivity to a service is high, the market is not especially competitive, and if switching costs are high, the outsourcing activity is high risk. From a patient's or physician's perspective, for example, a hospital's laundry service clearly is much more important than, say, its publications department. Patients and physicians are very concerned about clean and available linens and scrubs, but only minimally concerned about printing quality.

Exhibit 4-5 **The Three Dimensions of Outsourcing Risk**

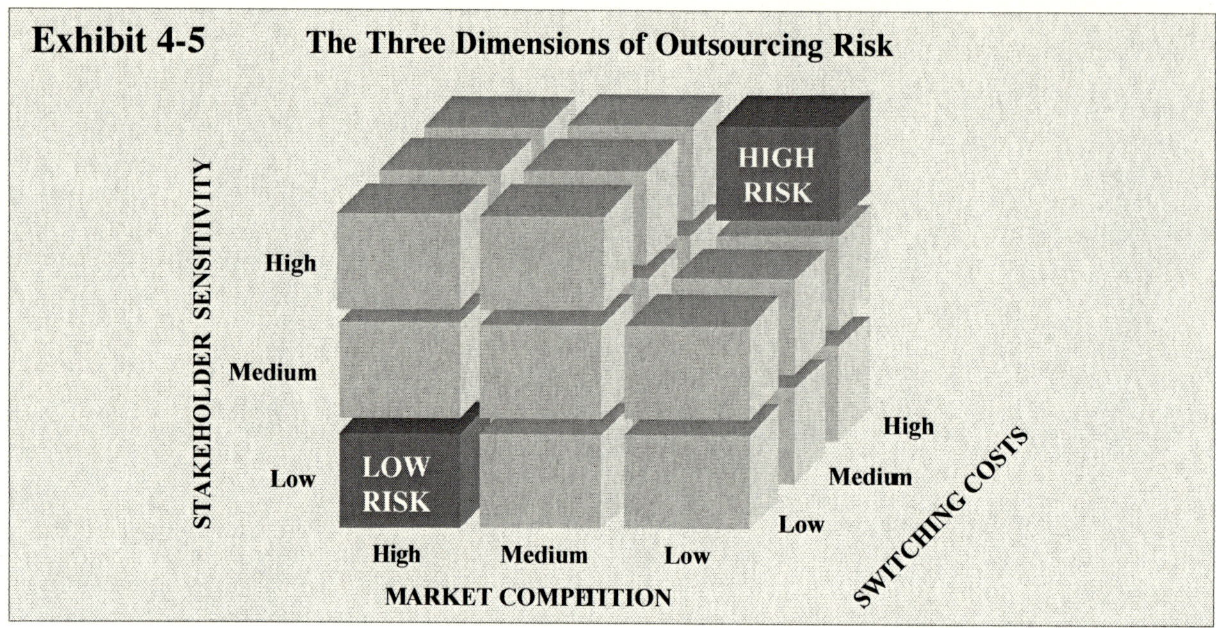

The low-risk cube embodies services such as the publication department with a combination of low stakeholder sensitivity, high competition, and low switching costs—situations with a high probability of successful outsourcing without the need for careful vendor management. A service such as snow removal might be in the northwest front corner, where stakeholder sensitivity is high but where a poorly performing vendor can be replaced easily and quickly.

It is in the northeast rear portion of the cube (high stakeholder sensitivity, low competition, high switching costs) where outsourcing is high risk. It is here that an organization must give very careful consideration to how a vendor will be managed.

Example Some years ago in Massachusetts, the state outsourced its Medicaid Management Information System, a system that mailed several hundred thousand checks each month to indigent citizens. Citizen sensitivity was high, and there were almost no vendors with computer systems of sufficient size and sophistication to undertake the various activities (only one of which was sending out checks). Moreover, due to the need to transfer software (or rewrite code in some instances), plus the difficulty of moving data files from one vendor to another and performing the needed audits, the switching costs were high. When the vendor went bankrupt, the state and several hundred thousand Medicaid recipients learned, quite painfully, the true meaning of "high risk" outsourcing.

Managing High-Risk Outsourcing

Even though a service may fall into the high-risk area of Exhibit 4-5, outsourcing still may have considerable cost-saving potential. To achieve this potential, the organization must manage the vendor carefully. To do so, managers must focus on three separate activities: output measurement, ongoing communication and coordination, and linkages to its responsibility accounting system. As Exhibit 4-6 indicates, for a high-risk outsourcing contract to be successful, there must be a high level of output measures, a great deal of ongoing communication and cooperation, and a full linkage with the organization's responsibility accounting system.

Exhibit 4-6 Three Key Activities for Managing High-Risk Outsourced Services

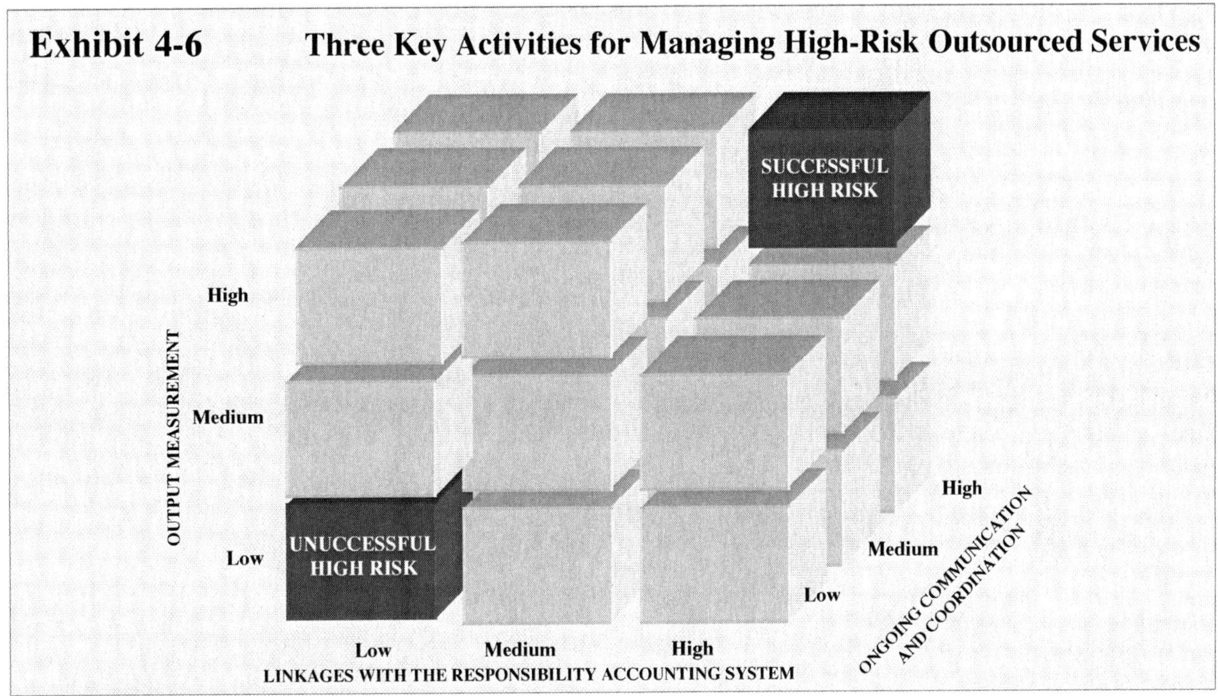

This latter requirement is especially important. In particular, an outsourced service must be included in an organization's ongoing process of programming, budgeting, reporting, and evaluating. Changes in a organization's programmatic activities, for example, may mean that a vendor needs to consider new or expanded services. Similarly, if new programmatic activities are to be initiated in the upcoming year, the budgeting phase of the responsibility accounting process must incorporate a revised vendor budget; otherwise the organization's budget will be unrealistic.

Similarly, the various results measures for the outsourced services need to be an integral part of the reporting phase of the responsibility accounting process. Indeed, unless reports focus on the results being produced by the vendor, the organization's senior management may learn too late of emerging problems.

In short, when an organization engages in high-risk outsourcing (the northeast, rear corner of Exhibit 4-5), and wishes to assure its stakeholders that the savings realized from the outsourced activity are not matched by a reduction in service quality and features, it must develop an appropriate set of activities to manage the vendor. Given that many outsourcing arrangements are of a high-risk nature, a focus on these activities is essential for organizations that wish to assure their stakeholders of effective services at a reasonable cost.[4]

[4] For additional details on high-risk outsourcing, see Emanuele Padovani and David W. Young "Managing High Risk Outsourcing," *Public Management*, Jan/Feb 2006, and Federica Farneti and David W. Young "A Contingency Approach to Managing Outsourcing Risk in Municipalities," *Public Management Review*, 2007.

Example The importance of both measuring performance when outsourcing a service, and also linking performance measures to appropriate motivational tools for the vendor, was learned somewhat painfully by the Metropolitan Boston Transportation Authority (MBTA) following revelations that the vendor running the commuter rail system was being paid $5 million a year in bonuses for on-time performance at the same time as the percent of on-time arrivals was declining.

Part of the problem was the nature of the contract. According to one official "the current contract... is quite complicated and [it is] hard to know how it works, unless you are a lawyer or a mathematician." Unfortunately, the contract period had two years remaining.

A related problem the MBTA faced was an absence of strong market competition. Nine years earlier it had contacted 16 companies around the world about operating the commuter rail service and received three bids, one of which was disqualified on technical grounds. The MBTA also was considering bringing the operation back in-house, but, if it did so, the switching costs no doubt would be very high.[5]

SUMMARY

Differential costs provide the proper analytical focus for keep/drop, make/buy, special-price, and obsolete-asset decisions. However, they do not make either the decisions themselves or the analytical efforts that underlie them easy. Indeed, a variety of strategic and other non-quantifiable factors usually enter into these decisions. These factors go beyond the financial analysis, and can create highly complex situations. An adequate differential analysis must incorporate all of them.

Suggested Cases for Classroom Use with this Chapter

See the Appendix at the end of the book for a more complete description of each case and ordering information.

Huntington Hospital	Developing a cost equation for a dietary department
Carlsbad Home Care	Conducting a breakeven analysis for a home health agency
Springfield Handyman Program	Performing a tricky breakeven analysis
Abbington Youth Center	Computing breakeven with multiple programs
Abbington Health Center	Computing breakeven with multiple departments
Opportunities Unlimited, Inc.	Computing breakeven with multiple programs in a job retraining organization
Jiao Tong Hospital	Computing breakeven with multiple departments in a Chinese hospital
Museo de la Casa	Analyzing a keep/drop decision in a small museum
Lowalos General Hospital	Doing a contribution analysis for two different DRGs
Lakeside Hospital	Analyzing a keep/drop decision in a hospital
Cittá di Forenna	Analyzing outsourcing risks and management in two Italian municipalities
Town of Rovereto	Making an alternative choice decision concerning snow removal

5 S.P. Murphy, "MBTA Looks to Alter Rail Pact," *Boston Globe*, 17 May 2011

Practice Case: Narcolarm

Not long after completing her residency in neurology, Mary Lou Black, M.D., became quite disenchanted with the practice of medicine. Shortly after she began her private practice, she was beset with more administrative and regulatory reporting requirements than she had ever thought possible. Moreover, the hospital at which she had admitting privileges began to insist that all its physicians participate in determining clinical treatment pathways for patients with the most common diagnoses, a practice that Dr. Black found completely repulsive.

BACKGROUND

During her residency and for the years that followed, she had specialized in the treatment of narcolepsy, a neurological disorder that resulted in individuals falling asleep during periods of high emotional activity or stress, and occasionally during periods of relative inactivity. Although drug treatments had been found that would allow narcoleptics to lead relatively normal lives, the one area where they frequently encountered difficulty was in driving. For obvious reasons, if a narcoleptic's drugs should fail to work while the individual was driving, the results could be fatal. As a result, many narcoleptics were very reluctant to drive.

During her work with narcoleptics, Dr. Black had begun experimenting with a device that could be used to keep them awake while driving. The device was quite simple: a small alarm, powered by a miniature battery, all of which could be inserted in an elongated plastic case that hooked over the driver's ear, much like a hearing aid. When the driver's head was erect, the device was silent, but if the driver's head began to tip forward or backward, as it would if he or she were falling asleep, the alarm would sound a shrill tone directly into the ear. If the head did not return to an erect position within 3 seconds, the device then would administer a small electric shock.

Her increasing disenchantment with medical practice, coupled with the potential for her "Narcolarm," as she called the device, led her to resign her position on the hospital staff and devote full attention to the invention. She obtained a patent for it, formed a nonprofit organization to manufacture it, and obtained a foundation grant that provided the start up funding to allow her to begin producing the device.

DECISIONS

In conjunction with her efforts to get her production and marketing activities underway, there were several questions that she thought important to answer. First, at her anticipated sales price of $10 per unit, how many Narcolarms would she need to sell to cover all her costs? Second, if she were successful, demand would grow, and she realized that she would need to earn a modest surplus to provide the cash needed to support the growth. She thought that that earning a surplus of $60,000 in her first year of operations, would be about right, and wondered how many units she would need to sell to attain it.

These decisions were complicated by her assessment of the market for the Narcolarm. Dr. Black estimated that, if the Narcolarm were priced appropriately, her annual sales could be on the order of 25,000 units. If this were the case, she wondered how much she would have to charge to cover all her costs, and how far this price was from her anticipated price of $10 per unit.

While pondering these matters, Dr. Black received a phone call from a local businessman who informed her that he was interested in manufacturing the electronic shock devices for the Narcolarms. He told her that he would charge her a fixed amount of $7,500 per year for his work. Dr. Black calculated that by having the businessman's company manufacture the devices, she would be able to reduce her variable costs by $.50 per unit.

If she did not accept the businessman's offer, Dr. Black thought that Narcolarm's annual costs would be as follows:

	Fixed	Variable (per unit)
Direct labor	$110,000	$2.30
Direct materials		5.90
Power	4,000	.10
Rental of plant and equipment	100,000	
Maintenance	20,000	.20
Administration and general	66,000	
Total	$300,000	$8.50

Assignment

1. How many units must Narcolarm produce and sell to break even? How many units would it have to produce and sell in order to cover all costs and earn a surplus of $60,000?

2. If sales of 25,000 units a year can be reached, how much must Dr. Black charge per Narcolarm in order to break even?

3. What price should Dr. Black use for a Narcolarm?

4. Based on cost considerations only, should Dr. Black accept the local businessman's offer?

5. In addition to cost information, what else should Dr. Black consider in her decision to accept or reject the offer?

6. What do you think of Dr. Black's venture?

Solution to Practice Case

This case helps you to develop your skills in CVP analysis, and also to examine some of the issues that arise in the context of an outsourcing decision. The outsourcing decision is interesting in that it can be turned into a CVP analysis.

Question 1 Part A

$$px = a + bx$$
$$\$10.00x = \$300{,}000 + \$8.50x$$
$$\$1.50x = \$300{,}000$$
$$x = 200{,}000 \text{ units}$$

Part B

$$\$1.50x = \$300{,}000 + \$60{,}000$$
$$x = 240{,}000 \text{ units}$$

Question 2

$$p(25{,}000) = \$300{,}000 + \$8.50\,(25{,}000)$$
$$p = \$20.50$$

Question 3

This is a tricky decision, and most likely will require some market surveys. It is interesting to note, however, that doubling of the price (from \$10 to \$20.50) lowers the breakeven from 200,000 units to only 25,000 units. Dr. Black needs to determine (a) how many potential buyers there are for the Narcolarm, and (b) how price sensitive they are. If the potential demand is low (say 25,000) but buyers are unwilling to pay \$20 for the device, she may not have much of a business. These, of course, are matters that Dr. Black might have considered before starting the organization.

Question 4

Yes. It lowers the breakeven. Calculations are as follows:

New FC	=	\$307,500
New Unit VC	=	\$8.00
New UCM	=	\$2.00
New B/E	=	153,750 (\$307,500 ÷ \$2.00)
Old B/E	=	200,000

Alternatively, since fixed costs are reduced by \$7,500 and unit VC are reduced by \$.50, the "breakeven" for this offer is 15,000 units (\$7,500 ÷ \$0.50). That is, if you are selling more than 15,000 units, it makes sense to subcontract.

Question 5

Some of the issues to be considered are the following:

- Will the quality be comparable?
- What is the term of the contract, and will next year's price be \$7,500 or something else?

- What is the rate of inflation and how does it compare to the projected price increases in the contract?
- Are there ceilings on volume?
- How accurate is the projected decrease in variable cost?

Question 6

A great deal of the success of Dr. Black's venture depends on the demand for the Narcolarm. How many potential customers (individuals who get sleepy while driving) are there? How many other people might be candidates to buy the device (such as for friends)? If 25,000 such people can be induced to pay $20 or so for the device, it looks as though she has a going concern. She needs to convince these people that $20 is not too much. Considering the stakes, it should not be too difficult for her to accomplish this, but a big question is the number of narcoleptics (or other people who need assistance staying awake while driving).

Chapter 5

Pricing Decisions

Setting prices is a tricky proposition in many organizations, but especially in nonprofits. Full costs, differential costs, or a variety of other configurations can be used to assist in the effort, but the choice depends in large measure on the scenario under consideration. Unfortunately, many nonprofit managers give insufficient thought to their pricing policies. In fact, many tend to regard all marketing activities (of which pricing is only one) as something to be avoided. Such an attitude can result in their giving insufficient attention to client needs. It also can result in the organization pricing its services in a way that is unfair to some clients, or developing pricing policies that inhibit the achievement of strategic goals. This chapter addresses these issues, and discusses several matters that affect pricing decisions in nonprofit organizations.

IMPORTANCE OF APPROPRIATE PRICING

Pricing policies are important in most nonprofit organizations because prices can (1) influence the behavior of clients, (2) provide a measure of output, and (3) influence the behavior of managers. The issues to consider differ in each of these areas.

Client Behavior

The amount that a client (or third-party payer on behalf of a client) pays for a service indicates that the service is worth at least that much to the client. Indeed, the better a pricing scheme fits with client decision-making options, the more powerful its impact on client behavior.

Example Residents of a city or town can be charged for water usage in at least three different ways: (1) everyone can be charged the same amount; (2) everyone can be charged a monthly or quarterly flat-rate, based on the number of water outlets in their residences; or (3) everyone can be charged individually for the water they actually consume, as measured by a meter. In the first case, residents are not motivated to conserve water, and consumers who use little water subsidize those who use more. In the second case, the charge is somewhat more equitable because water usage tends to vary with the number of outlets. However, such a system does not motivate consumers to conserve water (although it may influence their decisions to add or delete bathrooms). If meters are installed, however, consumers are more likely to conserve water. Indeed, some years ago, the installation of meters in New York City led to a drop in consumption of nearly 50 percent.

Prices that affect clients directly tend to have the greatest influence on consumption. Normally, as the price for a unit of service increases, clients consume fewer units. In some situations, however, price is a mere bookkeeping charge with no direct effect on client behavior. Some universities, for example, provide students with monetary allowances for printer usage that entitle them to a certain number of printed pages from the university's printers. These allowances may be set so high, or may be so easily supplemented, that they do not motivate at all, and do little more than track usage. The motivating force of such systems would be much stronger if clients were allowed to trade "dollars" of unprinted pages for other resources, or receive a refund for pages not printed.

Measure of Output

Measurements of output in nonmonetary terms, such as the number of visitors to a community center, or the number of faculty contact hours in the classroom, are likely to be more crude than monetary measurements. If, for example, each service furnished by an organization is priced at its cost, total revenue for a period approximates the total amount of service provided during that period. Even if reported prices do not measure the real value of an organization's services to individual clients or society, the revenue-based approximation may provide useful information to managers. For example, if revenue in one year is lower than that of the previous year (after adjustments for inflation), managers have a good indication that the organization's real output has decreased.

If the quantity of service provided varies among an organization's clients, a single price will not accurately measure the variations. At one time, for example, hospital patients were charged a flat rate per day, even though the services they received varied greatly based on their illnesses. Today hospital charges vary more directly with the type and quantity of services provided. Moreover, if the unit price of a service reflects its relative magnitude, then total revenue is, in effect, a weighted measure of output, i.e., it incorporates differences in the services rendered.

Behavior of Managers

If services are sold, the responsibility center that sells them frequently is a "profit center."[1] In general, profit center managers are motivated to think of ways to (a) render additional services so as to increase revenue, (b) reduce costs, or (c) change prices. Under these circumstances, the manager of a profit center in a nonprofit organization behaves much like a manager in a for-profit company.

Example In an organization with an automobile pool, if automobiles are furnished without charge, the manager of the pool may assign them according to his or her perception of users' needs (or sometimes friendship with users). The manager has little financial incentive to provide the vehicles in a cost effective manner. On the other hand, if the automobile pool were set up as a profit center, and dissatisfied users were free to go elsewhere, the manager would be motivated to offer the vehicles at competitive prices—or risk underutilized facilities, unmet revenue goals, and poor performance. In addition, when internal clients must pay for their use of the automobiles (which reduces the profit in their profit centers), they tend to think much more carefully about their use of them.

In this and other pricing situations, if customers do not buy a product in the quantity that managers think is reasonable, there is an indication that something is wrong. Perhaps not enough people believe the product is worthwhile at the stated price. Perhaps they can obtain a similar or better product at a lower price elsewhere. Whatever the reason, management no doubt will want to reexamine the product and its price.

Prospective Prices. In general, prices should be set prior to the delivery of services. When this happens, managers have an incentive to keep costs within prescribed amounts. No such incentive exists for managers who know that costs will be recouped no matter how high they are. Of course, this principle is feasible only when the cost of a service can be estimated with reasonable accuracy. With many research and development projects, for example, there is no reliable basis for estimating how much money should be spent to achieve the desired result.

---

[1] A profit center is an organizational unit in which both outputs and inputs are measured in monetary terms, i.e., using revenues and expenses. The manager of a profit center is responsible for operating the unit in such a way that it achieves the budgeted difference between revenues and expenses. Profit centers are discussed in Chapter 6.

NORMAL PRICING

Ideally, the price of a product or service provided by a nonprofit organization is its full cost plus an appropriate margin. This is the same approach that is used in normal pricing in the for-profit sector, except that, in for-profit companies, the margin ordinarily is higher due to the need to provide a return to shareholders.

Rationale for Normal Pricing

While the basic goal of a nonprofit organization is to provide services, it nevertheless must generate revenues that are at least equal to its expenses or it will go bankrupt. Beyond this, however, a nonprofit also must earn an excess of revenue over expenses if it is to generate some of the funds needed to grow, acquire new assets, and replace existing assets as they wear out. In this respect, there is no difference between for-profit and nonprofit organizations. Like their for-profit counterparts, nonprofit organizations need an excess of revenue over expenses to finance working capital (such as for inventories and accounts receivable) and fixed assets (such as new or replacement buildings and equipment). Moreover, because inflation usually increases replacement costs, depreciation on existing assets does not provide sufficient funds for their replacement.[2]

Approach to Normal Pricing

In setting a price, a nonprofit faces three tricky issues. First, the relevant costs are not historical costs, but estimates of future costs. Making these estimates can be difficult at times, especially when the organization faces an uncertain environment.

A second issue is whether the cost analysis should include depreciation on buildings and equipment that were financed with contributions. Some people argue that such buildings and equipment were acquired at zero cost, and, because one of the purposes of depreciation is to recover the cost of fixed assets, there is nothing to depreciate. Others maintain that depreciation is necessary to help provide for replacement of these assets. Some people also argue that the services a nonprofit organization provides are just as valuable as the services provided by a for-profit company, and that clients should pay a comparable amount for them. Thus, by including depreciation as an element of cost, nonprofits are in keeping with the pricing practices of for-profit companies. Indeed, many clients of nonprofit organizations, including government agencies, are willing to have depreciation on contributed assets included as an element of cost.[3]

The third issue concerns revenue offsets. Some services are partially financed by revenue from endowments or other contributed sources, and opinions differ as to whether these revenue offsets should be deducted from costs to arrive at the price a client should pay. For example, in a university, endowment spending that is specifically designated for financial aid to students clearly should be taken into account in arriving at annual tuition. When this is done, however, it may be desirable to report this amount as a component of the program's or service's revenue on the operating statement, rather than as an offset to costs. Then the operating statement will show the total revenue earned by the program or service.

---

[2] This issue and several related ones, are discussed in detail in Appendix 2A

[3] The government does not permit inclusion of depreciation on equipment that it has contributed (or otherwise paid for already), since to do so would be double counting.

Estimating the Margin

As discussed in Appendix 2A, the best conceptual way for managers to estimate their required margin is to work backwards from their organization's needed return on assets (ROA) and their forecasted asset turnover. Most managers do not make such calculations, however, and rely on rules of thumb instead. For example, there is a widespread belief among hospital managers that their margin should be three or four percent of revenue. There is little empirical justification for this figure, however. Moreover, since each hospital has a different strategy (resulting in a different required ROA, and a different asset turnover), its required margin quite likely will differ from the rule of thumb.

Some organizations base their prices on a conservative estimate of volume and plan for no surplus. When actual volume exceeds the estimate, the incremental contribution (i.e., revenues minus differential expenses) provides the necessary margin. For example, a college may base its tuition on an enrollment that is five percent lower than what it actually expects. If its actual enrollment reaches the expected level, the difference in contribution is its surplus for the year. Similarly, an organization may make a conservative estimate of its revenue from annual giving, with the expectation that the anticipated excess will be its surplus.

This approach works well when the estimate of volume is truly conservative. When volume falls below the anticipated level, however, an organization's revenues do not cover its expenses. In such circumstances, continued existence is precarious and often rests on the belief that, in times of crisis, special appeals to donors will bail out the organization.

Example It is said that for many years the Metropolitan Museum of Art presented its annual deficit to its board of trustees, and the trustees then wrote personal checks that totaled the needed amount. Today, few nonprofit organizations (including the Metropolitan Museum) have this luxury.

The Role of Outside Forces

Some prices are set by outside agencies. Examples are the Diagnostic Related Group (DRG) prices that are used by Medicare to reimburse hospitals, and the price ceilings specified by some government agencies as a condition for providing a grant. In these instances, managers still need to make cost calculations even though their selling price is given.

Example Some hospitals, upon discovering that the full cost of treating a patient with a particular diagnosis was greater than the associated DRG price, attempted to avoid treating these patients, giving rise to a phenomenon known as "DRG orphans." If the phenomenon extends to too many hospitals, it is a fairly clear signal to the payer (Medicare in this case) that its price is too low.

Price also may be influenced *indirectly* by outside forces. For example, if a college charges significantly than its competitors, there is an indication that it was inefficient. Nor would most colleges charge less than their competitors because they could make good use of any additional amount to strengthen their curricula. Furthermore, most colleges are convinced that small differences in tuition do not influence a student's decision as to which college to attend.

Example Some years ago, the Department of Justice considered investigating the possible incidence of illegal price fixing by a group of colleges whose tuition charges were within five percent of one another. Its decision not to pursue this matter quite likely was influenced by the recognition that such a situation is likely among competing organizations of comparable quality in the same industry.

THE PRICING UNIT

In general, the smaller and more specific a pricing unit, the better. Such a unit improves senior management's knowledge of, and decisions about, cross-product subsidization, and also measures output more accurately than otherwise. By contrast, a price that includes several discrete services with different costs is not a good measure of output because it masks the actual mix of services rendered.

The practice of isolating small units of service for pricing purposes is called unbundling, and managers who unbundle services should be mindful of two qualifications. First, and an obvious problem, beyond a certain point, the paperwork and other costs associated with pricing tiny units of service outweigh the benefits. Some hospitals charge for individual aspirin tablets, for example, a practice that is difficult to defend.

The second qualification is that the consequences of such pricing should be consistent with the organization's overall policies and goals. This qualification extends beyond the size of the unit to matters that are much more strategic in nature.

Examples Undergraduate English instruction costs less than undergraduate physics instruction, and these differences could be reflected by charging different prices for these courses. However, a separate price for each course might cause students to select courses in a way that university management considers to be educationally unsound. On the other hand, in most universities there are significant differences in the overall costs of graduate and undergraduate programs, such that there may be good reasons for charging different tuition rates to graduate students than to undergraduate students. University administrators who unbundle in this way do not believe that the differences motivate students to make unwise choices.

The Port Authority of New York and New Jersey charges the same amount for a tunnel crossing of the Hudson River as for a crossing using the George Washington Bridge, despite a lower cost per vehicle for bridge traffic. The pricing decision is based on transportation policy, rather than on the cost of the separate services.

Hospital Pricing as an Example of Unbundling

Exhibit 5-1 shows several approaches that could be used to price a hospital's services. Moving from Approach A to Approach D, one can see pricing practices that involve (1) an increase in record keeping, (2) a corresponding increase in the amount of output information available for senior management, and (3) a basis for charging patients that more accurately reflects the services they received. At one extreme, for example, the hospital could charge an all-inclusive rate, say $2,000 per day. This practice (shown in Approach A) is advocated by some on the grounds that patients can know in advance what their bills will be (assuming their lengths of stay can be estimated), and because record keeping, at least for billing purposes, is simplified.

A common variation on the all-inclusive price is shown in Approach B. Here the hospital charges separately for the cost of each easily identifiable special service, and makes a blanket daily charge for everything else. In fact, rather than a price per radiology film (as shown here), radiology prices, could be calculated according to a rather detailed point system that takes into account the complexity of the procedure, with each point worth a few cents. (There is, of course, some incongruity in calculating prices for certain services in terms of points worth a few cents each, while lumping other service costs into a large overall rate.)

Exhibit 5-1 Pricing Alternatives in a Hospital

(A) *All-Inclusive Rate*	(B) *Daily rate plus Special Services*		(C) *Daily Charge per Type of Service*
$2,000/day	Patient care	$1,000/day	Medical/surgical:
	Operating room	$ 500/hour	1st day $1,000
	Pharmacy	$ 10/dosage	Other days 750
	Radiology	$ 50/film	Maternity:
	Special nurses	$ 100/hour	1st day $700
	Etc.		Other days 500
			(plus special services as in B)

(D)
Detailed

Admittance	$800
Workup, per hour	50
Medical/surgical bed, per day	800
Maternity bed, per day	500
Bassinet, per day	200
Nursery care, per hour	80
Meals, per day	70
Discharge	100
(plus special services as in B)	

Approach C unbundles the daily charge. Different charges are made for each department, and more is charged for the first day than for subsequent days. This pricing policy accounts for the admitting and workup costs associated only with the first day of a patient's stay.

Approach D is the job-cost approach that managers use in many for-profit companies. Managers of automobile repair shops, for example, cost each repair job separately. Each repair is charged for the services of mechanics according to the number of hours they work on the job, as well as for each part and significant item of supply required for the job's completion. The sum of these separate charges is the basis for the price the customer pays. Customers of a repair garage would not tolerate any other approach. They would not, for example, agree to pay a flat daily rate for repairs, regardless of the services provided.

Example Some years ago, the Massachusetts Eye and Ear Infirmary in Boston developed a three-tiered pricing system for its "routine care" costs. There was a hospitalization charge designed to cover the costs associated with admitting and discharging a patient; it was independent of the patient's length of stay. There was a per diem charge associated with the hotel and meal component of care that was the same for each day of stay. There also was a clinical care charge based on the acuity of nursing care needed on each day of the patient's stay; this varied depending on the diagnosis and the patient's progress toward discharge.

VARIATIONS FROM NORMAL PRICES

There are many situations in nonprofit organizations where circumstances call for variations from the normal approach to setting prices. In some instances, these situations arise because of the requirements of third-party payers. In others, they arise because the organization wishes to distinguish between services provided as part of its main mission and those that are more peripheral. As a result, there are several areas where the organization may wish to use some approach other than normal pricing.

Cost-Plus Pricing

With cost-plus pricing, the purchaser of an organization's goods or services agrees to pay full cost plus an agreed-upon increment, usually a percentage. Many government contracts are written this way, especially in the defense industry, where the argument is made that the activities needed to design and manufacture the product are so uncertain that it would be impossible to determine the cost in advance, and hence to set a reasonable price.

Although the intent of cost-plus pricing usually is to pay the full cost of the service, the definition of full cost can vary among purchasers. In particular, some purchasers define certain costs as "unallowable." These are costs that, although incurred by the organization, may not be included in the cost computation used to arrive at the payment rate. Purchasers also may specify ceilings for certain items, such as the compensation of executives or the daily amount that can be spent for travel.

Market Based Pricing

Nonprofit managers may use normal prices for services that are directly (or closely) related to their organization's principal objectives, but market prices for peripheral services.

Example Many universities use normal pricing for room and board charges because students live in dormitories and eat in dining rooms as a necessary part of the educational process. By contrast, they will use market prices for space rentals to outside groups since these activities are not closely related to the main mission. Similarly, many universities use normal pricing for tuition for graduate and undergraduate programs but market rates for executive education programs.

In making pricing decisions, managers often have difficulty drawing the line between programs that are closely related to the organization's mission and those that are more peripheral. For example, market rates seem appropriate for a university's executive education programs while their use for the university extension courses or community education programs is much less clear.

Subsidized Pricing

A subsidy exists when price is set below full cost, and most subsidies are intended to encourage clients to use a service. For example, many public bathing beaches and other recreation facilities charge a lower price on weekdays to encourage off-peak use. More generally, nonprofit organizations use three types of subsidies: (1) for certain services, (2) for certain clients, and (3) for all clients.

Subsidizing Certain Services. A nonprofit organization may decide to price a certain service at less than the normal price to encourage use by clients who are unable or unwilling to pay the normal price. Or, as a matter of policy, the organization may want clients to select services on some basis other than their ability to pay. Examples are public education and public housing. In most circumstances, providing a service at a subsidized price is preferable to providing it for free, since a price, even if low, motivates clients to give thought to the service's value. However, an organization should be careful to determine whether the price deters clients from using *needed* services.

Example Some years ago, the MediCal (Medicaid) program in California instituted a charge of $1 per visit for primary care. The result was a sharp decline in the number of primary care visits. Some months later, however, there was an increase in these patients' rates of hospitalization, which could have been avoided if the patients had received timely primary care. Overall, the cost to MediCal was higher as a result of this pricing policy.[4]

An organization may decide to use the same price for all services even though some cost more than others. In this case, the higher-cost services are subsidized by the lower-cost ones. Although cross subsidization is frowned upon in some settings, there may be sound reasons for its use.

Examples Latin and Greek courses in a college typically have small enrollments, resulting in a higher faculty cost per student than in more popular courses. Because the college does not want to discourage enrollment in these courses, however, it charges the same tuition to all students. Thus, low-enrollment courses are subsidized by high-enrollment courses.

The U.S. Postal Service subsidizes rural post offices because its mission is to provide convenient mail service to everyone; this principle is rarely challenged.

Even if managers do not use cost as the basis for pricing, they may find it helpful to calculate the costs of subsidized services. Knowing the difference between price and full cost can help flag areas for managerial decision making. For example, if a service does not cover its full costs, managers have several possible courses of action:

- Accept the loss, recognizing that the service is either a loss leader or sufficiently important to the organization's strategy to warrant subsidization
- Reduce the variable costs or fixed costs directly associated with the service in an effort to have its revenue cover its costs
- Increase volume (if the service makes a contribution, there is some breakeven volume at which full costs will be covered)
- Raise the price of the service
- Phase out the service

Subsidizing Certain Clients. A client who is not charged the same amount as other clients who receive the same or comparable services is being subsidized. The usual reason for the subsidy is that the organization's objective is to provide the service to all qualified clients, even those who are unable to pay the normal price.

Examples Colleges and universities provide subsidies to certain students in the form of scholarships and other financial aid.

---

[4] Milton Roemer et al. "Copayments for Ambulatory Care. Penny-Wise and Pound-Foolish," *Medical Care,* June 1975, pp. 457-66.

Nonprofit hospitals, as charitable (and therefore tax-exempt) organizations, are obligated to provide certain levels of care to indigent patients.

In some instances, a *class* of clients is subsidized even though some members of the class have ample resources. Examples are subsidies given to handicapped and elderly persons for transportation, movies, restaurants, drugs, and a variety of other goods and services. Conceptually, the subsidy should be limited to those in need, but finding a practical way to do so is difficult. A "means test" usually is not feasible because it is expensive and time consuming, and, more importantly, because many people resent being classified as needy. Moreover, such a subsidy tends to be politically popular, and any attempt to eliminate or modify it would encounter considerable resistance from lobbying groups.

Subsidizing All Clients. Some organizations receive contributions or appropriations intended to subsidize their services for all clients. When this happens, no client pays the normal price for services. Museums, symphony orchestras, and state universities are examples.

FREE SERVICES

Some services are provided free. This can happen when public policy officials decide that it would be discriminatory to charge for a particular service, or when managers determine that attempting to collect a fee for a service would be impossible, unfeasible, or politically untenable.

Public Goods

The most important class of free services is public goods, which are services provided for the benefit of the public in general, rather than for specific users. Examples include community safety, public parks, foreign policy, and national security. In effect, public goods are goods (and services) that simply cannot be provided through the market because (a) they are supplied to users as a group rather than to specific individuals and (b) there is no way of withholding them from users who refuse to pay for them.

Example Road and traffic light maintenance is provided to all persons in a municipality. Everyone receives the same services, whether they are willing to pay for them or not. There is no way to withhold the service, or create a market that separates those who pay from those who do not. In fact, in this type of situation, rational consumers will never pay since they will get the benefit in any event.[5]

Quasi-Public Goods

Many services that seem to meet the definition of public goods turn out upon analysis to be services for which prices could be charged.

Example A somewhat classic example of a public good is a lighthouse. One ship's "consumption" of the warning light does not leave less warning light for other ships to "consume," and there is no practical way that the lighthouse keeper could prohibit ships from consuming it. At the same

[5] Otto Eckstein, *Public Finance*, 2nd ed. (Englewood Cliffs, N.J.: Prentice-Hall, 1967), p. 8.

time, a ship cannot refuse to consume the light. It can be argued, however, that ship owners, *as a class,* should pay for lighthouses. Then, if lighthouse costs become too high, the objections of ship owners may help bring them back in line.[6]

The lighthouse example is similar to the practice of charging users of highways for their cost via tolls or fuel-related taxes, or of charging airlines and owners of private aircraft for the cost of operating the air traffic control system. In some countries, the air waves are considered a quasi-public good and users are charged for them through a tax on television sets; in the United States, the air waves are regarded as a public good.

Within local governments (cities, towns, municipalities, counties, etc.), there can be considerable debate about the distinction between public and quasi-public goods. Some of the issues that managers need to consider are discussed in Appendix 5A.

Peripheral Services

Even when an organization's principal service is a public good, managers may be able to charge for certain peripheral services. For example, the Congress charges a fee for copying certain documents in its files, federal agencies charge fees for copying documents made available under the Freedom of Information Act, municipal governments charge for dog licenses, and some public school systems charge for extracurricular programs, such as after-school athletics.

Other Free Services

In addition to the general class of public goods, there are other situations in which prices should not normally be charged for services. These include the following situations:

- Services are provided as a public policy, but clients cannot afford to pay for them. Examples include welfare investigations and legal aid assistance.

- Services are not rationed on the basis of ability to pay. Examples include legislators, who do not charge fees for assisting constituents, even though a legislator's time is a valuable resource.

- A charge is politically untenable. Examples include guided tours of the White House and the Capitol. The public clamor over such charges could be harmful to overall organizational objectives, even though a charge would be equitable and would promote good management control.

- Client motivation is unimportant. A nominal charge to a public park or bathing beach will not measure actual output, nor will it influence a client's decision to use the facilities. A charge equal to full cost, by motivating less wealthy individuals to avoid using these facilities, may be inconsistent with public policy.

---

[6] In a fascinating article, Coase describes the history of British lighthouses, showing that they in fact successfully charged fees from the 17th century until the present. R. E. Coase, "The Lighthouse in Economics," *Journal of Law and Economics* 17 (October 1974), pp. 357-76.

SUMMARY

The prices that a nonprofit organization charges (or decides not to charge) for its services influence the behavior of its clients, provide a measure of output, and influence the behavior of managers and professional service providers. The price that is usually charged is called the "normal price." It is the sum of the full cost of a service plus an appropriate margin.

Prices charged for subsidized services are less than normal prices. Subsidized prices may be charged only for certain services, only to certain clients, or to all clients. In some instances, for sound public policy purposes, a service may be provided free of charge.

Pricing decisions exist not only between an organization and its clients, but between two responsibility centers as well. The latter price is called a transfer price. The principles of transfer pricing are similar to those for external pricing. Properly designed, transfer prices can have important and beneficial motivational effects on managers' behavior. They also can be used to measure the efficiency of an organization's responsibility centers. They are discussed in Chapter 6.

Suggested Cases for Classroom Use

See the Appendix at the end of the book for a more complete description of each case and ordering information.

Harlan Foundation	Determining the breakeven price for a camp, and computing the price for a seminar
Town of Levinton	Pricing water and sewer services
B.U. Medical Center Hospital	Pricing DRGs in a competitive environment
Massachusetts Eye and Ear Infirmary	Pricing based on three different pricing units
Central Valley Primary Care Associates	Devising a methodology to compute a sub-capitation rate
Sonsonala (A)	Determining the appropriate markup for drugs for community pharmacies in a developing country
Boise Park Health Care Foundation (B)	Deciding whether cash or accrual accounting should be used to measure the adequacy of a request for a rate increase
The Meredith Center	Analyzing a tricky pricing problem in a center for the blind.

Appendix 5-A
Conceptual Issues in Pricing Public and Quasi-Public Goods and Services

The distinction between public and quasi-public goods often is made at the local government (LG) level. Local governments include cities, towns, municipalities, counties, and other similar entities. This distinction, and the resulting design and implementation of a good pricing system (or of a decision not to charge for a good or service) is influenced by four conceptual issues: (1) the principle of generational (or inter-year) equity, (2) the principle of consumer equity, (3) the juxtaposition of positive externalities and pricing units, and (4) the pricing of programs and services without positive externalities. Many of these can be overcome with some creative thinking on the part of a LG's senior management team.[7]

The Principle of Generational Equity

According to the principle of generational equity, the current year's taxpayers should pay only for the expenses of the current year's programs and services, and not for any expenses incurred in operating those programs or services in a prior year, or to fund the expenses a program might incur in a future year. In effect, an operating deficit this year means that future years' taxpayers will pay for this year's programs (or, if the deficit is financed from a prior year's surplus, that prior year's taxpayers helped to pay for this year's programs). An operating surplus means that this year's taxpayers will help to pay for future years' programs.

In part, the generational equity principle underlies the need for a LG to have a balanced budget each year, coupled with restrictions to assure that no accounts are overspent. What the principle fails to recognize, of course, is that the revenues for many programs are not fully predictable. If they fall below the budget, and if the LG's spending restrictions are not sufficient, there will be a deficit. If they exceed the budget, and no mechanism is in place to raise the spending ceilings, there will be a surplus.

Despite having balanced annual budgets, many LGs violate the generational equity principle in two ways. First, they fail to account properly for pensions and other post-retirement benefits earned by their employees. In the United States, this accounting (and audit!) failure can reach billions of dollars in any good sized LG. Despite recently passed corrective legislation, many LG's taxpayers nevertheless will be called on to fund retirement benefits earned over several prior decades.

The second violation of the generational equity principle arises because most LGs do not depreciate their infrastructure and other fixed assets. A LG's infrastructure includes roads, bridges, tunnels, dams, and even some smaller capital items, such as a fire house. A LG also has fixed assets with somewhat shorter economic lives, such as a police cruiser. As with all fixed assets, the economic life is unknown at the time of construction or purchase. Moreover, because these assets have economic lives of several years, a LG has difficulty assuring that the individuals who receive their benefits pay for them in their entirety.

---

7 For a discussion of the different types of local governments see, Emanuel Padovani and David W. Young, *Managing Local Governments: Designing Management Control Systems that Deliver Value*, London, Routledge, 2012, Chapter 1. For additional discussion of the issues in this appendix, see Chapter 3.

In part, these difficulties are the same as those that any organization—in either the private or public sector—has in selecting an economic life for a new asset. As a consequence, the failure to depreciate fixed assets is not due to the difficulty of estimating their economic lives. Rather, it is a consequence of the use of cash- or commitment-based accounting. The result is that the current year's taxpayers pay for an asset that will be used by other taxpayers for several, if not many, years into the future.

Some observers have argued that the generational equity issue associated with an absence of accounting for depreciation is less problematic than it might appear to be, at least for infrastructure projects and other large fixed assets. Their reasoning is that these assets ordinarily are financed with municipal bonds or other forms of long-term debt. Under this scenario, the term of the debt effectively constitutes the economic life of the asset, such that the annual principal payment on the debt is a reasonable surrogate for the asset's depreciation expense.

Thus, the argument goes, if a LG finances an infrastructure asset with a bond (or a similar long-term debt instrument), and chooses a repayment period that approximates the economic life of the asset, there is no need to incorporate depreciation into the management control system. With infrastructure projects that benefit the entire community, and where no pricing units can be established, the LG need only assure that property tax and other general tax revenues are sufficient to cover the bond's debt service payments (principal and interest), in addition, of course, to the LG's other general operating expenses.

Unfortunately, a violation of the generational equity principle can occur when an asset's economic life extends well beyond (or is much shorter than) the term of the debt instrument that financed it. If the economic life is longer than the debt term, some future generations of taxpayers will benefit from an asset for which they did not pay. If the economic life is shorter than the debt term, the current generation of taxpayers will not fully pay for the cost of the asset they used.

Because of these complications, and because not all fixed assets are debt financed, LGs need to incorporate depreciation into their accounting systems. Using principal payments on debt as a surrogate for depreciation is a poor substitute.

Example In 2011, the Town of Lexington, Massachusetts, announced that it would be spending $60 million for renovations to two schools, both of which were 45 years old. The renovations were to be financed by a 20 years construction loan. At issue was the term of the loan. If the schools had lasted 45 years without the need for renovations, perhaps the loan should have had a longer duration. Unfortunately, the town's residents were not given the expected economic life of the project. Yet, unless the term of the debt was equal to this economic life, there would be a violation of the generational equity principal.

The Principle of Consumer Equity

The principle of consumer equity holds that user fees should support a program or service when there is an easily measurable unit of output and when consumption is a matter of choice. This principle underlies the creation of what in some locales are called "enterprise funds," such as Off-Track Betting in New York City.

Between enterprise funds and programs that are supported entirely by general taxpayers (such as road maintenance or street lighting) lies a somewhat amorphous middle ground where application of the consumer-equity principle can become contentious. To illustrate the dilemma, consider the water and sewer department shown in Exhibit 1.

Exhibit 1 Pricing Municipal Water and Sewer Services (In $000)

	New Users	Existing Users	Pre-tax Surplus (Deficit)	LG Taxpayers	Total
Revenues					
Access Fees	$46,700				
Usage Fees		$139,000			
Total Revenues	$46,700	$139,000			
Expenditures					
Operating		$67,900			
Debt service	$197,600				
Total expenditures	$197,600	$67,900			
Operating Surplus (Deficit)	-$150,900	$71,100			
Grant from region	$55,300				
Surplus (Deficit)	-$95,600	$71,100	-$24,500	$40,000	$15,500

In this situation, there has been a minor violation of the generational equity principle, since the LG's taxpayers have over-funded the $24.5 million deficit, thereby paying for $15.5 million of the services that will be received by future years' citizens. This situation could be corrected with little difficulty.

More significantly, the consumer-equity principle has been violated in several ways, most of which are more difficult to correct than the generational-equity problem. First, the department incurred a deficit prior to receiving taxpayer support, meaning that users, as a group, did not pay for the full costs of the services they received. The LG's taxpayers, who paid for their consumption directly via user fees, also paid for it *indirectly* (i.e., without regard to their consumption) via their property or other general taxes.

Second, as the line just above the Surplus (Deficit) computation for new users shows, the *region*'s (as opposed to the LG's) taxpayers subsidized some of the cost of new users gaining access to the water and sewer system. One must ask what benefits accrued to the region's taxpayers from providing a $55.3 million subsidy to support the construction of water and sewer facilities in a LG where most of them do not live.

Finally, and perhaps less obviously, existing users have helped to subsidize the cost of new users gaining access to the system. This violation of the consumer-equity principle arises because there are two separate services: *access* to the water and sewer *system* and *use* of water and sewer *services*. The access fees for new users (plus the regional subsidy) did not cover the debt service costs associated with the infrastructure to which they were gaining access, resulting in a $95.6 million shortfall. At the same time, existing users (who had paid their access fees in some prior period) have paid $71.1 million more than the full cost of the department's ongoing operations.

The water and sewer department in Exhibit 1 is not an anomaly. Similar situations arise regularly in the management of a LG. To address them, senior management must answer three questions about its programs and services: (1) Which should be paid exclusively by users with no taxpayer subsidies? (2) Which should be paid—in whole or in part—from property tax or other general tax revenues? (3) Which should be supported by state or regional taxpayers?

To make these questions more concrete, consider the following services, and assess whether they should be paid entirely by user fees. Alternatively, if they should be subsidized by general taxpayers, how should a LG's senior management team compute the amount of the subsidy? And, once the amount of the subsidy is determined, how should state or regional taxpayers decide on the support they should provide?

- *Education.* Property tax revenues, sometimes a specified percentage of each property tax dollar, are used in most U.S. LGs to pay for the operating costs of the LG's school system. Sometimes state or regional aid contributes to the system's operations, meaning that taxpayers in other LGs help to pay for a given LG's school system. In addition, the use of property taxes means that families who live in the LG but have no school-age children (i.e., families receiving no educational services) help to pay for the system's costs. And it means that families with few school-age children help to pay for the educational costs of families with many school-age children.

- *Water and Sewer.* As the example in Exhibit 1 demonstrates, some LGs use property tax revenues and state (or regional) aid to support a portion of the cost of running their water and sewer system. This means that all families pay a portion of the cost of the system, regardless of their consumption. It also means that those families in the LG with artesian wells and septic systems, i.e., those who use no municipal water or sewer services, help to pay the cost of water and sewer services for other residents. And the presence of state aid for new users means that people living outside the LG help to support construction of its water and sewer infrastructure.

- *Trash pickup and disposal.* When the pickup and disposal of non-recyclable trash is paid with general tax revenues, small families subsidize large families, abstemious families subsidize wasteful families, and families who recycle subsidize those who do not.

- *Public transportation.* When public transportation deficits are funded with property taxes, or with state (or regional) subsidies, public transit passengers do not pay the full cost of their transportation. They are subsidized by automobile drivers, cyclists, pedestrians, and shut-ins.

- *Police protection.* When funded with property taxes, or with state (or regional) subsidies, police protection for individuals who live in high-crime neighborhoods is subsidized by individuals who live in low-crime neighborhoods. In addition, individuals who live in rural areas (where crime rates typically are low) subsidize those living in urban areas.

- *Fire protection.* People who are safety conscious subsidize those who are careless with fire.

Positive Externalities and Pricing Units

In many respects, an answer to whether a program or service should be subsidized by general taxpayers hinges on two factors: the presence of positive externalities and the ability to identify an output (or pricing) unit. According to this view, a LG's taxpayers should subsidize the police protection, since the entire community benefits from having police protection in high-crime neighborhoods (a positive externality). In addition, using general tax revenues for funding the police department is appropriate, since it is all but impossible to develop a unit of output for pricing the service.

With a fire department, by contrast, there is an easily measurable unit of output (responding to a fire), and hence a cost and a price that can be determined relatively easily. Clearly, a positive externality exists in terms of preventing a fire's spread to other buildings, but, since the basic users of the service (those who started the fire) have a choice (use fire safely or carelessly), and since a pricing unit can be established (a response to a call), there would appear to be little reason to have the fire-extinguishing service (as opposed to the department's standby service) subsidized by general taxpayers.

The presence (or absence) of positive externalities and pricing units perhaps can be useful for arriving at a *conceptual* answer to the question of whether there should be a subsidy. But taking the next step requires a LG to address two important and related issues: the definition of the community and the amount of the subsidy. With public education, for example, the usual argument is that the LG's taxpayers should provide a subsidy because the entire community benefits from having an educated citizenry (a positive externality). But this begs the question of how to define the benefiting community. It also explains why public education in many countries is funded with *national* rather than *local* tax revenues.

With regard to the amount of the subsidy, a LG must answer two questions. First, is the department that receives the subsidy operating as efficiently as possible? Second, could the funds being used for the subsidy be put to better use for some other purpose? The first is a question of efficiency and can be answered rather easily. The second is a question of priorities and is much more difficult to answer.

Pricing Programs and Services Without Positive Externalities

A logical extension of the above thinking is that when an output (or pricing) unit can be established, and when no positive externalities can be identified, each user or user group should pay its own way with no general taxpayer support. With water and sewer services, trash collection and disposal, public transportation, after school programs, snow removal, and host of other municipal services, there is a measurable output unit. Under these circumstances, if the LG's senior management cannot identify a positive externality that accrues to a community from the consumption of the service (or use of the program), there would appear to be no basis for taxpayer subsidies. Thus, by identifying these programs and services, and designating the departments that provide them as "profit centers" in its management control system, a LG can begin to move toward the principle of consumer equity, and, at the same time, toward a more appropriate use of its general tax revenues.

Practice Case: Job Enrichment Center (A)

Job Enrichment Center (JEC), was a small nonprofit organization located in the southwest corner of Texas. JEC had been formed approximately two years ago, when several prominent members of the local community realized that many newly arrived immigrants were having a difficult time finding jobs due to problems with literacy and English-language skills.

JEC's mission was to provide basic training in these skills. It charged local companies for each person they hired who had successfully completed one or both of the center's training programs. Many companies needed employees who had a basic level of literacy in English, and most realized that it made economic sense to pay JEC rather than to try to train the employees themselves.

JEC conducted two types of training programs: Basic Literacy and English as a Second Language. JEC ran its programs for 40 weeks of the year, closing during the remaining weeks for breaks and vacations. Each program was run by a separate program manager, who also was a faculty member. The remaining faculty were hired on a per-session basis, based on the actual number of trainees in the session and the budgeted trainee-to-faculty ratio.

JEC determined its prices annually based on expected enrollment, its anticipated costs, and the need for a small (5 percent) operating margin. Since not all of JEC's students needed training in both programs, each program had a separate price. Budgeted data on the two programs for the upcoming fiscal year are shown in Exhibit 1. Administrative and general costs were allocated to programs based on the number of trainees.

Assignment

1. Use the data for the upcoming fiscal year to determine the price per trainee for each program. Given these prices and other estimates, what is the total operating surplus that JEC will obtain for the year?

2. What concerns, if any, should JEC's senior management have about its prices or other estimates?

Exhibit 1. Data

	Basic Literacy	**English as a Second Language**
Number training sessions	4	2
Length of each training session (in weeks)	10	20
Average number trainees per session	100	30
Number trainee-weeks	4,000	1,200
Number trainees	400	60
Trainee:faculty ratio	20:1	10:1
Number faculty needed	5	3
Average faculty salary	$20,000	$25,000
Books/workbooks per trainee	5	2
Average price per book/workbook	$15	$20

Administrative and general costs: $92,000

Solution to Practice Case

The purpose of this case is to calculate prices when there is a reasonably clear set of assumptions.

Question 1. The analysis should look something like the following:

	Basic Literacy	English as a Second Language	Total
Faculty:			
5 @ $20,000	$100,000		$100,000
3 @ $25,000		$75,000	75,000
Books:			
5 x 400 x $15	30,000		30,000
2 x 60 x $20		2,400	2,400
Total direct costs	$130,000	$77,400	$207,400
Administration and general			
$92,000 ÷ 460 x anticipated # of trainees	80,000	12,000	92,000
Total costs	$210,000	$89,400	$299,400
Anticipated number of trainees	400	60	
Full cost per trainee	$525	$1,490	
Price with margin of 5 percent	$551.25	$1,564.50	
Revenue	$220,500	$93,870	$314,370
Less Total costs	210,000	89,400	299,400
Total budgeted surplus	$10,500	$4,470	$14,970

In calculating these prices, you needed to pay attention to the following:

- Distinguishing between programs, with each program analyzed separately
- Allocating administrative and general costs to programs
- Calculating total costs and an average cost per trainee
- Increasing the average cost per trainee by 5 percent to arrive at the price
- Computing the total margin at the anticipated costs and prices

Question 2. Since JEC has been operating for two years, it presumably has good knowledge about the acceptability of its prices, and what its various costs will be. Its main source of uncertainty would appear to be the number of trainees. Since local companies pay the prices, the number of trainees is not the number of people who desire JEC's programs or even who are trained, but rather the number of people that the local companies hire after they have completed one or both of the training programs.

Part III

Management Control Systems

As discussed in Chapter 1, a management control system consists of both a structure and a process. Structure describes what the system is, and process describes what it does—in the same way that anatomy and physiology describe the human body.

This part of the book discusses some of the important aspects of a management control system. Chapter 6 focuses on the structure, placing it in the broader context of the management control environment. Because an organization's management control structure is governed in large measure by its external and internal environments, understanding the management control environment is essential to analyzing and/or designing the management control system.

Chapters 7-13 describe the management control process—a set of activities encompassing a wide variety of interactions among individuals in an organization. Each phase of the management control process—programming, budgeting, operating and measuring, and reporting and evaluating—is the subject of at least one chapter, sometimes two.

Some chapters consider specific aspects of a phase in detail. For example, Chapter 9 looks in depth at the control of operations—a significant part of the operating and measuring phase. Similarly, Chapter 10 examines a topic of considerable importance to nonprofit organizations: measuring non-financial performance.

Chapter 13 is devoted to program evaluation—an aspect of the management control process that is particularly important for nonprofit organizations. In most for-profit organizations, profit is the primary means to evaluate the success of a program (or a product line), but nonprofit organizations must use criteria other than financial performance. This chapter discusses some approaches to evaluation that can be used when profit (or surplus) is not an appropriate measure.

Chapter 14 summarizes the characteristics of a good management control system, and also puts the management control systems into its broader organizational context. The chapter also addresses some of the tricky behavioral issues that senior management encounters when it attempts to introduce a new management control system or make significant changes to an existing one.

Chapter 6

The Management Control Environment

A nonprofit organization can be affected by many forces in its *external environment,* including legal constraints, uncertain funding sources, absence of competition, and public scrutiny. These forces vary greatly among organizations. For example, one nonprofit might have relatively certain revenues, almost no competition, and programs that are essentially unchanged from one year to the next; a good example is a public school. Another, such as a museum, might have relatively uncertain sources of funding, numerous competitors, and programs whose emphases shift rapidly. Similarly, government organizations, as well as organizations that receive substantial funds from government sources, are subject to a variety of pressures and scrutiny from legislative bodies and the general public. In these cases, the desires of the press and the public for information constitute an important management control issue.

An organization also has an *internal environment*, and senior management must give careful consideration to the fit among its elements. These elements include the authority and influence structure, the program structure, the measurement and reporting structure, and a variety of administrative, behavioral, and cultural factors. Not only must these elements fit well with each other, but they also must fit with the management control system.

THE AUTHORITY AND INFLUENCE STRUCTURE

Organizational structure refers to the *formal* reporting relationships among managers and other individuals in an entity. There also is an *informal* structure that is unwritten and perhaps unintended. The informal structure encompasses a network of interpersonal relationships that has important implications for management. Because it is unwritten, however, the informal structure is difficult to identify and describe. For this reason, the focus here is on the formal structure.

Senior management weighs many considerations in determining the best formal structure. These considerations involve questions such as the most appropriate division of tasks, the activities that should be carried out by specialized staff units versus those that should be the responsibility of line managers, and the decisions that should be made at or near the top of the organization versus ones that can be delegated to lower levels.

An organization's formal structure can take one of several basic forms. In a functional structure, tasks are classified according to their relative similarities, and all personnel who work in the same functional area are under the direction of a manager. In a social service agency, for example, all social workers might report to a director of social work, or in a hospital all nurses might report to a director of nursing.

As an organization grows and becomes more diverse, it may shift from a functional to a divisional structure. In a divisional structure, functional tasks are grouped into logical clusters which might be according to clients served, regions, or programs. For example, if a large visiting nurse association had a divisional structure, its personnel might be grouped into teams according to geographic region. If so, its home care workers would report to a regional manager, rather than a director of home care. If a hospital had a divisional structure, nurses would report to a department head, such as the chief of surgery or chief of medicine, rather than to a director of nursing.

The most complex organizational structure is the matrix. In this form, individuals have two supervisors—a divisional or program supervisor and a functional supervisor. Social workers might report to a team manager for their day-to-day activities, for example, and to a director of social work for their professional development and training. In a hospital, nurses might have similar dual reporting responsibilities. In some universities, faculty report to both a department chair and a program director.

Responsibility Centers

The formal organizational structure for management control purposes is defined in terms of responsibility centers. A responsibility center is an organizational unit headed by a manager who is in charge of its activities. Line control is exercised by the managers of these responsibility centers.

Although the type and degree of control exercised by a manager may be difficult to pinpoint, at some level someone in an organization has control over each resource-related decision. In some cases, control is infrequent and has long-term implications, such as the acquisition of a fixed asset or the commitment to a long-term lease. In other cases, it is of shorter duration, such as the decision to sign a one-year supply contract. In still other cases, control is very short-term, such as the decision to ask employees to work overtime.

Types of Responsibility Centers

A key issue in designing a management control system is how senior management wishes to decentralize financial responsibility throughout the organization. To do so, it chooses among five different types of responsibility centers: revenue centers, standard expense centers, discretionary expense centers, profit centers, and investment centers. These different types of responsibility centers were discussed briefly in Chapter 1. Exhibit 6-1 lists them and the management control implications of each.

Exhibit 6-1 **Types of Responsibility Centers and Associated Responsibilities**

Type	Responsible for
Revenue center	Revenue earned by the center
Discretionary expense center	Total expenses incurred by the center regardless of the volume of activity
Standard expense center	Expenses per unit of output, but not total expenses, incurred by the center
Profit center	Total revenues minus total expenses of the center
Investment center	Total revenues minus expenses of the center, computed as a percent of the center's assets, i.e. the center's return on assets (ROA)

From the viewpoint of senior management, trustees, or even oversight bodies, the whole organization is an investment center. As discussed in Appendix 2A, it must obtain a satisfactory return on assets if it is to remain financially viable. The role of senior management is to decide how to decentralize ROA responsibility throughout the organization. As a result, in any organization except a very small one, there is a hierarchy of responsibility centers. At the lowest level, there are responsibility centers for sections or other small units. At higher levels, there are departments or divisions that consist of several smaller units, and may include staff and management people.

The principal factor in selecting one type of responsibility center over another is *control*. That is, senior management's objective in choosing a given type of responsibility center is to hold the center's manager accountable for those inputs and outputs over which he or she can exercise a reasonable degree of control. As a result, all five types of responsibility centers can be found in some nonprofit organizations. The most common types are discretionary expense centers, standard expense centers, and profit centers.

As Exhibit 6-1 indicates, the focus of a discretionary expense center is on *total expenses* regardless of the volume and/or mix of activity, whereas the focus of a standard expense center is on *expenses per unit of output* rather than total expenses. A standard expense center's budget each period is a *flexible budget* ; that is, it is adjusted based on the actual volume and mix of units of output. The actual costs incurred by the center during the period are then compared to the flexed budget in order to measure the manager's financial performance.

In a profit center, the focus is on both revenues and expenses. In some organizations, revenues may be generated by sales of services to other responsibility centers as well as to outside clients. The prices for these internal transactions, called *transfer prices*, are discussed later in the chapter.

Designing Effective Profit Centers

To some people, the idea of profit centers in a nonprofit organization seems peculiar, but the profit center idea can be an important way of facilitating management control. As such, it is not at all inconsistent to have a profit center in a nonprofit organization—the term simply refers to a manager's scope of financial responsibility. If a profit center is to be effective, however, senior management must pay careful attention to several important design matters.

Record-Keeping Costs. Because a profit center encompasses more elements of managerial performance than an expense center, it also requires more record keeping. Clearly, the benefits of having a profit center should be greater than this extra record-keeping cost and other administrative activities that are required. The cost of measuring the output of most accounting departments, for example, is quite difficult, such that establishing the accounting department as a profit center probably would not be worthwhile.

Dysfunctional Incentives. The competitive spirit that a profit center fosters should not have dysfunctional consequences to the organization.[1] For instance, the creation of a profit center may encourage managers to place too much attention on the revenue side of the equation, or to cut expenses in a given accounting period without concern for the longer term consequences of the cuts. Moreover, senior management's desired degree of cooperation with other responsibility centers may not occur—profit center managers may make decisions that add to the profit of their own units to the detriment of other units in the organization. They may be reluctant to incur overtime costs, for example, even though the services may be badly needed by another responsibility center. Senior management can avoid or minimize these dysfunctional consequences by designing the manage-

[1] For a discussion of dysfunctional consequences in a hospital context, see David W. Young "Profit Centers in Clinical Care Departments: An Idea Whose Time Has Gone," *Healthcare Financial Management*, March 2008.

ment control system in such a way that cooperative actions have a positive impact on the profit center's reported performance (or at least do not affect it adversely).

Despite the potential for dysfunctional consequences, a profit center generally is desirable if a manager has a reasonable amount of influence over both the revenues and expenses of his or her responsibility center. In many nonprofit organizations, managers who carry out identifiable programs, especially ones that are geographically separate, have their units designated as profit centers.

Managerial Autonomy. Organizations vary considerably in the autonomy they give to their profit center managers. In most organizations, although a profit center may operate almost as if it were an independent entity, its manager does not have all the autonomy of a chief executive officer. This is because profit centers are part of a larger organization, and their managers are subject to the organization's policies. Profit center managers rarely have the authority to initiate new programs or commit to major capital expenditures, for example. Those decisions, like others that influence the organization's overall strategy, usually are made by senior management.

Apart from these restrictions, a manager of a responsibility center should be able to exert *reasonable* influence over both the revenues and expenses of the center. This does not imply that he or she must have *complete* control over these items, for few, if any, profit center managers have such authority. However, a profit center manager should be able to exercise some control over the center's volume of activity, the quality of the work done, the center's unit variable costs, and its direct fixed costs. Sometimes he or she also can influence the prices charged.

Restrictions on autonomy imposed by senior management may be communicated by formal rules described later in this chapter or by other means. No matter how carefully these *formal* devices are constructed, however, informal mechanisms constitute powerful indicators of a manager's autonomy. These mechanisms include unwritten rules concerning, for example, what decisions are made independently by a profit center manager versus those that require approval of higher authority or consultation with (but not necessarily approval of) staff offices. In general, chief executives tend to give more autonomy to subordinates whom they know well and whose judgment they trust. As a result, despite the presence of a variety of formal devices in an organization, some profit center managers may have considerably more decision-making latitude than others.

Fairness. A profit center manager should perceive that the profit reported for his or her unit fairly measures the unit's financial performance. This does not mean that the reported profit is completely accurate, or that it encompasses all aspects of performance, for no profit measure does this. If a service center is designated as a profit center, its usual financial objective is to break even; that is, to provide services whose revenues approximate the center's costs. If this is the case, both the manager and his or her superior need to agree that breakeven is good financial performance.

Transfer Prices. When one profit center receives goods and/or services from another and is charged for them, the charge is called a *transfer price*. A transfer price is used exclusively for transactions *within* an organization, as contrasted with an external price, which is used for transactions between an organization and its clients.

In general, transfer pricing provides a mechanism for encouraging the optimal use of an organization's resources. This is because the behavior of profit center managers frequently is influenced considerably by the way the transfer prices are structured (or by the requirement that goods and services be furnished without charge under certain circumstances).

Ordinarily, internal users of a responsibility center's services should pay for them via transfer prices. If there are internal users and no transfer prices, senior management should not designate the providing unit as a profit center. An internal audit organization, for example, usually provides services without charge and therefore should not be a profit center. Similarly, if senior management encourages operating units to use the services of certain staff units, these staff units probably should not be profit centers, at least not until operating units come to accept the value of the staff services and are willing to pay for them.

In most instances, if a service is free, users are not motivated to consider its value. They tend to request as much of it as they can get without considering how much it is worth to them, or how its value compares with alternative services.

Example An organization had a motor pool that delivered its products by trucks without charging the shipping departments. It found that managers were requesting trucks to deliver small shipments that could have been delivered less expensively by private trucking companies. The private company price was a charge against the shipping department's budget, however, whereas the use of the motor pool truck was free. When the organization started to charge for motor pool deliveries, managers of shipping departments gave thought to the cost of alternative methods of transportation. They also were motivated to combine shipments to a given destination so as to further reduce costs.

It might appear that because a responsibility center does not sell its services to outside customers, there is no reliable way to establish its transfer prices. But this is rarely the case. Many service centers have counterparts in for-profit organizations. Motor pools are like car rental agencies, for example. Similarly, maintenance, housekeeping, laundry, and other service centers frequently have private sector counterparts. The principles used to set prices in the counterpart organizations usually can be adapted rather easily to the nonprofit organization. While there is no single best way to establish transfer prices, there are three approaches that can be used. Many organizations use all three at varying times, depending on the circumstances of each situation.

1. Market Price. If a valid market price exists for a good or service, it ordinarily is the basis for the transfer price. It may be adjusted downward to eliminate the profit component in prices charged by for-profit companies, or to eliminate bad debt or selling expenses that do not exist with internal transactions. Of course, valid market price information is not always available, or it is available for some, but not all, internally provided goods and services.

Example In setting transfer prices for a pathology laboratory in a hospital, it is likely that a market price for a complete blood count and several other standard tests is readily available from a free-standing laboratory. Because most free-standing labs do not analyze frozen sections, however, it would be difficult to determine a market price for these and other sophisticated tests.

A market price above the selling unit's full cost is an indication that the selling unit is operating efficiently, whereas a market price below full cost suggests inefficiency. If a selling center cannot furnish products at competitive prices, or if the revenue it earns is not equal to its costs, its operating statement will report a loss. This is an indication that something is wrong. Thus, the use of transfer prices provides senior management with information about the efficiency (and sometimes the quality) of the goods and services being provided by selling centers.

2. Full Cost. If no valid market price exists, the transfer price ordinarily is based on the product's full cost. This rule corresponds to the practice discussed in Chapter 5 for arriving at normal selling prices to outside customers, except that it generally has only a small margin above full cost. As with market prices, some organizations exclude bad debts and selling expenses in setting a full-cost transfer price.

Arriving at the full cost for a unit of service can be tricky. In particular, as discussed in Chapter 3, if Stage 2 of the full-cost accounting effort has not been well designed, the full cost of some service units may not reflect true resource consumption.

Ordinarily, if the full-cost approach is used, the transfer price should be set at a standard cost, rather than based on the actual costs incurred by the selling unit. Otherwise, the selling unit could pass its inefficiencies on to the receiving units.

3. *Negotiated Cost.* In some situations, buying and selling units may negotiate the transfer price. If the selling unit is operating below capacity, for example, it may be willing to accept a lower price than either market or full-cost—one that will make a contribution to its overhead. Conversely, if the selling unit provides an especially high quality product or certain special services or guarantees, the buying unit manager may be willing to pay a higher transfer price than otherwise.

THE PROGRAM STRUCTURE

Most nonprofit organizations exist to carry out programs. Fixing responsibility for control over programs would be relatively easy if each program (1) sold its services, (2) were staffed by personnel who worked in no other program, and (3) were run by a manager who had reasonable control over hiring, other personnel decisions, and decisions on program supply purchases. Under these circumstances, each program could be designated as a profit center.

Most nonprofits are not organized in a way that permits such a tidy and well-defined control structures. Many operate over large geographic areas, and must consider this fact when designing their structure. For example, does a multi-hospital system have one director of substance abuse services with broad geographic responsibilities, or several area directors, each with responsibility for all programs in his or her area, including the substance abuse program?

In other organizational settings, the program and functional lines become similarly blurred. Does the director of the summer festival program for a symphony orchestra have control over the number of personnel taking part in the festival or their salaries? Does the director of a master's degree program in a large university control the number of applications received, the tuition charged, or the salaries of the faculty who work in the program? Moreover, while performers in the orchestra or faculty in the university may take part in a particular program, their reporting relationships within the organization generally are to more than the director of one program only.

In summary, a separate program structure is needed when responsibility for a program involves more than one responsibility center. A municipality organized so that each responsibility center performs a defined type of service (e.g., public safety, highway maintenance, education, etc.) does not need a separate program structure. By contrast, a federal government agency that provides many separate programs through several regional offices does. So does a research organization that draws on the resources of several departments to carry out its research projects.

Example In the Department of Defense (DOD) in the 1960s, the lines of organizational responsibility ran to the Secretary of the Army, the Secretary of the Navy, and the Secretary of the Air Force, whereas defense programs cut across these lines. For example, the DOD had a strategic mission (or program) that was related to a possible nuclear exchange with the Soviets. Different parts of this program were the responsibility of the Army (antiballistic missiles), the Navy (Polaris submarines), and the Air Force (strategic missiles and bombers). A mechanism that facilitated decision making about the program as a whole was necessary.

The mechanism developed by the DOD turned out to be valuable when reductions in its expenses were needed following the end of the Cold War. To a great extent, the DOD's success in

> making cutbacks was facilitated by its structure, including transfer prices linking mission and support centers' interactions.[2]

Many organizations have found that selecting a good program structure is not easy. Indeed, it generally is quite difficult to align responsibility with control, and to overlay an appropriate set of responsibility centers on the broad organizational structure. Therefore, senior management must devote considerable time and effort to the task.

Components of a Program Structure

In a large organization, the program structure usually consists of several layers. At the top are a few major programs, and at the bottom are a great many program elements—the smallest units in which information is collected in program terms. A program element is a definable activity or related set of activities that the organization carries out—either directly, to accomplish its objectives, or indirectly, to support other program elements.

Between programs and program elements are summaries of related program elements, or "program categories," and, depending on how many layers are needed, "program subcategories." In a relatively flat organization, there may be no need for program categories or subcategories; program elements can be aggregated directly into programs. In a more hierarchical organization, there may be several levels of program categories. Exhibit 6-2 contains a simple example of programs, program categories, program subcategories, and program elements in a public school system.

Exhibit 6-2 Hierarchy of Programs, Program Categories, and Program Elements

Program	100. Formal Education
Program Categories	101. Pre-Elementary School Service
	102. Elementary and Secondary School Service
	103. Post-Secondary School Education Service
	104. Special Education Service for Exceptional Persons
Program Subcategories	1. Kindergarten
(for Program Category 102)	2. Primary or Elementary School Education
	3. Secondary or High School Education
	4. Vocational and/or Trade High School
Program Elements	a. Language instruction
(for Program Subcategory 2)	b. Music instruction
	c. Art instruction
	c. Social sciences instruction

Types of Programs. In designing the program structure, senior management typically focuses its attention on several different types of programs. The most basic division is between mission programs and support programs, with some variations within the support category.

In general, programs can be classified as either *mission* or *support*. Mission programs relate to the organization's objectives and usually are focused on clients. Support programs provide services to more than one other program but usually don't work directly with clients. In making decisions about the allocation of resources, management usually focuses its attention on mission programs. Within limits, the amount of resources required for support programs is roughly dependent on the size and character of the mission programs.

[2] See Fred Thompson, "Management Control and the Pentagon: The Organizational Strategy-Structure Mismatch," *Public Administration Review*, Vol. 51, Iss. 1, January-February 1991.

Example In a college or university, mission programs would be related to instruction and research. Support programs would include buildings and grounds maintenance, publications, and financial aid.

Administration. Ordinarily, there should be a separate program for administration. This support program typically includes certain miscellaneous program categories or elements that, although not strictly administrative in character, do not belong logically in other programs and are not important enough to be set up as separate program categories or elements.

The rationale for a separate program for administration is that it permits senior management to focus special attention on the organization's administrative activities. Senior management usually wishes to devote as much of the organization's total resources as possible to mission programs, and as little as possible to administration. In the absence of special attention, however, administrative activities tend to grow. A program for administration encourages senior management to direct attention to these activities.

Development. In organizations that obtain some of their resources from contributors, there typically is a separate program for development (or fund raising) costs. This is because contributors usually are interested in how much of the donated amounts were used for mission programs versus development (and other support) activities.

Occasionally there are practical difficulties in separating development and mission costs, but this should not deter senior management from attempting to keep track of development costs as accurately as possible. A separate program facilitates this effort.

Example Major contributors to a symphony orchestra or other arts organization may be given special preferences, such as the use of a patrons' lounge. Although conceptually these are fund-raising costs, the amounts are rarely segregated as such. As a result, the organization's reported development costs are understated.

Program Elements. Ideally, a program element is the responsibility of a single manager. If this is not feasible, senior management should attempt to relate program elements to the responsibility of a relatively small number of persons. Items for which responsibility is widely diffused, such as "utilities," are not good program elements. Such items should appear not as program elements but as functional categories or expense elements in the responsibility structure.

Management decisions about program elements cannot be enforced unless these elements are related to personal responsibility. An alignment of individual responsibility with specific program elements also leads to an increased sense of personal identification with programs, and thus helps foster a greater degree of commitment among responsibility center managers.

Example A museum of natural history might have a program on prehistoric animals. This program might have several program elements, such as individual exhibits, gift shop items, and educational activities. Each of these is the responsibility of a manager. One job of the program manager is to coordinate the work of these program element managers.

As is the case with programs, program elements can be classified as either mission or support. Many programs also have a separate program element for administration which includes activities associated with the program (as contrasted with the administration of the organization as a whole), and may also include miscellaneous catchall activities.

Criteria for Selecting a Program Structure

Since the primary purpose of the classification of programs is to facilitate senior management's judgment on the allocation of resources, the program structure should correspond to the principal objectives of the organization. It should be arranged so as to facilitate decisions having to do with the relative importance of these objectives. Stated another way, it should focus on the organization's outputs—what it achieves or intends to achieve—rather than on its inputs—the types of resources it uses or the sources of its support. A structure that is arranged by types of resources (e.g., personnel, material, services) or by sources of support (e.g., tuition, legislative appropriations, and gifts in a university setting) is not a program structure.

Exhibit 6-3 illustrates the difference between a program structure and a more traditional line-item structure in a public safety department of a municipality. As it indicates, a program structure is much more closely aligned with the overall strategy and objectives of the organization.

Exhibit 6-3 Line-items versus Programs for a Public Safety Department ($000)

Line Item Structure	Cost	Program Structure	Cost
Wages and salaries	$4,232	Crime control and investigation	$2,677
Overtime	217	Traffic control	1,610
Fringe benefits	783	Correctional institutions	470
Retirement plan	720	Inspections and licenses	320
Operating supplies	216	Police training	182
Fuel	338	Police administration	680
Uniforms	68	Fire fighting	1,427
Repairs and maintenance	340	Fire prevention	86
Professional services	71	Fire training	64
Communications	226	Fire administration	236
Vehicles	482	Other protection	563
Printing and publications	61	General administration	282
Building rental	447		
Other	396		
Total	$8,597	Total	$8,597

The designation of major programs also helps clarify the objectives of the organization. The development of the program structure may also clarify the organization's purpose, and thus suggest improvements in its overall structure. Therefore, the program structure should correspond to those areas of activity that senior management expects to use for decision making purposes.[3]

The idea that programs should be related to decision-making is, of course, a general one. The following questions can be used to make the idea more specific:

---

[3] The optimal number of programs in an organization is approximately 10. The rationale for this limit is that senior management cannot weigh the relative importance of a large number of disparate items. There are many exceptions to this generalization, however.

1. Is the program structure output-oriented? Specifically, does it focus on what the organization does and the target groups it serves or plans to serve?

2. Does the program structure assist senior management to decide whether to expand or contract a program?

3. Within a program, are there opportunities for tradeoffs; that is, are there different ways to achieve the objectives? Benefit/cost analysis, for example, is often feasible within a program but rarely between programs.

4. Is there an identifiable outside pressure group interested in all or a part of the organization's activities? If so, is there a program that corresponds to the interests of this group?

5. When a criticism arises that not enough (or too much) effort is being devoted to a certain activity, can information to address this criticism be obtained from the program structure?

6. Does the structure identify all important activities so that none is hidden from management's view? For example, if a research organization has no separate program for basic research, the pressure to devote resources to more attractive applied projects will be strong and basic research may be slighted. Or, basic research may be conducted clandestinely within a supposed applied project.

7. Does the structure require a relatively small amount of cost allocation? If a large fraction of the program cost is an allocated cost, the structure is suspect.
8. Is the structure of some help to operating managers? At a minimum, it should not impede the work of operating managers.

9. Can program elements be associated with a quantitative measure of performance? At the broad level of programs, no single reliable measure of performance ordinarily can be found. But as one moves down the hierarchy in the program structure, it should be possible to identify rather specific quantitative measures of performance.

Matrix Organizations. Although the program structure need not match the organization structure, there should be some person who has identifiable responsibility for each program (as well as for each program category and each program element in large organizations). This need for a fit between the organizational structure and the program structure often results in a matrix organization. The matrix consists of program managers along one dimension and functional managers along the other. Program managers may have other responsibilities, and they may call on other parts of the organization for much of the work that is to be done on their programs, but they nevertheless are advocates for their programs, and they are held accountable for their program's performance.

Example Faculty members of a business school typically have a home base in a subject-area department (such as organizational behavior, accounting, or marketing). They also may be assigned to one or more programs, such as undergraduate education, graduate education, or executive education. Program managers call on departments for work to be done on their programs. Under these circumstances, responsibility is divided between the department head and the program head.

An example of a matrix structure is contained in Exhibit 6-4. This is for a large agency—the Department of Mental Health in a state government. As it shows, complexity exists along several dimensions that affect the agency's management control structure. Some of those dimensions include the following:

- The agency does not generate revenues. Therefore it is an expense center. Since its budget probably cannot be changed with changes in volume during the year, the agency quite likely is a discretionary expense center.

- Resource allocation is along two dimensions. One is field operations and facilities, which corresponds to the agency's organizational structure (the left side of the matrix). The other is the agency's major programs, such as community mental health (the right side of the matrix). The major programs correspond to appropriation accounts in the state's budget, and are the responsibility of "account executives" (program managers).

- Both field operations and the major programs have several layers of responsibility. The field operations activity is comprised of regions at the highest level, followed by facilities, areas, and units within the facilities. The major programs are comprised of program categories (or subprograms as they are called here).

- Overall program control is the responsibility of the account executives, who may not spend more than the amount allotted to their appropriation accounts. Programs cut across all regions, although not all regions or all facilities have all programs or all subprograms. Thus, an account executive must determine the regions and facilities that can best meet the needs of each major program and its various subprograms.

- Control over the activities in regions and facilities is the responsibility of the field operations and facility managers. They receive budgets from the account executives, and must adhere to them while striving to meet the objectives of the programs and subprograms that the budgets fund.

- Although the agency is a discretionary expense center, some of its units might be set up as standard expense centers. This is because the managers of these units have no control over the number or mix of individuals who need their services. Since the appropriation account budgets are fixed, account executives should assure that increases in one region or facility are matched by decreases in other regions or facilities. With an appropriate flow of information to both account executives and managers in charge of field operations and facilities, such a structure might provide greater motivation to the field operations and facility managers to run their operations more effectively and efficiently—each would be competing for resources from the appropriations accounts.

THE INFORMATION STRUCTURE

Information is needed for both program planners and analysts, as well as for responsibility center (or operating) managers. Program planners and analysts need information to facilitate decision making about programs and to provide a basis of comparison of the cost and output of similar programs. Responsibility center managers need information on the outputs and inputs of their organizational units, which facilitates their ability to control revenues and expenses.

Exhibit 6-4 Matrix Structure in a Large State Agency

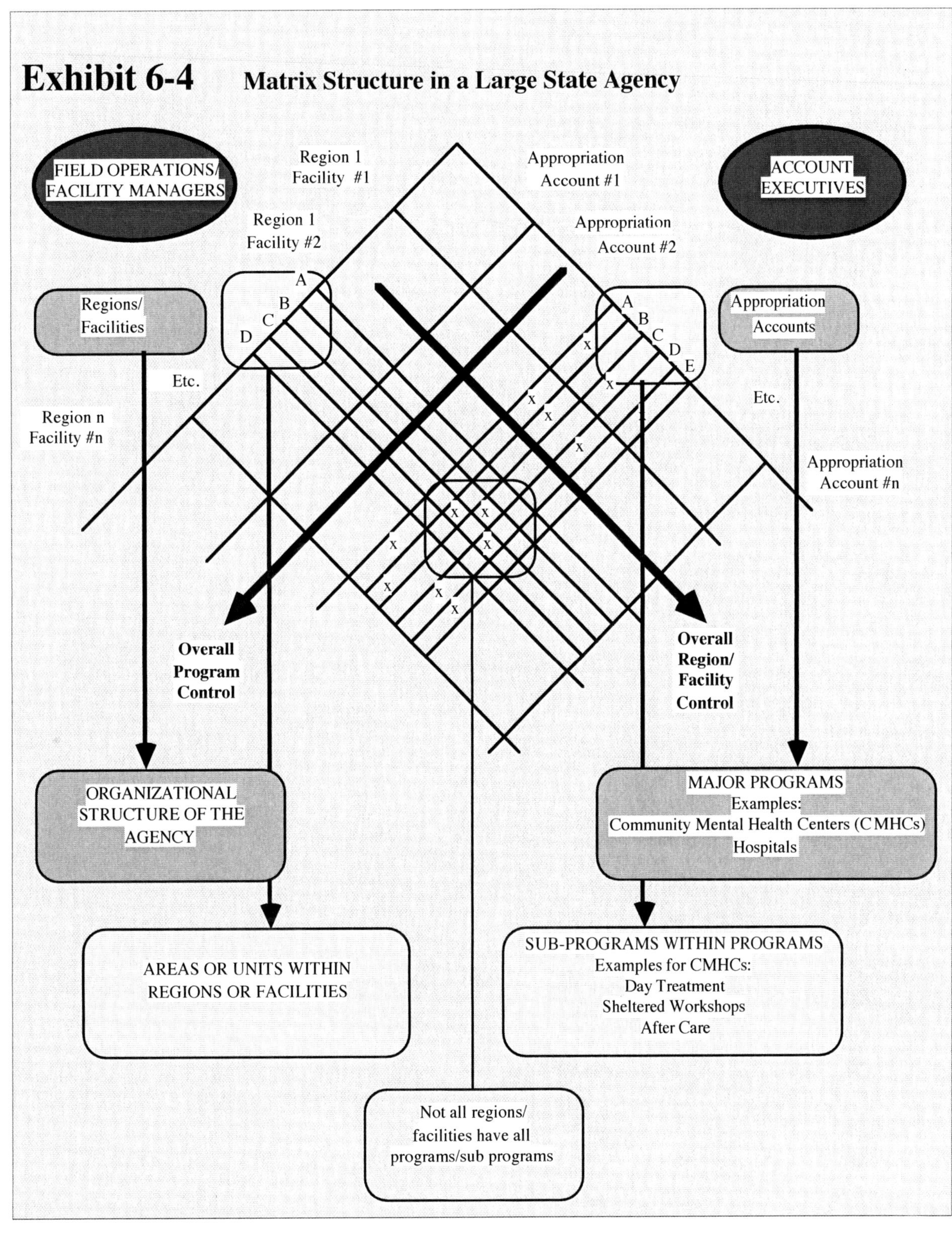

These information needs relate to the distinction between the program and organizational structures. The program structure is designed principally to meet the needs of planners and analysts, and emphasizes the full costs of carrying out programs. The organizational structure is designed to meet the needs of operating managers, and emphasizes the controllable costs of operating the organization's responsibility centers.

In designing a program structure, the needs of planners and analysts are dominant. For example, a program structure may cut across lines of operational responsibility, even though such a structure is not as useful to operating managers. In designing a responsibility structure, however, operating managers' needs are paramount. Such a structure must be consistent with lines of responsibility, and this principle cannot be compromised to meet the needs of the planners.

To ensure that these conflicts are resolved in the most equitable way, senior management must be certain that the team designing (or modifying) the management control system not be dominated by either planners or operating managers. Ideally, systems designers should be independent of both types of users, and should weigh equally the needs of each.

The information structure should be able to reconcile most needs. This is especially important since senior management usually is interested in summaries of information provided to all other groups. An information structure that will serve these multiple purposes is complicated since the information needed for one purpose may differ from that needed for another. In some cases, compromises in designing the structure may be necessary, but in most situations, the information structure can be designed to serve both sets of needs.

Example The director of a Latin American studies program in a university needs information on courses, enrollment, student satisfaction, and job placement. For the most part, this information is used for operating the program and not for comparisons with other similar programs. On the other hand, the dean of the school may wish to compare the Latin American studies program with similar programs in other universities. To do this, he or she will need information on applications, standardized test scores, admission yields, and so forth. A well-designed program structure will provide information for both the program director and the dean.

Information for Comparative Purposes

Using information for comparative purposes can be tricky, even with a well-designed program structure. If, for example, a number of similar organizations (e.g., schools, colleges, hospitals) use the same program structure, and wish to make comparisons, great care needs to be taken to assure that the participating organizations agree on the kinds of data they will provide, and their meaning. By having comparable data, managers can compile averages and other measures, and they can compare data from their own programs with these averages.

Example Good inter-program comparison structures exist for healthcare organizations, colleges and universities, social service organizations, and certain municipal services. In some areas there are good structures for primary and secondary education, higher education, municipal activities, and certain other functions. Some religious organizations have systems for their local units, for example, as do other membership organizations such as college fraternities, professional associations, chambers of commerce, and civic organizations.

Compromises frequently are necessary in designing a structure for comparisons. This is because the participating organizations rarely view their programs in the same way. Because of this, the program structure that is used for comparisons should be quite broad, specifying only the data that actually will be used for comparative purposes. Each participating organization can then modify this structure (usually by subdividing the program into program elements) to collect the more detailed information that is needed by its own management.

The Account Structure

To provide information needed by all relevant parties, the accounting system should contain an account structure that is responsive to multiple demands. In addition to providing information to program planners, analysts, and operating managers, the account structure must provide information to two other groups:

- *Senior managers and governing bodies*. These parties make policy decisions regarding the division of resources among programs and the relation of programs to objectives. Both groups need information on how the organization is performing.

- *Resource providers*, including contributors, legislative bodies, grantors, dues-paying members, taxpayers, third-party payers, oversight bodies, and regulatory agencies acting on their behalf. These groups need information about what the organization did with the resources they provided. The needs of some resource providers can be met by general-purpose financial statements. Other resource providers, particularly legislatures and grantors, require reports prepared according to their specifications.

Conflicts Among Information Needs. Since the needs of these diverse parties frequently conflict with one another, the accounting system must strike a balance. A well-designed account structure should be able to reconcile most needs, however. This is especially important since senior management usually is interested in summaries of information provided to all other groups. The system also must represent a balance between users' needs for information and the cost of collecting and processing that information.

The Need for Articulation. Ideally, all the accounts in the account structure make up a single, coordinated system. Technically, such a system is called an articulated system; each account is related to all other accounts. Serious management control problems can arise if program accounts are not linked with responsibility accounts, or if the actual costs in each set of accounts cannot be compared to the budgeted costs.

In some systems, a well designed program structure is used for planning and budgeting purposes, but after the programs have been planned and the budget approved, the structure is not rearranged according to the responsibility centers that must carry out the programs. Instead, a separate budget is prepared for responsibility centers, often without any relationship to the program budget. As a result, both budgets and actual spending are recorded by responsibility centers but not by programs. Indeed, some systems do not even collect actual spending according to the same account structure used for budgeting. When this happens, actual results cannot be compared to planned ones in any meaningful way.

There are two problems with systems that don't articulate. First, since the system cannot ascertain costs by program, program planners do not have the information they need to estimate future program costs. Second, without program-based costs, senior management has no adequate way of determining whether its program decisions are actually being implemented. If senior management decides that $1 million should be spent on a certain program, it needs to know whether the organization is in fact carrying out the program at the level of effort that $1 million represents. It cannot find this out unless the records classify actual spending in terms of programs.

One may ask why defective accounting systems are permitted to exist. One possible explanation is that the idea of a program structure is relatively new in many nonprofit organizations. Some nonprofits that have adopted a program structure have not yet had the time to design accounting systems that permit the recording of costs by program elements as well as responsibility centers. Such changes are complicated and time-consuming, and involve training many people, both accountants and managers.

ADMINISTRATIVE FACTORS

Another aspect of the internal environment is the set of rules, practices, guidelines, customs, standard operating procedures, and codes of ethics that exist in any organization. For brevity, these items are clustered together as administrative factors, or rules. Unlike the elements of the management control system, administrative factors typically change infrequently. Some rules, such as those set forth in manuals, are formal; others, such as understandings about acceptable behavior, are informal. They relate to matters that range from the most trivial (e.g., paper clips will be issued only on the basis of a signed requisition) to the most important (e.g., capital expenditures of over $200,000 must be approved by the board of trustees).

Types of Rules

Some rules are guides. An organization's members are permitted (and expected) to depart from them under specified circumstances or if a manager judges that departure is in the best interests of the organization overall. For example, a guideline may state that overtime is not ordinarily paid, but managers may approve overtime payments under certain circumstances, either on their own authority or after obtaining approval from their superior. Other rules are literally rules—they should never be broken. Rules that prohibit paying bribes or taking illegal drugs are examples. Some specific types of rules, procedures, and similar actions are listed below:[4]

1. *Physical control procedures.* Security guards, locked storerooms, vaults, computer passwords, television surveillance, and other physical controls are part of the internal control environment. Most of them are associated with task control, rather than with management control.

2. *Administrative control procedures.* There also are actions specifically designed to enhance task control, such as requiring that checks for more than a specified amount be countersigned. Their enforcement frequently is the responsibility of the controller's office.

3. *Administrative rules.* These are prescribed ways of performing certain functions, such as how to use time cards or how to complete expense reports.

Role of Manuals. Much judgment is required in deciding which rules and procedures should be made formal (i.e., put in a manual), which should be guidelines rather than fixed rules, and which should be subject to managerial discretion. There are no clear cut prescriptions for these judgments, although there are some fairly obvious patterns. Bureaucratic organizations tend to have more detailed manuals than other organizations, large organizations have more than small ones, and centralized organizations have more than decentralized ones. Additionally, with the passage of time, some formal rules become obsolete. Manuals and other sets of rules therefore need to be reexamined periodically to ensure that they are consistent with current needs.

---

[4] This list is derived from the work of Kenneth A. Merchant. He calls them "specific action controls." See Kenneth A. Merchant, *Control in Business Organizations* (Marshfield, Mass.: Pitman Publishing, 1985), chap. 3.

The Motivation Process and Reward Structure

An important administrative factor is the reward structure. Ideally, managers should be rewarded on the basis of actual performance compared with expected performance under the prevailing circumstances. This ideal frequently cannot be achieved for two basic reasons. First, the performance of a responsibility center is influenced by many factors other than the actions of its manager. As a result, the performance of the manager usually cannot be cleanly separated from the effects of these other factors. Second, managers are supposed to achieve both long- and short-run objectives, but the management control system usually focuses primarily on the short-run. This is because the system can only report on what has happened; it cannot report on what will happen in the future as a consequence of the manager's current actions. As a consequence, responsibility center and program managers are motivated to focus on achieving short-run goals. Indeed, a lack of knowledge about how best to measure and reward a manager's performance for achieving long-term results is probably the most serious weakness in the management control systems of many, if not all, nonprofit organizations.[5]

BEHAVIORAL FACTORS

Management control involves interactions among human beings. The behavior of people in organizations is therefore an important element of the internal environmental. The major issue that senior management must address here is the congruence between the *personal* goals of managers and professionals, and the goals of the *organization* itself.

Personal Goals

People join an organization because they believe that by doing so they can achieve some of their personal goals. Once they have joined, their decision to contribute to the work of the organization is based on their perception that their activities will help them achieve those.

An individual's personal goals can be expressed as needs. Some of these needs are material and can be satisfied by the money earned on the job. Others are psychological. People need to have their abilities and achievements recognized; they need social acceptance as members of a group; they need to feel a sense of personal worth; they need to feel secure; they need to be able to exercise discretion; they need to feel good about themselves.

These personal needs can be classified as either extrinsic or intrinsic. Extrinsic needs are satisfied by the actions of others. Examples are money received from the organization and praise received from a superior. Intrinsic needs are satisfied by the opinions people have about themselves. Examples are feelings of achievement or competence, or a clear conscience.

The relative importance of these needs varies with different persons, and their relative importance to a given individual varies at different times. Moreover, the relative importance that people attach to their own needs is heavily influenced by the attitudes of their colleagues and superiors. For some people, earning a great deal of money is a dominant need; for others, monetary considerations are less important than serving society. A few individuals attach considerable importance to the need to exercise discretion or to achieve results; they tend to be the leaders of the organization.[6]

---

[5] For-profit organizations sometimes use stock options as a way to motivate managers to think about the long-term consequences of their decisions. Some nonprofit organizations have used sabbatical leaves as a form of long-term incentive, but it is difficult to link leave time to long-run performance.

[6] David McClelland argued that there is a relationship between the strength of the achievement need of the leaders of an organization and the organization's success. See David McClelland, *The Achieving Society* (New York: Irvington Publishers, 1961).

How do people behave to satisfy their needs? One answer is based on the expectancy theory model of motivation. This theory states that the motivation to engage in a given behavior is determined by (1) a person's beliefs or expectancies about what outcomes are likely to result from that behavior, and (2) the attractiveness of these outcomes; that is, their ability to satisfy needs.[7]

Individuals are influenced by both positive and negative incentives. A positive incentive, or reward, is an outcome that is expected to result in increased need satisfaction; a negative incentive, or punishment, is the reverse. Incentives need not be monetary. Praise for a job well done can be a powerful reward. Nevertheless, many people regard monetary rewards as extremely important. Such rewards may include a bonus based on a comparison between planned and actual results. Indeed, many nonprofit organizations use bonuses as incentives.

Goal Congruence. Since an organization does not have a mind of its own, it literally cannot have goals. Organizational goals are actually the goals of the board of trustees and senior management. Senior management wants the organization to attain these goals, but the goals are not always congruent with the personal goals of operating managers and professionals. Because participants tend to act in their own self-interest, the achievement of organizational goals may be frustrated.

This distinction between organizational and personal goals suggests that a central purpose of a management control system is to assure that the actions participants take in accordance with their perceived self-interest are also actions that are in the best interests of the organization. That is, the incentives inherent in the management control system should encourage *goal congruence*.[8] If this condition exists, a decision that a manager regards as sound from a personal viewpoint also will be sound for the organization as a whole.[9]

Perfect congruence between individual and organizational goals does not, and cannot, exist. For example, many individuals want as much compensation as they can get, whereas from the organization's viewpoint there is an upper limit to salaries. At a minimum, however, the management control system should not encourage individuals to act against the best interests of the organization.

Example An organization has a goal of low cost, high quality services, but its management control system rewards managers exclusively for reducing costs. If some managers decrease costs by reducing the quality of service, there is an absence of goal congruence.

Given these and similar difficulties, senior management must ask two separate questions when evaluating its management control system: (1) What action does it motivate people to take in their own perceived self-interest? (2) Is this action in the best interest of the organization overall?

---

[7] Texts on industrial psychology expand on these points at length. See Paul R. Lawrence and Jay W. Lorsch, *Organization and Environment* (Homewood, Ill.: Richard D. Irwin, 1969); and B. F. Skinner, *Beyond Freedom and Dignity* (New York: Appleton-Century-Crofts, 1971).

[8] There actually are two levels of analysis here: (1) between *organizational goals* and *personal goals* and (2) between *organizational goals* and *incentives*. The determination of organizational goals and incentives is part of the management control system. However, senior management also can *influence* the personal goals of the organization's managers and professionals. It does so by using its hiring, promotion, and termination policies to select and retain individuals who have personal goals that are closely aligned with the organization's goals.

[9] For an elaboration of this idea see Douglas McGregor, *The Human Side of Enterprise*, New York: McGraw-Hill, 1960. This book is considered a classic in management literature.

Cooperation and Conflict

Generally, the lines connecting the boxes on an organization chart imply that organizational decisions are made in a hierarchical fashion. Senior management makes a decision, which is communicated down through the hierarchy, and operating managers at lower levels proceed to implement it. Clearly, this military model is not the way most organizations actually function.

Operating managers react to an instruction from senior management in accordance with their perception of how it affects their personal needs. Interactions between managers also affect what happens. For example, the manager of the maintenance department may be responsible for maintenance work done in all departments, but work in one operating department may be slighted if there is friction between the maintenance manager and the operating manager. Also, actions that a manager takes to achieve personal goals may adversely affect other managers. Managers may argue about which departments should get to use the limited funds in the capital budget, or other scarce resources, for example. For these and many other reasons, there is organizational conflict.

Clearly, an organization will not achieve its objectives unless managers work together with some degree of harmony. Thus, there also must be cooperation in an organization. Participants realize that without cooperation the organization will flounder or even dissolve, and they will then be unable to satisfy the needs that motivated them to join it in the first place.

Senior management must maintain an appropriate balance between the forces of conflict and cooperation. Some conflict is both inevitable and even desirable. It results from the competition between participants for promotion or other forms of need satisfaction; within limits, such competition is usually healthy. Conflict also arises because different members of an organization see the world differently, and believe that different actions are in the organization's best interests. For example, conflict arises in museums over the most appropriate exhibits, in school systems over the most appropriate courses, and in hospitals over the most appropriate treatment patterns for patients. To a certain extent, this sort of conflict is beneficial in that it frequently brings out the best ideas of an organization's members. Thus, if undue emphasis is placed on fostering a cooperative attitude, the most able managers and professionals may be denied the opportunity to use their talents fully.[10] Somehow, senior management must seek to foster the right balance.

The Bureaucracy

Many observers have suggested that in government organizations, and in certain other large nonprofit organizations, effective management control is inhibited by the existence of the *bureaucracy*. Bureaucracy is often used as a label for any organization that operates by complicated rules and routines, or that is characterized by delays and buck passing, or that treats its clients impolitely. In particular, government organizations are typically labeled as bureaucracies with the implication that non-governmental organizations are not bureaucracies.

In fact, any large and complex organization is necessarily a bureaucracy. The classic analysis of bureaucracy was by Max Weber,[11] who described such an organization as one in which the chief executive derives his authority by law or through election by an authorized body, rather than by tradition or charisma. Subordinates are responsible to the chief executive through a clearly defined hierarchy and are selected on the basis of their technical competence. They are promoted according to seniority or achievement, or both, and they are subject to systematic discipline and control.

In the Weberian bureaucracy, complex problems are solved by segmenting them into a series of simpler ones, and delegating authority for solving each segment to the appropriate experts in spe-

[10] For further discussion on conflict and its benefits, see Lawrence and Lorsch, *Organization and Environment*.

[11] Max Weber, *The Theory of Social and Economic Organization* (1922). See the English translation by A.M. Henderson and Talcott Parsons (New York: Oxford University Press, 1947).

cialized subunits. Such technical superiority, based on increased specialization, is supposed to lead to objective and impersonal decision making at the sub-unit level. Weber noted that an individual who applied personal or subjective values to policy or decision making could seriously lessen the effectiveness of the organization. A bureaucracy avoided this possibility by replacing the subjective judgment of individuals with routine work tasks, and by establishing a set of rules, values, attitudes, or goals which are approved by each individual's superior.[12]

Bureaucracy is essential in an organization where several different units perform the same function. For example, each office of the Internal Revenue Service is supposed to give the same advice to a taxpayer. There would be no way of coming close to that goal without a comprehensive set of rules and regulations used by all offices.

Researchers have paid considerable attention to the bureaucratic form of organization. Some have suggested that senior management can achieve the consistency needed in an organization such as the IRS without the complex hierarchy and red tape that generally characterize these organizations, and that give the word bureaucracy such a pejorative flavor. In part, this combination of consistency and flexibility can be achieved through the design of a good management control system.[13]

Role of the Controller

In most organizations, the controller is responsible for the operation of the management control system. The controller department is a staff unit. Its responsibility is similar to that of a telephone company: it assures that messages flow through the system clearly, accurately, and promptly. It is not responsible for the content of these messages, however, or for the way managers act on them.

The controller ordinarily works with senior management to design the management control system in such a way that fairness and goal congruence are maximized. Most of this effort is associated with designing the responsibility center structure and the transfer pricing arrangements along the lines discussed earlier. The controller also works with senior management to design the phases of the management control process. Because of the major impact that design choices can have on managers' and professionals' behavior, senior management should be heavily involved in these choices. In many organizations, senior management delegates these choices to the controller, which is a mistake since the controller typically does not have a sufficiently broad perspective of the organization and its goals.

CULTURAL FACTORS

Every organization has its own culture—a climate or atmosphere in which certain attitudes are encouraged and others are discouraged. Cultural norms are derived in part from tradition, in part from external influences, such as unions and societal norms, and in part from the attitude of the organization's senior management and directors. The 1980s bestseller, *In Search of Excellence*, was primarily an attempt to describe the culture in several companies that were judged at the time to be well-managed. The failure of that book to provide an accurate assessment (as evidenced by the fact that several of these companies ran into serious trouble shortly after the book was published) illustrates the difficulty of explaining the influence of culture. Nevertheless, cultural norms are extremely important. They explain why each of two entities may have an adequate management control system but why one has much better performance than the other.

---

12 For an argument that just the opposite takes place in a bureaucracy, see Michel Crozier, *The Bureaucratic Phenomenon* (Chicago: University of Chicago Press, 1964).

13 For a discussion of this idea, see David W. Young, "Management Control in the Public Sector: Overcoming the Barriers to Progress," in A.P. Kakabadse, P.R. Brovetto, and R. Holzer (eds.), *Management Development and the Public Sector: A European Perspective*, Aldershot, England, Gower Publishing Company, 1988.

Cultural norms are almost never written down, and attempts to do so almost always result in platitudes. Instead, norms are transmitted partly by hiring practices and training programs. They also are conveyed by managers, professionals, and other organization members using words, deeds, and body language to indicate that some types of actions are acceptable and others are not.[14]

Management Attitude

The aspect of culture that has perhaps the most important impact on management control is the attitude of a manager's superior toward control. In a well managed organization, the chief executive officer sets the tone, and can communicate it in a number of ways. If performance reports typically disappear into the executive suite and no response is forthcoming, managers soon decide that these reports are not important. Conversely, if a report is discussed at length with a manager, the signal is that taking action on the basis of the report is important. Conversations of this sort convey senior management's expectations about performance as powerfully as the formal budget does.

Other Aspects of Culture

The management control climate also is affected by the attitudes of a manager's peers and by staff units. The culture *within* a responsibility center is also important, but it may be difficult for a manager to affect it. This is because the employees in an organization, especially a large one, may have ways of behaving that are influenced by a long tradition.

Example Despite the prestige and power of the office, a cabinet officer in the federal government may find it impossible to create the desired control climate no matter how hard he or she tries. Usually, the bureaucracy has firmly accepted certain behavioral norms and has found ways to perpetuate them. There is little that a political appointee can do to influence this in the short tenure he or she has with the organization.

Finally, the culture in the *external* environment affects the control climate within the organization. Some attitudes appear to be industrywide. For example, when times are tough, people tend to take the control process more seriously than when the economy is booming. In many nonprofit settings, the cultural norms of a professional group (e.g., physicians, nurses, social workers, artists, musicians) will have a major influence on the culture of the organization itself.

SUMMARY

One of the most difficult aspects of designing a management control system is defining the system's structure—its network of responsibility centers. In determining what sort of responsibility center a given manager's unit will be, senior management needs to pay careful attention to the resources the manager can control. This is the driving force behind responsibility center design.

Beyond this, senior management needs to consider ways to attain congruence between the personal goals of each responsibility center manger and its goals for the organization as a whole. In part, a responsibility center manager's goals are determined by the incentives that senior management creates to reward certain forms of behavior. One of the major aspects of this incentive system is the organization's transfer prices, and senior management must be careful to establish the trans-

[14] For a discussion of how managers can use the management control system to influence their organization's culture, see David W. Young, "The Six Levers for Managing Organizational Culture," *Business Horizons,* September-October 2000.

fer pricing structure in such a way that it promotes behavior on the part of individual managers that is supportive of the organization's overall goals.

Beyond these considerations, senior management also must pay close attention to the fit between programs and responsibility centers. Programs represent the operational definition of an organization's strategy, and can be broken into program categories, subcategories, and elements. Each aspect of a program must be assigned to a responsibility center, and the management control system must be designed in such a way that it can provide information on both program and responsibility center activities. This calls for a careful design of the account structure, a task that ordinarily is carried out by the accounting staff but needs considerable guidance from senior management. Otherwise there is a danger that the accounts will not articulate.

Senior management must constantly bear in mind that management control is fundamentally behavioral. The various control tools are effective only to the extent they influence behavior, and they will influence behavior only to the extent that the culture of the organization is conducive to their doing so. A delicate balance must be struck between cooperation and conflict so that individuals —both managers and professionals—work together toward the attainment of organizational goals and yet are able to have legitimate and healthy conflicts over the best ways to attain them.

Suggested Cases for Classroom Use with this Chapter

See the Appendix at the end of the book for a more complete description of each case and ordering information.

Franklin Health Associates (A)	Determining the link between strategy and programs, and analyzing responsibility centers in a small group practice
Piedmont University	Considering the potential for profit centers in a university
Southern Seattle University Health System (A)	Assessing responsibility centers in a faculty practice plan
Commonwealth University	Resolving a relatively simple transfer pricing situation
Milan Sanitation Department	Using shadow prices to create a profit center in a municipality
White Hills Children's Museum	Resolving a transfer pricing dispute
National Youth Association	Resolving a transfer pricing dispute
Converse Health System	Resolving a tricky transfer pricing problem in an integrated healthcare delivery system

Practice Case: Valley Hospital

First they tell me that I'm a profit center, which seems to be a good idea. Then they tell me to run the department as though it were a little business, which I like. Then they tell me that I have to buy lab tests at prices much greater than what I would have to pay to Biolab, despite the fact that Biolab can give me equally fast turnaround time and equal quality. Now what do I do?

Phyllis Martin, M.D., Director of the Ambulatory Care Division of Valley Hospital, had received both good and bad news. The good news, which came several months ago was that her division, along with most other divisions in the hospital, had been reorganized into a profit center. Each profit center had been given responsibility for its own bottom line, and profit center managers and their key staff members were to be paid annual bonuses based on the profit (surplus) of their units. The bad news was that Dr. Martin had just been told that she had to purchase all of her laboratory tests from the Laboratory Division, another profit center. She continued:

Here's a good example. We charge our patients $21.00 for a CBC [complete blood count], which typically is required in conjunction with a diagnostic workup. The $21.00 charge covers the time spent by nurses in my division assisting the patient, the processing of paperwork by our administrative staff, the supplies needed for the test, and the time spent by our PA [physician's assistant] or physician reporting the results to the patient. However, we don't have the capability to do the actual lab work needed to analyze the patient's blood. This I must "purchase" from somewhere else. I've been using the hospital's Lab Division, but I now find out that its price is totally unreasonable.

The Laboratory Division charged all of the hospital's divisions $16.00 for a CBC. According to Joseph Goodman, the manager of the laboratory:

My $16.00 price for a CBC is very reasonable. It is based on our variable costs of $12.00, which is for the technician labor, reagents, and some miscellaneous supplies, plus $3.00 of our fixed costs, and only $1.00 of surplus, which is a fair amount.

Dr. Martin's concern arose because her staff had found that they could purchase CBCs of comparable quality for $14.50 each from Biolab, a free-standing laboratory located nearby. By doing so, she could improve her division's bottom line considerably.

The conflict had reached the office of Sam Black, the hospital's Chief Financial Officer. According to him:

They keep talking about what's fair and what's not fair. Fair is a summer event with cows and baked goods! We have a hospital to run. If we let Phyllis buy her CBCs from Biolab, then we have to let all our profit centers buy from Biolab. What happens to our own lab at that point? Answer: All it does are the really expensive tests that the labs-in-a-box can't or won't do. Can you imagine what would happen to our cost per test at that point, not to mention our vulnerability in the marketplace. Biolab could hold us up and we'd have no recourse. You can't have a hospital without a lab, and you can't have a lab doing only the esoteric stuff.

Although Dr. Martin was sympathetic to both Mr. Black's and Mr. Goodman's points of view, she also felt quite strongly that there had to be a better solution to the problem.

> I understand where Joe's coming from. He runs a profit center, too, and he and his staff get a bonus based on his department's bottom line. But his bonus shouldn't be at my division's expense. Each time we purchase a CBC from him, our surplus is $1.50 less than if we bought it from Biolab, and, along with that, our bonuses fall too. And we do a lot of CBCs!

Mr. Black knew that the conflict would not dissipate without some intervention from his office. He wondered what he should do, and what the implications of his decision would be for other departments in the hospital, such as radiology, that also were profit centers.

Assignment

1. Complete the following table showing each profit center's financial performance under the two options shown.

	Ambulatory Care Division	Laboratory Division	Hospital Overall
Option 1 - Buy from Hospital's Laboratory Division			
Revenue			
Variable costs	______	______	______
Contribution			
Option 2 - Buy from Biolab			
Revenue			
Variable costs	______	______	______
Contribution			

2. What problems, if any, are illustrated by your computations? Please be as specific as you can.

3. What should Mr. Black do about the conflict between Dr. Martin and Mr. Goodman over the price of a CBC? What should he do about the prices for other lab tests and other procedures (such as x-rays)?

Solution to Practice Case

This is a fairly basic case on transfer pricing, but one that illustrates the problems of fairness and of goal congruence rather neatly. You should have had little or no trouble making the computations, so that you can focus on the bigger question of how to resolve the various issues that have arisen as a result of the computations.

Question 1. The computations on a per-test basis are as follows:

	Amb Care Division	**Laboratory Division**	**Hospital Overall**
Option 1 - Buy from Hospital Lab Division			
Revenue	$21.00	$16.00	$21.00
Variable cost	16.00	12.00	12.00
Contribution	$ 5.00	$4.00	$ 9.00
Option 2 - Buy from Biolab			
Revenue	$21.00	$0.00	$21.00
Variable cost	14.50	0.00	14.50
Contribution	$ 6.50	$0.00	$ 6.50

Question 2. One problem depicted by the figures in this table is an absence of goal congruence. Specifically, although Dr. Martin could improve the surplus of her division by having CBCs prepared by Biolab, the overall surplus of Valley Hospital would decline if she were to do so. That is, the hospital pays $12.00 "out of pocket" for every CBC the Laboratory Division does. All other costs are fixed. Therefore each CBC done by the Laboratory Division reduces the hospital's surplus by $12.00.

If Dr. Martin buys CBCs from Biolab, the hospital incurs an incremental cost of $14.50 instead of $12.00, and its surplus therefore is reduced by $14.50. This is because, when CBCs are purchased from Biolab, the hospital pays a price that includes not just variable costs, but a portion of Biolab's fixed costs, plus a profit margin. Clearly, the hospital would prefer to have Dr. Martin purchase CBCs from the Laboratory Division rather than from Biolab.

The problem is that when she purchases CBCs from the hospital's Laboratory Division, Dr. Martin is charged $16.00, not $12.00. As a result, for each CBC she purchases from the Laboratory Division, her division's surplus falls by $16.00, as compared to only $14.50 if she purchases it from the freestanding laboratory. With revenue of $21.00, the result is a contribution $5.00 if she purchases from the Laboratory Division but $6.50 if she purchases from Biolab.

In summary, to allow Dr. Martin to purchase from outside the hospital increases her division's surplus but reduces the hospital's overall surplus. To force her to buy from the Laboratory Division maximizes the hospital's overall surplus but reduces the surplus of Dr. Martin's division. Since she is paid a bonus, it also reduces her bonus. Clearly, Dr. Martin's goals are not congruent with those of the hospital as a whole. Moreover, by not allowing her to buy from Biolab, the hospital has violated the fairness criterion: Dr. Martin has los the ability to control one of her costs.

Question 3. The resolution of transfer pricing problems such as these is one of the most complicated aspects of designing a management control structure. As discussed in the chapter, in arriving at a transfer price, senior management typically chooses among three options: (1) market price,

(2) full cost, and (3) negotiated cost. Different organizations use different options depending on a variety of circumstances, including matters such as the availability of information concerning market price, and the effect of the choice on managers' motivation. As such, there is no option that can be called the "right" option.

Although there is no right answer to the resolution of this problem, there are four basic issues that senior management must consider in making a transfer pricing decision.

1. **Rules of the Game.** The "rules of the game" must be clear. In the above example, Dr. Martin must know her options at the beginning of her budget year. If she must buy from inside the hospital, this needs to be well understood and agreed to, and her budget perhaps should be adjusted accordingly.

2. **Incentives.** The price (or pricing formula) needs to be established in advance, and held constant throughout the budget year. Dr. Martin should not be forced to pay for inefficiencies in the laboratory if its actual costs diverge from its budgeted costs. To allow this would be to remove any incentive for the laboratory manager to control costs.

3. **Setting a Fair Transfer Price.** If Dr. Martin is to be required to buy from inside the hospital, the transfer price probably should be a negotiated one. In many organization's the rule is that the transfer price must be at the "market rate," or $14.50 in the above situation, but this is not always possible due to the unavailability of market price information. In the above situation, the market price for a CBC is readily available from a free standing lab, but free standing labs most likely do not do some of the sophisticated tests that Dr. Martin needs; hence market prices for these tests would be difficult to determine.

4. **Autonomy versus Central Control.** Perhaps most importantly, senior management must decide how much autonomy it wishes to give to its individual divisions. Will it allow them to set their own prices without intervention, or will it intervene to set negotiated prices? Will it allow purchasing divisions to go outside if they can get a better deal than selling divisions offer them?

If senior management chooses to give its selling divisions the autonomy to set prices at the level they choose, and purchasing divisions the autonomy to buy from the outside, it must be prepared to lose some intra-organizational transactions, and to have the organization's overall surplus fall as a result. It must believe, therefore, that the increased autonomy will give individual division managers the motivation to increase their surpluses, and that the resulting increases will more than offset the declines in its overall surplus caused by the use of outside purchases.

If, on the other hand, senior management intervenes in the price setting and outside purchase decisions of is divisions, it must be prepared to engage in many detailed price-setting activities, and to assist in the resolution of the frequent conflicts that will arise between divisional managers.

Both courses of action have advantages and disadvantages, and successful organizations can be found that have chosen each course. The key question that must be asked is the following: *Does the responsibility center structure that is in place (including the transfer pricing rules) motivate managers to take actions that are simultaneously in the best interest of both their individual responsibility centers and the organization as a whole?* If not, then there would appear to be good reason to change the transfer pricing rules.

Chapter 7

Programming

As Chapter 1 discussed, management control systems have a structure and a process. Chapter 6 examined the management control structure and its relation to an organization's external and internal environments. With this chapter, we begin our examination of the management control process.

The management control process includes two phases that deal with organizational planning: programming (this chapter's subject) and budgeting (the subject of Chapter 8). The former represents long-range planning; the latter represents short-range planning.

Programming decisions frequently involve investments in fixed assets that senior management expects will be used for several years, and that will result in a financial return. Ordinarily, the end result of the programming phase is a capital budget, and often there are some commitments to initiate new programmatic endeavors.

By contrast, the budgeting phase typically has a one-year focus and is concerned only with operating activities. The end results usually are an operating budget and a cash budget. Although this chapter focuses on programming, it is important to keep in mind that an organization's programming decisions will have an impact on its operating budget.

Programming decisions that call for the purchase of a new fixed asset (such as a new building or new piece of equipment) usually rely on one or more analytical techniques that incorporate the multiyear period over which the new asset will be used. The chapter looks at three of these techniques (payback period, net present value, and internal rate of return). Although there are instances where an organization may decide to make a capital investment without giving much formal consideration to the financial analysis, most organizations use at least one of these analytical techniques in the programming phase.

Next, the chapter discusses the choice of a rate of return (or discount rate, as it frequently is called). This segues into the issue of risk and how an organization can deal with the risk inherent in an investment proposal.

We next examine the general topic of benefit/cost analysis, followed by a discussion of an issue that frequently confronts a public sector organization: quantifying the value of a human life, and how doing so relates to a benefit/cost analysis. The chapter concludes with a description of ways that programming relates to several other organizational activities.

AN OVERVIEW OF PROGRAMMING

Programming is a key activity in implementing an organization's strategy, and, properly done, takes place within the context of the existing strategy, coupled with whatever information is available concerning new opportunities, increased competition, new or pending legislation that might affect ongoing efforts, and other similar considerations. During the programming phase, senior management makes a variety of decisions of a long-term nature concerning the approximate resources it will devote to new products or services it will offer, new programs it will undertake, and new fixed assets it will acquire.

Decisions made in the programming phase involve long-term commitments. For example, a new piece of equipment usually will last for three to five years, sometimes longer. A new or renovated facility may last twenty years. Thus, the programming phase of the management control process frequently looks ahead by at least five or ten years. In some large organizations there is a lengthy program document that describes each program proposal in detail, estimates the resources needed to accomplish it, and calculates the expected returns.

Although decisions such as these ordinarily are based on the long-term impact on financial status, there also are some short-term consequences. For example, the purchase of a new fixed asset will affect cash management via either the use of existing cash or the need to increase long-term debt. In this latter instance, the short-term impact on cash is mitigated, resulting in a series of annual debt service outlays (principal and interest payments) rather than the large initial cash outlay that otherwise would be necessary.

ANALYTICAL TECHNIQUES FOR CAPITAL INVESTMENT ANALYSES

A typical capital investment proposal involves an outlay of money this year so as to realize a stream of benefits in some future years. Consider, for example, a proposal to install storm windows at a cost of $10,000, with an estimated savings in heating bills of $3,000 per year. In evaluating this proposal one asks: Is it worth spending $10,000 now to obtain benefits of $3,000 per year in the future? There are several approaches to answering this question.

Payback Period

One approach determines the number of years the benefits will have to be obtained to recover the investment. This is the payback period, calculated as follows for the storm window example:

$$\text{Payback period} = \frac{\text{Initial Investment}}{\text{Annual benefits}} = \frac{\$10{,}000}{\$3{,}000} = 3.3 \text{ years}$$

If the storm windows are expected to last fewer than 3.3 years, the investment is not worthwhile. If more than 3.3 years, the storm windows will have "paid for themselves."

Present Value

The payback period approach assumes that savings in the second and third years are as valuable as savings in the first year, but this is not realistic. No rational person would give up the right to receive $3,000 now for the promise to receive $3,000 two years from now. If a person loans $3,000 to someone now, he or she expects to get back more than $3,000 at some time in the future. The promise of an amount to be received in the future therefore has a lower *present value* than the same amount received today.[1]

Use of present value is important in capital budgeting. By incorporating the time value of money into the analysis, the present value technique recognizes that money received in the future does not have as much value as money received today. *Net* present value (NPV) is the difference between the present value of a project's estimated financial cash inflows and the amount to be invested in the project. The estimated benefits often are called the project's "cash flows." The approach involves the following steps:

1. Determine the estimated annual cash flows (CF) associated with the project. These may be either increased revenues (net of increased costs) or decreased costs to the organization, but they must result exclusively from the project itself and not from any activities that would have taken place without the project.

---

[1] The concept of present value is discussed in Appendix 7A.

2. Determine the estimated economic life of the investment. This is not necessarily its *physical* life, but rather the time period over which the cash flows will be received. The economic life may be shorter than the physical life because of obsolescence, change in demand, or other reasons.

3. Determine the net amount of the investment (I). This is the purchase price of the new asset, plus any delivery or installation costs, plus any disposal costs for the asset it is replacing, less the salvage value of the asset being replaced.

4. Determine the required discount rate, or rate of return (discussed in greater detail later), and combine it with the economic life to get the present value factor (pvf).

5. Compute the proposed project's net present value (NPV) according to the formula:

   $$NPV = (CF \times pvf) - I$$

6. If the NPV is greater than zero, the investment is financially feasible. That is, once we have determined a desired rate of return, a project that yields a NPV of zero or greater is earning the desired rate and therefore is acceptable from a pure financial perspective.

As discussed in Appendix 7-A, when the cash flow is the same every year, the present value factor can be obtained from Table B (in the appendix) by looking at the intersection of the year row and the percent column selected in steps 2 and 4 above. Present value factors for one-time cash flows can be found in Table A. The (CF x pvf) portion of this equation is known as *Gross Present Value*. The *Net Present Value* is determined by deducting the investment from it.

Example Assume we estimate that the storm windows in the above example will last 5 years, and that our required rate of return is 8 percent. The analysis would be performed as follows:

Step 1. Annual cash flow = \$3,000
Step 2. Economic life = 5 years
Step 3. Net investment amount = \$10,000
Step 4. Rate of return = 8%
Step 5. NPV = (CF x pvf) - I
= (\$3,000 x 3.993) - \$10,000
= \$11,979 - \$10,000
= \$1,979

Step 6. The investment has a NPV that is greater than zero, and therefore is financially feasible.

Points to Consider. Several important points should be made about an analysis of net present value. First, the above example assumed identical cash flows in each of the years, which permits us to use Table B. If the cash flows were not the same in each year, we would need to calculate the term (CF x pvf) for each year separately (using Table A) and add the results together.

Second, although an analysis of this sort appears to be quite precise, we should recognize that its significant elements are estimates or guesses, and may be quite imprecise. Specifically, cash flows projected beyond a period of two to three years ordinarily are not very precise, nor are estimates of the economic lives of most investments. Thus, we should be careful about attributing too much credibility to the precision that the formula seems to provide us. Because of this, many managers look for the NPV to be a *comfortable margin* above zero. Of course, what is comfortable for one manager may not be so for another.

Third, inflation is a factor. It is quite likely, for instance, that potential increases in wage rates, will cause labor savings from an investment to be greater five years from now than they are today. If, however, we are to adjust our cash flow factor for the effects of inflation, we also need to adjust the required rate of return to reflect our need for a return somewhat greater than the rate of inflation. By excluding an inflation effect from both the cash flow calculations and the required rate of return, we neutralize the impact of inflation. We thus do not need to undertake the rather complex calculations that otherwise might be necessary.

Finally, the financial analysis is only one aspect of the decision-making process. Clearly, there are many more considerations, including political and strategic analyses. Managers must be careful not to let the financial analysis dominate a decision with political or strategic consequences that cannot be quantified. In these instances, a manager's judgment and "feel" for the situation may be as important as the quantitative factors. Moreover, if a project is *required* by, say, a regulatory agency, its net present value is irrelevant. In short, almost all capital budgeting proposals involve a wide variety of non-quantitative considerations that will influence the final decision. The use of present value or any related techniques serves mainly to formalize the quantitative part of the analysis.

Benefit/Cost Ratio

Since most organizations do not have sufficient capital investment funds to engage in all financially feasible projects, managers must devise some method to rank projects in order of their financial desirability. One such method is to calculate their *benefit/cost ratio*, as follows:

$$\text{Benefit/cost ratio} = \frac{\text{Gross present value}}{\text{Investment}}$$

To illustrate this approach, suppose we have two proposals, one requiring an investment of $2,000 that yields a cash inflow of $2,400 one year from now, and the other an investment of $3,000 that yields a cash inflow of $900 a year for five years. If the required rate of return is 10 percent, the benefit/cost ratio indicates that the second proposal is preferable, as indicated below:

Proposal	*Investment*	*Cash Inflow*	*Present Value Factors at 10 percent*	*Gross Present Value*	*Benefit/Cost Ratio*
A	$2,000	$2,400, Year 1	0.909	$2,182	1.09
B	$3,000	$900, Years 1-5	3.790	$3,411	1.14

In this instance, Proposal B is more valuable on a benefit/cost basis than Proposal A.

Internal Rate of Return

Another way of ranking projects is by their *internal rate of return (IRR)*. The IRR method is similar to the net present value method, but instead of determining a required rate of return in advance, we set net present value equal to zero and calculate the *effective rate of return* on the investment. Proposed projects can then be ranked in terms of their rates of return.

To use this method, we usually assume identical cash flows in each year of a project's life. The IRR method thus begins with the net present value formula:

$$\text{NPV} = (\text{CF} \times pvf) - \text{I}$$

but sets NPV equal to zero, so that

$$\text{CF} \times pvf = \text{I}$$

or

$$pvf = \text{I} \div \text{CF}$$

Once we have determined the present value factor, we can use it in conjunction with the project's economic life to determine the effective—or *internal*—rate of return. We do this with Table B. For instance, in our storm window example, if we divide the $10,000 investment amount by the $3,000 annual cash flows, we get 3.33. We now find the figure 3.33 in Table B in the row for five years, and can see that it lies between 15 and 16 percent. This is the internal rate of return for the storm window project.

Choice of a Discount Rate

In any capital investment analysis, the choice of a discount rate is an important consideration, either for computing the NPV or for comparison with the IRR. The approach used by many organizations, both for-profit and nonprofit, begins by calculating their weighted cost of capital (WCC), followed by incorporating it into a computation of their weighted return on assets. The general approach is shown in Appendix 7-B.

Weighted Cost of Capital. An organization's assets are financed by a combination of liabilities and equity. Some liabilities, such as accounts payable, usually are interest free, but short- and long-term debt carry an interest rate. Equity generally comes in two forms: (1) contributions and grants, which generally are restricted in their use (and are the rough equivalent of contributed capital in a for-profit organization), and (2) operating equity (sometimes called "unrestricted net assets," which is equivalent to retained earnings in a for-profit entity).

Cost of Equity. The trickiest aspect of computing the WCC is choosing an interest rate for equity, which is an ongoing debate in many nonprofit organizations. Although some people argue that these funds are essentially free, and therefore should be assigned a zero interest rate, most managers believe there is at least an opportunity cost for their use.

While managers may agree on the relevance of *including* an interest rate for equity, there is considerably less agreement on how to determine it. One argument is that permanently restricted equity (where the principal may not be used legally for operating purposes) typically is invested in stocks, bonds, or similar investments. If some of these funds are used for a particular project, there is a reduction in the amount available for investments, and hence an opportunity cost. This opportunity cost (i.e., the rate the organization is earning on its investments) is an appropriate rate to use for equity in computing the WCC. A similar argument can be made for unrestricted equity.

Weighted Return on Assets. If the overall return on assets (ROA) is not at least equal to the weighted cost of capital, the organization is paying more to finance its assets than it is earning on them, and is atrophying. This gives rise to the need to compute a "weighted return on assets" (WRA).

The need for a WRA arises because not all assets earn a return. Accounts receivable and inventory, for example, do not earn any return. It thus is necessary to determine how much an organization's property, plant, or equipment must earn if the overall ROA is to be equal to the WCC. Appendix 7-B shows how this computation can be made.

Problems Associated with Low Discount Rates

There are many instances in which nonprofit organizations, especially those in the public sector, have analyzed capital investment proposals using discount rates that are too low. This problem is particularly important with respect to proposals for public works projects and other capital expenditures whose benefits accrue over a long period. Until fairly recently, many government agencies either did not discount the streams of cash flows at all, or they used the interest rate on government bonds as the discount rate. Most government officials now agree that a government bond rate is too low, since its use can result in the approval of projects that actually should not be undertaken.

There are two errors that can result from using a discount rate that is too low (or from the failure to discount at all). First, and most obvious, projects may be undertaken that are financially unfeasible. Second, and less obvious, projects that are capital-intensive and long-lived will appear more attractive than they actually are. In India, for example, the mistake of using low discount rates led to the construction of large cement plants built at infrequent intervals, rather than to the construction of smaller plants built more frequently.

In the 1960s there was considerable discussion about the appropriate discount rate to use for the federal government. The eventual consensus was that the rate should approximate the average rate of return on private sector investments. In March 1972, the U.S. Office of Management and Budget (OMB) effectively ended the controversy with Circular A-94, which specified that in most circumstances a rate of 10 percent should be used. In 1992, the rate was lowered to 7 percent.[2]

Incorporating Risk into the Analysis

Capital investment proposals are not risk free. Since they involve future cash flows, there is always the possibility that the future will not be as anticipated. This risk element needs to be incorporated into the analysis. If risk is not considered explicitly, then a very risky proposal might be evaluated in the same way as one that has a high probability of success.

There are a number of ways to incorporate risk into an analysis. With all of them, an increase in risk reduces the net present value of a proposal. For example, many organizations adjust their discount rate either upward or downward to account for perceived risk. The problem with this approach is that there is no easy way to establish a meaningful risk scale or otherwise make adjustments to the discount rate. Statistical techniques are available for incorporating the relative riskiness of a project, but they require analysts to estimate the probabilities of possible outcomes. This is quite difficult to accomplish.

Another approach, taken by many organizations, is to heavily discount any projected cash flows beyond some predetermined time period. They use a discount rate based on the WCC and WRA for all cash flows in, say, the first five years of an investment, and then use a much higher rate for all subsequent years. Some even exclude all cash flows beyond a certain number of years. In all instances, the reasoning is that the future is highly uncertain, and the farther out the projections, the greater the uncertainty. While this approach tends to bias decisions in favor of projects with short payback periods, many organizations in industries experiencing rapid technological change believe that short payback periods are justified.

Finally, in considering risk, some organizations give greater weight to projections of cost savings than to projections of additional contribution (incremental revenues less incremental costs). When a particular technological improvement, say a new piece of equipment, has demonstrated its ability to produce certain cost savings in other organizations, managers reason that projections of cost savings are quite reliable. By contrast, a projection that a certain investment will result in new business and hence additional revenue is far more uncertain. Factors such as clients' willingness to use the new service, competition, and so forth will affect a new investment's return. Some organizations incorporate this risk into the analysis by using lower discount rates for projects with cost savings and higher ones for projects that are expected to yield additional contribution.

In summary, when we consider the formula:

---

[2] For details, see http://www.whitehouse.gov/omb/circulars_a094#8. Circular A-94 also gives concise, useful guidance on applying the discounting principle.

$$NPV = (CF \times pvf) - I$$

the only element that is reasonably certain is the amount of the investment. Both cash flow estimates and economic life can be highly speculative. Organizations can include adjustments for uncertainty either by shortening the proposal's economic life or by raising the required rate of return. Either approach requires managers and analysts to exercise considerable judgment.

BENEFIT/COST ANALYSIS

So far, we have examined only one dimension of a technical analysis: estimating the benefits of a proposed program that can be stated in monetary terms, i.e., cash inflows, and comparing them with the investment amount. We also must make an overall judgment about a proposed program, recognizing that not all relevant factors can be expressed monetarily. This leads to the idea of a benefit/cost analysis.

Status of Benefit/Cost Analysis

The idea of comparing the benefits of a proposed course of action with its costs has existed for many years. Certain government agencies, such as the Bureau of Reclamation, have made such analyses for decades; proposals to build new dams, for example, frequently were justified on the grounds that the benefits exceeded the costs. Nor are such comparisons unique to nonprofit organizations. Techniques for analyzing the profitability of proposed investments in a for-profit enterprise involve essentially the same approach.

Interest in benefit/cost analysis grew rapidly in the 1960s when the U.S. Department of Defense applied it to problems for which no formal analysis previously had been attempted. During this time, a variety of promotional brochures, journal articles, and proposals implied that benefit/cost analysis did everything, including "...taking the guesswork out of management."

Example A proposal for a $275,000 research project submitted to the National Institute of Education promised to address " ...the Benefit/Cost question by making a Macro Management and Policy analysis of alternate Cost opportunities in Elementary-Secondary and Post-Secondary Education," and to provide the results in nine months. Translated, this means that the proposer promised to use benefit/cost analysis to find the optimum amount and character of educational programs from kindergarten through college, in nine months, and all for $275,000!

As a result of the burgeoning interest, nonprofit organizations began to apply benefit/cost analysis to all sorts of proposed programs. When these efforts produced mixed results, public policy officials began to question the merits of the approach. Nevertheless, although over-exuberant advocates of benefit/cost analysis (and outright charlatans) do exist, and their works are properly criticized, there is no doubt that many benefit/cost analyses have produced valuable information. To assure useful results, however, decision makers must consider two essential points:

1. A benefit/cost analysis focuses on those aspects of a proposal that can be estimated in quantitative terms. Because there is no important problem where all relevant factors can be reduced to numbers, benefit/cost analysis will never provide the complete answer. Not everything can be quantified, and no one should expect a benefit/cost analysis to do so. Analyses that claim to have quantified everything are of dubious merit.

2. To the extent that analysts can express some important factors in quantitative terms, they are better off doing so than not. This narrows the area where the decision maker must operate in the more judgment-based dimension of technical analysis. Thus, while the need for judgment is not eliminated, it can be reduced.

In short, the issue is not whether benefit/cost analysis is a panacea or a fraud, for in general it is neither. Rather, the issue is to define the circumstances under which it is likely to be useful. There are many. There are, however, some important factors to be considered in the decision to employ it. They are discussed below.

Clarifying Goals

The benefit in a benefit/cost analysis must be related to an organization's goals; there is no point in making a benefit/cost analysis unless all concerned agree on these goals. The purpose of benefit/cost analysis is to suggest the best alternative for reaching a goal, but the formulation of goals is largely a judgmental process. Various members of management and various staff people may have different ideas of an organization's goals, and unless they reconcile their views, middle managers will find it difficult to formulate and implement appropriate programs.

Example Several years ago, the federal government began to support local transportation for the handicapped. Since the U.S. Department of Transportation then subsidized local bus and subway lines, its natural inclination was to finance the modification of buses to provide lifts that would permit easy access for wheelchairs. The extra capital and maintenance costs of such equipment turned out to be substantial, and usage was not high because handicapped individuals had no way of getting from their homes to the buses. Consequently, the cost per passenger was high—$1,283 per trip in one study. Subsequently, transportation was provided by vans that picked up these individuals at their doors and took them directly to their destinations. This was more convenient and less expensive—between $5 and $14 per passenger trip in most cities that tried it.

A focus on the goal of transporting the handicapped, rather than one of modifying existing modes of transportation, might have avoided the costly installation of passenger lifts in buses. Moreover, speculating on alternative ways of reaching the goal could have produced a more effective solution.[3]

Just as it is important to agree on goals, it also is important to make sure that the goals are reasonable and achievable. Stated somewhat differently, the problem being presented must be real, and the program being proposed must help to alleviate it.

Example In the late 1980s, locusts threatened the crops of many African nations. The U.S. Agency for International Development and other international aid agencies responded with a fleet of aircraft that helped bomb crops with millions of liters of pesticides. A few years later, a report by the Office of Technology Assessment (OTA) said the campaign may have been a wasted effort. The OTA concluded that "Massive insecticide spraying... tends to be inefficient in the short-term, ineffective in the medium term, and misses the roots of the problem in the longer term." Moreover, the study suggested that the justification for the entire operation may have been flawed because locusts aren't as big a threat as had been thought.[4]

---

[3] See Alice L. London, "Transportation Services for the Disabled," *The GAO Review,* Spring 1986, pp. 21-27.

[4] Ann Gibbons, "Overkilling the Insect Enemy," *Science,* August 10, 1990.

Proposals Susceptible to Benefit/Cost Analysis

Benefit/cost analysis has two general principles: (1) management should not adopt a program unless its benefits exceed its costs; and (2) when there are two competing proposals, the one with the greater excess of benefits over costs is preferable. To apply these principles, we must be able to relate benefits to costs.

Economic Proposals. For many proposals in nonprofit organizations, an analyst can estimate both benefits and costs in monetary terms. These economic proposals are similar to capital budgeting proposals in for-profit companies. A proposal to convert a heating plant from oil to gas involves the same type of analysis in either a for-profit or a nonprofit organization. Problems of this type are common in all organizations, and while important administratively, they frequently have little programmatic impact. Conversely, for problems that do have programmatic effects, analysts have difficulty making monetary estimates of benefits. Frequently, because benefits are elusive, analysts cannot make a reliable estimate at all.

Alternative Ways of Reaching the Same Objective. Even if benefits cannot be quantified, a benefit/cost analysis is useful in situations where there are several ways to achieve a given objective. If each alternative will achieve the objective, then management ordinarily will prefer the one with the lowest cost. This approach does not require that the objective be stated in monetary terms, or even that it be quantified. We need not measure the degree to which each alternative meets the objective, but only make the go-no-go judgment that any of the proposed alternatives will achieve it. Of these, we seek the least costly.

Examples The output of an educational program is difficult to measure. It is especially difficult to find a causal relationship between a certain teaching technique and the resulting quality of education. Nevertheless, educators can compare the costs of alternative teaching techniques, such as team teaching, computer-assisted instruction, and conventional tests and workbooks. In the absence of a judgment that one method provides better education than another, an educational manager presumably would prefer the technique with the lowest cost.

The objective of one benefit/cost analysis was to provide the optimal ground transportation for passengers arriving and departing Washington, D.C. by air. Analysts estimated the costs of various airport locations and associated ground transport services. Senior management chose the proposal that provided adequate service with the lowest cost. There was no need to measure the benefits of "adequate service" in monetary terms.

Equal Cost Programs. If competing proposals have the same cost but one produces more benefits than the other, it ordinarily is the preferred alternative. This conclusion can be reached without measuring the absolute levels of benefits. Analysts often use such an approach to determine the best mix of resources in a program.

Example Will $1,000,000 spent to hire more teachers produce more educational benefits than $1,000,000 spent on a combination of teachers and teaching machines, or $1,000,000 on team teaching rather than individual teaching? The analysis involves estimating the amount of resources that $1,000,000 will buy, and a judgment of the results that will be achieved by using this amount and mix of resources. It requires only that benefits be expressed comparatively, however, not numerically.

Different Objectives. A benefit/cost comparison of proposals intended to accomplish different objectives is likely to be worthless. For example, an analysis that attempts to compare funds to be spent for primary school education with funds to be spent for retraining unemployed adults is not worthwhile. Such an analysis would require assigning monetary values to the benefits of these two programs, which is an impossible task.

On the other hand, since funds are limited, policy makers recognize that there is an opportunity cost for any given program. While experienced managers may have an intuitive feel for these opportunity costs *within* their organizations, relatively few managers have sufficient experience or skill to make such tradeoffs *across* organizations, particularly when those organizations have disparate goals and clientele. Nor do many managers have the *authority* to make such tradeoffs. Funds not used for pollution-control programs, for example, are not necessarily available for social welfare programs.

Causal Connection Between Cost and Benefits. Many benefit/cost analyses implicitly assume a causal relationship between benefits and costs, i.e., that spending X dollars produces Y benefits. Unless a causal connection actually exists, such a benefit/cost analysis is fallacious.

Example An agency defended its personnel training program with an analysis indicating that the program would lead participants to get new jobs, which would increase their lifetime earnings by $25,000 per person. Thus, the $5,000 average cost per person trained seemed well justified. However, the assertion that the proposed program would indeed generate these benefits was completely unsupported; it was strictly a guess. There was no plausible link between the amount requested and the projected results.

Benefit/Cost as a Way of Thinking

Because of difficulties in quantifying benefits, benefit/cost *analysis* is feasible for only a small portion of the problems that arise in nonprofit organizations. These tend to be well-structured administrative-type problems. Nevertheless, a benefit/cost *way of thinking* is useful for a great many problems. One of the characteristics of competent managers is their ability to evaluate program proposals, at least in a general way, by comparing the expected benefits with the proposed costs. They may not be able to quantify the relationship, nor do they need to do so in many cases. Nevertheless, the analysis can help to distinguish factors that are relevant from those that are not.

Example The president of a liberal arts college was considering a proposal to join a consortium of three other colleges in the general area. Advocates of the proposal argued that the consortium movement originated in Oxford in the 15th century, and the idea therefore was good because it had a long and noble history. They also pointed out that there were 67 American consortia at the time, compared with only 7 three years earlier, and that the idea therefore was good because it was growing rapidly. They said that it was good for college faculties to cooperate with one another, that central purchasing would be more efficient than each college doing its own purchasing, and so on.

The president said that, although these statements were interesting, none of them directly addressed the questions that were on his mind: How many students were likely to benefit from the activities of the consortium? Was the benefit likely to be worth the annual fee? What would a central purchasing office cost, and would it be likely to reduce costs sufficiently to pay for itself plus the cost of the consortium? Could a central purchasing office be created without having a formal consortium? In effect, the president was engaging in a benefit/cost analysis, even though he had no quantified measures of benefits available to him.

Over Reliance on the Benefit/Cost Approach. Benefit/cost thinking can be carried to extremes. If a manager rejects all proposals in which no causal connection between costs and benefits has been demonstrated, middle managers will be reluctant to submit innovative program proposals. A primary characteristic of many new, experimental—and promising—schemes is that there is no way to estimate their benefit/cost relationships in advance. Undue insistence on a rigorous benefit/cost analyses can therefore result in overly conservative programs. The risk of failure of an innovative proposal may be high, but it frequently is worth taking the risk if an organization wishes to serve its clients in the best way possible.

Whither Benefit/Cost Analysis. Despite its limitations, a benefit/cost approach may be better than any alternative. It may show that a proposal is outside a reasonable boundary in either direction—that it is obviously worthwhile or obviously not worth its cost from an economic standpoint. Unfortunately, this does not guarantee either its acceptance or rejection.

Example Some studies of the effect of a 55-mile-per-hour speed limit showed that the benefits were not worth the costs. Benefits were lives saved. Costs could be measured in terms of the additional time taken to reach a destination. Even when time was valued at low amounts per hour, and lives were given a high value, the cost exceeded the benefits in most of these studies. Nevertheless, the 55 mile-per-hour speed limit persists in many states.

QUANTIFYING THE VALUE OF A HUMAN BEING

In undertaking benefit/cost analyses, nonprofit organization managers frequently encounter a factor that rarely is relevant in proposals originating in for-profit companies: the value of a human being. This dilemma arises because some programs are designed to save or prolong human lives. Such programs include automobile safety, accident prevention, drug control, and medical research. In these programs, the value of a human life, or of a workday lost to accident or illness, is a relevant consideration in measuring benefits.

Analysts are often squeamish about attaching a monetary value to a human life since there is a general belief in our culture that life is priceless. Nevertheless, such a monetary amount often facilitates the analysis of certain proposals. In a world of scarce resources, it is not possible to spend unlimited amounts to save lives in general.

There are, of course, circumstances in which society is willing to devote significant resources to saving a specific life, as when hundreds of people, supported by helicopters and various high technology devices, are brought together to hunt for a child who is lost in the woods. In most situations, however, the focus is not on saving a single life, but rather on saving the lives of a class of people (such as motorcyclists or cancer victims) or on valuing a life that already has been lost (such as in cases of litigation for medical malpractice).

Analytical Approaches to Valuation. There are several approaches to estimating the value of a human life, all of which present difficulties. One discounts the expected future earnings of the person or persons affected by the program; this discounted present value presumably represents the person's *economic value* to his or her family or to society. A related approach subtracts the person's food, clothing, and other costs from the earnings to find the *net* value of his or her life.

These two approaches frequently are used in litigation involving "wrongful deaths." They are relevant to cases involving deceased persons, automobile accidents, industrial pollution, or the release of toxic chemicals.

Example In a study of the costs of firearm injuries, the U.S. General Accounting Office (GAO) reported on a study that determined the average lifetime cost of a firearm injury. The costs used in the study included actual dollar amounts spent for hospital and nursing home care, physician and other medical professional services, drugs and appliances, and rehabilitation. The cost estimates also included life years lost, plus the indirect cost associated with loss of earnings from short- and long-term disability or premature death from injury. The study concluded that injuries not requiring hospitalization cost $458 per person; those requiring hospitalization were $33,159 per person. The average lifetime cost of a firearm *fatality* was $373,520, which the GAO called "... the highest of any cause of injury." Using annual figures for injuries and deaths attributable to firearms, the GAO concluded that the estimated lifetime costs for accidental shootings was close to $1 billion every year.[5]

Among the problems encountered in applying these approaches is the difficulty of (a) estimating the amount of future earnings and related costs, (b) choosing an appropriate time period, and (c) selecting the correct discount rate. Perhaps more important, these approaches tend to discriminate against persons with relatively low expected lifetime earnings, such as the elderly, homemakers, school teachers, ministers, artists, and retired college professors.[6]

A third analytical approach computes the value of a life in terms of society's willingness to spend money to prevent deaths. One might imagine, for example, that the development and enforcement of occupational safety regulations and building codes are based on benefit/cost comparisons. This is rarely the case, however. Spending on many of these programs frequently is based on emotional arguments or political posturing, as happens, for instance, when legislators suggest that economic costs are irrelevant for questions related to human lives.

Example In the early 1990s, the state of Oregon planned to modify the strategy of its Medicaid program by covering more poor residents but offering fewer services. The state ranked 1,600 medical procedures according to costs, benefits, and patients' "quality of well-being." Under the scheme, immunizations ranked higher than treatment for gallstones and depression; cosmetic surgery and sex-change operations fell in the lowest rank. Ultimately, the state drew a line through the list, with funding to be provided for procedures above the line and denied for those below it.

The state needed a federal waiver to implement the plan since Medicaid rules required that states fund "all medically necessary" services. In 1992 (a presidential election year), the waiver was denied based, in part, on the argument that the plan valued some human lives higher than others, and that such a valuation was unfair.

A fourth approach seeks to measure the value people place on their own lives as indicated by, say, the amount they are willing to spend on life or disability insurance, or by risk premiums they earn in hazardous occupations. This implies that these individuals' decisions are based on economic considerations, but many other considerations may be involved.

---

[5] U.S. General Accounting Office, *Accidental Shootings: Many Deaths and Injuries Caused by Firearms Could be Prevented,* Report to the Chairman, Subcommittee on Antitrust, Monopolies, and Business Rights, Committee of the Judiciary, U.S. Senate, Washington, D.C., March 1991.

[6] Ralph Estes makes an attempt to adjust for some of these factors in *Estes® Economic Loss Tables,* Wichita, Kansas, A.U. Publishing. He provides separate data for different education levels, different genders, whites and nonwhites, persons with and without established earnings histories, and for persons who earn the minimum wage. In cases of wrongful death, he also provides data that adjust for terminated personal consumption.

Examples At one time, the exposure standard for benzene was 10 parts per million averaged over an eight-hour working day. At this rate, one benzene worker would die of benzene-related cancer every third year. According to the Occupational Safety and Health Administration (OSHA), a standard of 1 part per million would have eliminated the risk, but would have cost $100 million annually for the 30,000 workers who were exposed to benzene.

One analyst asked the following questions: Would each of the 30,000 benzene workers be willing to pay $3,333 a year (his or her share of the $100 million) to eliminate the risk? If not, would the $100 million be better spent in a highway-improvement or cancer-screening program that could save more than one life every third year?[7]

Merril Eisenbud, the former chairman of the North Carolina Low-Level Radioactive Waste Management Authority, criticized some states' regulations concerning the design of low-level radioactive waste disposal sites. He argued that, in response to public pressure, some states require more protection be provided than is specified by the Nuclear Regulatory Commission. According to Mr. Eisenbud, "The additional protection involves expenditures of more than $100 million over the life of a facility, which is the equivalent to many *trillions* of dollars per premature death averted!"[8]

Alternatives to Valuation. The cost of saving lives may be a useful way of choosing among alternative proposals even when it is not possible or feasible to measure the value of a life. Specifically, the alternative that saves the most lives per dollar spent generally is considered preferable from an economic viewpoint. The Federal Highway Administration uses this approach in ranking the attractiveness of various highway safety alternatives. Such an analysis is limited to judging whether a particular program saves more lives per dollar spent than other lifesaving or life-prolonging programs. It does not attempt to assign a value to a life.

LINKS TO OTHER ORGANIZATIONAL ACTIVITIES

Beyond its role as a phase of the management control process, programming is directly or indirectly linked to several other activities of importance to senior management. Recognizing these linkages is essential if the programming phase is to be as effective as possible.

Link to Strategy Formulation

Programs and product lines are among the most readily observable aspects of an organization's strategy. Thus, if new programs and large capital expenditures are to remain consistent with strategy, line managers must understand the linkages between their programs or product lines and the organization's overall strategic directions. Indeed, if an organization's strategy is to evolve over time because of shifting environmental opportunities and threats, and changing organizational strengths and weaknesses, senior management must find ways to monitor and manage the organization's programs so they remain consistent with, and supportive of, the evolving strategy.

---

7 From Steven E. Rhoads, "Kind Hearts and Opportunity Costs," *Across the Board*, December 1985.

8 Merril Eisenbud, "Disparate Costs of Risk Avoidance," *Science*, September 9, 1988, p. 1277-8.

Link to Culture

Programming also can be an especially important tool for managing an organization's culture, in that senior management can use it to influence the basic assumptions of decision-making.[9] Specifically, the constraints senior management establishes on programming, and the way it makes use of the "programming purse," can have a profound impact on line managers' understanding of what is acceptable and unacceptable in the organization. This, in turn, can help to either maintain or change the organization's culture.[10]

Link to Conflict Management

Because many of the benefits of new program proposals are difficult to quantify, and because line managers (especially profit center managers) tend to be quite optimistic about their program proposals, a new program bias tends to characterize the programming phase of the management control process. In particular, many proposals tend to overestimate volume and prices. Some may underestimate costs.

Senior management typically counteracts this bias by using its staff to analyze the proposals. When this happens, there can be considerable friction between line managers and the staff. Designing a conflict management process to deal with this friction so that the final result is a tough but realistic analysis is one of the most challenging tasks senior management faces in programmatic decision making.

Link to Authority and Influence

While many large nonprofit organizations have decentralized considerable decision-making authority to their divisions, frequently establishing them as profit centers, most stipulate that programming decisions for amounts that exceed some ceiling require senior management approval. Their reasoning is that large programming decisions, if not carefully managed, may lead the organization in strategic directions that senior management does not want to take. Thus, there are constraints on the authority of almost all profit center managers.

In addition, there is an internal political dimension to programming, which is not always well understood. For a variety of reasons, some managers may have the "ear" of senior management, or they may run units or programs that are seen as key to the organization's future, or they may simply be more articulate or more forceful than some of their colleagues. As a result, they may receive a favorable decision on a proposed project that has a much lower IRR than a project in another unit with a manger who, for one reason or another, is not seen in such a favorable light. There is not much that can be done about this; it is simply a reality of organizational life.

SUMMARY

Managers frequently must choose between two or more competing programs. When this happens, an attempt to quantify both benefits and costs usually can assist in the decision-making effort.

When two or more proposals have roughly the same benefits, the comparison is relatively easy since only costs need to be calculated. Similarly, when competing proposals have the same costs but

---

9 For a discussion of culture, see Edgar H. Schein, *Organizational Culture and Leadership,* Second Edition, San Francisco, Jossey Bass Publishers, 1992. In Shein's model, basic assumptions about decision making are at the core of an organization's culture.

10 For additional discussion on this point, see David W. Young, "Managing Organizational Culture," *Business Horizons,* September-October 2000.

one clearly produces more benefits than the other, the decision usually is quite easy. The decision becomes complicated, however, when benefits and costs extend over several years (as is the case with almost all proposed new programs), and when competing proposals have both different benefits and different costs.

When both benefits and costs can be expressed easily in monetary terms, calculating either present values or internal rates of return can facilitate a decision When these analyses are being used, the choice of a discount rate is a key decision; many relatively undesirable projects have been undertaken because analysts used a discount rate that was too low.

Frequently, benefits and costs cannot be expressed easily in monetary terms. This happens, for example, when managers attempt to incorporate risk into the analysis, since risk is inherently difficult to measure. It also happens when managers attempt to quantify the value of a human being, and include that in the analysis. Additionally, there are a variety of other non-quantitative considerations that are part of almost every proposed program. In all instances, managers must be careful not to allow the quantitative factors to dominate the decision. They need to recognize that their judgment occasionally must override the results of the quantitative analysis.

Suggested Cases for Classroom Use with this Chapter

See the Appendix at the end of the book for a more complete description of each case and ordering information.

Yoland Research Institute	Assessing a capital investment decision when behavioral factors are involved
Dovetown Parking Authority	Making a tricky present value computation, with an unusual twist
Green Valley Medical Center	Including non-financial considerations in an investment decision
The Heartbreak of DRGs	Analyzing a tricky programming computation for treating psoriasis
Stonehill Family Practice	Valuing a family practice for purposes of acquisition
Disease Control Programs	Making programmatic tradeoffs that require valuing a life

Appendix 7-A
The Concept of Present Value

The concept of present value rests on the principle that money has a *time value*, such that a dollar received one year from today is worth less than a dollar received today. To illustrate the concept, consider the following situations:

> *Question:* A colleague offers to pay you $1,000 one year from today. How much would you lend her today?

Presumably, unless you were a good friend or somewhat altruistic, you would not lend her $1,000 today. You could invest your $1,000, earn something on it over the course of the year, and have more than $1,000 a year from now. If, for example, you could earn 10 percent on your money, you could invest your $1,000 and have $1,100 in a year. Alternatively, if you had $909, and invested it at 10 percent, you would have $1,000 a year from today.

Thus, if your colleague offers to pay you $1,000 a year from today, and you are an investor expecting a 10 percent return, you most likely would lend her only $909 today. With a 10 percent interest rate, $909 is the *present value* of $1,000 received one year hence.

> *Question:* Under the same circumstances as the previous question, how much would you lend your colleague if she offered to pay you $1,000 *two years* from today?

Here we must incorporate the concept of compound interest, i.e., the fact that interest is earned on interest. For example, at a 10 percent rate, $826 invested today would accumulate to roughly $1,000 in two years, as shown by the following:

Year 1 $826 x .10	=	$ 82.60
Year 2 ($826 + $82.60) x .10	=	$ 90.86
Total at end of Year 2 = $826 + $82.60 + $90.86	=	$ 999.46

Thus, you would be willing to lend her $826.

> *Question:* The previous question consisted of a promise to pay a given amount two years from today, with no intermediate payments. Another possibility to consider is the situation where your colleague offers to pay you $1,000 a year from today and another $1,000 two years from today. How much would you lend her now?

The answer requires combining the analyses in each of the above two examples. Specifically, for the $1,000 received two years from now, you would lend her $826, and for the $1,000 received one year from now you would lend her $909. Thus, you would lend her a total of $1,735.

Our ability to make these computations is simplified by present value tables. Two such tables, A and B, are contained in this appendix. Table A, "Present Value of $1," is the table we would use to determine the present value of a single payment received at some specified time in the future. For instance, we could find the answer to the first question above by looking in the column for 10 percent and the row for one year; this gives us 0.909. Multiplying 0.909 by $1,000 gives us the $909 we would lend our colleague. Similarly, if we look in the row for two years and multiply the entry of 0.826 by $1,000, we arrive at the answer to the second example: $826.

Table B, "Present Value of $1 Received Annually for N Years," is used for even payments received over a given period. Looking at Table B, we can see that the present value of 1.735 (for a payment of $1 received each year for two years at 10 percent) multiplied by $1,000 is $1,735. This is the amount we calculated in the third example above. We also can see that the 1.735 is the sum of the two amounts shown on Table A (.909 for one year hence, and .826 for two years hence). Thus, Table B simply sums the various elements in Table A to facilitate calculations.

PRESENT VALUE TABLES

Table A. Present Value of $1

Years Hence	1%	2%	4%	6%	8%	10%	12%	14%	15%	16%	18%	20%	22%	24%	25%	26%	28%	30%
1	0.990	0.980	0.962	0.943	0.926	0.909	0.893	0.877	0.870	0.862	0.847	0.833	0.820	0.806	0.800	0.794	0.781	0.769
2	0.980	0.961	0.925	0.890	0.857	0.826	0.797	0.769	0.756	0.743	0.718	0.694	0.672	0.650	0.640	0.630	0.610	0.592
3	0.971	0.942	0.889	0.840	0.794	0.751	0.712	0.675	0.658	0.641	0.609	0.579	0.551	0.524	0.512	0.500	0.477	0.455
4	0.961	0.924	0.855	0.792	0.735	0.683	0.636	0.592	0.572	0.552	0.516	0.482	0.451	0.423	0.410	0.397	0.373	0.350
5	0.951	0.906	0.822	0.747	0.681	0.621	0.567	0.519	0.497	0.476	0.437	0.402	0.370	0.341	0.328	0.315	0.291	0.269
6	0.942	0.888	0.790	0.705	0.630	0.564	0.507	0.456	0.432	0.410	0.370	0.335	0.303	0.275	0.262	0.250	0.227	0.207
7	0.933	0.871	0.760	0.665	0.583	0.513	0.452	0.400	0.376	0.354	0.314	0.279	0.249	0.222	0.210	0.198	0.178	0.159
8	0.923	0.853	0.731	0.627	0.540	0.467	0.404	0.351	0.327	0.305	0.266	0.233	0.204	0.179	0.168	0.157	0.139	0.123
9	0.914	0.837	0.703	0.592	0.500	0.424	0.361	0.308	0.284	0.263	0.225	0.194	0.167	0.144	0.134	0.125	0.108	0.094
10	0.905	0.820	0.676	0.558	0.463	0.386	0.322	0.270	0.247	0.227	0.191	0.162	0.137	0.116	0.107	0.099	0.085	0.073
11	0.896	0.804	0.650	0.527	0.429	0.350	0.287	0.237	0.215	0.195	0.162	0.135	0.112	0.094	0.086	0.079	0.066	0.056
12	0.887	0.788	0.625	0.497	0.397	0.319	0.257	0.208	0.187	0.168	0.137	0.112	0.092	0.076	0.069	0.062	0.052	0.043
13	0.879	0.773	0.601	0.469	0.368	0.290	0.229	0.182	0.163	0.145	0.116	0.093	0.075	0.061	0.055	0.050	0.040	0.033
14	0.870	0.758	0.577	0.442	0.340	0.263	0.205	0.160	0.141	0.125	0.099	0.078	0.062	0.049	0.044	0.039	0.032	0.025
15	0.861	0.743	0.555	0.417	0.315	0.239	0.183	0.140	0.123	0.108	0.084	0.065	0.051	0.040	0.035	0.031	0.025	0.020

Table B. Present Value of $1 Received Annually for *N* Years

Years *N*	1%	2%	4%	6%	8%	10%	12%	14%	15%	16%	18%	20%	22%	24%	25%	26%	28%	30%
1	0.990	0.980	0.962	0.943	0.926	0.909	0.893	0.877	0.870	0.862	0.847	0.833	0.820	0.806	0.800	0.794	0.781	0.769
2	1.970	1.941	1.887	1.833	1.783	1.735	1.690	1.646	1.626	1.605	1.565	1.527	1.492	1.456	1.440	1.424	1.391	1.361
3	2.941	2.883	2.776	2.673	2.577	2.486	2.402	2.321	2.284	2.246	2.174	2.106	2.043	1.980	1.952	1.924	1.868	1.816
4	3.902	3.807	3.631	3.465	3.312	3.169	3.038	2.913	2.856	2.798	2.690	2.588	2.494	2.403	2.362	2.321	2.241	2.166
5	4.853	4.713	4.453	4.212	3.993	3.790	3.605	3.432	3.353	3.274	3.127	2.990	2.864	2.744	2.690	2.636	2.532	2.435
6	5.795	5.601	5.243	4.917	4.623	4.354	4.112	3.888	3.785	3.684	3.497	3.325	3.167	3.019	2.952	2.886	2.759	2.642
7	6.728	6.472	6.003	5.582	5.206	4.867	4.564	4.288	4.161	4.038	3.811	3.604	3.416	3.241	3.162	3.084	2.937	2.801
8	7.651	7.325	6.734	6.209	5.746	5.334	4.968	4.639	4.488	4.343	4.077	3.837	3.620	3.420	3.330	3.241	3.076	2.924
9	8.565	8.162	7.437	6.801	6.246	5.758	5.329	4.947	4.772	4.606	4.302	4.031	3.787	3.564	3.464	3.366	3.184	3.018
10	9.470	8.982	8.113	7.359	6.709	6.144	5.651	5.217	5.019	4.833	4.493	4.193	3.924	3.680	3.571	3.465	3.269	3.091
11	10.366	9.786	8.763	7.886	7.138	6.494	5.938	5.454	5.234	5.028	4.655	4.328	4.036	3.774	3.657	3.544	3.335	3.147
12	11.253	10.574	9.388	8.383	7.535	6.813	6.195	5.662	5.421	5.196	4.792	4.440	4.128	3.850	3.726	3.606	3.387	3.190
13	12.132	11.347	9.989	8.852	7.903	7.103	6.424	5.844	5.584	5.341	4.908	4.533	4.203	3.911	3.781	3.656	3.427	3.223
14	13.002	12.105	10.566	9.294	8.243	7.366	6.629	6.004	5.725	5.466	5.007	4.611	4.265	3.960	3.825	3.695	3.459	3.248
15	13.863	12.848	11.121	9.711	8.558	7.605	6.812	6.144	5.848	5.574	5.091	4.676	4.316	4.000	3.860	3.726	3.484	3.268

Appendix 7-B
Selecting a Discount Rate

Selecting an appropriate discount rate requires, as a minimum, computing a weighted cost of capital (WCC) and a weighted return on assets (WRA). Each is discussed below, along with some of the associated complications. The balance sheet on which the computations are based is contained in Exhibit 1.

Weighted Cost of Capital

The computations for the WCC and WRA are contained in Exhibit B2. Note that the interest rate for equity is 10 percent. This is a debatable number; as footnote *a* indicates, it was assumed to be the average return on the organization's investments. The result is a WCC of 6.5 percent.

The weighted cost of capital tells us what, on average, it is costing us to finance our assets. Over time, we need to be earning that rate on our assets to remain financially viable.

Not all assets earn a return, however. Therefore, we also must compute a weighted return on assets to determine what our plant and equipment needs to earn.

Weighted Return on Assets

The computations for the WRA are shown in the lower half of Exhibit 2. The process is as follows:

- Start with a breakdown of the assets, as shown, and compute their weights.
- Determine the returns of all *except* the Property, Plant and Equipment (PP&E) account. Current assets other than investments usually do not earn anything, for example. Assume, for purposes of these computations, that all cash is invested, and earns 10 percent, as indicated in footnote *a*.
- Insert the WCC (6.5 percent here) as the required weighted return on total assets, and determine what the weighted rate for PP&E must be to achieve it. To do so, we subtract from 6.5 the weighted return on our invested cash, meaning that the weighted return on PP&E in this case must be 6.2 percent.
- Using the weight for PP&E and the *weighted* rate from the above item (6.2 percent in this case), compute the absolute rate that is needed for PP&E projects on average. In this case, it is 13 percent.
- Therefore, in this case, our PP&E assets must earn a 13 percent return if our overall ROA is to be equal to our 6.5 percent WCC.

There are three issues issues to keep in mind when using this approach:

1. Some new PP&E projects will not yield the required return (13 percent here). Some renovations, for example, will probably lead to very little additional cash flows

(although there may be some savings in maintenance). Thus, incremental projects that generate significant cash flows will need to subsidize those that do not. This means that we will need to find some projects that give us greater than a 13 percent return.

2. This analysis is based on a weighted cost of capital of 6.5 percent. As we undertake additional borrowing, and as our composition of liabilities changes, our weighted cost of capital will change. This means that our required ROA also will change. As a practical matter, these changes ordinarily will be rather small, and therefore of little consequence.

3. To include the effects of the above changes, some organizations will use a forecasted weighted cost of capital. That is, they will decide how much borrowing they are planning to do for the upcoming year, how their current liabilities will shift, and what rates they will pay for borrowed funds. They then will compute the estimated WCC for the next year. Of course, this is only for one year in the future, and new assets will last for much longer, but it is more realistic than using an historical WCC.

Exhibit 1 Balance Sheet for a Large Nonprofit Organization

As of the End of the Fiscal Year ($000)

Assets		**Liabilities and Equity**	
Current Assets		Current liabilities	
Cash	$ 1,155	Accounts payable	$ 12,307
Accounts receivable	7,742	Current portion of mortgage	1,160
Inventory	10,010	Total current	13,467
Prepaid expenses	4,644	Long-term liabilities	
Total current	23,551	Bonds (7%)	8,300
Non-current assets		Mortgage (9%)	5,339
Property, Plant and Equipment (net)	20,609	Equity	
Total	$ 44,160	Permanently restricted net assets	11,000
		Unrestricted net assets	6,054
		Total	$ 44,160

Exhibit 2 Weighted Cost of Capital and Weighted ROA

Dollar amounts in thousands

Weighted Cost of Capital

Liabilities and Equity	Amount	Weight	Rate		Weighted Rate
Current liabilities					
Accounts payable	$ 12,307	0.279	.00		.000
Current portion of mortgage	1,160	0.026	.09		.002
Total current	13,467				
Long-term liabilities					
Bonds	8,300	0.188	.07		.013
Mortgage	5,339	0.121	.09		.011
Equity					
Permanently restricted net assets	11,000	0.249	.10	*a*	.025
Unrestricted net assets	6,054	0.137	.10	*a*	.014
Total	$ 44,160	1.000			.065

a Assumed to be the organization's desired return on equity

Weighted Return on Assets

Assets	Amount	Weight	Rate		Weighted Rate
Current Assets					
Cash	$ 1,155	0.026	.10	*a*	.003
Accounts receivable	7,742	0.175	.00		.000
Inventory	10,010	0.227	.00		.000
Prepaid expenses	4,644	0.105	.00		.000
Total current	23,551				
Non-current assets					
Property, Plant and Equipment (net)	20,609	0.467	.13		.062
Total	$ 44,160	1.000			.065

a Assumed to be the return on the organization's invested cash

Practice Case: Erie Museum

Christian Larson, Executive Director of Erie Museum, was contemplating the proposal recently submitted to him by Francesca Michaels, the head of Curatorial Services. Ms. Michaels' request was for the purchase of some new equipment to perform operations currently being performed on different, less efficient equipment. The purchase price was $300,000, delivered and installed.

BACKGROUND

Erie Museum was a nonprofit organization located on the shores of Lake Erie in Cleveland, Ohio. It had been in existence for some 40 years, specializing in art from the European Renaissance, with a special focus on the Italian City States. Many of its art works were extremely fragile, and for this reason, the museum needed to regulate its air temperature and humidity at all times. Doing so required a rather constant upgrading of its equipment as new technology emerged. However, because of increased financial pressures, the museum's board of trustees was taking a harder and harder look at all capital equipment proposals that did not have grant funding.

THE REQUEST

In the case of Ms. Michaels' request, no grant funds were available, and hence the investment's cost would need to be financed from internal funds. Ms. Michaels had worked closely with the equipment manufacturer to determine the potential benefits of the new equipment, however, and she estimated that it would result in annual savings of $60,000 in electricity, maintenance, and other direct costs. She also estimated that the proposed equipment's economic life was 10 years, with zero salvage value.

The museum had recently borrowed long-term to finance another project. Paul Hershenson, the Vice President of Fiscal Affairs, had informed Mr. Larson that, because of this, he was certain the museum could obtain additional funds at 12 percent, although he would not plan to negotiate a loan specifically for the purchase of this equipment. He did feel, however, that an investment of this type should have a return of at least 20 percent, even though the museum paid no taxes.

COMPLICATING FACTORS

There were four complications. First, Mr. Larson's computation of the museum's weighted cost of capital, shown below, indicated the Mr. Hershenson's 20 percent rate was very high.

	Percent of Total	*Average Interest Rate*	*Weighted Interest Rate*
Debt	40.0	12.0	4.8
Equity	60.0	0.0	0.0
Total	100.0		4.8

Second, the present equipment was in good working order and probably would last, physically, for at least 15 more years. Third, this request was for what Ms. Michaels called "even better equipment," to replace some equipment purchased two years ago involving the same economic life and dollar amounts. Ms. Michaels had informed Mr. Larson that the new equipment would render the existing equipment completely obsolete with no resale value.

Fourth, at a recent board meeting, the chair of the board's finance committee had discussed the inconsistency between weighted cost of capital computed by Mr. Larson and the 20 percent rate of return that Mr. Hershenson was recommending. She had pointed out that Erie's equity consisted of donations and other gifts which were essentially free. As a result, she thought the proper discount rate to use for capital investment proposals was Mr. Larson's (roughly) 5 percent, and not the 20 percent suggested by Mr. Hershenson.

THE DECISION

Although funds could be obtained to finance the purchase of Ms. Michaels' proposed new equipment, Mr. Larson and Mr. Hershenson were both concerned about the mistake made two years ago, and wanted to be sure that a similar mistake would not be made this time. Mr. Hershenson also was not certain that Ms. Michaels' request was justifiable.

Assignment

1. What is the internal rate of return of Ms. Michaels' proposal?

2. What is the proposal's net present value, using a discount rate of 20 percent? A discount rate of 5 percent? What is the appropriate discount rate to use? Why?

3. If the museum decides to purchase the new equipment for Ms. Michaels, a mistake has been made somewhere, because good equipment bought only two years ago is being scrapped. How did this mistake come about?

4. What non-quantitative factors should the museum consider in making this decision? How important are they?

Solution to Practice Case

This case allows you to work through some of the basic elements of capital budgeting. It also introduces some tricky issues that go beyond the basic computations, including the questions of sunk costs, the weighted cost of capital, and the appropriate interest rate to use for donated funds.

Question 1. The internal rate of return of Ms. Michaels' proposal can be calculated as follows:

Investment ÷ annual cash flows = present value factor
$300,000 ÷ $60,000 = 5.000
Economic life = 10 years

Internal rate of return = 15 percent (The present value factor that lies at the intersection of the 10-year row and the 15 percent column is 5.019.

Question 2
Part A

At a discount rate of 20 percent, the net present value can be calculated as follows:

Cash flows:	$ 60,000
Economic life:	10 years
Investment amount:	$300,000
Discount rate:	20%
Net present value:	= ($60,000 x 4.192) - $300,000
	= $251,520 - $300,000
	= ($48,480)

At 20 percent, the investment is not financially feasible. This makes sense, of course, since its internal rate of return was only 15 percent.

Part B

At a discount rate of 5 percent, we need to estimate the present value factor using the midpoint between 4 percent and 6 percent. When we do so, the net present value is calculated as follows:

Cash flows:	$ 60,000
Economic life:	10 years
Investment amount:	$300,000
Discount rate:	5%
Net present value	= ($60,000 x 7.736) - $300,000
	= $464,160 - $300,000
	= $164,160

The investment now is financially feasible. Again, this makes sense since the internal rate of return is 15 percent.

Part C

The appropriate rate to use is the weighted cost of capital (WCC) or, more specifically, the weighted cost of capital after the additional borrowing takes place (which is not, incidentally, the same as the interest rate on the incremental borrowing). This raises the question of how to calculate the WCC.

A key point here is that donated funds are not free. In the first place, there usually is some fundraising cost associated with donations. Second, donors may expect that the earnings on their funds are to be used rather than the principal; under these circumstances, the rate of return must be equivalent to the interest that could be earned on the funds. Finally, in an inflationary economy, unless donated funds earn a rate of return equivalent to inflation, their purchasing power will be eroded. Thus, the interest rate used should be at least equal to inflation, and possibly should reflect the opportunity cost of the funds.

Let's use a rate of 10 percent, which is a fairly reasonable amount over a long time period for a conservatively invested portfolio of funds. The result is the following weighted cost of capital:

	Percent of Total	Average Interest Rate	Weighted Interest Rate
Debt	40.0%	12.0%	4.8%
Equity	60.0	10.0	6.0
Total	100.0%		10.8%

Given the arbitrary nature of these computations, 11 percent would serve the purpose. We might even use 12 percent if we were expecting to take on some additional debt during the coming year at a higher interest rate than we now pay. Alternatively, if the cost of debt were declining, we might lower the rate to 10 percent. The result will be a figure that is somewhat higher than 4.8 percent but probably not as high as 20 percent.

Question 3. The mistake is because the economic life was estimated at 10 years when it in fact was only two years. If Ms. Michaels' proposed new equipment has an economic life of only two years, it would have an internal rate of return of less than 1 percent, as the following calculations show:

Investment ÷ annual cash flows = present value factor
$300,000 ÷ $60,000 = 5.000
Economic life = 2 years

The present value factor that lies at the intersection of the 2-year row and the 1 percent column is 1.970. Therefore, the internal rate of return is less than 1 percent. If a two year economic life had been used for the previous request, it would not have been financially feasible either.

The fact that a mistake was made in the past does not change the conclusion that the new investment is financially feasible at 15 percent, *assuming* that the economic life and cash flows have been estimated accurately. Thus, the past decision is a sunk cost and should not be incorporated into the calculations for the present decision.

What is important here, however, is Ms. Michaels' ability to estimate economic lives. Mr. Larson should question Ms. Michaels' 10-year estimate carefully, in order to satisfy himself that it is as accurate as possible. No matter how much he questions Ms. Michaels, though, it is impossible to predict the future with certainty, and thus a similar mistake may be made again.

Question 4. There are a variety of non-quantitative factors to consider in this decision. Product quality, competition, curator satisfaction, the kind of technology needed to preserve the art, and others. Indeed, it is non-quantitative factors that would usually tip the balance, especially if preserving the integrity of the art is at stake. The three non-quantitative issues that seem the most important are the following:

- Erie's strategy. How does this proposed investment help to achieve it?
- The credibility of Ms. Michaels. She did not do a good job of estimating the economic life of her last project. What confidence do we have in her estimate for this one?
- The pace of technological change. What will happen a few years from now with the technology in her area?

Chapter 8

The Operating Budget

In the programming phase of the management control process, an organization makes a variety of long-range decisions, frequently resulting in investments in assets that senior management expects will be used over some future period of time (usually several years in duration), and that will result in a "payback" of some sort to the organization. Often, the result is a capital budget.

By contrast, the budget formulation phase of the process typically has a one-year focus and is concerned only with operating activities. Operating activities usually are assessed in two ways. First, via the *operating budget,* which is the subject of this chapter. It focuses on revenues and expenses on an accrual basis, and is used to measure the performance of operating managers. Second, with the *cash budget,* which analyzes cash inflows and outflows associated with ongoing operations; this budget is used by the controller's office as a means of forecasting the organization's cash needs. The cash budget is discussed in many accounting textbooks, but not in this book.[1]

The general character of operational budgeting in a nonprofit organization is similar to that in a for-profit one, but there are significant differences in emphasis. This chapter focuses on both the similarities and the differences. It looks at the operating budget through several lenses, beginning with the organizational and strategic context in which operational budgeting takes place, and distinguishing between the mechanical and behavioral aspects. It then looks in some detail at the mechanical aspects of building a budget. It concludes with a discussion of *budgeting misfits*—areas where the budgetary phase does not work as well as it might because it does not fit well with other organizational systems or processes.

GENERAL NATURE OF THE OPERATING BUDGET

Preparing the operating budget is an important phase in the management control process. It is during this phase that an organization sets out its plans for the upcoming year and attaches monetary amounts to its various activities and programs. Moreover, in many organizations, the budget is used as a central aspect of measuring managerial performance, which means that the budgeting phase has behavioral as well as mechanical aspects.

The operating budget always applies to a specific time period, usually one year, although some organizations use a different time frame.[2] For example, the state of Nevada prepares a budget biennially (once every two years). Some theaters and symphony orchestras, by contrast, have semiannual budgets: one for the winter season and one for the summer season.

Relationship Between Programming and Budgeting

In concept, operational budgeting follows programming but is separate from it. The budget is supposed to be a "fine tuning" of an organization's programs for a given year. It incorporates the

---

1 Readers interested in cash budgeting in health care, can find a discussion in David W. Young, *Management Accounting in Health Care Organizations,* San Francisco, Jossey Bass, 2008, Chapter 10.

2 Budget (or fiscal) years end in different months of the calendar year. In colleges and universities, for example, the fiscal year frequently ends on June 30. In many non-governmental organizations, the budget year is the calendar year. In the federal government, the fiscal year ends on September 30.

final decisions on the amounts to be spent for each program, and specifies the organizational units that are responsible for carrying out each program. In some organizations, these decisions take place within the context of basic decisions made during the programming phase of the management control process, but in most organizations there is no clean separation between programming and budgeting. Even organizations that have a well-developed programming phase occasionally discover circumstances during the budgeting phase that require revision of programming decisions. In organizations that do not have a clearly defined programming phase, program decisions are made as part of the budgeting phase.

Example In the town of Lexington, Massachusetts, program proposals and the operating budget were submitted simultaneously. The operating budget contained a line item called "capital," which was $1.5 million. In other parts of the document there were capital requests for "community preservation" ($5.8 million), recreation ($75,000), municipal projects ($3.8 million), water system improvements ($1.8 million), sewer system improvements ($100,000), school projects ($952,000), and public facility projects ($2 million). These requests totaled $14.5 million. Nowhere in the document was the $13 million discrepancy explained. Moreover, there were overlaps among the categories of proposed capital projects (e.g., school roofing, flooring, and other improvements were not included in the "school projects" category). It thus was very difficult for taxpayers (and probably some of the town's line managers) to understand the separation between programming and budgeting.[3]

Despite this overlap, it is useful to think about the two activities separately as they have different characteristics. As discussed in Chapter 7, programming decisions usually have multiyear consequences, and occasionally provide rough estimates of the associated revenues and costs. Budgeting, by contrast, requires careful estimates of revenues and expenses, and usually is formulated within a ceiling of estimated available resources. Moreover, since a budget is a plan against which actual performance is compared, senior management must be certain that it corresponds to the organization's responsibility centers. It then provides a basis for measuring the performance of each responsibility center manager. This can be complicated because, as discussed previously, some nonprofits have matrix structures where several departments are responsible for different aspects of a program. In these instances, if a program earns revenue, it should be designated as a profit center. Departments can then be established as either break-even profit centers or standard expense centers, with transfer prices used to account for the program's use of each department's resources. Under this sort of arrangement, program managers and department managers must interact on a regular basis.

Two-Stage Budgets

This chapter refers to the operating budget as if there were only one, which usually is the case. In government organizations, and in some other nonprofit organizations, there actually are two budgets: the legislative budget, which is essentially a request for funds, and the management budget, which is prepared after the legislature has decided on the amount of funds to be provided.

The focus here is on the management budget, which corresponds to the budget prepared in a for-profit company—a plan showing the amount of authorized spending for each responsibility center. If the amount of revenue is known within reasonable limits, the management budget can be an accurate reflection of the organization's profitability plans for the year.

[3] Town of Lexington, *Warrant to the 2010 Annual Town Meeting*, Lexington, Massachusetts, March 1, 2010.

Contrast with For-Profit Companies

Budgeting is an important part of the management control process in any organization. It is more important in a nonprofit organization than in a for-profit company, however, for two reasons: cost structure and spending flexibility.

Cost Structure. In a for-profit company, especially a manufacturing company, many costs are engineered. The amount of labor and the quantity of material required to manufacture products are determined within close limits by design and engineering specifications. Consequently, little can be done to affect these costs during the operational budgeting phase. By contrast, in most nonprofit organizations many costs are discretionary—the amount to be spent can vary widely depending on decisions made by managers and professionals. Many of these decisions are made during the budget formulation phase of the management control process.

Example Many hospitals have developed "clinical pathways" for patients with different diagnoses or diagnosis-related groups (DRGs). A clinical pathway is like an engineered cost, in that it specifies the ideal mix of resources for a "typical" patient with a given diagnosis: length of stay, lab and radiology tests, physical therapy, and so forth. However, unlike a manufacturing company, where the products of any given type are identical, all patients are not the same. Therefore senior management must be willing to accept some deviation from the standard. How much deviation, under what circumstances, and for what kinds of patients are topics that must be addressed during the budgeting phase.

Spending Flexibility. In a for-profit company, a budget is a fairly tentative statement of plans, and is subject to change as conditions change. Volume and mix of sales can change during the year, for example, and there is general agreement that managers need to react to such changes by making revised plans that are consistent with the overall objective of profitability.

In many nonprofit organizations, conditions are more stable and predictable. In a university, the number of students enrolled in September governs the pattern of spending for the whole year. A federal agency or a public school system has a certain authorized program or set of programs for the year that it must carry out. Under these circumstances, the budget is a fairly accurate statement of both the activities and resources to be used. It is therefore important to prepare the budget carefully. Significant time, including that of senior management, should be devoted to it.

MANAGERIAL CONTEXT FOR THE OPERATING BUDGET

Clearly budgeting has a mechanical aspect. Revenue forecasts must be made, the associated expenses must be estimated, and an overall budgeted surplus or deficit figure must be calculated. For organizations to use the budget as a managerial tool, however, they must view it from a broader perspective than just its mechanics. Let's look first at this "contextual perspective," and then use the resulting context as a basis for discussing the mechanical side of budgeting.

Organizational and Budgeting Contexts

Operational budgeting has both a formulation and a monitoring phase. In this chapter, our emphasis is on formulation. Nevertheless, to put operational budgeting in context, we need to look at both phases. Doing so allows us to view budgeting's mechanical and a behavioral aspects in a broader context. Further, the whole process exists in an organizational context that gives it a contingent nature, thereby explaining why different organizations have different approaches to budget formulation. This idea is shown schematically in Exhibit 8-1. To better understand it, let's examine some of the key elements, beginning with the organizational and budgeting contexts, and then moving to the budget formulation and monitoring activities.

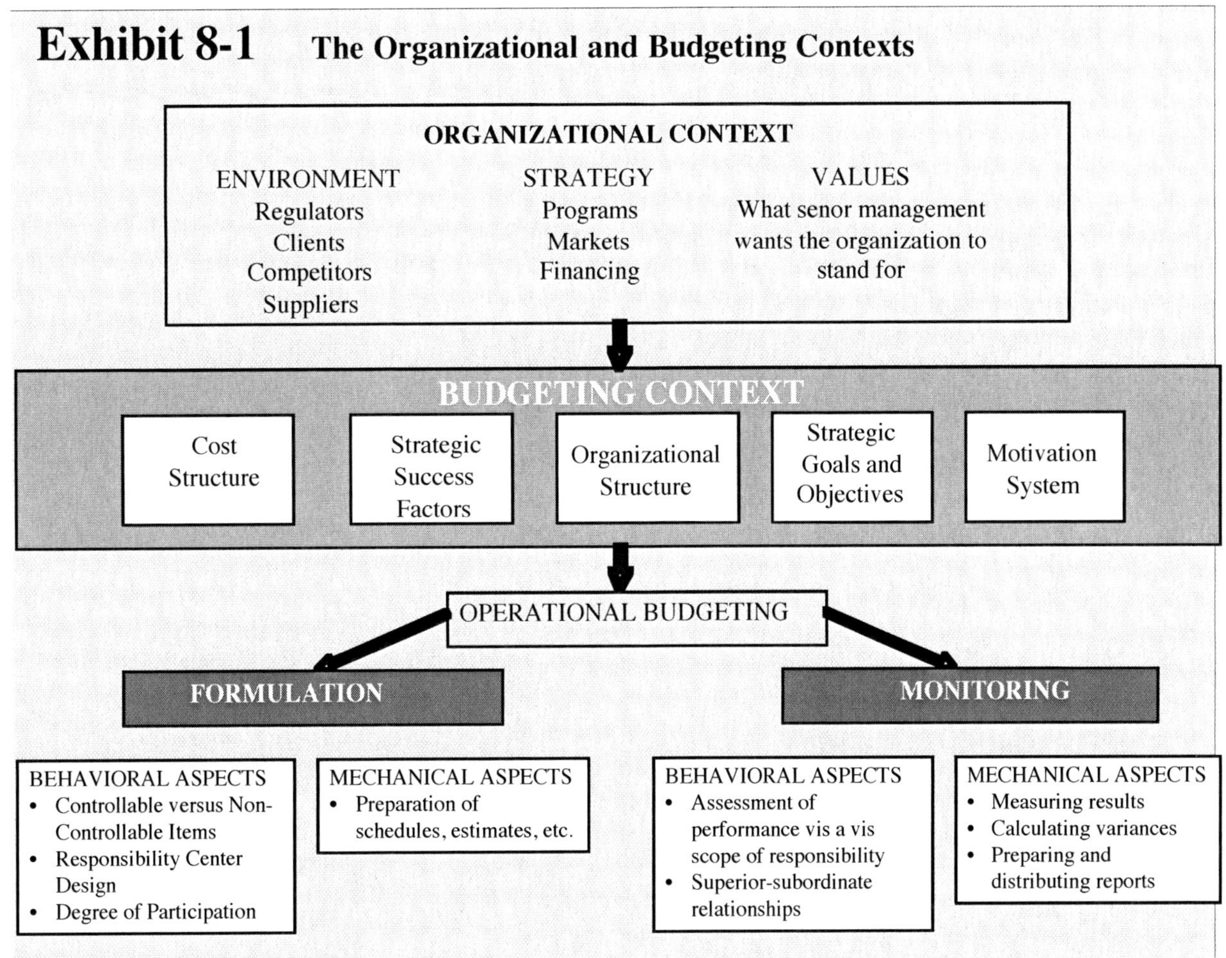

Organizational Context. One way of thinking about the context for a budget is in terms of the organization's environment, its strategy, and the values of its senior management team. Each is discussed below.

Environment. In many respects, an organization's environment governs much of what happens in the formulation of its operating budget. If, for example, an organization exists in a highly regulated environment, such as a public utility, its budget must be geared in part to the needs of the regulatory agencies and their constraints. On the other hand, if an organization operates in a highly competitive environment, as with, say, a municipal parking lot, it quite likely will need to use the budget to eliminate as much "slack" as possible. By contrast, an organization that is the sole provider of a particular service may not need to pay much attention to its costs.

Strategy. An organization's strategy also will have a great deal to do with the formulation of its operating budget. In part, strategy can be defined in terms of the organization's programs, the markets where it operates, and its sources of financing. As a result, there is a great deal of room for strategic differences among organizations that might otherwise appear quite similar. For example, a small community hospital with minimal capitation contracts would need a different budgetary process than a large teaching hospital that has many capitation contracts.

Values. Finally, senior management's values will influence the way the operating budget is formulated. If, for example, a university's senior management team values a highly collegial atmosphere among its faculty, it quite likely will have a different budgetary process than a university that thinks of its faculty as "hired help." In the former instance, department chairs might be expected to play an important role in formulating the budget, whereas in the latter, each would simply be given the department's budget.

Budgeting Context. The budgetary context arises out of the organizational context, and consists of at five features of the organization that will both influence and constrain the way the budget is prepared. The five features are cost structure, strategic success factors, organizational structure, programmatic goals and objectives, and motivation systems.

Cost Structure. An organization's environment, strategy, and values will influence its cost structure, which in turn will influence its budget. For example, a day care center that believes it is important to have a full-time, salaried labor force will have a different cost structure than one that uses many part-time, hourly workers. Full-time, salaried labor generally can be considered a fixed cost, whereas part-time, hourly workers can be thought of as variable costs.

Strategic Success Factors. Because of its environment and strategy, each organization will tend to have two or three activities that are crucial to its success. Attaining these strategic success factors ordinarily will influence the budget. For example, in many colleges and universities, a strategic success factor is average class size. Variations in this factor will have a major impact on the budget.

Organizational Structure. The way the organization is structured also will influence how it goes about formulating and monitoring its budget. Some nonprofits are organized into departments, while others have structures that are more product line- or program-based. Some organizations are highly authoritarian, while others are more collegial. All of these factors will influence how the budget is structured and who plays a role in its formulation and monitoring.

Strategic Goals and Objectives. Some organizations specify their strategic goals and objectives clearly, while others do not. When these goals and objectives are specified clearly, managers who are responsible for attaining them soon will begin to develop relationships between their attainment and the costs associated with doing so. When this happens, an organization has the opportunity to budget for both strategic goals and objectives, as well as revenues and expenses, and can begin to make tradeoffs among them.

Motivation Systems. Some organizations have reward systems that pay bonuses to key operating managers. Others encourage managers to behave in an entrepreneurial way, and provide extra budgetary resources to those who are successful. Clearly, there is a link between these kinds of motivation systems and the way the budget is formulated and monitored. Indeed, in many organizations, the budget is used along with actual results as a major performance evaluation tool. When this is the case, managers' annual bonuses, salary increases, and promotions may be closely linked to how well they performed against their budgets.

Budget Formulation. As indicated earlier, budget formulation has both mechanical and a behavioral aspects. We will look at the mechanical aspect in greater detail later in the chapter. For the moment, it is important to see it in its broader context.

Mechanical Aspect. From a purely mechanical perspective, schedules, estimates of revenues, hours, unit costs, and the like all must be made. In the last 35 years or so, the use of spreadsheet technology has greatly facilitated the mechanical side of budget formulation. Managers can incorporate key budget drivers into a spreadsheet program in such a way that "what if?" scenarios can be tested for their budgetary implications. Moreover, when spreadsheets are used, decisions made in budget meetings about reductions or increases can be incorporated into individual managers' budgets quickly and accurately.

Example A program director in a business school can relate a wide variety of expenses to the number of students enrolled in the program: curriculum materials, books, student travel, special memberships, etc. Most of the other expenses are fixed. When the number of students is changed, a spreadsheet can automatically recalculate tuition revenue and variable expenses, and determines the new contribution the program makes to its fixed expenses. The advantage of having the budget on a spreadsheet is that it allows the program director to calculate the budgetary implications of a variety of "what if?" scenarios. Moreover, the impact of changes in tuition or reductions in fixed expenses, can be assessed quickly and easily.

Behavioral Aspects. If a budget is to be useful as a management tool, its formulation must be more than a mechanical exercise, with arbitrary reductions across line items when the first pass leads to unacceptable results. Indeed, if the budgetary process is to be useful for managers at all levels in the organization, it must assist them in making a commitment to achieving a set of agreed-upon results. Because the "bottom line" in a nonprofit organization does not fully measure performance, these results need to be both strategic and financial. In most instances, if managers are to commit themselves to achieving the strategic and financial aspects of the budget, they must have some degree of participation in setting the budget targets. In this regard, it is essential for managers be held accountable for items they can control and not for those outside of their control.

The budget also can help different departments and divisions to communicate their plans and needs to each other, and it can help managers at all levels to anticipate potential problems. This *communication* aspect of the budgeting process is perhaps one of its most important benefits. When it is combined with the goal of managerial commitment, it gives the budget formulation process a significant behavioral aspect.

Budget Monitoring. The mechanical side of budget monitoring consists of measuring the same elements that were used to formulate the budget, and structuring the information in a way that is useful for review and action by program and department managers. In many instances, the most useful way to structure information is in terms of variances. In addition, however, this information must be distributed via regular reports to the appropriate managers and used by them for decision-making purposes. Variances and reports are discussed in Chapters 11 and 12.

In using information from the budget monitoring phase to assess the activities of their units, managers must carefully consider some important behavioral aspects of the process. Subordinates' performance should be assessed in terms of the scope of their responsibilities, and individuals should not be held accountable for variances that they cannot control. In carrying out this process, managers need to be careful not to put too much emphasis on the elimination of negative variances to the exclusion of the organization's more strategic objectives.

Example In a hospital, too much emphasis can be placed on reducing the negative variances in technician time per procedure in the radiology department. Technicians may respond by attempting to work faster, and in so doing may lower the level of quality of their work. As a result, many procedures may need to be redone, which both costs the hospital more and lowers the overall quality of patient care. This may result in considerable physician and patient dissatisfaction.

COMPONENTS OF THE OPERATING BUDGET

In all but the simplest of organizations, the budget is formulated in a context like the one shown in Exhibit 8-1. It also is formulated in light of the decisions that senior management has made about the organization's responsibility centers. For example, profit center managers will build their budgets differently from standard expense center managers, whose budgets will be different still from those of managers who run discretionary expense centers. These budgets will be quite different from those of managers of revenue centers. In general, however, the operating budget consists of three components: revenues, expenses and expenditures, and output measures.

Revenues

As discussed in Chapter 2, the general purpose of a nonprofit organization is to provide as much service as it can with available resources. In many nonprofit organizations, the total amount of resources (revenue) in any given budget year is, for all practical purposes, confined within quite narrow limits. The goal in preparing the operating budget, therefore, is to decide how best to spend it. This suggests that the basic approach should be to first estimate the available resources.

Most managers would agree that the policy of anticipating revenues first, and then budgeting expenses below or equal to them, is fiscally sound. The policy also provides a bulwark against arguments, often made by highly articulate and persuasive people, that an organizations should undertake a program even though it cannot afford to do so.

In federal or state governments, application of this principle requires that managers make careful estimates of the level of funds that the legislature is likely to appropriate. In state and municipal governments, it requires judgment as to feasible taxation and other revenues. In other organizations, it requires estimating the revenues to be derived from a variety of sources.

Discipline Required for a Revenue-First Policy. Carrying out a revenue-first policy requires considerable discipline in two respects. First, it requires a careful and prudent estimate of total revenues from all sources, including client fees, gifts, grants, contracts, third-party payments, and endowment earnings. Once this figure has been established, it is "locked in."

Second, it requires a commitment to engage in cost cutting if the first approximation to the budget indicates a deficit. Although the least painful course of action is to anticipate additional sources of revenue that will eliminate the deficit, this is a highly dangerous course of action. If the original revenue estimates were made carefully, all feasible sources were included. New ideas that arise subsequently may produce additional revenue, but the evidence that they will do so frequently is not strong. The safer course of action is to take whatever steps are necessary to reduce expenses so as to bring them into balance with revenues.

Examples Some churches and religious organizations have a "God will provide" approach to budgeting. Many have discovered, much to their dismay, that the Lord works in mysterious ways.

During one fiscal year, the Baltimore Ballet budgeted its expenses first, and then compared them with estimates of earned revenue. The excess of expenses over revenue was labeled "to be raised" through contributions. The sum was overly optimistic as were estimates of earned revenue. Although monthly statements indicated unfavorable revenue and expense variances, no corrective action was taken for eight months. The result was a deficit of several hundred thousand dollars.[4]

Exceptions to the Revenue-First Policy. The policy that budgeted revenue sets the limit on expenses is not applicable under certain conditions. Some of these are discussed below.

The Federal Budget. The considerations discussed above do not apply to the federal budget, which may have either a surplus or a deficit. The amount of either is determined by the administration's conclusion (with the concurrence of Congress) as to the proper fiscal policy in a given year. The federal government rarely plans for a balanced budget.

Discretionary Revenue. In some organizations, management has an ability to increase revenues. For example, it may be able to undertake an intensified fundraising effort so as to increase gifts and donations. This idea of "spending money to make money" is the nonprofit counterpart of a for-profit company's marketing budget. To the extent that this argument is valid, it is appropriate to speak of discretionary revenue as well as discretionary expenses.

Such opportunities are not of major significance in many nonprofits, however. In most situations, the organization has already used all the fund-raising devices it can think of, and managers must take the revenues from such efforts as a given.

Anticipated Revenue. Some organizations, such as universities, research institutes, and social service agencies include anticipated grant revenues in their budgets. This is because they frequently apply for grants, but do not learn whether the funds will be approved until well into the fiscal year. If the budget were prepared only on the basis of *known* revenues, key professional staff might be laid off, obtain employment elsewhere, and not be available when the grant is awarded. Thus, some organizations decide to incur deficits in anticipation of receiving grant awards. Such a strategy is risky, and clearly can be sustained only if grants of sufficient magnitude are received.

Example Some years ago, New York University embarked on a major expansion program. Substantial amounts of additional revenue were obtained from additional enrollments, fund-raising campaigns, and government grants. Several years later, funds from these sources began to shrink. Instead of cutting costs to meet the lower level of revenues, however, deficits were permitted, which reached a peak of $14 million. Drastic steps were finally taken to bring costs in line with revenues, but by then a considerable portion of the university's capital had been dissipated.[5]

Short-Run Fluctuations. When managers expect short-term revenue fluctuations around an average, it is appropriate to budget for the average revenue, rather than for a specific level of revenue anticipated in a given year. In some years expenses may exceed revenue and in others revenue will exceed expenses. Over time, the two should net out. Indeed, some nonprofit organizations con-

[4] From a report by Rosemary Dougherty (personal correspondence).

[5] Condensed from a report in *Science,* December 8, 1972.

sciously adopt a "counter-cyclical" fiscal policy. They reason that when the economy is in a downswing, more clients who cannot pay will need their services, with the opposite effect taking place during an economic expansion. Thus they plan to incur deficits in bad times and surpluses during good times. Clearly, this strategy must be carefully managed to make sure the organization can, in fact, weather the bad times.

The Promoter. Occasionally, the amount of resources available can be increased by a dynamic individual. The governing board then may authorize an operating budget with a deficit in anticipation of the new resources that the promoter will bring in. Such a decision obviously is a gamble. If it works, the organization may be elevated to a permanently higher plateau. If it does not, painful cutbacks may be needed to bring expenses back in line with revenues.

Deliberate Capital Erosion. There are situations in which the current revenue is deliberately not regarded as a ceiling, and part of the organization's permanent capital is used for current operations. This may represent a gamble in anticipation of new resources, or it may reflect a conscious policy to go out of business after the capital has been consumed.

In effect, any budget with a deficit consumes permanent capital. Thus, decisions to use permanent capital for current operations should be made with great care. No organization can live beyond its means indefinitely.

Example One university had its schools organized as profit centers. Each school was responsible for achieving a balanced budget every year. One year, when one of the schools was facing its third substantial deficit in three years, the university's central administration informed the school's dean that if there were a deficit this year, it would be financed with the principal from the school's endowment. Faced with the prospect of capital erosion, the dean balanced the budget.

Preliminary Versus Final Budgets. Some colleges and private schools approve a *preliminary* budget in early summer, just prior to the beginning of their fiscal year (usually on July 1). This gives department heads the spending authority needed to prepare for fall classes. In September, when actual enrollments are known with almost total certainty, each department head prepares a final budget, which uses total revenue as the ceiling for total expenses. Such a process works well if the total revenue is known with reasonable certainty early in the fiscal year, and if line managers have enough discretionary items in their budgets (such as part-time faculty) so they can make reductions in expenses if necessary.

Hard and Soft Money. A college with a reasonable expectation of meeting its enrollment quota can count on a certain amount of tuition revenue; this is *hard money*. Income from endowment investments is also hard money. It is prudent to make long-term commitments such as tenured faculty appointments, when they will be financed with hard money. By contrast, revenue from annual gifts or short-lived grants for research projects is *soft money*. In an economic downturn, gifts may drop drastically and grantors may decide not to renew their grants. Managers must be careful about making long-term commitments that are financed with soft money.

Expenses and Expenditures

There are two general formats for the spending portion of the budget. The traditional format, called the *line-item budget*, focuses on expense elements, such as wages, fringe benefits, supplies, and other similar resources. The other format, called a *program budget*, focuses on programs and program elements. The contrast between the two was shown in Exhibit 6-3. Importantly, although the focus of a program budget is on programs, there almost always is a line-item listing of the appropriate expense elements within each program or program element.

The program budget permits a decision maker to judge the appropriate amount of resources for each activity. It also permits senior management to match spending with measures of each activity's planned outputs. These are important advantages of the program budget format.

Link to the Capital Budget. If the operating budget is prepared on an expenditure (rather than expense) basis, it may include amounts for equipment and other long-lived assets. When this is the case, only buildings and major capital acquisitions will be included in the capital budget. Minor capital items, such as computers, photocopying equipment, and the like will be contained in the operating budget, even though their economic lives extend over several years. Often the magnitude of the expenditure dictates which budget is used. For example, a nonprofit's governing body might require that any asset costing more than, say, $5,000 be included in the capital budget.

When the operating budget is prepared on an expenditure basis, senior management should make a clear distinction between expenditures and expenses. Otherwise, there is a temptation to balance the operating budget by moving some expenditures from it into the capital budget, rather than reducing expenses.

Example Some years ago, officials in New York City made many maneuvers to hide the city's true operating deficit. One was shifting operating items to the capital budget, where they presumably would be financed by bonds rather than current revenues. An extreme example was vocational education expenses, which were shifted to the capital budget on the grounds that students would reap the benefits for many years, and that vocational education therefore was a long-lived asset!

There also may be a temptation to sell some assets to provide the funds needed for the operating budget. In general, however, such an activity is dangerous as it constitutes a one-time solution only, and therefore only postpones to future years the need to find a more permanent solution

Output Measures

The third component of the operating budget is information on planned outputs. As will be discussed in Chapter 10, output information usually consists of process and results measures. Some organizations commit themselves to specific targets for each as part of the budgetary process.

Examples In one public school system, principals' budgets were determined in part by a combination of expected enrollments and centrally mandated student-to-teacher ratios, which are *process measures*. The principals also committed themselves to achieving certain levels of reading scores for students completing different grades. Senior management believed that these *results measures* indicated, in part, how well teachers achieved the school system's objectives.

An article on university budgeting listed several output criteria that could be used to determine merit salary increments for faculty: dollar amounts of research grants generated, number of Ph.D.s graduated, number of publications in refereed journals, and teaching quality.[6] These criteria can help link the budget to the university's objectives.

---

[6] Allen G. Schick, "University Budgeting: Administrative Perspective Budget Structure, and Budget Process," *Academy of Management Review,* 10, No. 4 (1985), pp. 794-802.

STEPS IN FORMULATING THE OPERATING BUDGET

Although each organization formulates its operating budget somewhat differently from all others, the mechanical aspect of the effort generally follows a timetable, which typically includes five steps. Each is discussed below.

Step 1. Disseminating Guidelines

Senior management usually begins the process by distributing a set of guidelines for managers to follow in preparing their budgets. These guidelines include dates when various documents are due. Sometimes managers are asked to submit partial budgets (such as revenue budgets) to headquarters (or division headquarters, depending on the size of the organization) before preparing the remainder of their budgets. Sometimes, managers are asked to submit only complete budgets.

If approved programs exist, one guideline is that the budget should be consistent with them. This does not necessarily mean that the budget should consist only of approved programs, since this can be frustrating for operating managers. Indeed, desirable innovations may come to light if managers are permitted to propose activities that are not part of approved programs. These improved activities should be clearly distinguished from those in the approved programs, however, and operating managers should understand that the chances for approval of new programs during budget formulation are slight. Otherwise, senior management may be downgrading the programming phase of the process.

Senior management also must make sure that operating managers are aware of any other constraints that exist, such as a requirement that the budget not be for more than 105 percent of the prior year's budget. Constraints also can be quite detailed, such as stipulating that the budget must be consistent with: (1) planned changes in the organization's activities, (2) senior management's assumptions about wage rates and other input prices, (3) the conditions under which new employees may be recruited, (4) the number of employees who may be promoted, (5) expected productivity gains, and/or (6) services to be provided by support centers and the corresponding transfer prices.

In addition, there often are guidelines about the format and content of the proposed budget. These are intended to ensure that the budget estimates are submitted in a fashion that both facilitates analysis and permits their subsequent use in comparing actual to planned performance.

Step 2. Preparing the Revenue Budgets

For managers of profit centers, the first step usually is to prepare a revenue budget. Doing so provides the organization with some reasonable assurance that anticipated revenue is based on the market. If expenses were estimated first, there could be a tendency to assume that revenue would be high enough to cover them, which might be unrealistic.

In preparing the revenue budget, the manager of each profit center in a large organization may ask his or her revenue centers to estimate their revenues for the year. If a profit center is responsible for one or more programs, the profit center manager may ask each program manager to estimate the revenues for his or her program. Conversely, if the organization has a program structure, each program manager will need to prepare an estimate of his or her program's revenue, which is sent directly to senior management.

Sometimes revenue estimates are evaluated by senior management's staff to assure that they are realistic in light of general economic conditions, competitive forces, production capabilities, and so forth. In large, complex organizations, revenue budgets contain considerable detail on exactly what types of services or goods will be sold, in what quantities, and where. These projections may go through divisional management for approval before being sent to senior management.

Step 3. Preparing Expense Budgets for Profit and Standard Expense Centers

Each program's expense budget usually is constructed by beginning with the volume and mix estimates used for the revenue budget, and attaching variable cost elements to the units. The results are multiplied to give total variable costs, after which the appropriate step-function costs and fixed costs are added. In the case of a standard expense center, although no revenue is received, the manager still will need to estimate expenses by beginning with the anticipated volume and mix of its outputs.

Examples In a prison cafeteria, the total variable cost for food can be estimated by using the average variable cost per meal, multiplied by the number of meals a day and the number of inmates. If the variable cost is different for each meal (breakfast versus lunch and dinner), a mix factor will be needed. To this total can be added the step-function costs of the cafeteria's service personnel, various nonfood supply costs, and the cafeteria's fixed costs.

In a welfare office, if the number of cases can be predicted, the budget for social worker salaries can be obtained by using a standard workload factor (cases per social worker) multiplied by the average salary of a social worker. If there are are different levels of social workers (MSW versus BA, for example), a mix factor will be needed, with the possibility that each level will have a different workload factor. To this total can be added the fixed costs of the office.

In a research program, the expense budget may be prepared by estimating the number of professional work years, and by estimating the personnel-related costs per work year.

Step 4. Preparing Expense Budgets for Discretionary Expense Centers

The manager of each discretionary expense center prepares a budget for the center's expenses. Since these expenses are unrelated to volume or mix of outputs, the budget is a fixed amount, based on assumptions about the kinds and amounts of activities that staff will need to engage in during the year. For example, if litigation is pending, the budget for legal services might be higher this year than last. Or if there are plans to undertake a major revision of the management information system, the budget might be higher. Similarly, if activities that took place last year won't take place this year, the budget should be reduced.

Step 5. Preparing the Master Budget

The various profit center budgets are assembled to determine the forecasted contribution to standard and discretionary expense centers for the year. Standard and discretionary expense center budgets are then subtracted to give the overall surplus. This budget usually is taken to the board of directors for approval.

If the master budget is not approved (usually because the surplus is not sufficiently high, but sometimes because some flaws in forecasts are identified), it may be returned to one or more responsibility center managers for reworking. For reasons discussed earlier, profit center managers usually are not permitted to adjust their revenue forecasts. Instead, they (and sometimes standard and discretionary expense center managers) must reduce their expenses. Reduced expenses in a profit or standard expense center can be achieved by either lowering fixed costs or variable costs per unit, but ordinarily not by assuming a different volume or mix of output.

Exhibit 8-2 shows how these various pieces might be brought together in a hospital. As it indicates, *clinical care departments* (such as surgery and medicine) forecast the number and mix of patients they will serve as well as the payer mix and prices for each case type. They also forecast the resources they will use to treat each case, such as the length of stay (LOS), radiology procedures, lab tests, and so forth. And they forecast the resources they will need from the patient service departments, such as laundry, housekeeping, medical records, and dietary.

The *clinical service departments* (such as radiology) and *patient service departments* (such as dietary) are treated as standard expense centers. They compute their variable costs and arrive at a transfer price for each of their services. The transfer price for each service is combined with the resources needed by the clinical care departments to treat each case, which leads to the budgeted variable cost per case type (or DRG). After each clinical care department's step-function and fixed costs are subtracted, the result is its contribution to the hospital's surplus.

From the sum of the contributions from all clinical care departments, the hospital subtracts the step and fixed costs of its clinical service and patient service departments, which gives the contribution to the administrative service departments (which are discretionary expense centers). The final result is the hospital's surplus (or deficit).

Important Features

The above process is only a rough guide to what actually happens in most organizations, and there are many variations on the general theme. Despite the specific approach an organization takes, however, there are several important features associated with preparing the operating budget:

- *The budget is taken seriously by senior management.* Senior management is involved in budget meetings with key managers and in setting the tone for the process. It does not turn the budget process over to the controller, but instead relies on the controller to assemble the information and to conduct any needed analyses.

- *The timetable remains roughly the same each year.* It is adhered to closely so that managers and others who are involved know what to expect and when.

- *Staff analyses are used as a check.* They are conducted principally by personnel in the controller's office, and are designed to verify (or contradict) forecasts by responsibility center mangers and their staffs. When staff analyses contradict a forecast, neither is allowed to dominate the decision-making. Instead, areas of disagreement are identified, discussed, and resolved. Where corporate staff and operating managers cannot resolve their differences, senior management makes the final decisions.

- *There is a negotiation phase.* Operating managers have an opportunity to present their case to senior management, and to defend their forecasts.

- *The final budget represents a serious commitment.* Operating managers commit to achieving the budgeted level of surplus, usually with the stipulation that highly unusual circumstances can result in a budget revision, but nothing else. Highly unusual circumstances can include acts of nature (such as floods) or events such as fires, prolonged strikes, or major economic events.

Exhibit 8-2 Budgeting in a Hospital

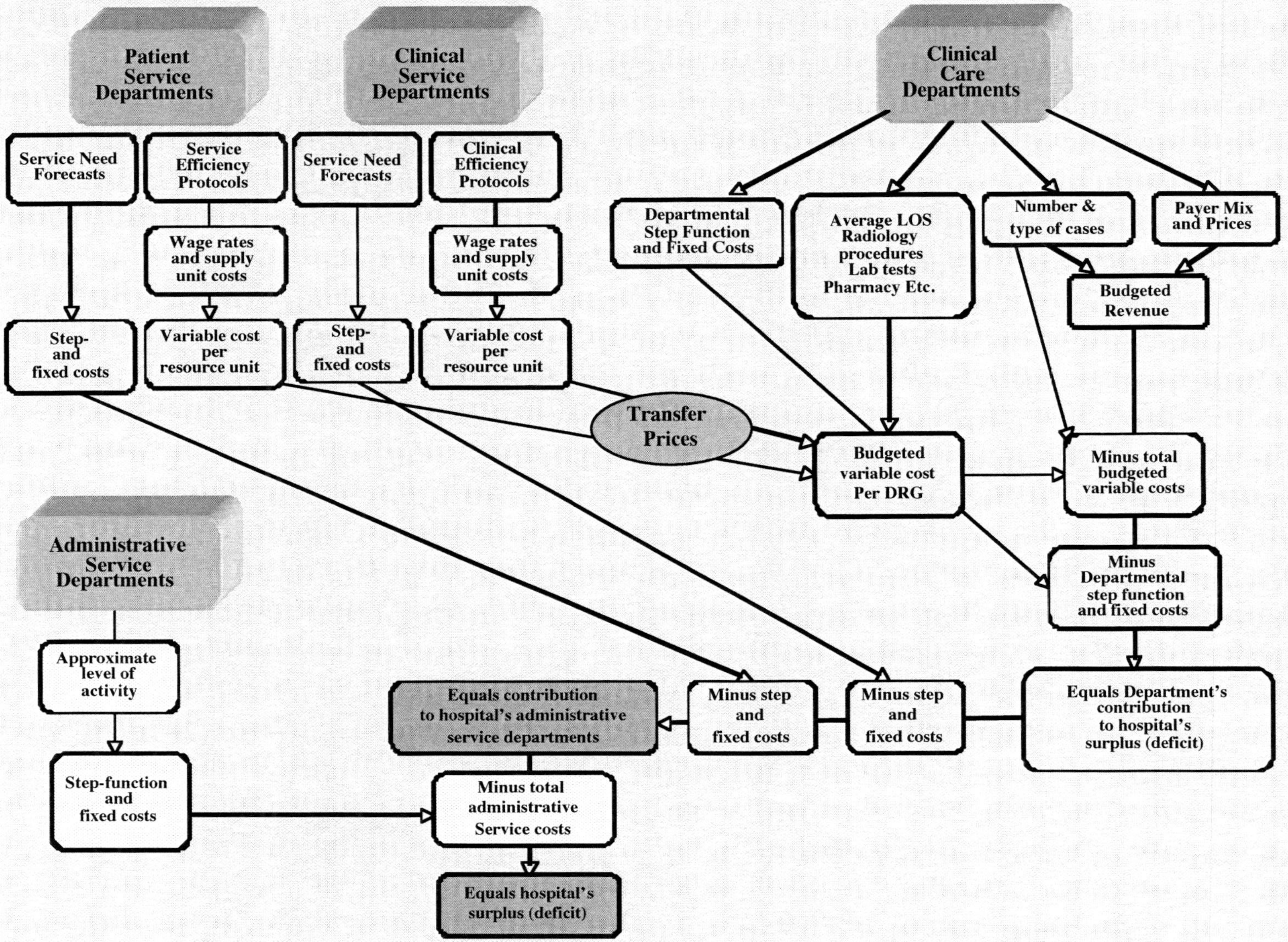

- *Within operating units or programs, budgets also represent serious commitments.* Sometimes these commitments are different than the division's commitment to senior management. For example, managers of standard expense centers are expected to adhere to budgeted levels of unit variable costs and total fixed costs, but not to total costs, since total costs will be affected by the volume and mix of output (which is not under their control). Revenue center managers, on the other hand, are expected to adhere to budgeted revenue forecasts. They may be allowed to change the volume and mix of sales, as long as total revenue forecasts are met.

RELATED ORGANIZATIONAL ASPECTS

There are several organizational aspects that bear upon the budget formulation activity in many organizations, some of which are more applicable to nonprofits than others.

Expense Creep

There is a tendency for support costs to creep upward, especially in affluent organizations. Because of this, staff analysts need to make special efforts to detect and eliminate unnecessary increases in these costs. If unit costs or ratios can be calculated, comparison can be made with similar numbers in other responsibility centers or with external benchmarks. In the absence of such comparison bases, analysts may use historical ratios to help get a feel for the nature of the changes and whether they are reasonable.

This problem is particularly troublesome in responsibility centers whose output cannot be reliably measured (such as a human resources department). Under these circumstances, not only are budgetees motivated to acquire as many resources as they can, but it is extremely difficult for senior management to measure the effectiveness of their resource use.

Behavioral Issues

The negotiation phase of the budget formulation effort, tends to be *zero-sum* in many organizations, with each budgetee negotiating for a larger slice of the fixed budget pie. In instances where resources are not abundant, such an arrangement generally produces a great deal of conflict and game playing by budgetees. Appendix 8-A discusses some of the games (called "budged ploys") used by budgetees and their superiors.

Example One study of budget game playing identified five major activities: (1) understating volume estimates, (2) undeclared or understated price increases, (3) undeclared or understated cost reduction possibilities, (4) overstated expenses (such as for research), and (5) undeclared shift in a program's mix. A principal reason given by one manager was "senior management just doesn't have time for checking every number you put into your plans . . . so one strategy is to 'pad' everything. If you're lucky, you'll still have 50 percent of your cushions after the plan reviews."

Conflict and game playing can be mitigated somewhat if there is a culture with some well-established norms. In some organizations, these norms include: (1) trust between supervisors and their subordinates, (2) an assumption of competence, goodwill, and honesty on everyone's part, (3) a recognition that disagreements do not mean threats, (4) a spirit of openness and sharing of information, (5) a willingness to allow subordinates to develop their own solutions to budget-related problems, and (6) confidence in the computations and other work of staff analysts. This sort of culture is somewhat rare in most nonprofit organizations.

Role of Professionals

The role of professionals is a particularly important factor in nonprofit organizations. In a hospital, for example, the budgetee may be a physician and the supervisor a hospital administrator. Physicians are primarily interested in maintaining or improving the quality of patient care, improving the status of the hospital as perceived by their peers, and increasing their own prestige. Their interest in the amount of costs involved generally is secondary. By contrast, hospital administrators are primarily interested in costs, although they realize that costs must not be so low that the quality of care or the status of the hospital is impaired. Thus, the two parties weight the relevant factors considerably differently.

Use of Models

Many budgetary analyses can benefit from a model that describes the underlying variables and the relationships among them. Such a model need not be complicated, and frequently can be prepared with a relatively simple spreadsheet. Exhibit 8-3 shows how a model might be designed for the budget process described in Exhibit 8-2. The categories have been simplified (only four DRGs, for example and only four service departments), and the numbers are hypothetical. It would be rather easy to increase the number of categories and service departments, however, and to insert actual numbers.

Once the appropriate number of DRGs, service departments, and costs have been included, the consequences of budgetary decisions can be seen in terms of their impact on the hospital's surplus. If the surplus is too small, or if there is a deficit, the options available (other than increasing prices, changing payer mix, changing case mix, or increasing volume) are the following: (1) change the treatment patterns for a given case type, (2) decrease the variable cost per resource unit, (3) decrease step-function and/or fixed costs in clinical care departments, clinical service departments, or patient service departments, or (4) decrease costs in the administrative service departments. With a properly designed spreadsheet, the impact on the hospital's surplus of various options can be explored rather easily. Similar models can be constructed for many nonprofit organizations. Exhibit 8-4, on page 190, shows how such a model might be designed for a college.

BUDGETING MISFITS

The budgetary process is not only an integral part of an organization, but an essential ingredient in its success. The role of budgeting depends to a large extent on its fit with a variety of other organizational elements, however. For this reason, the failure of the budget to play a useful role in some organizations might be assessed in terms of "misfits" with these other elements.

Misfit #1: Between the Cost Structure and the Budget Formulation Phase

Budget formulation frequently is not built around the organization's cost structure. For example, many nonprofit organizations—particularly those in the health and human services—are reimbursed by the public sector (or third-party payers) via a per-diem rate. Although the rate is designed to cover three types of costs—fixed, step-function, and variable—it ordinarily is based exclusively on volume, i.e., units of service or care provided. Since fixed costs and a portion of step-function costs are time-based, i.e., dependent on the passage of time, not on the number of units of service provided, there is a misfit between the payment system and the cost structure.

Exhibit 8-3 Model for the Master Budget in a Hospital (Part A)

	Case Mix				
	DRG A	DRG B	DRG C	DRG D	Total
FORECAST REVENUE					
DEPARTMENT #1					
PAYER #1					
Forecast number of cases	60	200	100	50	
Expected revenue per case	$7,350	$1,430	$2,020	$7,650	
Total Revenue	$441,000	$286,000	$202,000	$382,500	$1,311,500
PAYER #2					
Forecast number of cases	100	50	300	150	
Expected revenue per case	$6,800	$1,500	$3,000	$7,400	
Total Revenue	$680,000	$75,000	$900,000	$1,110,000	$2,765,000
TOTAL REVENUE					$4,076,500
DEFINE CLINICAL PATHWAYS	DRG A	DRG B	DRG C	DRG D	
Resources from Clinical Service Departments					
No. of patient days per case	10	5	6	12	
No. of x-rays per case	5	1	2	3	
No. of CBCs per case	10	5	3	12	
Resources from Patient Service Departments					
No. of meals per case	30	15	18	36	
No. of pounds of laundry per case	15	7.5	9	18	
No. of medical records per case	1	1	1	1	
STEP FUNCTION AND FIXED COSTS AT FORECAST VOLUME AND MIX					
Step-function costs (e.g., nursing)					$1,000,000
Fixed costs (e.g. departmental administration)					1,500,000
TOTAL STEP AND FIXED COSTS AT ESTIMATED VOLUME AND MI:					$2,500,000
DETERMINE VARIABLE COST PER RESOURCE UNIT					
CLINICAL SERVICE DEPARTMENTS	DRG A	DRG B	DRG C	DRG D	
CLINICAL EFFICIENCY PROTOCOLS					
No. nursing minutes per patient day	60	40	50	40	
No. technician minutes per x-ray	40	40	40	40	
No. technician minutes per CBC	20	20	20	20	
No. units of nursing supplies per patient day	10	3	5	8	
No. units of supplies per x-ray	3	3	3	3	
No. units of supplies per CBC	4	4	4	4	
WAGE RAGES AND UNIT SUPPLY COSTS					
Cost per minute for nurses	$0.50	$0.50	$0.50	$0.50	
Cost per minute for x-ray technicians	$0.20	$0.20	$0.20	$0.20	
Cost per minute for lab technicians	$0.20	$0.20	$0.20	$0.20	
Cost per unit for nursing supplies	$3.50	$3.50	$3.50	$3.50	
Cost per unit for x-ray supplies	$5.00	$5.00	$5.00	$5.00	
Cost per unit for CBC supplies	$2.00	$2.00	$2.00	$2.00	
VARIABLE COST (TRANSFER PRICE) PER RESOURCE UNIT IN CLINICAL SERVICE DEPARTMENTS					
Patient day	$65	$31	$43	$48	
X-Ray	$23	$23	$23	$23	
CBC	$12	$12	$12	$12	
PATIENT SERVICE DEPARTMENTS	**DRG A**	**DRG B**	**DRG C**	**DRG D**	
SERVICE EFFICIENCY PROTOCOLS					
No. minutes per meal	10	10	10	10	
No. minutes per pound of laundry	1	1	1	1	
No. minutes per medical record	5	5	5	5	
No. units of ingredients per meal	5	5	5	5	
No. units of laundry supplies per pound	3	3	3	3	
No. units of supplies per medical record	2	2	2	2	
WAGE RAGES AND UNIT SUPPLY COSTS					
Cost per minute for meals	$0.25	$0.25	$0.25	$0.25	
Cost per minute for laundry	$0.15	$0.15	$0.15	$0.15	
Cost per minute for medical records	$0.30	$0.30	$0.30	$0.30	
Cost per unit for dietary supplies	$1.50	$1.50	$1.50	$1.50	
Cost per unit for laundry supplies	$0.30	$0.30	$0.30	$0.30	
Cost per unit for medical record supplies	$1.00	$1.00	$1.00	$1.00	
VARIABLE COST (TRANSFER PRICE) PER RESOURCE UNIT IN PATIENT SERVICE DEPARTMENTS					
Meals	$10	$10	$10	$10	
Laundry	$1	$1	$1	$1	
Medical Records	$4	$4	$4	$4	

Exhibit 8-3 Model for the Master Budget in a Hospital (Part B)

ESTIMATE SERVICE DEPARTMENT STEP AND FIXED COSTS AT FORECASTED VOLUME					
CLINICAL SERVICE DEPARTMENTS			**STEP**	**FIXED**	**TOTAL**
Nursing			$350,000	$700,000	$1,050,000
Radiology			250,000	800,000	1,050,000
Laboratory			320,000	600,000	920,000
Total					$3,020,000
PATIENT SERVICE DEPARTMENTS			**STEP**	**FIXED**	**TOTAL**
Dietary			$180,000	$600,000	$780,000
Laundry			100,000	400,000	500,000
Medical Records			150,000	300,000	450,000
Total					$1,730,000
CALCULATE VARIABLE COST/CASE	**DRG A**	**DRG B**	**DRG C**	**DRG D**	
From Clinical Service Departments					
Nursing	$650	$153	$255	$576	
Radiology	115	23	46	69	
Laboratory	120	60	36	144	
From Patient Service Departments					
Dietary	$300	$150	$180	$360	
Laundry	16	8	9	19	
Medical Records	4	4	4	4	
TOTAL VARIABLE COST PER CASE	$1,204	$397	$530	$1,171	
COMPUTE THE SURPLUS (DEFICIT) FOR EACH CLINICAL CARE DEPARTMENT					
Revenue	$1,121,000	$361,000	$1,102,000	$1,492,500	
Minus Variable Costs	192,680	99,219	211,980	234,280	
Equals Contribution to Step and Fixed	$928,320	$261,781	$890,020	$1,258,220	$3,338,341
Minus Step and Fixed Costs					2,500,000
Equals Contribution to Clinical and Patient Service Step and Fixed Costs					$838,341
COMPUTE CONTRIBUTION TO HOSPITAL OVERHEAD					
Contribution from Clinical Care Departments (assumes 10 with same contribution)					$8,383,413
Minus Step and Fixed Costs of Clinical Service Departments					3,020,000
Minus Step and Fixed Costs of Patient Service Departments					1,730,000
Equals Contribution to Hospital Overhead					$3,633,413
ESTIMATE ADMINISTRATIVE SERVICE COSTS			**STEP**	**FIXED**	**TOTAL**
Legal			$250,000	$300,000	$550,000
Human Resources			300,000	600,000	900,000
Fiscal Affairs			300,000	850,000	1,150,000
Total					$2,600,000
COMPUTE HOSPITAL'S CLINICAL SURPLUS (DEFICIT)					
Contribution to Hospital Overhead					$3,633,413
Minus Estimated Administrative Costs					2,600,000
Equals Hospital's Surplus (Deficit)					$1,033,413

The resolution of this dilemma consists of holding managers responsible only for those costs over which they exercise reasonable control, resulting in a need to distinguish between controllable and non-controllable costs. While some fixed costs are controllable in a budget period, many others are not. They exist because the organization has committed itself to be "ready to serve," and will continue to exist even if no units of service are provided. The classic examples of this situation are fire departments and hospital emergency rooms.[7] By contrast, most variable costs and some step-

7 The classic solution to this problem is a two-part transfer price. It has been used extensively in industry (Solomons, 1965) but has seen almost no application in the nonprofit sector. For a discussion of its applicability to integrated delivery systems in health care, see David W. Young, "Two-Part Transfer Pricing Improves IDS Financial Control," *Healthcare Financial Management*, August 1998.

function costs *are* controllable, but only on a *per-unit* basis. As a result, while a manager can be asked to control variable costs per unit, he or she cannot be expected to control total variable costs. Total variable costs are affected by volume, which frequently is outside the manager's control.

Example A budget for snow removal will never be completely accurate because weather conditions will dictate the amount of snow to be removed. A city or town therefore should budget for the average amount of snow to be removed, knowing that in some years the actual amount will be below the budget and in some it will exceed the budget.

Exhibit 8-4 Budget Model for a University

Line I.D. Formula	Name of Variable	Value
a	Number of students	1,700
b	Number of course sections per student per year	12
c	Average number or students per section	25
d = (a x b) ÷ c	Number of sections offered per year	816
e	Number of FTE faculty	200
f	Number of sections per FTE teaching faculty per year	6
g = (d ÷ f)	Number of FTE teaching faculty needed per year	136
h = f - g	Number of FTE non-teaching faculty per year (sabbaticals, research buyouts, slippage)	64
i	Average compensation per faculty	$80,000
j = e * i	Total faculty compensation	$16,000,000
k	Instruction cost other than faculty compensation (e.g., faculty support staff, admissions, registrar, career center)	$10,000,000
l = j + k	Total instruction cost	$26,000,000
m	Non-tuition revenue available for instruction (e.g., earnings from endowment)	$1,700,000
n = l - m	Tuition revenue needed	$24,300,000
	Management Decisions	
Option #1	Tuition is dependent variable	
o = n ÷ a	Tuition per student	$14,294
Option #2	Number of students is the dependent variable	
p	Tuition is fixed at	$12,000
q = n ÷ p	Number of students needed	2,025

Misfit #2: Between the Cost Structure and the Budget Monitoring Phase

In the budget monitoring phase, a misfit exists when the reporting system does not adequately specify the reasons underlying a variance between budgeted and actual figures. Although an accounting technique called variance analysis has been developed to distinguish among these different cost drivers, it is not always utilized. As a result, managers frequently find it extremely difficult to determine the reasons underlying a deviation between budgeted and actual performance. Variance analysis is discussed in Chapter 11.

Misfit #3: Between Strategic Success Factors and the Budgetary Process

Most organizations can identify one or two factors that are crucial to their success. For a health maintenance organization, it is hospital days used per thousand enrollees; for a fire department it is response time; for an organization selling newsletters, it is renewal rate; for a university, it is "yield," i.e., matriculants as a percent of accepted applicants. Serious misfits can occur when these critical success factors are excluded from the budgetary process. A fire department that does not include response time estimates in its budgeting effort quite likely will find that it has difficulty making tradeoffs between operating costs and its overall measures of performance, such as loss of lives and property. Similarly, many HMOs have encountered serious financial problems when their hospitalization rates per 1,000 enrollees exceeded budgeted levels. A university that does not build yield into its budget also can be expected to face budgetary problems, since revenue can fluctuate greatly with only a small change in yield.

Example The Pleasant Street Home Health Agency charges $60 per visit and has a staff of 50 nurses. Nurses make an average of 6 visits a day. If there is a change to an average of 6.1 visits a day (about a 1.7 percent increase) per nurse over the course of a year, revenue changes by $72,000, which can be a substantial sum for an agency such as this. Calculations are as follows:

Change in average visits per nurse (6.1 - 6.0)	=	0.1
Number of work days in a year	=	240
Number of nurses	=	50
Revenue per visit	=	$60
Change in revenue (0.1 x 240 x 50 x $60)	=	$72,000

Misfit #4: Between the Organizational Structure and the Budgetary Process

Many organizations are organized into product lines, and many departments within an organization are organized into sub-departments. Occasionally, however, the budget is not prepared in accordance with this structure. As a result, managers who make decisions that can affect the budget frequently do not have appropriate budgetary responsibility. Situations of this sort can exist between, say, the support departments in a hospital (housekeeping, laundry, and the like) and the "mission" departments (medical/surgical, and outpatient clinics). Problems can occur when a mission department's costs are affected by the costs in several service departments, but when the managers of service department have no budgetary responsibility for the costs in their departments.

Misfits also can occur when budgetary units either overlap or fall between organizational units. This situation can occur when the budget for a department has been disaggregated into some sections but not others, or where budgetary categories do not correspond to organizational sections.

Example The Department of Medicine at Arlmont Hospital has several sections: internal medicine, pediatrics, gastroenterology, and cardiology. Each section is managed by a chief of the specialty, and the department itself is under the direction of the chief of medicine. The budget report, which contains both budget and actual cost data, is prepared monthly and contains direct cost information classified into salaries, supplies, and depreciation. The information is broken down by ward, including two adult medicine wards and a pediatrics ward. Each specialty chief is asked to prepare a budget and to assist the hospital in its cost-containment efforts.

Until the cost data are classified by specialty, rather than ward, only the chief of pediatrics will have the requisite information to prepare and monitor a budget.

Misfit #5: Between Programmatic Goals and the Operating Budget

Organizations that engage in program budgeting have the opportunity to be explicit about any lack of congruence between strategic objectives and financial constraints. By so doing, they can address this lack of congruence during budget formulation, and make tradeoffs as needed. Alternatively, issues concerning the congruence between financial and strategic objectives may be resolved by default, as happens when budget cuts are necessary but managers do not have sufficient information to determine which products or product lines are most successful in meeting the organization's overall goals.

Misfits of this sort can be corrected by revising budget formulation to include a component in which department managers are asked to specify strategic objectives, and to commit themselves to their attainment in the same way as they committed themselves to the financial objectives of the budget. Generally, the problem is not a particularly easy one to solve, however, and managers often are forced to consider the budget as a financial constraint, rather than a pool of resources designed to assist in the attainment of some strategic ends.

Misfit #6: Between Motivation Systems and the Budgetary Process

While managers and other professionals in most nonprofit organizations appear to derive some motivation from non-financial sources, the budget can play a role in providing them with incentives to work toward the organization's strategic goals. To the extent that managers are committed to strategic objectives that are not financially feasible, for example, or are encouraged to develop new program ideas that are then thwarted during programming or budgeting, there is a misfit between the organization's motivation systems and the programming and budgeting phases of its management control process. In many instances, the budget is seen as a hurdle to overcome rather than an integral part of the planning process.

In some hospitals, for example, the entire budgetary process in some departments is one of generating statistics in an attempt to convince the controller's office that the department will provide at least as much service as it did in the prior year. In other organizations the budget is used as a way to obtain funds from corporate headquarters. In these instances, the budget is not looked upon as a useful management tool by either managers or professionals in the organization. Indeed, under circumstances such as these, budgeting is at best divorced from the organization's motivation system; at worst, it is inconsistent or incompatible with them.

While no simple solution exists to attaining a good fit between motivation systems and budgeting, organizations can attempt to interest their responsibility center managers in budgeting by an attractive structuring of financial incentives. For example, year-end bonuses tied to the accomplishment of both strategic and financial objectives effectively include the organization's managers and professionals in the strategic side of budgeting without creating an external control mechanism that would interfere with their decision-making autonomy.

Misfit #7: Between the Budget Formulation and Budget Monitoring Phases

In addition to the six misfits discussed above, which are between the budgeting context and the budgetary process, there is the possibility of misfits *within* the budgeting phase of the management control process. The area where this problem occurs most frequently is between the budget formulation and monitoring phases. Even if managers have made strategic and financial commitments, and are prepared to take them seriously, the entire process is weakened, and perhaps incapacitated, if the organization's reporting phase does not provide information that is complete (i.e., allows managers to assess the extent to which they are meeting their commitments), accurate, and timely. Yet, the reports in many nonprofit organizations arrive with such long time-lags that the information is of little managerial use when it arrives, and, as mentioned above, even those reports that are timely frequently do not provide sufficient detail on the reasons underlying a budget variance. Managers thus find it quite difficult to assess the action that should be taken to correct a problematic situation.

SUMMARY

Many aspects of operational budgeting in nonprofit organizations are similar to those in for-profit companies. Perhaps the most important difference is on the revenue side of the budget. Many nonprofit organizations are not "self-financing." Therefore, they must be careful to forecast their revenues accurately, and to assure themselves that expenses will not exceed revenues. Although there are some exceptions to this rule, and most organizations can have a year or two where expenses exceed revenues, the effective result of such a policy is to erode the organization's capital.

Three other important differences between nonprofit and for-profit organizations are (1) the existence of soft money coupled with uncertainty about grant revenue in some nonprofits, (2) the need for output measures as well as measures of revenues and expenses, and (3) the role of professionals. Moreover, in many organizations, for profit and nonprofit, the budget has a game-like quality to it. Because of this, some managers and supervisors have developed ploys to assure their success in the game. Some of these ploys are described in Appendix 8-A.

Suggested Cases for Classroom Use with this Chapter

See Appendix for a More Complete Description and Ordering Information

Moray Junior High School	Making budget tradeoffs
Los Reyes Hospital (A)	Building a budget using cost drivers
Southern State University Health System	Assessing responsibility centers and a line-item budget Combines Southern Seattle (A) and (B)
Southern Seattle University Health System (B)	Building an activity-based budget in a faculty practice plan
Urban Arts Institute (A)	Building a budget in a small college
Urban Arts Institute (B)	Assessing additional budgetary issues in a small college
LaSalle Hospital (A)	Assessing the budgetary process for a pathology department
Centro Italiano Sviluppo	Creating "decision packages" in a ZBB system
North Lake Medical Center	Building a budget using cost drivers
Rush-Presbyterian-St. Luke's Medical Center	Dealing with some tricky issues in building a budget
North Lincoln	Preparing a state government budget with many ploys at work

Appendix 8-A
Some Budget Ploys

Ever since there has been budgeting, there have been budgetees who engage in various activities (what here are called *ploys*) to help improve their chances of obtaining the resources they desire, and supervisors who engage in their own ploys to try to prevent an inappropriate or wasteful use of resources. Observations in both for-profit and nonprofit organizations, spanning several decades, have led to a conclusion that these ploys fall into four categories:

1. Ploys for new programs (Numbers 1-14)
2. Ploys for maintaining or expanding ongoing programs (Numbers 15-19)
3. Ploys to resist cuts (Numbers 20-25)
4. Ploys used primarily by supervisors (Numbers 26-32)

There are some overlaps among the categories, and Category 1 clearly relates to the programming (rather than the budgeting) phase of the management control process. In all instances, however, the ploys are about obtaining or maintaining resources. Each ploy is described briefly, followed by some speculation about an appropriate response to it.

PLOYS FOR NEW PROGRAMS

1. Foot in the Door

Sell a modest program initially with the idea of concealing its real magnitude until after it has been initiated, and has built a constituency.

Example In a certain state, the legislature agreed to fund a program to educate handicapped children in regular schools rather than in the special schools then used. The costs were said to be for transportation and a few additional teachers. Within five years, the definition of handicapped had been greatly broadened, and the resources devoted to the program were four times the amount originally estimated.

Response This ploy can elicit one of two responses: (1) Detect it when it is proposed, consider that it is merely a foot in the door and that actual costs eventually will exceed estimates by a wide margin, and therefore disapprove the program initially (difficult to do). (2) Hold to the original decision, and limit spending to the original cost estimate, despite pleas for more funds (effective only if the ploy is detected in time).

Variation A variation on this ploy is the *bait and switch* ploy*:* initially request an inexpensive program but increase its scope (and cost) after approval has been obtained. This differs from the "foot in the door" ploy in that the changes take place before the program begins rather than after is has been operating for a while.

2. Foot in the Mouth

Underestimate the real cost of a program, and apologize contritely when actual expenditures exceed the approved amount.

Example In its proposal for a new B-1 bomber, the Air Force "certified" that the cost would not exceed $20.5 billion. However, two independent audit groups within the Pentagon estimated its cost as $23.6 billion and $26.7 billion. The Congressional Budget Office (perhaps more objectively) estimated the cost as $40 billion!

Response Use staff analysts (such as people in the Congressional Budget Office) to examine and verify (to the extent possible) the budgetee's estimates. Also use staff analysts to assess whether the overall goal could be accomplished in a less expensive way.

3. Hidden Ball

Conceal the nature of a politically unattractive program by hiding it within an attractive one.

Example At one time, the Air Force had difficulty obtaining funds for general-purpose buildings, but could obtain them easily for intercontinental ballistic missiles. One year, it included in its missile program budget an item for constructing a new office building. The missile program used the building initially, but later it became a general-purpose Air Force office building.

Response Break down programs so that such items become visible.

4. Divide and Conquer

Seek approval of a budget request from more than one supervisor.

Example The New York City Planning Commission was organized so that each member represented a specified area. The distinctions were not clear, however, so budgetees would deal with more than one member, hoping that one of them would react favorably.

Response Define responsibilities clearly defined (easier said than done).

Caution In some situations, especially in research, it is dangerous to have a unitary decision point. With this and similarly ambiguous areas, it is often desirable to have two places where a person with a new idea (such as for a research project) may obtain a hearing. New ideas often are extremely difficult to evaluate, and a divided authority, even though superficially inefficient, can help to lessen the possibility that a good idea will be rejected.

5. Hocus Pocus

Base a request on the premise that an overall program has been approved, when it has not.

Example At a legislative committee hearing, a state university president presented a proposal to replace some buildings as part of his plan to double the capacity of one of the university's professional schools. His argument was that the replacement buildings would be more useful and efficient than the existing ones. The merits were discussed in terms of the return on investment arising from the greater efficiency of the new buildings. This discussion went on for some time until a committee member asked who had approved the plan for expansion of the school in the first place. It turned out that the expansion had never been approved; approval of the new buildings would have, de facto, approved the expansion.

Response Expose the hidden aims, but this is sometimes very difficult.

6. Shell Game

Use statistics and the fungibility of money to mislead supervisors as to the true state of affairs.

Example The head of the Model Cities program for a certain city wanted the program's available funds to be used primarily for health and education programs, but knew that his superiors were more interested in economic development programs (new businesses and housing). He drew up the following table:

Purpose	Federal Funds	Other Funds	Total
Health and education	$ 2,000,000	$ 15,000	$ 2,015,000
Economic development	50,000	2,300,000	2,350,000

The budgetee emphasized to the mayor and interested groups that over half the funds were intended for economic development purposes. The catch was that the source of "other" funds was not known, and there were no firm plans for obtaining them. This fact was not discovered by the supervisor until just prior to the deadline for submitting the request for federal Model Cities funding. At that point, it was too late to make the needed revisions.

Response Careful analysis

7. It's Free

Argue that someone else will pay for the project so the supervisor might as well approve it.

Example Since the federal government reimburses 95 percent of the cost of highway construction, states often have built a highway because their outlay was low. Many overlooked the fact that highway maintenance is 100 percent a state cost.

Response Require analysis of a project's lifetime costs, not merely the costs for next year. This technique is called *life-cycle costing*.

8. Not My Idea

The budgetee says that, although the budget request is not something that he or she personally is enthusiastic about, it is for a program that someone higher up in the organization has asked to have included in the budget. Preferably this higher-up person is not well known to, but more prestigious than, the budgetee's superior. The budgetee hopes that the supervisor will not take the time to bring this third-party into the discussion.

Response Examine the documentation. If it is vague, not well justified, or nonexistent, check with the alleged sponsor.

9. End Run

This is like the "Not My Idea" ploy, but the budgetee actually goes to the supervisor's boss without discussing the matter with the supervisor first.

Response This tactic should not be tolerated by the supervisor's boss. Moreover, anyone who attempts an end run should be reprimanded and the request denied. Otherwise, the entire authority system in the organization may be compromised.

10. Keeping Up with the Joneses

They (the competition, perhaps, or similar organizations elsewhere) have it, so we need it also if we are to remain on a par with them.

Example Minneapolis must have new street lights because St. Paul has them.

Response Analyze the proposal on its own merits. Attempt to shift the discussion from emotional grounds to logical ones by analyzing the request to see if the benefits are even remotely related to the cost.

11. Keeping Up to Date

This differs from the above ploy in that it does not need a "Jones." The argument is that the organization must be a leader and must therefore adopt the latest technology. This is a fashionable ploy for computers and related equipment, and for new medical technology.

Response Require that a benefit be shown that exceeds the cost of adopting the new technology. Emphasize that in a world of scarce resources, not everyone can get all that is desired, or even deserved.

Caution Sometimes the state of the art is such that benefits cannot be conclusively demonstrated. If this leads to a deferral of proposals year after year, opportunities may be missed.

Variation A "nothing but the best for our people" variation sometimes is used to justify expenditures that affect employees or clients directly, including such items as new cemeteries, office decor, or various facilities in public schools and colleges. Here, the issue is not necessarily related to technology or the "Jones," but to the budgetee's desire that his or her unit maintain an impressive public image.

12. Don't be Last

Appeal to supervisor's innate fear of being inferior to either the competition or organizations carrying out similar activities.

Example A university budgetee argued that a proposed program was breaking new ground, and was important to the national interest. She stated that if her university didn't initiate the program, some other university would. Moreover, the other university would obtain government funding, thus make it more difficult for her university to start the program later on.

Response Point out that there is a long list of possible programs with this characteristic, and the university must select those few that are within its capabilities.

13. Call It a Rose

Use misleading, but appealing, labels.

Example The National Institutes of Health were unable to obtain approval for the construction of new buildings but were able to build annexes. It is said that Building 12A (the annex) is at least double the size of Building 12.

Response Look behind the euphemism to the real function. If the disguise is intentional, deny the request and discourage recurrence.

14. Expert Opinion

The agency hires outside experts to support its request, either formally in hearings, or informally in the press.

Response Determine whether these experts are biased, either because they have connections with the agency or because they are likely to benefit if the request is approved. Seek other experts with contrasting views.

PLOYS FOR MAINTAINING OR EXPANDING ONGOING PROGRAMS

15. Show of Strength

Arrange demonstrations in support of a request. Threaten violence, work stoppages, or other unpleasant consequences if the request is not approved.

Response Have fair criteria for selecting programs, and have the conviction to stand by your decisions.

16. Razzle-Dazzle

Support the request with voluminous data, arranged in such a way that their significance is not clear. The data need not be valid.

Example A public works department submitted a 20-page list of repairs to municipal buildings that were said to be vitally needed, couched in highly technical language. This was actually a "wish list," prepared without a detailed analysis.

Response (a) Ask why the budget should be greater next year than the current year. (b) Find a single soft spot in the request and use it to discredit the whole analysis.

17. Delayed Buck

Submit the data late, arguing that the budget guidelines required so much detailed calculation that the job could not be completed on time.

Example In one state, the budget guidelines required a "complete justification" of requested additions to inventory. The state's motor vehicle repair shop submitted its budget at the last minute. The budget contained an itemized list of parts to be ordered, based on a newly installed system of calculating economic order quantities. The shop's manager argued that his tardiness was a consequence of getting the bugs out of the new system.

Response This is a difficult ploy to counter. Complaining about the delay may make the supervisor feel better but it will not solve the immediate problem. One possible response, designed to prevent recurrence, is to penalize the delay by making an arbitrary cut in the amount requested, although this runs this risk that needed funds will be denied. Alternatively, the supervisor could use the delay as part of an annual personnel evaluation.

18. Sacred Cows

Whatever was spent last year must have been necessary to carry out last year's program. Therefore, the only items to be negotiated this year are proposed increments above this sacred base.

Response As a practical matter, because there is insufficient time to zero-base every manager's budget, this approach must be accepted for a great many programs. However, a supervisor can conduct a "zero-base review" for a few programs each year.

19. Sprinkling

This is a subtle ploy in which the budgetee "sprinkles" small increments in many line items across the entire budget, especially in areas that are hard to detect. It often is done in anticipation that the supervisor will make arbitrary reductions, and with the hope that the final budget will be what it otherwise would have been if neither the sprinkling nor the arbitrary cuts had taken place.

Response Since this ploy, when done by an expert, is extremely difficult to detect, the best response is to remove the need to do it. Specifically, a supervisor must create an atmosphere in which the budgetees trust him or her to be fair, and not to make arbitrary cuts.

PLOYS TO RESIST CUTS

20. Make a Study

The budget guidelines contain a statement that a certain program is to be curtailed or discontinued. The budgetee responds that the proposed action should not taken until its consequences have been studied thoroughly.

Response If the consequences are clear, take the action. Otherwise, make the study, and use its recommendations as part of making a final decision.

21. Gold Watch

When asked to cut a budget, propose ways that do more harm than good.

Example This well-known ploy derives its name from an incident at Ford Motor Company when, in a period of stringency, all division heads were asked to make special efforts to cut costs. Most responded with genuine belt tightening. However, one division manager, with $100 million sales, reported that the only cost reduction opportunity he had found was to eliminate the gold watches that were customarily given to employees retiring with 30 or more years of service.

Response Reject the proposal. (In the example, disciplinary action was also taken with the division manager.)

22. Stoke the Fires

When a budget cut is ordered, cut a popular program, thereby provoking complaints from clients that will pressure the supervisor to restore it.

Examples In a classic case, known as the "Washington Monument Elevator Ploy," the manager of the Washington Monument proposed to reduce his budget by eliminating the elevator service. He knew that doing so would arouse considerable antagonism from hundreds of thousands of visitors each year.

In New York City, as part of a 1975 federal government financial bailout, Mayor Abraham Beame was asked to reduce spending to avoid bankruptcy. He responded by dismissing 7,000 police officers and firefighters, and closing 26 fire houses. Many believe he did this to inflame public opinion against budget cuts. It, in fact, had this effect, and the order was reversed.

Response Reject the proposal, and tell the budgetee to focus on areas where cuts are feasible.

23. Sword of Damocles

The budgetee asserts that if the request is not approved, dire consequences will occur.

Example Some years ago, the Department of Defense recommended an antiballistic missile system as a counter defense to the "Talinin System" that the Soviets were alleged to be building. In fact, the Soviets were not building such a system.

Response Base the analysis on evidence rather than on emotion or speculation without any substantiation.

24. Professional Expertise

The budgetee asserts that a proposal must be accepted because he or she has professional knowledge that the supervisor cannot possibly match. This ploy is used by professionals of all types: military officers, scientists, social workers, nurses, professors, physicians, curators, and clergy.

Response If the basic premise is accepted, the budget process cannot proceed rationally, because many supervisors tend to be a generalists, and many budgetees are specialists. The supervisor should insist that professionals express the basis for their judgments in terms that are comprehensible to the generalist.

25. Use Another Door

Go outside normal channels to reverse a decision. This is like the end run, but it is used in government organizations where there frequently is antagonism between the legislative and executive branches.

Example In Massachusetts in the early 1980s, when the public health council (an executive branch agency) denied a hospital a certificate of need (CON) for a capital building project, the hospital would ask its state representative to introduce a bill overriding the decision. Other representatives, knowing that the next CON denial might be in their district, supported their colleague, and the entire CON process was undermined.

Response Under these circumstances, and especially where political priorities are such that the veto pen must be used sparingly, the executive branch probably has no choice but to grin and bear it. Leaks to the press and the "bully pulpit" can draw the voters' attention to the special-interest deals, however, which may help to curtail the practice eventually.

PLOYS USED PRIMARILY BY SUPERVISORS

26. Keep Them Lean and Hungry

The supervisor tells the budgetee that his or her unit will work harder and possibly more effectively if it doesn't carry so much fat.

Response Show that the analogy with human biology is false, or go along with the analogy and show that the cuts represent muscle rather than fat.

27. Leverage Productivity Improvements

In the entire economy, productivity increases by about 3 percent annually. Therefore, it is reasonable to assume that management improvements will lead to lower operating costs in the aggregate. Some nonprofits, reasoning that they are only about half as likely to achieve productivity gains as the economy as a whole, reduce their personnel-related costs by about 1.5 percent from the previous year's level.

Response Point out that retirements and resignations may not be rapid enough to permit costs to be reduced to the desired level, and that layoffs can be politically undesirable.

28. Cuts Tied to Capital Expenditures

In some organizations cost reductions can be traced to specific capital expenditures.

Example If the approved budget for last year contained an item for the installation of a new computer system that was designed, in part, to reduce clerical expenses, the budgeted clerical expenses for this year should reflect the promised reduction.

Response If the budgetee proposed the new capital expenditures on the basis of cost reductions, he or she should be expected to carry them out. If the proposed cost reductions came from a predecessor, the new budgetee should either implement them as planned, or explain why they were erroneous, and propose a new plan.

29. Because I Said So

Target certain discretionary (and perhaps low budget) areas for expense reduction, even though there may be no precise rationale for the reduction, or, for that matter, for the area.

Example A supervisor, who was director of research of a large company, followed the practice of reducing the budget each year for certain discretionary items (travel, publications, professional dues) in certain departments by approximately 10 percent. Although the supervisor did this on a purely random basis, he achieved a reputation for astute analysis.

Response Challenge the rationale for the cuts (but the items often are so unimportant and difficult to defend that such challenges may consume more time than they are worth.)

30. I Only Work Here

The supervisor says she cannot grant the budgetee's request because it is not within the scope of the ground rules that her superiors have laid down.

Response Ask that the issue be brought to the appropriate decision-making authority. This, of course, relies on a trusting relationship between the budgetee and the supervisor.

31. Backdoor Exit

Eliminate a program without going through normal channels with the idea that it's better to apologize than be turned down.

Example The dean of a business school was not in favor of a small program that had been developed by the school's department of accounting. However, the program had considerable support both from the school's faculty and the local accounting community. To eliminate the program formally would have required faculty approval, which the dean knew he could not obtain. Thus, when asked by the university's central administration to cut the school's budget, the dean cut the budget of this program to such an extent that it could not survive. One year later, the program was no longer in existence.

Response Higher authorities should be sure that there is a process for budget reductions that is followed in any given program for an amount greater than some predetermined percentage. Otherwise, by starving a program until it is eliminated, a supervisor could have a detrimental impact on the organization's overall strategy. Unfortunately, this is not always easily accomplished.

32. The White Rabbit

The supervisor uses various tactics to bring the negotiation to a close. A simple one is to glance at his or her watch. Another is to "split the difference" between the amount requested and the amount he or she initially wanted to approve. Still another is to propose that the parties settle on a small amount now, with an indication that a larger amount will be considered later on.

Response Suggest that another meeting be scheduled to complete the negotiation. If this is not possible, be sure to clarify in writing those decisions that have been made.

Practice Case: Bandon Medical Associates (A)

Preparing this budget requires a lot of assumptions, and I'm not even sure that we're using the right approach. But if the group is to have something that's realistic, and if we're going to survive within the IDS [integrated delivery system], we've got to push ahead.

Charlene King, M.D., the senior physician member of Bandon Medical Associates (BMA), a small physician group practice located in Oregon, was commenting on the frustration she felt in trying to prepare the group's budget for the upcoming fiscal year. She realized that, although BMA's budget process had come a long way in just a few months, much remained to be done.

BACKGROUND

BMA had been established about 20 years ago by Dr. King and a colleague she had met during her residency. Over the years, the group had grown, and currently comprised six physicians and two medical assistants, who functioned as "extenders" for the physicians. The extenders assisted the physicians by completing a variety of tasks such as taking patients' blood pressure, drawing blood samples, and so forth. They did not bill for their time.

Two years ago, BMA had joined Coos Bay Health System, a large IDS that included several primary care and multi-specialty group practices, a free-standing laboratory, a freestanding radiology unit, two acute care hospitals, a nursing home, a home health agency, and a hospice. Coos Bay coordinated care, negotiated contracts with third-party payers, and provided some central services, such as information systems support.

FINANCIAL MATTERS

Recently, Coos Bay's chief financial officer, had told Dr. King that BMA along with the other physician practices in the IDS were going to be treated as "profit centers." He had emphasized that, even though Coos Bay was a nonprofit organization, each provider entity nevertheless would be required to generate sufficient revenue from its outpatient activities to cover its own expenses plus the costs of the Coos Bay central services that would be allocated to it. Each entity also would need to generate an operating surplus to provide the cash required for any capital purchases (such as office and testing equipment) that it wished to make to support its outpatient activities.

The CFO also pointed out that, in accordance with the contracts signed with various provider entities at the time they had been purchased by Coos Bay, all inpatient revenue—from both hospital and physician billings—would be retained by the hospital, and a portion distributed to physicians in accordance with the compensation formulas negotiated with them as part of Coos Bay's bundled-pricing and sub-capitation arrangements with its payers.

Additionally, the CFO had reminded Dr. King that, as had been the practice for the past two years, revenue from all outpatient laboratory and radiological testing would be retained by the free-standing facilities. Thus, all of the physician groups would need to earn a surplus on the basis of the revenue generated from their outpatient visits only.

Stunned by this news, Dr. King had held a retreat for the group's physicians and extenders at which they had discussed a wide variety of matters related to the new financial arrangements. After considerable debate, some of it acrimonious, they had reached the following conclusions:

1. Different visit types required different levels of physician intensity, and although there were several different approaches to measuring productivity, revenue generation would be the best method. Everyone had agreed that, since the payment for each visit type was a rough reflection

of its intensity, revenue generation was not only a simple way to measure each physician's productivity, but a good one as well.

2. While most third-party payers classified visits by precise codes, the BMA physicians had agreed that four visit types (initial consultation, routine physical, intensive visit, and routine visit) were sufficient for budgeting purposes.

3. Physicians would be available to see outpatients for 32 hours a week (eight 4-hour sessions). They also had agreed that, with time off for continuing medical education and vacations, they would be available for a total of 1,500 hours a year (about 47 weeks).

4. The extenders would be expected to see patients for 1,400 hours a year—less than the physicians since they had some other responsibilities in the group.

5. Physicians would be paid by a combination of base salary and bonus. The extenders would be on a straight salary with no bonus, although physicians could share their bonuses with one or more extenders who they thought were especially helpful.

6. Each physician's base salary would be set at 42 percent of his or her expected revenue generation. Ten percent of that amount would be kept in reserve until the end of the year, and paid out as a year-end bonus if the group reached at least 95 percent of its total revenue target.

7. The remaining revenue would be used to cover the group's operating expenses and to provide the surplus needed to fund office renovations, equipment purchases, and other similar items.

With these decisions in mind, Dr. King had met with each physician to discuss his or her plans for the upcoming year, and to arrive at a forecast for the different visit types. She and BMA's administrator, Gordon Hawkins, had then summed the individual physician forecasts to get the group's total volume forecast.

Dr. King and Mr. Hawkins next developed expense estimates. To do this, they decided to treat physicians, extenders and the group's medical supplies as "variable expenses." Dr. King commented:

> Clearly, the only truly variable expenses are the medical supplies, but if we're to find out how we're doing, we need to know both physician and extender costs for the different visit types. If we use straight salaries, and essentially treat the providers as fixed costs, we won't be able to do that. So I need to compute per-minute rates for both physicians and extenders, and then multiply those rates by the number of minutes that each provider type spends for each visit type. As I look at this, it all seems pretty daunting, and it's not something that Gordon has done before either, so we're both struggling a little.
>
> Medical supplies, on the other hand, are pretty easy. They include a wide variety of disposable items that we use in conjunction with a visit. To keep the budget simple, we've decided to measure them in terms of "units," and Gordon has computed an average cost per unit. We just need to multiply those out to get the budget for each visit type.

The group's fixed expenses included rent, cleaning, administrative staff, receptionists, office supplies, and similar items, which Dr. King expected to total $300,000 for the year. Allocated overhead was for a variety of administrative services provided by Coos Bay, such as billing, collections, and information services. Coos Bay's CFO had told Dr. King that he thought the allocations would total about $250,000, but since they were based on the formulas from Coos Bay's full cost allocation system, he could not be completely certain.

The Current Year's Budget

The elements of the current year's budget that Dr. King and Mr. Hawkins had developed are shown in Exhibit 1. This exhibit contains the anticipated revenue for each visit type, the anticipated provider time and medical supply units per visit, and the corresponding unit variable expense figures. Dr. King commented:

> I think we're almost there. We now need to calculate the total variable expense per visit for each visit type, multiply the revenue and total variable expense per visit by the anticipated number of visits to give total revenue and total variable expenses by visit type, deduct the latter from the former to get the contribution to fixed expenses from each visit type. Finally, we need to deduct our anticipated fixed expenses and allocated overhead from the total contribution to give our total budgeted surplus for the year.

Assignment

1. Using the information contained in the case and Exhibit 1, prepare a budget for BMA for the four visit types shown. Use the approach suggested by Dr. King at the end of the case, and organize your figures so that she will find them understandable and useful.*

2. Assuming Dr. King is unhappy with the "bottom line" of this budget, what options are available to change it? Which options seem the most feasible to implement?

3. What problems do you think Dr. King will encounter in attempting to implement this budget? What should be done about them?

* Try to set up a spreadsheet to calculate the budget. Make it as formula-driven as possible. This will allow you to easily test assumptions in answering Question 2.

BANDON MEDICAL ASSOCIATES (A)
Exhibit 1. Budget Data

Type of Visit	Expected Number of Visits	Expected Revenue per Visit	Expected Physician Time per Visit (1)	Expected Extender Time per Visit (2)	Expected Medical Supplies per Visit (3)
Initial consultation	3,000	$150	60	15	3
Routine physical	4,000	$110	45	10	2
Intensive visit	6,000	$80	20	10	2
Routine visit	6,000	$60	10	15	1

Notes:
1. In minutes at $1.35 per minute.
2. In minutes at $0.90 per minute.
3. In units at $4.00 per unit.

Solution to Practice Case

This case lends itself to the use of a rather simple spreadsheet, which can be used to both build the budget and to examine opportunities for increasing the budgeted surplus.

Question 1

Exhibit A contains a spreadsheet with the budget, and shows the three factors that will be useful for budget revision: number and mix of visits, resources per visit, and cost per resource unit. Exhibit B contains the formulas used in the computations.

Exhibit A demonstrates that an initial visit makes up about half of the contribution, and an intensive follow-up visit another third. Routine follow-up, in particular, contributes very little.

Question 2

Dr. King has several options, as follows:

- *Increase revenues*. In general, this option is the easiest to put into a budget but the hardest to actually pull off. It would be unwise for Dr. King to increase her budgeted surplus by taking this route. If she does, there are three ways to go about it:

    1. Raise prices. We are told little about the market, however, so it is hard to say whether a price increase could be instituted without a loss in volume. Frequently, HMOs and other third-party payers dictate prices, so the group practice quite likely is a price taker.

    2. Increase volume. Presumably, Dr. King is trying to do this already, however, and this set of figures represents her best guess. It may even be optimistic.

    3. Change the mix of business toward more higher contribution visits. This analysis is a little tricky, however. The question, assuming capacity constraints, is not which visit type has the highest contribution margin, but how much total contribution can be attained. If, for example, Dr. King's physicians could see only one more patient (and were interested primarily in the impact on surplus), they would see a patient for an initial consult. If, however, they have one hour of capacity available, they presumably would prefer to see six routine follow-up patients, which, since each visit is only 10 minutes, would provide total contribution of $174 ($29 x 6), compared to only $43.50 for a single initial consult (which lasts 60 minutes). These computations are shown in the first box in Exhibit C, which shows the impact of a shift of 333 hours from intensive follow-up visits to routine follow-up visits. As this exhibit indicates, the financial impact is $22,000.

        However, when the extender time is included (shown in the second box at the bottom of Exhibit C), the number of visits that are possible in an hour changes (assuming extender time cannot overlap with physician time). The result is the availability of 500 hours (rather than 333 hours). However, given the fact that total time is only 5 minutes less for the routine follow-up visits, the number of additional visits is only 1,200. Overall, the result is a decline in contribution.

- *Reduce costs*. This is probably the most viable option. There are two ways to go about it:

1. Reduce fixed costs. We are told little about these, however, so it is hard to say whether this is a viable option. In most organizations, it usually is a feasible option, since costs of this sort tend to grow over time. From all we can tell, the allocated overhead is something that is outside Dr. King's control.

2. Reduce variable expense per case. There are two ways to do this:

   a. Reduce the number of resource units per case. For example, fewer physician minutes, extender minutes or medical supplies per case.

   b. Reduce the expense per resource unit. This can be done by lowering factor prices (e.g., lower physician wages, extender wages, supply expense per unit).

   If we examine these options, we can see that it probably will be difficult to reduce factor prices. We could ask physicians and extenders to work for less, but depending on opportunities in the area, that would probably result in some of them leaving. Replacing them with lower wage people could be difficult. Similarly, we presumably have the best prices that we can get from suppliers, although this certainly is a possibility.

   This leaves us with options 2a. It appears that this area is where the greatest opportunities exist. By working with the physicians and extenders in the group, Dr. King should be able to reduce the time spent per visit. As Exhibit D shows, however, the big payoff is with physicians, not with extenders. That is, a 10 percent increase in productivity for physicians across all visit types improves the surplus by $72,900, whereas a similar increase for extenders improves it by only $21,150. All of this comes with no change in budgeted fixed costs, except that the implication is the use of fewer physicians: 5.4 FTEs rather than 6 FTEs. (Note, incidentally, that with the projected visit volume and productivity figures, the group will need another .8 FTE extender.)

Question 3

There are several problems that might arise. First, and perhaps most importantly, with the bonus based on revenue generation, there is a considerable incentive for physicians to obtain productivity increases by shifting some of the responsibility for a visit to an extender. Doing so will free up the physicians to either see more patients or spend time in other activities.

Second, Dr. King probably will want to see greater detail on the fixed expenses to see how they might be reduced. For example, some breakdown among the usual categories of rent, utilities, cleaning, administration, and the like might shed some light on the feasibility of reducing these expenses.

Third, Dr. King probably should work with Coos Bay's CFO to see if the allocation can be restructured either as a fixed commitment or, if there is a measurable unit of activity, based on a transfer price. Otherwise, excessive spending by Coos Bay will quite likely affect BMA's bottom line in a way that Dr. King cannot control. If transfer prices can be established, she will need to work with the CFO (and others in the hospital) to determine an appropriate amount. It should be easy to have a transfer price for laundry services, for example, but would be quite difficult to have one for "administration and general."

Finally, as Dr. King already has seen at the retreat, there no doubt will be considerable resistance from physicians to spending their time on financial matters. Developing per-visit standards and linking them to financial matters can be time consuming and frustrating. Developing transfer prices for service departments can be similarly difficult.

BANDON MEDICAL ASSOCIATES (A)

Overall Budget	Initial Consult	Routine Physical	Intensive Visit	Routine Visit	Total
Exhibit A Original Budget					
Number of visits	3,000	4,000	6,000	6,000	19,000
Price per visit	$150.00	$110.00	$80.00	$60.00	
Total revenue	$450,000	$440,000	$480,000	$360,000	$1,730,000
Variable expenses per visit	$106.50	$77.75	$44.00	$31.00	
Total variable expenses	$319,500	$311,000	$264,000	$186,000	1,080,500
Contribution	$130,500	$129,000	$216,000	$174,000	$649,500
Total fixed expenses					300,000
Allocated overhead					250,000
Surplus					$99,500
Variable expense detail:					
Physician care					
Average #minutes per visit	60	45	20	10	
Average wage per minute	$1.35	$1.35	$1.35	$1.35	
Total expense per visit	$81.00	$60.75	$27.00	$13.50	
Extender care					
Average #minutes per visit	15	10	10	15	
Average wage per minute	$0.90	$0.90	$0.90	$0.90	
Total expense per visit	$13.50	$9.00	$9.00	$13.50	
Medical Supplies					
Average # units per visit	3	2	2	1	
Average expense per unit	$4.00	$4.00	$4.00	$4.00	
Total expense per visit	$12.00	$8.00	$8.00	$4.00	
Total average variable expense per visit	$106.50	$77.75	$44.00	$31.00	
Exhibit B. Financial Implications of a Change in Visit Mix—Physicians Only					
Unit contribution margin	$43.50	$32.25	$36.00	$29.00	
# visits possible in an hour	1.0	1.3	3.0	6.0	
Potential total contribution in 1 hour	$43.50	$43.00	$108.00	$174.00	
# visits planned	3,000	4,000	6,000	6,000	
Planned contribution	130,500	129,000	216,000	174,000	$649,500
Change in visits			-1,000	2,000	
Hours used (saved) with visit change			-333	333	
New contribution	130,500	129,000	180,000	232,000	$671,500
Change in contribution	0	0	-36,000	58,000	$22,000
New Surplus					$121,500
Exhibit C. Financial Implications of a Change in Visit Mix—Physicians and Extenders					
Unit contribution margin	$43.50	$32.25	$36.00	$29.00	
# visits possible in an hour	0.8	1.1	2.0	2.4	
Potential total contribution in 1 hour	$34.80	$35.18	$72.00	$69.60	
# visits planned	3,000	4,000	6,000	6,000	
Planned contribution	130,500	129,000	216,000	174,000	$649,500
Change in visits			-1,000	1,200	
Hours used (saved) with visit change			-500	500	
New contribution	130,500	129,000	180,000	208,800	$648,300
Change in contribution	0	0	-36,000	34,800	($1,200)
New Surplus					$98,300
Exhibit D. Financial Implications of Productivity Changes					
Original Budget					
Number physicians needed	6.0				
Number extenders needed	2.8				
With 10% Physician Productivity Increase					
Minutes per visit	54	40.5	18	9	
Number physicians needed	5.4				
New surplus					$172,400
Increase over original surplus					$72,900
With 10% Extender Productivity Increase					
Minutes per visit	13.5	9	9	13.5	
Number extenders needed	2.5				
New surplus					$120,650
Increase over original surplus					$21,150

Chapter 9

Control of Operations

The third phase in the management control process is operations and measurement. Although described as a single phase, it actually consists of two separate but related activities: control of operations and measurement of inputs and outputs. This chapter describes some tools and techniques that can be useful in carrying out these activities.

Control of operations includes both financial and performance control. The former, as its name implies, is related to spending activities. Financial control systems are designed to assure that appropriate records are maintained, so as to preserve the financial integrity of the entity's activities.

Performance control focuses on the activities of line managers, professional staff, technical support staff, clerical employees, and other members of the organization. Its goal is to assure that performance is in accordance with the organization's objectives. It concentrates on matters of productivity, and on managers' motivation to operate their programs and responsibility centers effectively and efficiently.

Since many of their programs are not subject to market forces, nonprofit organizations must be especially concerned with performance control activities. Performance control can help to assure clients and other constituents that the organization's resources are being used as efficiently as possible in carrying out ongoing operations.

The first half of this chapter is devoted to financial control. It focuses on matters such as accounting systems and auditing. The second half discusses performance control, including both technical and behavioral matters.

FINANCIAL CONTROL IN GENERAL

The approved operating budget, consisting of both planned expenses and expected outputs, is the principal financial guideline for operations. Presumably, management wants the organization to operate in a way that is consistent with this plan unless there is a good reason to depart from it. This qualification is important, for it means that the control process is more complicated than simply insisting that the organization do what the budget prescribes. One of the principal purposes of management control is to assure that objectives are accomplished as efficiently as possible. If changed conditions suggest that a course of action other than the one specified in the budget will do a better job of attaining the objectives, that new course of action should be followed. Thus, the financial control activity should have two aspects: (1) to assure that, in the absence of reasons to do otherwise, the plan set forth in the budget is adhered to, and (2) to provide a way to change the plan if conditions warrant.

Types of Financial Control

In governmental agencies and some other nonprofits, the total amount in the approved budget is a ceiling that should not be exceeded. Indeed, as discussed below, if funds are received from a legislative appropriation, it is a ceiling that legally cannot be exceeded. Within this ceiling, there are more detailed controls, which usually take the form of ceilings for specific activities or programs.

Although the budget may contain a detailed listing of amounts for expense elements (e.g., wages, supplies, travel, utilities), these amounts are normally guides rather than ceilings. The primary focus should be on programs and responsibility centers, not on expense elements. Some years ago, financial control focused on individual line items of expense. Although some nonprofit organizations, especially government agencies, persist in using line-item controls, many have wisely shifted their focus to programs and responsibility centers.

Need for Some Line-Item Restrictions

Despite the shift to a focus on programs and responsibility centers, most organizations also require operating managers to obtain approval for shifts among line items above a certain amount or percentage. Although this policy may seem inconsistent with shift to program control, there are several reasons that justify it.

Lack of Experience. Many line managers are professionals (such as artists, teachers, physicians, or social workers), and have not had much experience with budgets. Overspending one line item by a large amount early in the fiscal year (such as for travel to professional meetings) may consume funds that are needed later in the year for ongoing program operations.

Example In a college of art and design, a department head gave out considerably more financial aid early in the fiscal year than he had in his budget. Later in the fiscal year, he informed management that there were no funds left in his budget to pay for models for art classes. Since models were essential for art classes, the department head was allowed to overrun his budget. The next year the CEO told the department head that all his budget expenditures needed to be approved in advance.

Potential Changes in Objectives. When the budget was agreed upon, it represented a commitment between the line manager and senior management that it was the most appropriate way to use the organization's resources to accomplish certain objectives. A large change in the use of resources implies a change in the activities of a program or responsibility center and hence may inhibit the attainment of certain objectives. Senior management needs to approve this sort of decision.

Long-Run Implications. Some expenses represent long-term commitments. If personnel are added, for example, the corresponding increase in costs tends to be relatively permanent. This is especially true if the newly hired person occupies a union or civil service position, or otherwise assumes a position with some sort of tenure commitment. Therefore, the number of personnel frequently constitutes a ceiling that cannot be exceeded without senior management approval.

Potential for Duplication. Since line managers do not have a complete view of the organization, senior management needs a way to avoid duplication in resource use. This was an important aspect of the budget preparation process. If line managers are permitted to make large changes in their operating budgets without the review and approval of senior management, they may be undertaking activities that overlap or conflict with activities of other programs or responsibility centers.

For these reasons, most organizations require program and responsibility center managers to obtain approval from higher levels of authority for major deviations from their budgets. Depending on the size of the organization and the dollar amounts involved, this approval may be required from several higher levels of authority.

Despite this approval process, line managers can have sufficient flexibility to carry out their programs as planned if two conditions are in place: (1) they are allowed to make minor shifts among line items in their budgets without higher level approval, and (2) there is an efficient and non-capricious approval process in place that will allow them to make larger shifts if necessary to attain programmatic objectives more efficiently.

Flow of Spending Authority

The flow of spending authority within an organization generally should follow the lines of operating management responsibility; that is, spending should be authorized from higher levels to lower levels according to the formal organizational hierarchy. Difficulties arise when funds are received directly by organizational units, rather than through the organizational hierarchy. If it does not control the distribution of spending authority, senior management often cannot exercise appropriate control over subordinate elements.

Example In one city, mental health services were provided to the public on a contractual basis by private institutions. These institutions were supposed to be accountable to the city's Department of Mental Health. However, operating funds for these institutions were provided directly by the state, and the institutions therefore tended to disregard the city agency.

Funds from Several Sources

A similar problem occurs when program managers have funding from several sources, and can play off one funding source against another. Thus, while senior management may desire that the overall level of spending be reduced, a program manager can sometimes defeat this desire by finding an alternative source for the additional funds.

Examples The manager of a program in a university wanted to purchase an expensive computer with funds from her operating budget but was denied permission by the dean, who was attempting to control overall spending. The manager then used grant funds to purchase the computer, and operating funds to pay for a research assistant who otherwise would have been paid with funds from the grant.

A university spent $1.7 million to renovate the official residence of the president. The money came from a $55 million reserve fund of "unrestricted private donations, interest on university investments, and surpluses from the campus food and housing services and the university's bookstore." Neither the Board of Regents, nor the state's legislators were aware of the existence of this fund. Further, although the Board of Regents was required to approve all capital expenditures in excess of $100,000, this project was carried out "through a series of smaller projects costing less than $100,000 each."

The chief administrative officer of a chapter of the American Cancer Society reportedly faxed a letter to the Society's bank stating that he wanted to transfer $6.9 million to a law firm in Austria to be disbursed for research purposes. The money was among funds raised by volunteers to support cancer research, education, and prevention programs.

He was arrested after returning to the United States from Zurich and accused of bank fraud. Of concern to at least some observers was the ease with which he allegedly moved almost half of the chapter's $15 million budget out of the country.[1]

Budget Adjustments

Changed circumstances often call for modifications in detailed spending requirements. This raises the problem of accommodating these modifications within the budget ceiling. There are two

[1] Anonymous, "American Cancer Society Executive Accused of Embezzling," *Fund Raising Management*, August 2000, p.8.

general techniques for solving this problem: contingency allowances and revisions. The choice between the two is largely a matter of management preference.

Contingency Allowances. In this approach, amounts are set aside for unforeseen circumstances at various levels in the organization . Thus, the budgeted expenses for each responsibility center and program are targets that can be exceeded, if necessary, with the excess being absorbed by the contingency allowance.

An advantage of contingency allowances is that increases in spending can be accommodated without the sometimes painful task of finding an offsetting decrease. A risk is that if there is, say, a 5 percent contingency allowance, there may be a tendency to regard the actual ceiling as 105 percent of the target in all responsibility centers. This defeats the purpose of the contingency allowances.

A variation of the contingency allowance is the practice of releasing somewhat less than the proportionate amount of funds in the early part of the year. For example, in an agency whose spending is expected to be spread evenly throughout the year, only 22 percent of funds, rather than 25 percent, might be released in the first quarter. As the year progresses and spending needs become clearer, subsequent releases of the contingency funds are made to those responsibility centers that need them the most.

Revisions. In this approach, 100 percent of the authorized amount is divided among responsibility centers. Changed circumstances are accommodated by increasing the budget of one responsibility center and making a corresponding reduction in the budget of one or more other responsibility centers. Under this plan, the budget for each responsibility center cannot be exceeded without specific approval. Moreover, if a given responsibility center receives an increase, one or more other responsibility center(s) will be asked to spend less than their budgets.

Mechanism for Making Changes. Whichever approach is used, senior management should be certain that the mechanism for making these changes is well understood. Otherwise, the budget may not conform to the demands managers face, and will not serve as a reliable instrument for measuring their performance.

Example Some states have three budgets: the originally approved one, a supplemental budget, and a deficiency budget. The supplemental and deficiency budgets are submitted to the legislature by the governor during the course of the fiscal year. The supplemental budget is for a request for a budget increase. The deficiency budget, by contrast, is submitted after the state incurs obligations that exceed the funds provided in either the original or the supplemental budget. This process calls the legislature's attention to the situation, and permits it to: (a) approve the proposal as warranted, (b) disapprove it (difficult if the money has already been spent), or (c) approve it, but publicly criticize the governor's performance.

FINANCIAL CONTROL VIA THE ACCOUNTING SYSTEM

The central device for reporting internal operating information is the accounting system. It is central because accounting data deals with monetary amounts, and money provides the best way to aggregate and summarize information about a wide variety of inputs, including labor, supplies, and purchased services. In this regard, the accounting system must serve several purposes.

Donor Restrictions

The accounting system must assure that restrictions placed on contributions are observed. If a donor specifies that a scholarship may be used only for residents of a particular state or community, for example, this restriction must be honored. Many organizations set up a separate account for each type of restriction as a device for exercising this control, even though there is no need to report the details of the restrictions in the financial statements. The result often is considerably more detailed in the accounting system than one typically would find in a for-profit setting. The principal purpose of this detail is to assure donors that their contributions were used only for the specified purposes. Since the auditor can provide this assurance (or identify an instance where restrictions were not observed), there is no need to report the detail.[2]

Consistency with the Budget

The accounting system should be consistent with the budget. The budget states the approved plan for spending, and the accounting system reports actual spending. Unless the two are consistent, there is no reliable way to determine if actual spending occurred according to plan. This does not mean that the accounting system should contain only the accounts that appear in the budget. Management may need more accounting detail than contained in the budget, and it needs rearrangements of the basic data for various purposes. Nevertheless, at a minimum, the accounting system should contain accounts that match (or that can be aggregated to total) each item on the budget.[3]

Need for Integrated Systems

Not only should budget and accounting data be consistent with one another, but the accounting system should be an integral part of a total information system. This means that it should be possible to report on both inputs and outputs and to compare them.

Encumbrance Accounting

An encumbrance occurs when an organization becomes obligated to pay for goods or services. This happens when a contract is signed or when personnel work. (This is because, at the time they work, they are entitled to salaries and benefits.) An appropriation by a state or local government usually is an authority to encumber (a federal appropriation is an authority to obligate, which is identical).

In the federal government, amounts appropriated in accordance with the budget cannot legally be exceeded, and violators are subject to criminal penalties. Most states have similar legislation.[4]

Appropriations for operating purposes usually cannot be encumbered after the end of the fiscal year; that is, they lapse. Therefore, there is a natural tendency to fully encumber all appropriated funds. Thus, while an encumbrance accounting system is designed to avoid spending more than the amount appropriated, it also discourages spending less than that amount.

---

[2] Some colleges and universities, where the number of separate funds typically is quite large, will not accept restricted contributions unless they exceed a given amount. They reason that the extra cost of controlling for the restrictions is only warranted for large contributions.

[3] If accounts do not match the budget, it generally is possible to develop a mechanism for reconciling the two. This mechanism, called a crosswalk, is a rearrangement of the accounts to match the budget categories. A crosswalk is not as reliable as recording amounts in the proper accounts in the first place.

[4] As a practical matter, punishment under these acts is rare, but the possibility of legal action is a deterrent.

FINANCIAL CONTROL VIA AUDITING

No matter how well an accounting system has been designed, there is always the possibility of error or fraud. To detect such irregularities, many nonprofit organizations have an internal audit function. In addition, most have their financial statements (and certain aspects of their financial control systems) audited by an external body, usually an independent public accounting firm.

Internal (or Compliance) Auditing

A well-designed management control system contains its own financial controls. Where there is an internal audit staff, its responsibility is to ensure that these controls are effective. Internal financial controls have three general purposes: (1) to minimize the possibility of financial loss by theft, fraud, or embezzlement; (2) to ensure adherence to senior management's rules governing the receipt and spending of money, and the use of other resources; and (3) to ensure that information flowing through the system is accurate.

Some organizations, including many state and municipal governments, do not have even a minimal level of such controls. This problem is revealed by frequent newspaper exposés of contracts entered into in a unauthorized manner, persons on the public payroll who do not actually work, or welfare payments made to persons not entitled to receive them.

Example For 11 years, the purchasing agent at the University of California, San Francisco, was considered to be an "extremely valuable employee." Three months after he left the university, it was discovered that during the preceding four years, he had embezzled $310,000 by billing fake purchases to dummy corporations. He was in complete charge of placing orders, receiving the goods, and paying for them.[5]

Internal controls are never perfect. Their limitations are well described in the AICPA's Statements of Auditing Standards (SAS)—promulgations that describe the objectives and difficulties of internal auditing.[6] Nevertheless, more attention needs to be devoted to designing good control systems.

Examples In one study of 77,000 cases, only 2.5 percent of the fraud that was exposed was uncovered through audit efforts. Much of the rest was uncovered by chance or by scheduled compliance and eligibility reviews by program units. Reports by alleged victims and private individuals also helped uncover the fraud.[7]

Federal prosecutors charged New York University Medical Center with overcharging the Federal Government for research costs, and announced that they had reached a $15.5 million settlement, by far the largest amount ever in any case involving research overhead at a university. While denying it did anything wrong, the university acknowledged that it had made some "administrative and accounting mistakes with respect to certain cost items." It insisted that none of the errors was intentional.[8]

---

5 *Chronicle of Higher Education*, April 10, 1991.

6 For details, go to www.aicpa.org/Research/Standards/AuditAttest/Pages/SAS.aspx#SAS1

7 Mortimer A. Dittenhofer, "Internal Control and Auditing for Fraud," *The Government Accounts' Journal*, Winter 1983-84.

8 Elisabeth Rusenthal, "N.Y.U. Hospital Settles Case on Research Billing Charges," *New York Times*, April 8, 1997.

Incorrect Charges

One possible reason for the relative ineffectiveness of internal auditing is its focus. Many non-profit organizations spend considerable effort assuring that certain rules are obeyed precisely (for instance, checking every travel voucher to ensure that the per diem calculations are accurate and that mileage between points is stated correctly). They also have voucher systems, locked petty cash boxes, and other devices that inhibit obvious possibilities for theft or losses by individuals. By contrast, these same organizations may pay little attention to procedures for assuring that expenditures are charged to the proper accounts, i.e., to projects or other items that correspond to those for which the costs actually were incurred. If the amounts charged to accounts are used as a basis for reimbursement by a client, as is often the case, deliberate mis-charging is tantamount to fraud. The situation is even more flagrant when the persons responsible sign their names to a certificate stating that costs were recorded correctly, knowing full well they were not.

In addition to the illegality of this practice, one obvious consequence is that recorded data are inaccurate. Reports prepared from such data give management an incorrect impression about current performance, and a misleading basis for future plans.

An interesting ethical question arises when the rules under which an agency is forced to operate are such that efficient (and sometimes effective) operations are inhibited. Should managers get the job done and cover up the fact that, to do so, they had to break the rules, or should they use the existence of the rules as an excuse for not getting the job done? Managers with different temperaments answer this question in different ways.

Example A certain state legislature set maximum payment rates for part-time psychiatrists employed by the state's mental health institutions. These rates were about half the going rate for psychiatrists. At these rates, few psychiatrists would work for the state. Consequently, administrators hired psychiatrists for half a day and paid them for a full day. They said that this was the only way they could hire a sufficient number of qualified psychiatrists. On balance, was this wrong? Whether or not it was wrong, the records showed that twice as many psychiatrist work-hours were provided as actually was the case.

EXTERNAL AUDITING

In many states, the Office of the Attorney General requires tax-exempt organizations to submit financial statements annually. For large organizations, these statements be must audited. Moreover, any organization that receives grants from a government agency is subject to audit. Although government auditors conduct many of these audits, independent public accountants increasingly are engaged to perform them.[9]

Even where audits are not required by law or by grantors, there is a general recognition that, for purposes of reliability and continuity, such reports should by prepared by an independent auditor. The audit determines whether: (a) financial operations were conducted properly, (b) the financial reports were presented fairly, and (c) the entity complied with applicable laws and regulations. When defects in an organization's financial control system prevent the auditors from undertaking a thorough analysis of compliance, the organization may need to upgrade its system.

[9] Because the requirements for conducting a government audit generally are somewhat different from those for a non-government audit, special training is needed. See "About Government Auditing Standards." The 2011 revision is available at http://www.gao.gov/yellowbook.

PERFORMANCE CONTROL

Apart from establishing systems to assure that funds are spent as intended, nonprofit managers also must be concerned with the effective and efficient performance of their organizations. The remainder of this chapter addresses several issues related to managers' need to exert control over the day-to-day operations of their organizations.

Relationship to Task Control

In many respects, performance control is concerned with the activities that Chapter 1 called task control: the rules, procedures, forms, and other devices that govern the performance of specific tasks to assure they are carried out effectively and efficiently. For example, professionals in a research organization must report the time they spend on various projects; payroll checks must be issued in a timely way; inventories must be replenished before they are depleted, but must not be maintained at excessively high levels; and accounts receivable must be monitored and steps taken to collect potentially delinquent accounts. The larger and more complex the organization, the larger the number of these rules. Also, a mature organization tends to have more formal rules and procedures than a young one.

Although most managers dislike rules, they also recognize that many are necessary to assure that members of the organization handle similar situations in a similar manner. Some rules, however, may have been devised to deal with situations that no longer exist, or they may unduly restrict the ability of managers to use good judgment. Because of this, an organization needs to review its rules from time to time, and eliminate those that no longer serve a useful purpose.

Example In the Department of Labor, a committee of OSHA employees and managers reviewed the agency's 400-page field operations manual. The new manual that emerged was fewer than 100 pages long, and, according to one manager, "Should help people spend less time on documentation and more time doing what they were hired to do."[10]

Relationship to Productivity

Many nonprofit organizations have instituted measures designed to improve employee productivity. These include attempts to classify costs into controllable and non-controllable categories so that managers can focus on costs that might be reduced without affecting the organization's programmatic outcomes.

In some instances, these measures call for consolidation of activities across two or more organizational units. In others, they attempt to assure that professionals' time is being used as much as possible in the activities for which they were hired.

Examples In one public school system, managers found that significant savings could be achieved by consolidating certain functions, such as that of a registrar. Since the optimum-size school was determined to be 1,500 students, principals of schools with fewer than 800 students were encouraged to share registrars with similarly small nearby schools.

A rural health clinic found that it could significantly improve the productivity of its physicians by using nurse practitioners (NPs). The NPs were able to screen patients, treat those who did not require a physician, and conduct many tests and procedures that physicians for-

[10] Bruce G. Posner, "Sowing the Seeds of Change at the Department of Labor," *Harvard Business Review*, May-June 1994.

merly conducted. As a result, the clinic greatly increased productivity of its physicians with consequent reduction in the cost of a patient visit and a higher volume of patients seen.

Selection of a Measure. Efforts to improve productivity require developing measures that managers can use to judge their success. The major difficulty in selecting a measure of productivity is choosing a unit that is sufficiently homogeneous to provide a reliable indicator of improved (or worsened) performance. In a membership organization, for example, clerical staff might be evaluated according to the number of applications processed per hour. Since each application is about the same as all others, this can be a reliable measure. In an ambulatory care clinic, on the other hand, there are many different types of patient visits and levels of severity associated with different patients. Therefore, a patient visit is at best only a rough measure of productivity.

Operational Auditing

Compliance auditing, described above, determines whether financial data are being recorded properly and whether financial rules (such as those concerning spending authorizations) are being followed. Another type of auditing, called operational auditing, has been important for many years. Its development was fostered by the U.S. Comptroller General, who said that it:

> . . . involves examining into the operating, managerial, or administrative performance of selected aspects of an activity or organization beyond that required for the audit of the accounts and financial transactions. The primary purpose of such extended auditing is to evaluate the quality of management or operational performance and to identify opportunities for greater efficiency and economy, or for increased effectiveness in carrying out procedures or operations. The basic objective is improvement in relation to the goals of the organization.[11]

By showing where changes in policies or procedures are desirable, operational auditing can help an organization improve both its effectiveness and efficiency. If properly conducted, it can be a valuable tool in the management of a nonprofit organization. If not properly conducted, however, it can be a source of friction and frustration, with no constructive results.

Example When James Watkins was head of the Department of Energy, he created "tiger teams" to serve as a special inspection force to enforce compliance with federal rules on environmental purity, worker safety, and public health. While some of the teams identified serious problems, others focused on the trivial. In one reported instance, a team member discovered a paint brush left under a fume hood in a laboratory. Someone in the lab had used it to apply ordinary paint to a piece of equipment, setting it down to dry so that it could be disposed of safely in the trash later. The tiger team threatened to cite the lab for a violation. As a result, the lab staffer was forced to wrap the brush in two layers of plastic, and dispose of it as costly hazardous waste.[12]

---

11 For an original presentation of the concept of operational auditing, see Ellsworth H. Morse, Jr., Assistant Comptroller General, "Operational Auditing and Auditing Standards," September 24, 1973. A complete description can by found in Andrew Chambers and Graham Rand, The Operational Auditing Handbook: Auditing Business Processes, New York, John Wiley and Sons, Limited, 2010. For a description of operational auditing in health care, see Charles Holley and Ross McDonald, "Operational Auditing of a Health Care Ancillary Department," *Internal Auditing*, 6, No. 1. For a description of its use in higher education, see John Krallman and Wayland Winstead, "Operational Audits in a University Environment," *Internal Auditing* 5, No. 2. For a description of its use in a municipality, see John D. Heaton, Linda J. Savage, and Judith K. Welch, "Performance Auditing in Municipal Governments," *Government Accountants Journal*, Summer 1993.

12 Eliot Marshall, "Tiger Teams Draw Researchers' Snarls," *Science*, 252 (April 19, 1991), pp. 366-69.

The operational auditor must recognize that all managers make mistakes, and that hindsight almost always permits identification of decisions that should have been made differently. There is no point, however, in publicizing such decisions if they were made in good faith, given the information available at the time. Operational auditing serves a useful purpose if, and only if, it shows how future decision-making can be improved.

Skills Required

Clearly, operational auditing requires a different approach and a different type of auditor than does compliance auditing. This is evidenced by the fact that the Government Accountability Office (GAO) hires approximately equal numbers of accountants and non-accountants. Operations analysts, economists, and social psychologists are well-represented among the non-accountants.

Process Flow Analysis. One technique that has proven effective in operational auditing is process flow analysis. Such an analysis can map levels of decision-making for a particular activity, thereby assisting managers to focus on potential problem areas or gaps in the way clients are handled by the organization's employees. While a process flow analysis can become highly complex, depending on the activity being analyzed, the technique itself is quite simple, identifying key decision points in a process, and analyzing the consequences of each.[13]

The value of process analysis is that it identifies in a very specific way the decisions that are made in conjunction with a particular activity. Since there can be no loose ends (i.e., paths that are left undefined), managers can view the decision-making process in its entirety and identify potential problem areas. Managers can monitor these areas and take corrective action when necessary.

Process analysis has become increasingly important in organizations implementing continuous quality improvement (CQI) and total quality management (TQM). These organizations ask line managers to engage in operational auditing. If senior management fosters an organizational environment that supports such an effort, line managers will be able to undertake operational analyses on their own. They do not have to wait for, or rely on, operational auditors to conduct them.

Controls on Effectiveness

Some management control systems omit effectiveness considerations, i.e., comparisons of actual and planned outputs. Indeed, the absence of information on effectiveness frequently is used as a reason for not giving appropriate attention to information that is provided by the system. For example, in a hospital, there may be no adequate formal mechanism for measuring the quality of care, and this fact leads some people to conclude that little attention should be given to the control of costs because of the danger that such attention might lead to a lowering of of quality.

Notwithstanding the absence of good data, there actually are powerful forces at work in hospitals and other nonprofit organizations where professionals deliver services, to ensure that the quality of service is adequate. If it becomes inadequate, this fact usually is brought to senior management's attention. Physicians, nurses, and other hospital professionals are vitally interested in patient welfare, and usually will not tolerate reductions in quality. Some hospitals also use patient care representatives to question patients about the quality of care they receive, and to bring patient complaints to the attention of management. Additionally, if there are problems with non-clinical quality, patients may complain directly. When these complaints are about poor food, dirty floors, or other matters within the patient's competence, they are relevant. They may even come to the attention of the general public or the trustees, which is an outcome senior management certainly wants to avoid.

---

[13] For a brief but very useful description of process analysis in a nonprofit contest, see Janelle Heineke, *Note on Process Analysis in Health Care* (Cambridge, MA: The Crimson Press Curriculum Center, 2006

The presence of competition also may affect quality, for if quality levels deteriorate in one hospital, physicians may threaten to use (or actually use) another. Accrediting and licensing agencies also make periodic inspections and check actual conditions against prescribed standards. Thus, physicians, nurses, patient representatives, patients, trustees, competition, and outside agencies are all of some help in assuring adequate quality levels, even in the absence of a formal method of measurement.

Example In one large medical center, a volunteer interviewed eight patients a month, following a printed interview guide. Serious problems, if any, were brought to the attention of management immediately. A summary report was discussed monthly at a meeting of management and the volunteer team.

Peer Review

Several professions have devised methods to ensure a satisfactory quality of service. Although the movements have different labels, they share in common the concept that a professional's work should be subject to review by other professionals. In a healthcare context, such a review would concern the accuracy and completeness of records, the accuracy of surgical diagnoses, and the clinical treatments and lengths of patient stays.

Peer review also exists in other organizations in which professional decision-making is a critical activity. Colleges and universities have mechanisms for reviewing the performance of faculty members, and the schools are themselves subject to review by accrediting agencies. In research organizations, work done by one group is reviewed by other groups.[14]

In general, when the principal output of an organization is the work of professionals, the quality of that output is best judged by other professionals. Professionals tend to resist peer review activities, however, and there is a strong possibility of back scratching, so the mechanism needs senior management attention if it is to be effective.

Results of Operational Auditing

Despite many years of emphasis on operational auditing, little in the way of management reform has taken place. In the federal government, for example, in 1984, the President's *Private Sector Survey on Cost Control* (the Grace Commission) identified programs where it claimed that waste reduction and improved management could result in savings of some $425 billion over five years. Relatively few of its proposals were implemented.[15]

By contrast, a detailed follow-up process was instituted for then-Vice President Gore's 1993 *National Performance Review*. Responsibility for implementing each of the *Review's* 1,250 recommendations was assigned to an agency or office, and each of these units was instructed to make annual reports to Congress. By 1995, according to Vice President Gore, 244,000 jobs had been eliminated, 2,000 obsolete field offices had been closed, and 200 programs and agencies had been eliminated. The result was a savings of $118 billion.[16]

---

[14] It should be noted that peer review focuses on the effectiveness of an organization's professionals and not on the broader question of the effectiveness of its programs. It may be, for example, that individual teachers in a bilingual education program are all extremely well qualified and carry out their responsibilities in a highly effective manner, but that the nature of the student population has changed such that the program no longer is needed. Questions such as these are part of an evaluation review, discussed in Chapter 13.

[15] *President's Private Sector Survey on Cost Control, War on Waste,* 1984. For current efforts to improve performance in the federal government, go to www.whitehouse.gov/omb/management.

[16] Al Gore, *The Best Kept Secrets in Government*, Washington, D.C., U.S. Government Printing Office, 1996).

Confusion with Compliance Auditing

Some organizations have not been successful at operational auditing because they do not identify the differences between operational auditing and compliance auditing. As a result, they use persons with an accounting background for operational auditing, simply because the auditing organization consists exclusively of accountants. When accountants imply that they know how to run a school, hospital, or any other organization better than the professionals who have spent their careers working in and managing such organizations, or when they attempt to recommend changes that are outside their areas of competence, their work is resented and frequently disregarded.

PROJECT CONTROL

The forgoing description has focused on the control of individual responsibility centers. Somewhat different techniques are appropriate for the control of projects, such as individual research projects or the construction of a major capital asset. Specifically, in controlling a responsibility center, the focus is on the work done in a specified period, such as a month or a quarter. In project control, by contrast, the focus is on the accomplishment of the project that, in some instances, may extend over a period of several years.

A project control system must consider three aspects of the project: cost, quality, and time. The elements of the system for controlling these items are work packages, budgets, cost and output reporting, and plan revisions.

Senior management begins the effort by specifying the responsibility centers that will be involved in the project. Responsibility center managers then estimate the activities to be completed and the resources and time required to complete them. These estimates should be made as near to the inception of the project as possible, and then organized in terms of work packages—relatively small, measurable increments of work that can be related to a physical product, milestone, or other measurable indicators of progress. These units should be of short duration, with clear starting and ending points, and should be the responsibility of a single organizational unit.

Based on the work packages, responsibility center managers prepare a work schedule and a budget showing (a) physical products, milestones, technical performance goals, or other indicators that will be used to measure output, (b) budgets for costs expected to be incurred for each work package and for overhead costs, (c) starting and completion time for each work package, (d) the organizational unit responsible for the work, and (e) any interdependencies among work packages.

During the project, the accounting staff maintains records of actual outputs and actual costs incurred. At frequent intervals, it prepares reports from these records showing, both for the interval and cumulatively, significant differences between budgeted and actual direct costs, overhead costs, work performed, and performance.

Based on these report, managers make revisions to the project plan and budget to reflect current estimates of the work schedule, the expected level of technical performance, and costs. Once they have revised plans and budgets, subsequent management reports should show comparisons both with the original (i.e., baseline) budget and with the current budget. The reasons for significant revisions should be readily identifiable in these reports.

BEHAVIORAL CONSIDERATIONS

Thus far, the focus of this chapter has been mainly on the technical aspects of performance control systems. While these matters are important, so too are the attitudes of those who use, and are affected by, the information from these systems. There are several behavioral matters that relate to the use of performance control information.

Senior Management Involvement

A management control system is likely to be ineffective unless operating managers and professionals perceive that their superiors consider it important. This requires that both senior management and line managers use information from the system in decision-making, in appraising the results of performance, and as a basis for salary adjustment, promotions, and other personnel actions. It also requires that superiors at all levels discuss the results of operations with their subordinates.

Some managers hold regular meetings to discuss performance of the entire organization. Others prefer individual discussions with responsibility center heads. Still others prefer to make comments in writing, holding only infrequent meetings. In all instances, in discussions of performance, subordinates should be given an opportunity to explain circumstances not revealed in the reports. If corrective action seems warranted, constructive suggestions for such action should be put forth and agreed upon. If the performance is good, managers should convey appropriate recognition.

Sometimes it is difficult for management to convey the correct impression about the importance of quantitative information, especially the comparison of budgeted and actual revenues and expenses. Inadequate attention leads to a common disregard of these numbers. On the other hand, if senior management places too much emphasis on numerical measures of performance, operating managers may act in such a way that their performance looks good according to the measures that are emphasized, but may be detrimental to the real objectives of the organization. These actions can be avoided only by convincing operating managers that they should concentrate on accomplishing the real objectives of the organization and that they will not be penalized if such efforts are not fully revealed in numerical measures of performance.

Importance of Adequate Staffs

Quantitative information for appraising performance cannot be used unless qualified people are available to make the calculations. Most managers do not have time to make the calculations themselves. Unfortunately, a great many nonprofit organizations, including some very large ones, do not have enough staff to undertake such analyses in a thorough and systematic way. For example, one state government agency with a multibillion dollar budget had only six professionals who were engaged in the regular analysis of operating reports. Some states have none at all.

Balance Between Freedom and Restraint

In any organization, for-profit or nonprofit, the right balance must be struck between freedom and restraint. Freedom is needed to take advantage of the ability and knowledge of the person on the firing line. Restraint is needed to ensure that management policies are followed and to mitigate the negative impact of poor judgments or counterproductive decisions by lower-level managers.

In nonprofit organizations, there are two complications to attaining an appropriate balance between freedom and restraint. First, the absence of profit as an overall basis for measuring performance usually calls for somewhat less freedom and somewhat more restraint than in a for-profit organization. Second, the presence of professionals in many nonprofits introduces a level of knowledge about client needs that senior management must consider carefully.

This is a matter of degree. Many nonprofit organizations, particularly government agencies, impose far too many (and far too detailed) restraints on line managers. Sometimes these restrictions are caused by the "goldfish bowl" problem. Errors are likely to be played up in the newspapers, and, as a protective device, managers prescribe rules, which they can point to when errors come to light: "I am not to blame; he (the sinner) broke my rule." The detailed restraints also result from encrustation: a sin is committed, and a rule is promulgated to avoid that sin in the future; but the rule continues even after the need for it had disappeared. Often, inadequate thought is given to whether the likelihood and seriousness of error is great enough to warrant continuation of the rule.

Motivation

A central purpose of any control system is to motivate operating managers to take actions that help accomplish the organization's objectives efficiently and effectively. The problem of inducing the desired degree and direction of motivation is difficult in any organization, but especially in nonprofit organizations. In a school system, for example, everyone is interested in better education, but teachers also are concerned with salary, educational advancement, and professional status.

The Problem of Budget Conformance

The fact that performance in a nonprofit organization is measured in part by how well managers conform to their budgets can have dysfunctional consequences. Suppose a manager has a $1 million budget, and by careful, hard work, performs the required job, but spends only $990,000. In many organizations, the budget for the following year, all else being equal, will be $990,000. In effect, the manager is punished, rather than rewarded, for reducing costs—his or her department now has less money to work with than would have been the case if the entire $1 million had been spent.

It is a difficult matter to create the right attitude in these circumstances. On the one hand, if the program can be run more efficiently, or if demand for it has fallen, its budget *should* be less than before. On the other hand, managers need incentives to be efficient this year that do not penalize them in future years. There are several possible ways to accomplish this.

One possibility is to guarantee managers that their budgets will not be reduced for the current year or the succeeding year, even if the job can be done at less than the amount budgeted. To make this policy work, senior management may need to expand the definition of operating expenses to include minor capital expenditures, for it is on items of this type that managers tend to spend the extra money.

A second possibility is to convince operating managers that a budget reduction, per se, should not be viewed as a punishment, and that senior management recognizes and rewards cost reductions. An effective and efficient manager is rewarded with a combination of promotion, salary, and the respect of peers, superiors, and subordinates. If senior management successfully stresses the importance of cost reduction, and provides appropriate rewards, it may be able to avoid negative reactions to a budget reduction.

The third possibility is to release substantially less (say, 20 percent less) than the funds managers need. They know that additional funds are available, but they can never be sure of getting them. This may lead them to be more careful than otherwise in spending available funds. There is a risk, of course, that this practice will stifle their initiative, and result in a reluctance to both introduce new programs and maintain existing facilities.

A fourth possibility is to hold next year's budget constant, but expect managers to accomplish more work with the same amount of resources. This approach increases efficiency just as much as a policy of expecting a unit to do the same amount of work with fewer resources. It also assumes that the organizational unit can, in fact, accomplish more work with the same amount of resources.

Use of Monetary Incentives

For-profit organizations often pay cash bonuses or give stock options when savings are realized or profits are high. Increasingly, as discussed in Chapter 2, nonprofit organizations are paying bonuses. Frequently, the bonuses are related to non-financial as well as financial performance, and sometimes they also emphasize the importance of collaboration and teamwork.

Example One nonprofit organization had an incentive system in which a portion of each manager's salary was withheld monthly with the understanding that it might not be paid at all. Depending on the extent to which the organization as a whole achieved its financial and programmatic objectives for the year, all or a portion of this withheld salary would then be paid out as a bonus. Since all managers received the same proportion of the amount withheld, and since the proportion was based on the performance of the entire organization, managers had a major incentive to collaborate, which was an essential activity for the success of the organization.

Short- versus Long-Term. A nonprofit's bonus arrangements usually relate to performances in the short-term. In general, nonprofit organizations have had difficulty designing incentive compensation plans that motivate managers to consider the long-term consequences of their decisions. One important reason is that they cannot use stock options, which frequently are used by for-profit companies to motivate managers to think in terms of the long-run.

Some nonprofit organizations have attempted to design incentive plans that encourage managers to adopt a long-term perspective. The accumulation of extra vacation days is one such approach, with the possibility of an extended sabbatical leave at some point in the future. If the system is designed in such a way that these days are not paid if the employee leaves the organization voluntarily, there also is an incentive for the employee to remain with the organization.

Gainsharing

Some nonprofit organizations have incorporated financial rewards into productivity improvement programs. Sometimes called *gainsharing,* these programs allow the savings generated by increases in productivity to be shared between the employee and the organization. At the federal level, the major barriers to gainsharing programs are the lack of legislation authorizing such programs, the presence of existing regulations that limit managers' flexibility in designing and operating the programs, and the absence of specific policies and guidelines from the Office of Personnel Management. Nevertheless, several instances have been reported of successful efforts, including elimination of work backlogs, decreased equipment downtime, reduction in time lost from on-the-job injuries, and substantial reductions in overtime and sick leave.

There are also gainsharing successes outside the federal government. For example, one hospital paid bonuses to employees of departments where productivity exceeded historical standards. The result was an increase in productivity of 8 percent, producing $2 million in savings; employee bonuses averaged 4.3 percent of base salaries.[17]

If properly designed, a gainsharing program takes advantage of the knowledge of possible improvements that usually exist in the lower levels of an organization. While there can be problems with gainsharing, such as a tendency to hold back some ideas for next year so there is constant evidence of effort, such a program nevertheless provides managers with a financial incentive to reduce costs.[18]

---

17 "Hospitals Adopt New Strategy to Keep Top Executives," *Journal of Accountancy,* March 1988, pp. 14-17.

18 For some early thinking on the issue, see U.S. General Accounting Office, "Gainsharing: DOD Efforts Highlight an Effective Tool for Enhancing Federal Productivity," *Briefing Report to the Chairman, Subcommittee on Defense,* Committee on Appropriations, House of Representatives, GAO, September 1986. For more recent thinking, see HRM04: Authorize Agencies to Develop Incentive Award and Bonus Systems to Improve Individual and Organizational Performance, Library, National Partnership for Reinventing Government, 21 May 2002. To obtain the report, go to http://govinfo.library.unt.edu/npr/library/reports/hrm04.html

SUMMARY

Control of operations consists of both financial and performance control. The former focuses on assuring that the spending limitations of the budget are adhered to. The latter is concerned with effective and efficient managerial performance. The distinction between the two types of control is highlighted by the kind of auditing that takes place in each. Financial control uses the compliance audit, an audit that is relatively narrow in scope, and is concerned with safeguarding the organization's assets against loss from unauthorized use or disposition. It also verifies the reliability of the records used for preparing financial statements. Its main focus is on the accounting system.

Performance control uses the operational audit, which is relatively broad in its scope, and focuses on how an organization is managing its resources. It attempts to identify the causes of any inefficiencies or uneconomical practices. The operational audit's main units of analysis are the management information system, administrative procedures, and the organizational structure.

Behavioral considerations are important in the control of operations. In particular, senior management should give program heads and responsibility center managers the freedom to exercise judgment in their operating activities, but they also must ensure that overall management policies are followed, and that the possibilities for poor judgment or counterproductive decisions by lower level managers are minimized. One tool to help attain this balance is a system of monetary incentives that rewards managers for attaining superior financial and programmatic operating results.

Rewarding managers for good performance is more difficult in a nonprofit organization than in a for-profit one, largely because the "bottom line" doesn't measure effectiveness or efficiency in the same way it does in a for-profit company. Thus, senior management must seek other ways to reward managers for the programmatic results they attain.

Suggested Cases for Classroom Use with this Chapter

See the Appendix at the end of the book for a more complete description of each case and ordering information.

Hospital San Pedro	Process flow analysis for a healthcare system in a developing country
WIC Program	Process flow analysis for food vouchers and detecting fraud in a food stamp program
Cittá di Forenna	Assessing a municipality's outsourcing strategy for trash collection
The Robert Wood Johnson Medical School	Assessing the role of an incentive system in controlling operations
Haas School of Business	Considering some ethical issues associated with supplemental payments to faculty in a business school

Chapter 10
Measurement of Output

No single overall measure of the performance of a nonprofit organization is analogous to the profit measure in a for-profit company. The goals of nonprofit organizations usually are complex and often intangible, and their outputs are difficult or impossible to measure. As a result, the performance measurement challenges nonprofits face are far greater than those of for-profit firms.

In general, output information is needed to measure (a) efficiency, which is the ratio of outputs (revenues) to inputs (expenses) and (b) effectiveness, which is the extent to which actual outputs correspond to the organization's goals and objectives.[1] In a for-profit organization, gross margin or net income can be used to measure both efficiency and effectiveness. In a nonprofit organization, no such monetary measure exists because revenues do not approximate true output as they usually do in a for-profit company. This chapter looks at alternative ways of measuring output in nonprofit organizations.

In the absence of a profit measure, analyses of efficiency and effectiveness require substitute measures of output. Despite the importance of devising such alternatives, the management control systems in many nonprofits tend to be deficient in this respect.

The problem of measuring output in nonmonetary terms is not unique to nonprofit organizations. The same problem exists in responsibility centers in for-profit organizations where discretionary costs predominate (e.g., research, law, personnel). Conversely, the output of many individual activities in nonprofit organizations, such as food service, vehicle maintenance, and clerical work, can be measured as easily as as the corresponding activities in for-profit entities.

Example A library estimated that it should take two minutes to re-shelve a book (including an allowance for personal time). One hundred books were replaced by a staff person who took 4 hours to complete the task. The output (100 books replaced) multiplied by the standard time per book (2 minutes) gave a total expected time of 200 minutes, or 3.3 hours (200 ÷ 60 minutes per hour). This can be compared with the actual total of 4 hours to measure productivity. This sort of analysis could be performed in a library of any sort, whether it is part of a nonprofit organization or a for-profit company.

BASIC MEASUREMENT CATEGORIES

Many terms are used to classify output measures according to what they purport to achieve. In this chapter, we will look at three: social indicators, result measures, and process measures.

Social Indicators

A social indicator is a broad measure of output that reflects the impact of an organization's work on society at large. Few if any social indicators can be related to the work of a single organization because in almost all instances they are affected by many different forces. The crime rate in a city may reflect the activities of the police department and the court system, but it is also affected by

[1] There often is some confusion about the distinction between goals and objectives. Here; the term "goals" means something broader than "objectives." Goals are related to a nonprofit's strategy; objectives are the focus of individual programs and/or departments.

unemployment, housing conditions, and other factors unrelated to the effectiveness of these organizations. Similarly, life expectancy (or its converse, mortality) is partly influenced by the quality of health care, but it is also affected by nutrition, environment, heredity, exercise, and other factors.

Example The Peace Corps sponsored an attempt to measure the effectiveness of its program in Peru, using measures that purported to show the change in Peruvians' well-being during a two-year period. Since there was no plausible way of relating the measures of well-being to the efforts of Peace Corps workers, the effort to measure the Peace Corps' effectiveness was of little value.

Additionally, valid social indicators are difficult to collect, and those that can be collected fairly easily are likely to be of dubious validity. Social indicators also are difficult to use properly because there ordinarily is no demonstrable cause-and-effect relationship between what an organization does and the change in a social indicator. Likewise, proxy indicators for intangible factors, such as percentage of registered citizens voting as an indicator of citizenship, or crime and disturbance statistics as indicators of social unrest, may be collected fairly easily, but frequently are of limited reliability.

Thus, social indicators are nebulous, difficult to obtain on a current basis, little affected by a single organization's current programmatic efforts, and much affected by external forces. As a result, for most nonprofits, they are only a rough indication of what a single organization has accomplished, and therefore are of limited usefulness for management control purposes.

Social indicators can be useful in strategic planning, however, in that they can help guide senior management's decisions about the overall directions the organization should take. Because of this, social indicators are often stated in broad terms, such as "the expectation of a high-quality life, free of serious disabilities."[2]

Example The American Cancer Society (ACS) devotes resources to activities that it knows have an impact on reducing the incidence of cancer, such as screening, education, and advocacy. One of its goals is a 50 percent reduction in cancer mortality rates and a 25 percent reduction in overall cancer incidence by 2015. It knows that other organizations will contribute to this goal but it has decided that using a social indicator serves as a rallying point for its programs.[3]

As discussed later in the chapter, social indicators also can be useful in a municipality or other government entity, where the work of several different departments can be coordinated toward a broad social goal. If the right departments are involved, and the work is well coordinated, a municipality can control many of the relevant forces (although it will not be able to control all of them).

Result Measures

Result measures attempt to express output in terms that are related to an organization's objectives. As such, they tend to avoid many of the difficulties inherent in social indicators. Ideally, objectives are stated in measurable terms, and output measures are stated in these same terms. When it is not feasible to express objectives in measurable terms, as is often the case, the result measure represents the closest feasible way management has to both specify the organization's objectives and measure progress toward them.

---

[2] The term *quality of life* refers to the general well being of individuals and societies. A comprehensive list of publications on the topic and its application to different contexts and wide variety of substantive areas can be found on the International Society for Quality-of-Life Studies. Go to www.isqols.org.

[3] John C. Sawhill and David Williamson, "Mission Impossible: Measuring Success in Nonprofit Organizations," *Nonprofit Management and Leadership,* Spring 2001.

Properly designed, a result measure relates to an organization's success in attaining its goals. If the organization is client-oriented, its result measures should relate to what it did for its clients. Organizations that render services to a class of clients, such as to alcoholics or unemployed persons, may measure output in terms of results for the whole class or a target group.

Although result measures usually are easier to collect and are more directly tied to a specific organization than social indicators, they still can pose difficulties. Indeed, the closer a result measure comes to a social indicator, the more difficult it is to establish a cause-and-effect relationship.

Example A program to rehabilitate alcoholics might measure results in terms of either the percent of enrollees successfully completing the program or the rate of recidivism. While the latter is a more accurate result measure, it is complicated by three factors: (1) the choice of an appropriate time period, (2) the difficulty of identifying clients who resume drinking but do not notify the program of this fact, and (3) the influence of forces outside the organization's control on an individual's decision to resume drinking. This latter complication is similar to a complication associated with social indicators.

Process Measures

A process measure (often called a *productivity* measure) relates to an organization's operational activities. Examples are the number of livestock inspected in a week, lines typed in an hour, requisitions filled in a month, or purchase orders written in a day. The difference between a result measure and a process measure is that the former is *ends-oriented,* while the latter is *means-oriented* (the terms *performance-oriented* and *work-oriented* are other names for the same distinction).

A process measure relates to what a responsibility center or an individual does to help an organization achieve its objectives. Thus, process measures help managers gauge efficiency. Since they do not measure effectiveness, however, they ordinarily are only remotely related to the organization's goals and objectives. Because of this, senior management should be careful not to put too much emphasis on process measures, especially if they are unrelated, or only tenuously related, to result measures.

Example A city measured the performance of its building inspectors by the number of miles they drove each day—a process measure. As a consequence, inspectors sometimes would build up a record of performance by crisscrossing town to make inspections, rather than by designing a route that would maximize the number of inspections in a day.

Need for Cause-and-Effect Relationships. In developing process measures, management must be careful to assure itself of a cause and effect relationship between the processes it wants employees to undertake and its desired results. There frequently is an implicit assumption that certain processes help the organization to achieve its objectives, but this is not always the case.

Example In an air pollution program, the change in the amount of ozone in the atmosphere is a result measure, while the number of inspections made of possible violators is a process measure. The implication of a causal relationship between the number of inspections made and the amount of air pollution may or may not be valid.

Process measures are most useful in the measurement of current, short-run performance, and are particularly helpful in the control of lower-level responsibility centers. They are the easiest type of output measure to interpret, presumably because there is a close causal relationship between them and inputs. Indeed, for those activities whose costs are related to inputs, process measures can be useful in constructing the relevant parts of a budget.

Example In a department of public health, restaurant inspections are considered an important process measure. If each restaurant inspection (including travel time, scheduling, report-preparation time, and other factors) should take approximately one hour and 15 minutes (a measure of efficiency), and there are 10,000 restaurant inspections to be made, there is a need for 12,500 inspector hours (10,000 restaurants x 1.25 hours per restaurant). This can be converted into the number of inspectors needed, which can be multiplied by the average inspector compensation to arrive at a budget.

Development of Standards. As the above example suggests, process measures require (a) identification of the activities of a person or a responsibility center and (b) development of a *unit standard*. A unit standard is the amount of time needed to complete a single activity. For instance, in the above example, a unit standard is the amount of time needed to inspect a single restaurant. When the total activity count is multiplied by the unit standard, the resulting amount can be compared with the actual time spent, and can be used to evaluate performance.

Example In the above example, if 3,000 restaurants were actually inspected during a given period of time, the 3,000 could be multiplied by the unit standard of 1.25 hours to give a total of 3,750 hours. This amount could be compared with the actual number of inspector hours used during the same period to obtain a measure of the efficiency of the inspectors. For example, if the inspectors did the job in 3,500 hours, they would be considered more efficient than anticipated.

In an office or clerical setting, there are three approaches to arriving at unit standards: (1) Using time standards for office operations developed by standard-setting organizations. (2) Having employees keep detailed records of the time taken to perform specific activities, and using averages of these records. (3) Having external observers record the time required to perform activities and the amount of idle time, according to a random plan of observations, and using averages of these records (often referred to as work sampling)

Example The National Institutes of Health established productivity measurement systems for its support activities. One was the Accounts Payable section, whose function was to examine roughly 30,000 vouchers monthly to determine whether they were completed properly.

Different types of vouchers required differing amounts of examination time; standard times were established by engineering studies. For convenience in calculating, unit standards were expressed as *equivalent units*. The simplest voucher, a transportation request, had a standard time of 7.37 minutes, and this was designated as one equivalent unit. Equivalent units for the 14 other types of documents were determined based on the ratio of their standard time to 7.37. For example, a purchase order accompanied by a record of the call had a standard time of 16.68 minutes, which was 2.3 standard units (16.68 ÷ 7.37).

These measures were used to calculate employee productivity each month. Assume, for example, that an employee worked 125 productive hours during the month and produced 2,163 equivalent units or 17.3 per productive hour. The standard per productive hour was 8.14 units (60 minutes ÷ 7.37). The employee therefore performed at 213 percent of standard.[4]

[4] From *Measuring Productivity in Accounting and Finance Offices*, Washington, D.C.: Joint Financial Management Improvement Program, September 1981, pp. 4-12.

Definitional Problems. Productivity typically is defined as output per unit of input. The inputs in the ratio should include labor, materials, energy, equipment, and all the other resources used to achieve the output. In practice, however, productivity usually has a much narrower definition. Specifically, because labor is the critical resource in most nonprofits, the term usually means output per person-hour or person-year. However, an increase in output per person-hour is equivalent to an increase in efficiency *only if* all input factors other than personnel remain constant.

Terminology Problems. Not everyone uses the above terms in the same way. For example, in developing service effort and accomplishment (SEA) measures, the Governmental Accounting Standards Board (GASB) used different terminology. Although the basic thrust was the same, the GASB used the terms inputs, outputs, and outcomes. Inputs were expenditures, outputs were process measures (e.g., number of visits per month in a clinic, number of student days in a school), and outcomes were result measures (e.g., infant mortality rates in a clinic, test scores in a school).

The GASB's work measured efficiency as a cost per unit (e.g., cost per immunization in a clinic, average cost per student-day in a school). Efficiency measures were computed for both outputs and outcomes. Exhibit 10-1 is an example of how these measures were structured for a maternal and child health (MCH) program in a public health agency.[5]

Exhibit 10-1 Recommended SEA Measures for Maternal and Child Health (MCH)

Indicator	*Rationale for Selecting Indicator*
Inputs:	
Expenditures (may be broken out by program or activity)	Measure of resources used to provide services in current and constant dollars
Outputs:	
Number of clients admitted to the MCH program Number of clinic visits per month	Widely reported measures that provide an indication of MCH program outputs
Outcomes:	
Infant mortality rate Low-birth-weight rate Teenage pregnancy rate Rate of lead poisoning cases Number of clients served by the(WIC) program	Widely accepted measures used by public health officials to measure MCH program outcomes
Percentage of low-birth-weight babies in target population Projected low-birth-weight births prevented Projected infant deaths prevented Cases of measles prevented	Widely reported measures by MCH programs to provide an indication of the accomplishment of short-term MCH program objectives
Efficiency:	
Cost per immunization	Indication of efficiency in purchasing immunizations
Cost of WIC supplements per unit	Indication of efficiency in purchasing supplements
Number of premature births/number of patients	Indication of efficiency in reducing premature births
Projected health care costs saved through routine checkups/costs of routine checkups	Indication of efficiency in reducing future healthcare costs

[5] For additional details, see Vivian L. Carpenter, "Improving Accountability: Evaluating the Performance of Public Health Agencies," *Association of Government Accountants Journal*, Fall Quarter 1990. Carpenter looks at the utility of GASB's recommended performance indicators for assessing performance in public health agencies.

In addition, the literature that has emerged over the past few years has several slightly different conceptual models. For example, in some instances social indicators are called "outcomes," and are differentiated in terms of results and impacts. Sometimes, the relevant time frame (short-term versus long-term) is important. Sometimes processes are included in what this chapter calls "results." Furthermore, there are differences in the use of terms, where different terms may mean the same concept (for example *activity* is sometime used as substitute for *process*) or where the same terms refer to different concepts (for example certain authors refer to results as outputs and others call them outcomes). Obviously, it is important to understand the concept at work, rather than to attempt to memorize the terminology.[6]

Measurement Problems. Beyond problems with definition and terminology, there also are problems occasionally in reaching agreement on the adequacy of the measure. That is, whether the measurement device actually gives useful information on the item in question.

Example For many years, the Nature Conservancy, a nonprofit organization dedicated to conserving biodiversity by protecting the lands and waters that rare species need to survive, used two measures of success: bucks and acres. Bucks referred to total revenue and its annual growth rate; acres referred to acres under protection in the United States. Despite growth in both measures, species extinction continued to grow at alarming rates. Even endangered species that had once lived on the acreage under the Conservancy's control had, over time, vanished from its properties.

As a result, the Conservancy began to develop new performance measures. The eventual result was a family of measures that addressed three areas: impact, activity, and capacity. Impact measures focused on the organization's mission; activity measures focused on goals and strategies; and capacity measures were oriented toward obtaining the required resources. These categories are similar to social indicators, result measures, and process measures.[7]

Linkages Among Measures

Some organizations have had success in linking process measures to result measures, and even in suggesting a link between result measures and social indicators. For reasons discussed earlier, the latter linkage is difficult to identify with any certainty, but the former is quite feasible. Specifically, for many activities, once an organization has determined its objectives, management can specify the corresponding result measures, and can link those measures to the process measures required to achieve them. The process measures also can be linked to the productivity of the organization's employees. Then, if objectives are not achieved, or if the cost of achieving certain objectives is higher than anticipated, the measurement system can help to pinpoint the reasons.

Example A social service agency ran a group home program for at-risk adolescent girls. In an effort to measure the program's success, the agency worked with each girl entering the home to determine: (a) her vocational and living goals, (b) the objectives that were related to each goal, and (c) the service needs for each objective. For example, if a girl wished to become a beautician, this was established as a vocational goal. The related objectives might be obtaining a high school diploma, completing beauticians' school, improving the girl's relationships with adults, and developing her ability to manage personal finances. Service needs then were established, such as

6 For further details see C. Talbot, *Theories of Performance. Organizational and Service Improvement in the Public Domain*, Oxford, Oxford University Press, 2010, and Theodore H. Poister, *Measuring Performance in Public and Nonprofit Organizations*, San Francisco Jossey-Bass, 2003.

7 John C. Sawhill and David Williamson, "Mission Impossible: Measuring Success in Nonprofit Organizations," *Nonprofit Management and Leadership*, Spring 2001.

10 hours per week of tutoring, tuition for beauticians' school, three hours a week of psychotherapy, and structured summer employment in a job entailing interaction with adults.

The entire structure of goals, objectives, and service needs was time phased, and progress was assessed every quarter. During the assessment, the following questions were asked:

1. Were service needs delivered as anticipated and at the budgeted cost? If not, what changes were made and why?
2. Were the objectives accomplished as scheduled? If not, why not? Was it because designated service needs were not delivered, because needed services were not identified, or for some other reason?
3. If the objectives were accomplished, did they have the anticipated effect? If not, why not?
4. Are any new objectives needed?
5. Does the girl still have the same goals, and are they realistically attainable? If not, what new goals, objectives, and service needs should be put in place?

The program aimed to develop a result measure that focused on the target population: percent of girls who achieved their goal. In addition, managers developed a number of related measures, such as percent of objectives accomplished, percent of services delivered as anticipated, and actual expenditures per girl versus the budget.

Linking the Measures in Public Sector Organizations. In some public sector organizations, especially municipal governments, it is possible to develop a relatively strong link between social indicators and the related result and process measures. It also is possible to link the process measures to the resources needed to carry them out, and hence to determine the cost of attaining certain results, and ultimately the cost of attaining the organization's social indicators.

To see how such an approach might work, consider a city or town that has a social indicator of clean and safe streets. Several of the municipality's departments contribute to this, such as road maintenance and repair, street cleaning, public safety, and trash collection. As Exhibit 10-2 indicates, each department could develop a set of result measures related to its contributions to achieving and maintaining clean and safe streets. It then could determine the activities it needed to undertake to accomplish the results, and estimate the cost of each. These estimates then would be submitted as part of its annual budget request.

ISSUES IN SELECTING OUTPUT MEASURES

In selecting output measures, senior management makes several choices, all of which affect the kind of output information that program and other line managers will see. The choices also have an impact on how these managers and others will view the effectiveness and efficiency of the organization. It therefore is important for senior management to consider these choices carefully.

In many instances, standard-setting bodies, laws, and governmental agency rules influence the selection of performance measures. Many of these can have an impact on a nonprofit's definition of "performance." Indeed, many nonprofits, especially local governments, deal with a multitude of entities that can affect or even constrain their performance. The list of potential entities includes government departments, ministries, legislatures, auditors, inspection and regulatory bodies, judicial bodies, professional institutes, and, finally citizens and other service users. As a result, senior managers and elected officials often find it difficult to select performance measures that satisfy all relevant stakeholders.

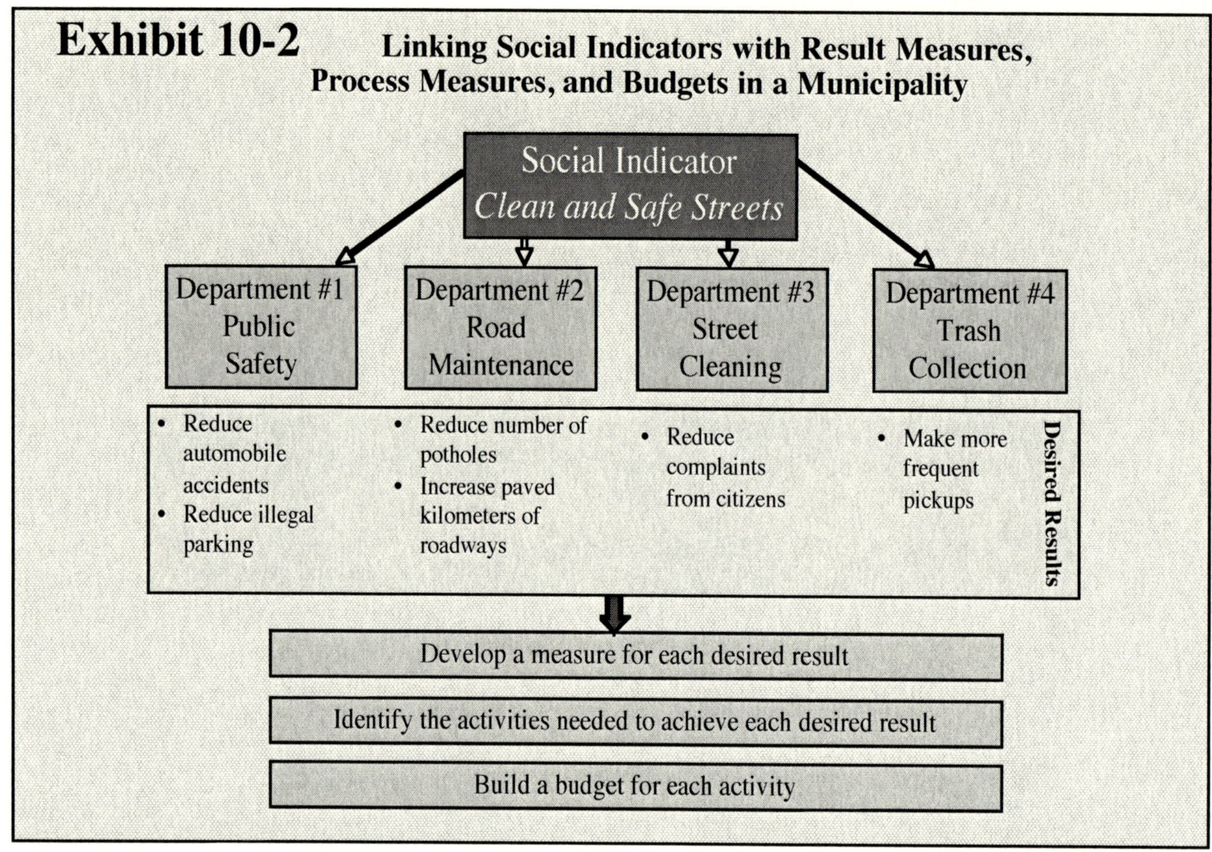

In addition to these matters, nonprofit managers must contend with several methodological issues in designing their performance measurement system. Each of these requires some tricky decision-making.

Subjective Versus Objective

An output measure may result from the subjective judgment of a person or a group of persons, or it may be derived from data that (unless consciously manipulated) do not depend on human judgment. Of course, in many instances, a judgment made by a qualified person can be a better measure of the quality of performance than any objective measure. This is because humans incorporate the effects of circumstances and nuances of performance into their judgment. No set of objective measures can take all of these factors into account.

Example Hospitals are usually reluctant to measure the performance of physicians by any means other than peer review. Professors also prefer peer review judgments, but will increasingly accept ratings made by students. Many will not accept the number of students electing a course or the number of articles published as valid measures of performance, however.

On the other hand, subjective judgments depend on the person making the judgment, and may be affected by his or her prejudices, attitudes, and even emotional and physical state at the time the judgment is formed. Objective measures, if properly obtained, do not have these defects. Ideally, an organization's output measures should include both.

Quantitative Versus Non-Quantitative

Information in a measurement system is usually quantitative so that it can be summarized and compared. Even some subjective information can be measured quantitatively. For example, grades in schools, even though numerical, indicate the instructor's judgment as to where a student's performance is located along some scale. Similarly, although performance in figure skating contests, gymnastics, and certain other athletic events is measured by the subjective assessment of the judges, the performer is ranked along a numerical scale by each judge, and these ranks are then averaged to give a quantitative measure.

Non-quantitative information also can be valuable in some instances, but it frequently is more useful for professionals than for supervisors or senior management. For example, most case files in a social service agency contain narrative statements of the social workers' assessments of clients. In many instances, these statements contain judgments about the kind of progress the client is making. While the statements frequently do a good job of measuring the progress of each client, and would be valuable for a replacement social worker taking over the case, or for review with a supervisor, they ordinarily cannot be summarized and reported to management in a quantitative way. Unless it reviews each case file, which is an impossible task, senior management has difficulty measuring client progress, and hence the overall performance of the agency in meeting its goals.

Discrete Versus Scalar

A measure of performance may be either discrete (a "satisfactory/unsatisfactory" or "go-no-go" dichotomy), or it may be measured along a scale. For example, to measure performance of a reading program in a school, a target could be established, such as "80 percent of students should read at or above grade level on a standardized test." If the measure were discrete, any performance of 80 percent or higher would be counted as success, and any performance below 80 percent would be counted as failure. If the measure were scalar, the percentage of students reading at each grade level on a standardized test would be used as the measure of performance.

In general, scalar measures are preferable to discrete ones. However, there are many situations where discrete measures are appropriate. For example, most colleges do not measure how close their applicants came to being admitted; they simply use a discrete measure: x percent of all applicants met the admission criteria.

Actual Versus Surrogate Measures

Whenever actual output can be measured, an organization should do so. If actual output cannot be measured, a surrogate measure may be useful, assuming it is closely related to an objective. By definition, however, a surrogate does not correspond exactly to an objective, and managers should keep this limitation in mind. If this limitation is not recognized, the organization may focus too much attention on the surrogate, which may be dysfunctional. Achieving the surrogate should not be permitted to become more important than achieving the objective.

Examples A city used "number of complaints" as a surrogate performance measure for the agency that managed low-cost rental housing. It was later discovered that, after this measure was introduced, the agency pressured tenants not to make complaints. As a result, performance, as measured by the surrogate, appeared to improve, whereas service to tenants actually had deteriorated.

When "effectiveness" of a Job Corps training program was being calculated by the contractor, "completions" were the mark of success; "dropouts" were the failures. When the latter appeared

> to be on the increase, "certificates of completion" were issued every other Saturday instead of the diploma originally given at the end of six months. Immediately, the number of completions rose, and the proportion of dropouts declined. As a result, the effectiveness of the enterprise was assured, as was its continued funding.
>
> The success of some U.S. Department of Labor employment programs was measured by the proportion of people placed in jobs. This led to the practice known as "cream skimming:" accepting as job applicants the cream of the unemployed (persons temporarily unemployed but with a high probability of being placed).
>
> Performance of Veterans Administration hospitals was measured in part by the percentage of beds occupied. Because many hospital costs are fixed, a high occupancy rate resulted in a low cost per patient day. Studies showed that some veterans hospitals tended to keep patients longer than their clinical need for hospitalization. The result was a low cost-per-patient-day, but a higher-than-necessary *total cost*.

An inappropriate surrogate output measure may cause the discontinuation of a useful program, but, more likely, it will support the continuation of a marginally useful one, with a corresponding waste of resources. Inappropriate surrogate measures also may cause agencies to be complacent even though they are not reaching their objectives.

Quantity Versus Quality

Although performance has both a quantity and a quality dimension, it usually is more feasible to measure the former. Nevertheless, the quality dimension should not be overlooked.

Frequently, the indicator chosen to measure quantity implies some quality standard. "Number of lines typed per hour" usually carries with it the implication that the lines were typed satisfactorily; there may even be an explicit statement of what constitutes a satisfactory line of typing, such as the requirement that it be free of errors. Similarly, the measure "number of students graduated" implies that the students met the standards of quality that were prescribed for graduation.

In some situations, judgments about quality are limited to discrete measures such as those given above: either a line of typing was error-free or it was not; either students met the requirements for graduation or they did not. In these situations, it is not feasible to measure quality along a scale, and this precludes a determination of, say, whether this year's graduates received a better education than last year's.

Importance of Quality. In nonprofit organizations, measures of quality tend to be more important than in for-profit ones, where the market mechanism provides an automatic quality check. If a pair of shoes is shoddy, people will not buy it. The company will then have to raise quality to stay in business. If it does not, other companies will take its customers away.

Similar market mechanisms exist for some nonprofit organizations. For example, a university that gives poor quality education quite likely will lose students to other universities. A museum that has poor quality exhibitions will not have as many visitors as otherwise. In some nonprofits, however, there is no such mechanism for consumer reaction to output. Hospital patients generally are not competent to judge the quality of their care, and, even if they are dissatisfied, there may be little they can do. Clients of welfare departments, courts, public safety departments, license bureaus, and other government offices cannot "vote with their feet" as customers of commercial businesses can; they have nowhere else to go. Because of the absence of market-oriented client checks on quality in nonprofit organizations, it is usually worthwhile for an organization to devote considerable effort to developing quality measures. If possible, these measures should be linked to the individuals responsible for attaining them.

Example U.S. Healthcare, Inc., a health maintenance organization (HMO), decided to integrate quality indicators with its physician payment and re-certification system. Twenty percent of each physician's payment was withheld, with return of the withheld amounts based on a 50/50 split—half on corporate utilization goals and half on four quality measures: (1) patient satisfaction, (2) chart audits, (3) transfer rates, and (4) a general assessment of the physician's ability to perform as expected. Re-certification of physicians took place yearly, and high dissatisfaction rates led to close scrutiny.[8]

In some programs where a market mechanism might provide a measure of quality, an individual's personal motive for participating in the program may diverge from the program's social objective, so that personal and social measures of quality differ. For example, if a job training program neither trains nor places its clients well, unemployed people may still participate in it out of boredom, or out of hope it will assist them, or because they receive a stipend for participation. In such circumstances, unless there are adequate measures of quality, management may be misled about the value of the program's services.

Measuring Quality. Many nonprofit organizations have initiated programs in Total Quality Management (TQM) or Continuous Quality Improvement (CQI). One of the dilemmas they face is measuring improvements in quality, which, as indicated above, is inherently subjective. Yet, unless management can find some way to measure quality changes in a relatively objective fashion, the claim that quality has improved will have little credibility.

There are three approaches that managers generally take to measure quality: crude measures, estimates, and surrogates. Each has advantages and disadvantages.

Crude Measures of Quality. The absence of quality measures may lead to an emphasis on quantity. For example, people may be pushed rapidly through an education program, or inspectors may make a large number of quick and careless pollution inspections, or construction jobs may be done in a quick and shoddy manner. Thus, managers should make every effort to find acceptable quality measures, even if they are crude.

Example In preschool programs, one can measure a child's degree of literacy, social acclimation, and so forth before and after the program. In personnel training, one can ask employers to rate graduates. In construction, one can test fulfillment of construction standards.

Even though these measures are crude, and even though they may not contain the "proper" attribute of quality, they may, if nothing else, serve as good motivators for the program's management and service delivery personnel. This assumes, of course, that there is a clear relationship between inputs and quality. If there is no demonstrable relationship between the two, senior management may not find it worthwhile to attempt to measure quality.

Example In what is now considered an infamous failure to measure quality, even crudely, Boston's "Big Dig" not only overran its original budget by several billion dollars, but, upon completion was

[8] Maria R. Traska, "HMO Uses Quality Measures to Pay Its Physicians," *Hospitals*, Vol. 62, Issue 13, July 5, 1988.

discovered to have water leakages that were so serious as to cause portions of the project's underground passages to be closed for repair. Then, when a portion of the ceiling in one of the underground stretches collapsed and killed a motorist, a substantial section of the underground roadway was shut down for months while repairs were made. While the repairs were underway, 15 separate entities, ranging from the Massachusetts Turnpike Authority to an adhesive manufacturer, all were suing each other over the quality failures.[9]

Estimates of Quality. In the absence of objective data, *estimates* of quality may be useful. For example, in a university, comparisons can be made between the standing of a college or department within its professional discipline, or between its position currently and its position in the past. Similar judgments can be made about the kinds of jobs graduates hold and the kinds of organizations that employ them.

Surrogates for Quality. In some nonprofit organizations, surrogates for the quality of services provided, such as response time, are important indicators. Often, objective measures of such surrogates are readily obtainable. Examples are the backlog of information requests, the number of checks returned due to of error, average time taken to process an application, and the number of applications completed within a specified number of days after their receipt. Clearly, in using surrogates, managers must be cautious to avoid some of the problems discussed earlier.

IMPLEMENTING OUTPUT MEASURES: SOME GENERAL PRINCIPLES

As the above discussion suggests, selecting and implementing output measures for a management control system is an extremely complex task. It also is highly situational—what works for one organization quite likely will not work for another. This is certainly true if two organizations have contrasting missions and clientele, but it also may be the case even if the two are similar.

Despite dissimilarities among organizations, some general principles are relevant for selecting and implementing the output measures in an organization's management control system. These principles are very general—there no doubt are exceptions to each. Nevertheless, they can provide some useful guidance to managers concerned with measuring an organization's output.

Principle #1. Some Measure of Output Usually is Better than None

Valid criticisms can be made about almost any output measure, since no measure is perfect. There is a tendency on the part of some managers to magnify the imperfections and thus downgrade the attempt to collect and use any output information. In most situations, a sounder approach is to take account of the imperfections and to qualify the results accordingly. In general, some output data, however crude, are more useful to a manager than none at all.

Although there is always a possibility of inappropriate output measures, most organizations can develop reasonable, albeit imprecise, indicators of output. Rather than using such indicators as absolute bases for judgment, managers can use them as a basis for asking questions to determine if a problem really exists. Thus, considerable effort in finding and developing output measures generally is worthwhile.

Inputs as a Measure of Outputs. Although generally less desirable than a true output measure, inputs are often better than no measure at all. For example, it may not be feasible to construct

[9] Sean A. Murphy and Scott Allen, "The Big Tangle," *The Boston Globe,* April 8, 2007.

output measures for research projects. In the absence of such measures, the amount spent on a research project may provide a useful clue to output. In the extreme, if no money was spent, it is apparent that nothing was accomplished. (This assumes that the accounting records show what actually was spent, which sometimes is not the case.)

Example The New Communities Program offered assistance to private and public developers of new communities. Although funds were available, no new projects were financed for 10 years. This was considered to be conclusive evidence that the program was not generating outputs.

As with other surrogates, when inputs are used as surrogates for output measures, managers must be careful to avoid undue reliance on them. An organization should continually try to develop usable measures of output.

Principle #2. Compare Output Measures to Measures from Outside Sources

Several professional associations, including those for hospitals, schools, colleges and universities, and welfare organizations, collect information from their members, and compile averages and other statistics. These statistics may provide a valuable starting point for analyzing the performance of an organization. Similar data are available from government sources, such as the Office of Productivity and Technology of the Bureau of Labor Statistics (although not much for nonprofit organizations), the U.S. Department of Health and Human Services, and various state agencies. In some cases, the measures reported are too detailed or not well suited to management needs, but some of the available statistics may nevertheless be useful.

Problems with Comparability. When one organization's output information is being compared with averages of other organizations, the data must be comparable. This requires that the definitions used in compiling the averages be studied carefully; the user should not rely on the brief titles given in the tables. Moreover, in using published statistics, an organization must be sure that its data are prepared according to the same definitions and ground rules as those used by the compiling organization.

Example The reporting system of the Department of Health of the state of New York defined a hospital bed three different ways: certified beds, bed complement, and total beds. Unless users knew which of these definitions was in use, they could not make valid comparisons.

Comparability is especially important when data are reported for costs per unit of output. If an organization's definitions do not correspond to those used for both the numerator and the denominator of a ratio, the comparison is invalid. "Cost per FTE (full-time-equivalent) student" can be a valuable statistic, but there are several different ways of defining the denominator of this ratio, and innumerable ways of defining the elements of cost that make up the numerator.

Problems with Reliability. Managers also should ensure that reliable data underlie the statistics. For example, many people believe that some statistics published by the Department of Education were compiled from data of dubious validity. Obviously, one cannot expect to obtain valid comparative information from poor raw data.

Within an organization, if costs per unit of output are desired, output measures must be comparable with expense measures. In some organizations, the output measurement system is developed by one group and the expense reporting system by another. Under such circumstances, comparability is unlikely. Furthermore, if the cost-per-unit ratio is for a responsibility center, the responsibility center must be defined in the same way for measuring outputs as for measuring inputs (expenses); this is also the case for program elements or other cost objects.

Principle #3. Use Measures that Can be Reported in a Timely Manner

There is no point in furnishing information after the need for it has passed. If managers need information quickly as a basis for action, the controller's staff must find a way to compile the information quickly. In this regard, the controller's office must keep in mind that, for management control purposes, a timely, but not completely accurate, output measure usually is preferable to a highly accurate but less timely one.

Example Mortality from emphysema, which can be measured only years after the occurrence of the cause of the disease, is less useful for control of air pollution programs than less accurate but more timely measures, such as the number of persons with eye, ear, nose, or throat irritations, the number of persons who are advised by physicians to move to another locality, or the amount of effluents in the air.

Reasons for Timeliness Problems. Timeliness requirements are different for different types of information, and timeliness is not necessarily equivalent to speed. Rather, it is related to when a manager needs information for taking action. In addition, the problem of timeliness is different in nonprofit organizations than in for-profit companies. There are several reasons for the differences.

Lack of Prompt Feedback. Output often cannot be measured immediately after a program's efforts have taken place. The results of funds invested in a school program in September may not be measurable until the following June, for example. The effect of interest rate subsidies on the supply of low-income housing may not be measurable for two or three years after the program has been initiated due to the time needed to design and construct buildings. The impact of reforestation programs may not be measurable for a decade or two.

Organizational Hierarchy. Because of the bureaucratic and political nature of many public sector entities, reports on a program may have to work their way through several organizational layers before they reach the key decision maker. At that point, they may be too old to be of much use.

Example Title I, an educational program, provided grants through a state educational agency, then through a local educational agency, and ultimately to the local Title I administrator. The data that worked their way back through this chain were several months old when they finally reached program analysts in Washington.

Principle #4. Develop a Variety of Measures

There is no such thing as a general-purpose report on output that is analogous to a general-purpose financial statement. Just as management accounting information must be tailor-made to the needs of individual managers, so too must output measures.

For most responsibility centers, and for an organization as a whole, there are usually a few *key result measures* that are important indicators of the quality and quantity of performance. In a given situation, opinions may differ as to what these are, but it is usually worthwhile to give careful thought to identifying them. When there are several measures, each tends to be used for a different purpose. For example, with respect to health care in a community:

1. The total cost of a health center can be used as a basis for comparison with the cost of other community services; this measures the relative emphasis given to each service. Expressed as a cost per person in the community, this can be compared with costs per person in other communities as another expression of relative emphasis.

2. There can be a measure of the cost per visit, or diagnosis, or episode of illness.

3. At a lower level, information can be collected on the overall cost per patient day in each hospital as a basis for detecting gross differences in the operating characteristics of the various hospitals. Patient-day costs for each service (medicine, surgery, pediatrics, psychiatry, and so forth) can be useful for similar reasons.

4. At a still lower level, one can measure the cost per unit of service rendered, such as cost per meal served, or cost per nursing hour.

A Continuum of Output Measures. When several types of output measures are used in a given organization, they tend to be arranged along a continuum. At one end are result measures (sometimes rough ones) that are closely related to the goals of the organization; at the other end are precisely stated process measures that are only remotely related to the organization's goals.

Example At one extreme, the U.S. Information Agency measured the degree to which its activities influenced international behavior. This is close to a social indicator. A second level measured the extent to which specific attitudes and opinions of the governing members of other nations had been changed by the agency's work. A third level measured the increase in understanding of people overseas in regard to specific issues. A fourth level counted the number of times people had been reached by media of different kinds. A fifth and lowest level counted the number of "media products" produced by the agency, which clearly was a process measure.

It is useful to think of output measures in terms of this continuum for two reasons. First, higher-level output measures generally are better indicators of the organization's or program's effectiveness than lower-level measures, which often are not closely related to goals. Second, lower-level indicators are easier to specify and quantify than are higher-level indicators. This fact explains the prevalence of measures of personnel efficiency in situations where personnel efficiency is only marginally related to overall program goals.

The continuum also corresponds to the relative usefulness of particular types of output indicators at various levels in the organization's hierarchy. Result measures (and sometimes social indicators) are most useful to senior management, governing bodies, and funding sources, whereas process measures are most useful to first-line supervisors.

Example A regional Air Pollution Control Administration headquarters had a wide variety of measures. It measured its own efficiency; that is, it had internal process measures, such as how fast a request was considered. At the other end of the spectrum, it had objectives for air quality in each region. The progress toward these objectives was measured by the appropriate instrumentation.

Between these process and result measures there were several measures related to the functioning of the regional administrator and the state programs within a region. For example, one agency had an objective to improve air quality in the New England region by more vigorous anti-pollution efforts on the part of the Commonwealth of Massachusetts.

Principle #5. Don't Report More Information than is Likely to be Used

Although a variety of output measures may be feasible, managers should avoid receiving too much information. In part, this problem arises because there is a reluctance in many organizations to discontinue the use of certain output measures when they no longer serve an important managerial purpose. This reluctance must be overcome if the management control system is to remain valuable and cost effective.

Example In response to a request from a manager, the Information Services Department in a social service agency developed a report that classified clients according to race and age. This was valuable output information to the manager at the time. Several years later, after that manager had left the agency, and the kinds of problems and issues the agency faced had changed, the Information Services Department continued to prepare the report, even though no one used it.

A similar problem also arises when output measurement systems are being designed initially. In developing a new system, the system's designers have a tendency to collect a great mass of data so that there will be information available to meet everyone's desires. However, too much data swamp the system, increase its "noise level," draw attention away from important information, and lessen the credibility of the system as a whole.

Principle #6. Don't Give More Credence to Surrogates than is Warranted

As discussed previously, a surrogate can be a useful approximation of actual output, but it never should be interpreted as a *substitute* for actual output. Its limitations must be kept in mind when developing a measurement system for output information.

USE OF OUTPUT MEASURES FOR STRATEGIC PLANNING VERSUS USE FOR MANAGEMENT CONTROL

The management control system should provide output information that is useful for both strategic planning and management control. Managers should recognize, however, that the criteria governing the output measures used for strategic planning tend to differ from those used for management control. They do so in several ways:

Precision

For strategic planning, rough estimates of output generally are satisfactory. For management control, the measure must be more precise (although, as indicated above, timeliness considerations sometimes outweigh the desire for precision).

Example One hospital's strategic planning activities included the purchase of a magnetic tape from the local telephone company; the tape contained information on new telephone installations. This information was used to identify the number of potential new patients in the hospital's service area. The fact that the tape contained data on people who had moved within the service area, and thus did not indicate precisely how many new residents there were, was not considered a serious limitation.

Causality

For strategic planning purposes, there should be a plausible, although perhaps only tenuous, link between a potential effort (i.e., inputs) of the organization and the output measure. For management control purposes, the connection needs to be stronger. If output measures are to be used in analyzing a proposal for a specific program, for example, there should be some connection between inputs and outputs. To include correlating but non-causal input and output numbers in a new program analysis is not only a waste of time, but may do more harm than good if it leads people to believe erroneously that such a connection exists.

Example In one rural community, there was a high positive correlation between the number of storks observed in the spring and the number of babies born in the following winter. If health planners wish to determine the demand for maternity services, a model that used the number of storks as a predictive indicator probably would suffice. If, however, health planners wish to lower the birthrate, the systematic extermination of storks would not work, since the causal factor for both storks and babies was something entirely different: the richness of spring crops. Rich crops caused the storks to come in the spring because there was plenty of food for them; the rich crops also were a cause for optimism among the farmers and their wives, resulting in higher birthrates.[10]

The absence of a demonstrated causal connection is no reason to avoid analyzing *plausible* connections to assess the impact of a certain program. When there is no causal connection, decisions must be based on judgments unaided by quantitative information. For example, it seems obviously desirable to spend money on a judiciary system even though no good measurement of output is available and there is evidence to suggest that some judges use bad judgment.

Responsibility

For management control, output measures must be related to the responsibility of a specific person or organization unit. For strategic planning, this is unnecessary. Thus, strategic considerations may require operating personnel to collect data for which they themselves have no use.

Example Title I education programs were intended to provide funds for improving the education of low-income and disadvantaged children. In connection with these programs, planners in Washington required the collection of data (e.g., test scores) that were of no use to operating managers. They were nevertheless necessary for reformulating program goals and strategies.

Timeliness

For management control purposes, data on outputs must be available shortly after the event. For strategic planning, this is less important.

Example The crime rate of an urban area is useful for strategic planning purposes, even if the data are lagged by a year or so. On the other hand, data on police surveillance hours by neighborhood is needed within a day or two; a delay of one or two weeks would be of marginal help for taking managerial action to correct a deficiency in a particular neighborhood.

---

[10] Richard Normann, *A Personal Quest for Methodology*, Stockholm, Sweden: Scandinavian Institutes for Administrative Research, SIAR Dokumentation AB, 1975, p. 7-9.

Cost

For both strategic planning and management control, the benefits of obtaining information about inputs and outputs must exceed the costs of obtaining it. For strategic planning, it may be possible to obtain certain data on an *ad hoc* or sampling basis to keep the cost low, whereas the continuous collection of the same data for management control would be prohibitively expensive.

Relation to Program Elements

If output measures are to be useful for strategic planning, they must be related to the organization's overall goals and objectives. If it is not feasible to do this directly, it may be necessary to relate the measures to program categories or even to individual program elements. Ideally, they should be related to all three.

THE BALANCED SCORECARD

One well-known approach to linking several output measures, including some that may be useful in strategic planning, is known as the Balanced Scorecard (BSC). The BSC can help senior management translate the organization's mission and strategy into a set of performance measures.

Although the BSC in for-profit organizations tracks financial results, it also monitors progress along three other dimensions: customers, internal processes, and innovation and learning,[11] all of which are considered to be drivers of successful financial performance. In a nonprofit organization, where successful financial performance typically means abiding by financial constraints, and is not the end goal, the other dimensions are important in and of themselves.

The designers of the BSC emphasize that both financial and non-financial measures should be part of the reports received by managers at all levels of the organization. Although all responsibility centers presumably are concerned with achieving the organization's mission and strategy, each of them usually has a different role to play in the effort. Thus, the the BSC can help a responsibility center manager to monitor his or her center's results and their contributions to the performance of both the center and the organization overall. Moreover, by reviewing the results of all responsibility centers, senior management can see each center's contribution to the organization's overall performance, both financially and non-financially, and can intervene when necessary to take corrective action. Additionally, since a BSC's measures are closely linked to the organization's mission, it can be a powerful tool for channeling employee energy into improved performance.

The BSC combines several elements discussed previously in this chapter. First, it includes both external and internal measures. In a nonprofit organization, the external category might include not only clients, but funders, the community, and perhaps regulators as well, whereas the internal category comprises service-delivery processes and employees' learning and growth. Second, the BSC attempts to achieve a balance between outcome measures and process measures. Third, it includes both objective, easily quantified, measures a well as more subjective, somewhat judgmental, ones, or perhaps surrogates. Finally, it attempts to include measures that have some causal relationship with overall organizational performance and the attainment of strategic goals.

---

[11] For details on the BSC, see Robert S. Kaplan and David P. Norton, "The Balanced Scorecard: Measures That Drive Performance," *Harvard Business Review*, January-February 1992. See also Robert S. Kaplan and David P. Norton, "Putting the Balanced Scorecard to Work," *Harvard Business Review*, September-October 1993.

Developing and Using a BSC

The BSC is based on the idea that no single measure, not even profit in the for-profit world, can adequately capture the performance of an entire organization. At the same time, senior management would be wasting resources if it attempted to track all measurable activities and outputs. A typical BSC therefore contains a limited set of measures that focus management's attention on the key activities that the organization must do well to succeed.

Adaptating the BSC to Nonprofit Organizations. Because profit is not the ultimate objective, some nonprofits have found they need to use a modified BSC structure. Robert Kaplan and David Norton, the architects of the BSC, have suggested placing both donor and recipient perspectives at the top of a nonprofit's scorecard, for example, thereby emphasizing the importance of these two classes of "customers." They also suggest that placing a social indicator at the top of the scorecard may serve the purpose equally well. Social indicators such as a reduction in poverty or illiteracy, or improvements in the environment, may provide a sufficiently broad focus that the remaining categories of the BSC can be developed to reinforce the social indicator.[12]

Examples The City of Charlotte, North Carolina, selected five themes of strategic priority: community safety, transportation, preservation of older urban neighborhoods, restructuring government, and economic development. A core project team translated these five themes into strategic objectives for a balanced scorecard. The customer (citizen) was placed at the top of the scorecard, and the team identified the elements needed to address the themes from a customer perspective. When the team moved to the other aspects of the BSC, it found that the financial, internal process, and learning and growth objectives were quite similar for all five themes.[13]

Henry Ford Health System divided its BSC measures into the categories of financial performance, customer service, growth, and system integration. Within each category, there were five items that were measured. In the financial performance category, for example, one item was cost per unit of service; in customer service, the HMO turnover rate was measured; in growth, total HMO enrollment was measured; and in system integration, employee satisfaction was surveyed and reported. Henry Ford's senior management team developed specific measures and targets for each item, and presented the information monthly to the board of directors.

After deciding what to measure, an organization must set targets for each item. Doing so makes the BSC a true "scorecard" on which actual performance can be compared with desired performance. Management then needs to periodically reevaluate both the target levels and the measured activities themselves to ensure that the indicators remain aligned with the organization's mission, and are responsive to changing environmental conditions.

SUMMARY

Just as the economy has many indicators of prosperity that various people interpret differently, nonprofit organizations have numerous ways of looking at their complex outputs. Several output measures, including a number of surrogates, often are necessary for a valid impression of the effectiveness of a nonprofit organization or one of its programs.

[12] Robert S. Kaplan and David P. Norton, "Balance Without Profit," *Financial Management*, January 2001.

[13] Ibid. See also Robert S. Kaplan, *City of Charlotte*, Harvard Business School Case 9-199-036, 1998.

In selecting a set of output measures, senior management must give consideration to four separate but related matters. First, it must find measures that strike a balance between (a) subjective and objective, (b) quantitative and non-quantitative, (c) discrete and scalar, (d) actual and surrogate, and (e) quantity and quality.

Second, it must respond to six principles concerning the implementation of output measures: (a) the need for *some* measurement, (b) the ability to make comparisons, (c) the need for timely information, (d) the importance of having a variety of measures, (e) the avoidance of an excessive quantity of information reported, and (f) the role of surrogates.

Third, management must recognize that the demands for management control purposes are quite different from those for strategic planning. It therefore must be careful to choose output measures that are appropriate for the intended purposes.

Finally, management must consider how performance objectives can be decentralized into individual responsibility centers and how the resulting information can best be summarized and reported for review and action. In this regard, a balanced scorecard can be extremely useful.

Suggested Cases for Classroom Use with this Chapter

See Appendix for a More Complete Description and Ordering Information

Carleton Fire Department	Evaluating non-financial measures of performance in a fire department
Barrington High School	Creating a balanced scorecard for a public school

Chapter 11

Reporting on Performance: Technical Aspects

Among other activities, managers make decisions. Ordinarily, an informed decision is better than an uninformed one. The difference, of course, is information. For this reason, the *measurement and reporting* phase of the management control process is key to successful operations.

Senior management in a nonprofit organization generally reviews performance in two somewhat different ways. First, it monitors current operations on a regular basis, using a set of reports designed for this purpose, combined with other information. This type of review is the subject of this chapter and the next. Second, it reviews programs at infrequent intervals, using information that is developed specifically for the review. These reviews, called *program evaluations,* are discussed in Chapter 13.

Reports concerning the performance of current operations customarily are called *management control reports* since their purpose is to aid in the management control process. The dissemination of such reports, coupled with an analysis of the information they contain, is only one facet of the process, however. The entire process consists of several activities as well as a variety of formal and informal devices. Many of these activities and devices were discussed in Chapter 6. They also will be discussed in a broader context in Chapter 14.

This chapter discusses the technical aspects of the management control reports. It focuses in particular on flexible budgeting and variance analysis—techniques that allow managers to determine in some considerable detail why actual revenues and expenses diverged from those that were budgeted. In Chapter 12, we look at how the reports themselves can be structured, and how variance analysis can be combined with other information to facilitate managerial action to improve organizational performance.

TYPES OF INFORMATION

In monitoring performance, managers typically rely on both quantitative and non-quantitative information. Quantitative information can be either financial or non-financial. For example, as we will see in this chapter, flexible budgeting and variance analysis use financial information. By contrast, as discussed in Chapter 10, output information, while frequently quantitative, is not usually financial.

Example A school system can measure output at each school by a combination of (1) attendance figures, (2) extracurricular activity participation, (3) number of diplomas earned, (4) number of scholarships given, (5) percent of students taking a certain number of courses, (6) percent of students with an 85 percent grade average or above, and (7) standard test results.

Quantitative information also can include nonmonetary information on inputs, such as the number of employees or the number of hours of service, which supplements the financial information on expenses. Output and input information frequently are shown on the same page as financial information, and the two types are related by reporting, say, the cost per unit of output.

Quantitative information usually is contained on reports that are prepared according to a regular schedule. The reports may arrive weekly, monthly, quarterly, or according to some other schedule that provides the information to managers in a timely way. As discussed in Chapter 10, timely means that the information arrives soon enough to help managers make the needed decisions.

In addition to receiving these routine reports, which tend to have the same format and content month after month, managers also can receive a variety of non-routine, unsystematic, and occasionally non-quantitative performance information. Some information comes from trade publications, newspapers, and other outside sources. Some comes from conversations within the organization, such as from memoranda, or from managers' personal observations as they visit responsibility centers and talk with people there.

Although the routine reports serve as a useful starting point in monitoring performance, additional information obtained from these other sources is essential to understanding how organizational units are performing and what factors are affecting them. Indeed, this non-quantitative information often is more important than that contained in the routine reports.

Role of the Accounting Staff

In many respects, it is during the measuring and reporting phases of the management control process that managers' needs and accountants' skills merge. Managers must be able to communicate their information needs to the accounting staff; otherwise, the accounting staff will not be able to design a measurement system that captures the appropriate information. At the same time, the accounting staff must recognize that they are staff, and thus need to make an effort to measure what managers think is important, rather than what they think is important.

TYPES OF ORGANIZATIONS

Some nonprofit organizations, or parts of them, have activities that are quite similar to those in for-profit businesses. Analysis of management performance in these *business-like* organizations is essentially the same as it is in a for-profit company. Other nonprofits are unlike a business in that they are not self-financing. Instead, the amount of resources they have available for operations in a given year is fixed in advance. These might be called *fixed-resource* organizations. Still other nonprofits are required to do a job that is relatively fixed, regardless of the amount of resources planned. These can be called *fixed-job* organizations.

Business-Like Organizations

A business-like organization obtains a substantial fraction of its revenues from fees charged to clients, either directly or through third-party payers (such as Medicare for hospitals, state governments for some mental health agencies, or city governments for some foster care agencies). A business-like organization ordinarily can exert a significant amount of influence over either the amount of revenue earned, the amount of expenses incurred, or both. Analysis of operating performance thus is similar to an analysis of the performance of a for-profit company.

Examples A hospital cannot influence the number of individuals in its community who need hospital care, but it can—through a variety of techniques—influence the number of those individuals who are admitted to its facility. Moreover, although management cannot directly influence physician-ordering patterns, it can have a direct effect on unit costs in terms of efficiency of personnel, average wage rates, and unit prices for supplies and materials.

A museum or symphony orchestra can engage in a wide variety of marketing activities in an attempt to increase the number of people who visit its exhibits or attend its concerts. Choices about programming, prices, promotional activities, and the like are all comparable in nature to a for-profit company. Furthermore, cost analysis and control are of equally great significance.

Fixed-Resource Organizations

In many nonprofit organizations, the amount of resources available for operations in a given year is essentially fixed. This is the case with many religious organizations and membership organizations, where the resources are fixed by the amount of pledges or dues. Colleges with a fixed enrollment know their available resources, within narrow limits, as soon as the students enter. Health maintenance organizations (HMOs) know their resources based on annual enrollments and monthly premiums.

Fixed resource organizations must carefully monitor their spending to assure that it does not exceed the amount of available funds. At the same time, their success is measured by how much service they provide with these funds. In such organizations, spending more than the budget could portend financial disaster, and spending too far below the budget could be the first sign of impending client dissatisfaction.

In some fixed-resource organizations, such as a welfare office or a job training program, the amount of service provided is a subjective judgment rather than a measured quantity (other than clients served). When this is the case, the reporting system cannot express the output for the whole organization in quantitative terms, meaning that overall measures of effectiveness and efficiency cannot be developed. Nevertheless, within such an organization, there may be service units, such as the client record department, whose output can be measured, and it may be possible to develop output and efficiency measures for these units. It also may be possible for managers to use quantitative information to help them determine where they need to take corrective measures.

Fixed-Job Organizations

A fire department has a specific job to do: it must be ready to fight all fires that occur in its service area. Differences between the budget and actual amounts of spending may exist in either direction because of the number and/or nature of the fires that it needed to fight. Similarly, if there are many snowstorms, the budget for snowplowing may need to be exceeded. Judgments about the performance of these types of fixed-job organizations therefore must be in terms of how well they did whatever they were supposed to do, and whether an appropriate amount of resources was used in doing so. It is more appropriate, for example, to consider the cost of snow removal per snowstorm, or per inch of snow plowed, instead of the total snow removal cost for the year.

In fixed-job organizations, there is a tendency to ascribe differences between actual and budgeted amounts in a general way to the requirements of the job, whereas a detailed analysis may reveal inefficiencies. It is not sufficient to explain away a budget overrun in the highway maintenance department on the grounds that the winter was severe. Analysis of the variable costs that were caused by snowstorms of varying depths may indicate that the overrun was greater than it should have been. Thus, in almost all of these situations, a quantitative analysis of the reasons why actual results diverged from the budget is an essential management tool.

Role of Responsibility Centers

All three types of organizations can use both quantitative and non-quantitative information. Because senior management usually acts by communicating with heads of responsibility centers, the information usually can be organized in terms of responsibility centers. For ease of comparison, the same format usually is used for all responsibility centers. Most examples in the discussion that follows assume that the computations are being made for a single responsibility center within a larger organization. In this context, two techniques stand out as particularly relevant and important: flexible budgeting and variance analysis. Both techniques have been used extensively in many for-profit organizations, and can be quite useful to nonprofit managers at all decision-making levels.

FLEXIBLE BUDGETING

The concept of flexible budgeting arises from the distinction between controllable and non-controllable costs. Standard expense center managers typically exert a great deal of control over their department's fixed costs and the variable costs *per unit* of activity, but almost no control over the *total units of activity*. As a result, they exercise little control over *total* variable costs. The management control solution to this problem is a budget that is adjusted for volume changes prior to measuring a manager's performance. This adjusted budget is known as the *flexible budget*.

A flexible budget contrasts with a *fixed budget*, which is a budget with no variable expense component that typically is used in a discretionary expense center. In a discretionary expense center, the manager is held responsible for spending no more than the budgeted amount each month (or other reporting period) unless there are compelling reasons to change the budget, such as a labor strike, a fire, or some catastrophic event.

A flexible budget is developed by classifying a responsibility center's expenses into their fixed and variable components. Rather than being a fixed amount, a flexible budget is expressed as a cost formula using agreed-upon fixed expenses and agreed-upon variable expenses per unit. An expected level of volume is specified to make sure the fixed expenses are within the relevant range. This gives rise to the original budget.

The original budget is then "flexed" each month (or other reporting period) by applying the actual volume (and sometimes mix) of activity to the cost formula. The result is the budget against which the responsibility center manager's performance is measured (because of this it sometimes is called a *performance budget*).

Example The manager of Tanglewood Dentistry, a large dental clinic, estimated that 2,000 patients would need exams and cleanings each month. She estimated that each exam and cleaning would take approximately 30 minutes of a dental hygienist's time, at an hourly rate of $20. Other costs associated with an exam and cleaning were supplies, electricity, and water; these totaled about $2 per cleaning. The monthly fixed costs associated with the exam and cleaning activity were $8,000. The result was the following budget:

Estimated number of procedures	2,000
Hygienist cost (1/2 hour at $20/hr.)	$10
Other variable costs	2
Total variable costs per procedure	$12
Variable-cost budget	$24,000
Fixed costs	8,000
Total budget	$32,000

During the reporting period, a total of 2,500 patients had an exam and cleaning, and the total costs of the department were $40,000. The flexible budget for Tanglewood would look as follows:

Actual number of procedures	2,500
Variable costs per procedure	$ 12
Variable-cost budget	$30,000
Fixed-cost budget	8,000
Flexed (performance) budget	$38,000
Less actual expenditures	40,000
Spending variance	$ (2,000)

Note that, although it would appear initially there was a budget overrun of $8,000 ($32,000 - $40,000), in fact only $2,000 was a "spending" overrun. The remaining $6,000 can be attributed to the volume change, which the manager could not control.

Factors Other than Volume

Although the flexible budget is a partial answer to the problem of aligning responsibility with control, it does not answer all the important questions. Returning to the above example, we might still have some questions about the negative $2,000 spending variance. Among the possible explanations are: (1) a higher hygienist wage rate, (2) higher per-unit supply costs, (3) more hygienist time per procedure, (4) more supply usage per procedure, (5) usage of different kinds of supplies, and (6) higher fixed costs.

Since the answer most likely is contained in one or more of the above factors, we might wish to explore the issue even further. If, for example, more hygienist time than budgeted were used, we might wish to know why. Were there new hygienists on the job who required training and thus were slower than anticipated in exams and cleanings? Or were there some patients for whom exams and cleanings were more complicated than others, resulting in more time needed to complete the procedures? Or perhaps patients arrived late, and scheduling was disrupted, slowing the hygienists down? And so on. While accounting techniques cannot answer all the above questions, the technique of variance analysis permits us to look into some of the possibilities.

VARIANCE ANALYSIS

Variance analysis is an accounting technique that permits a close examination of the difference between budgeted and actual information, and allows us to break the difference into categories that are potentially meaningful for managerial action. In most organizations, the difference, or *variance*, between budgeted and actual performance can be explained by five factors:

1. Volume (number of units of output of products or services)
2. Mix of units of output
3. Revenue per output unit (selling price)
4. Rates paid for inputs (such as labor wages and raw material unit costs)
5. Usage and efficiency of inputs (usage of raw materials and efficiency of labor)

Ordinarily, the variance for each factor is considered separately. There are three reasons for the separation: (1) each variance typically has a different cause, (2) different variances usually involve different managers, and (3) different variances require different types of corrective action. Thus, if responsibility for different factors has been assigned to a different managers, variance analysis can help senior management to work with them to determine the reasons for the variance and the kinds of corrective action that might be taken.

Basic techniques for calculating these variances are shown below; more sophisticated techniques are described in cost accounting textbooks. In many situations, computer programs are available, or can be developed easily on spreadsheet software, to perform the actual calculations.

A Graphic Illustration

The concept of variance analysis can best be illustrated graphically. Consider the example of labor costs. Total labor costs for a given employee or category of employees can be calculated using the number of hours worked and the wage rate per hour. Assume that our labor budget is $4,000, resulting from an estimate of 100 hours of work at $40 per hour. Graphically, this can be represented by a rectangle, with the vertical axis indicating the wage rate, and the horizontal axis indicating the number of hours, as follows:

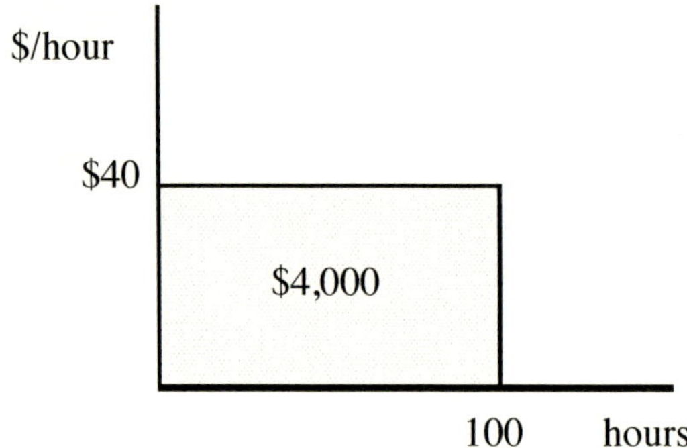

Assume now that our actual labor costs for the period in question were $6,000. A typical budget report might indicate the variance as follows:

Item	Budget	Actual	Variance
Labor cost	$4,000	$6,000	($2,000)

Although the report indicates a $2,000 negative variance, i.e., actual expenses greater than budget, it does not indicate *why* the variance occurred. More specifically, in this instance, it does not tell us whether the cause was a higher wage rate than anticipated, more hours than anticipated, or some combination of the two.

If the variance were solely the result of a higher wage rate, it could be viewed as follows:

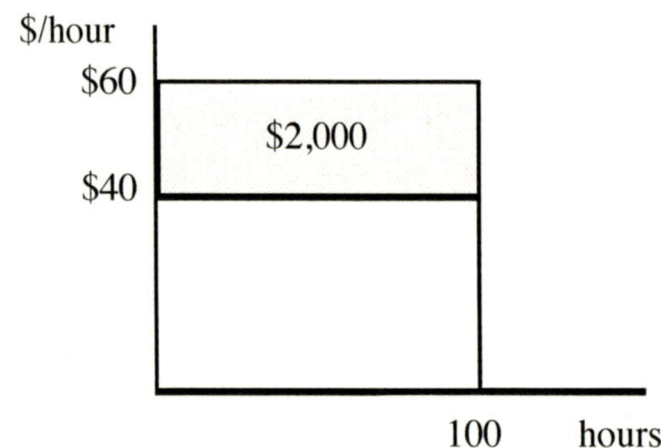

If, on the other hand, it were a result solely of more hours than budgeted, it could be viewed as follows:

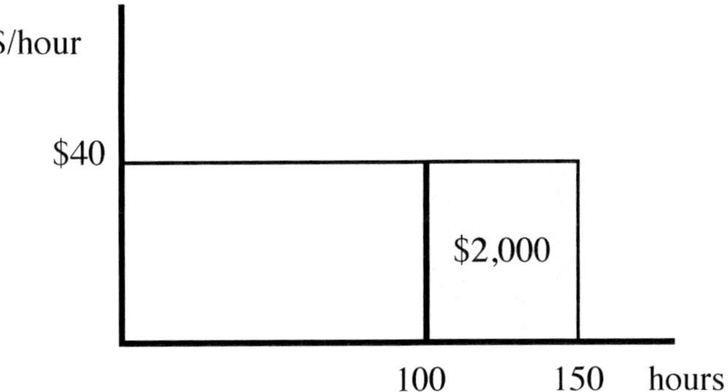

Finally, if it were a result of a combination of both a higher wage rate and more hours, the variance could be depicted by several wage/hour combinations; one example is shown below:

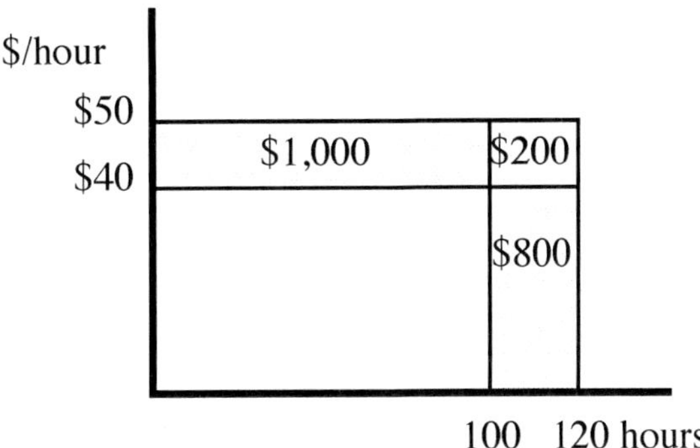

The small rectangle shown on the upper right portion of the graph results from a combination of the labor (or wage) rate variance *and* the hour (or use) variance. This combination variance sometimes is referred to as the "gray area" because it cannot be cleanly assigned to either the higher rate or the higher use, but rather to the *combined effect* of the two. In this instance, $1,000 of the total variance can be attributed to the higher wage rate, $800 to the greater number of hours, and $200 to the combined effect.

For ease of calculation, the combined effect ordinarily is included in the rate variance (here the labor wage *rate* variance). Not only does this approach simplify the calculation and presentation of information, it also seems reasonable. Specifically, whoever is responsible for the rate variance is responsible for it over as many units as actually were used (hours in this example). This means that the $200 combination effect described above would be added to the $1,000 to give a $1,200 labor rate variance. The details of variance calculations are discussed in Appendix 11-A.

Given this approach, the budget report might look as follows:

Item	Budget	Actual	Variance
Labor costs	$4,000	$6,000	($2,000)
Labor rate (wage) variance			(1,200)
Use variance			(800)

The managerial utility of this report comes directly from the fact that, in most organizations, different managers are responsible for different elements of a total variance. In line with the need to align responsibility with control, it is important to designate the portion of the total variance that is attributable to each individual manager. It then becomes possible to discuss the reasons for the variances with these managers.

It is important to emphasize that a negative variance should not be used as a "club." Rather, it is the first step in diagnosing the reasons *why* costs diverged from budget, and for exploring these reasons with the appropriate managers so that, where possible, corrective actions can be taken to bring costs back in line. Similarly, as we will see below, a positive variance is not necessarily a cause for celebration. It does suggest, however, that some improvement in operations have been achieved that could be examined for possible transfer to other operating units.

An Illustration of Variances in a Hospital Setting

To illustrate how variances can be used, assume that Nucio Hospital has prepared the somewhat simplified budget shown in Exhibit 11-1. Let's work through the details.

Exhibit 11-1 Original Budget

	Acute MI	Influenza	Pneumonia	Phlebitis	Total
Number of cases	300	200	100	50	650
Revenue per case	$6,000	$1,000	$1,500	$3,000	
Total revenue	1,800,000	200,000	150,000	150,000	$2,300,000
Variable expenses per case	3,590	910	1,031	1,218	
Total variable expenses	1,077,000	182,000	103,100	60,900	1,423,000
Contribution	$723,000	$18,000	$46,900	$89,100	$877,000
Total fixed expenses					800,000
Surplus					$77,000
Variable expense detail:					
Routine care					
Number days per case	21	5	6	7	
Expense per day	$150	$150	$150	$150	
Total expense per case	$3,150	$750	$900	$1,050	
Radiology					
Number films per case	5	1	2	0	
Expense per film	$25	$25	$25	$25	
Total expense per case	$125	$25	$50	$0	
Laboratory					
Number tests per case	10	5	3	7	
Expense per test	$15	$15	$15	$15	
Total expense per case	$150	$75	$45	$105	
Pharmacy					
Number units per case	55	20	12	21	
Expense per unit	$3	$3	$3	$3	
Total expense per case	$165	$60	$36	$63	
Total variable expense per case	$3,590	$910	$1,031	$1,218	

As this budget shows, the hospital anticipates four different kinds of cases: acute myocardial infarction (heart attack), influenza, pneumonia, and phlebitis. Its budgeted variable expenses per case are based on four different services: routine care (i.e., the hospital stay itself), radiology films, laboratory tests, and pharmacy units (such as prescriptions). Obviously, there are many more services and many more case types in a hospital than this, so the example is not totally realistic. Nevertheless, the numbers are sufficient for illustrative purposes.

Operating under a diagnosis-based form of reimbursement, the hospital is paid on a per-case basis. For each case type, the anticipated "selling price" is shown, along with the anticipated utilization of each service, and its variable expense per unit. The total variable expense per case for each case type is then calculated, and the revenue and total variable expense per case are multiplied by the anticipated number of cases to give total revenue and total variable expenses by case type. The latter is deducted from total revenue to give the contribution to fixed expenses from each case type. The fixed expenses are then deducted from the total contribution to give a total budgeted surplus for the accounting period, which, in this case is $77,000.

Exhibit 11-2 is a flexible budget based on the actual volume and mix of cases served. It shows what the surplus *would have been* if everything had remained the same as in the original budget except volume and mix. That is, the calculations use budget figures for both revenue per case and variable expense per case. Fixed expenses are shown as budgeted based on the assumption that the change in mix and volume did not affect them. The result is that there would have been a surplus of $43,450 instead of the original $77,000. Moreover, the exhibit also shows revenue and expense variances related to volume, and a contribution margin variance.

Exhibit 11-2 Flexible Budget and Variances

	Acute MI	Influenza	Pneumonia	Phlebitis	Total
Actual number of cases	250	150	200	75	675
Revenue per case	$6,000	$1,000	$1,500	$3,000	
Total revenue	1,500,000	150,000	300,000	225,000	$2,175,000
Variable expenses per case	3,590	910	1,031	1,218	
Total variable expenses	897,500	136,500	206,200	91,350	1,331,550
Contribution	$602,500	$13,500	$93,800	$133,650	$843,450
Total fixed expenses					800,000
Surplus					$43,450
Revenue Volume Variance					
Actual-budgeted cases	-50	-50	100	25	
Budgeted unit revenue	$6,000	$1,000	$1,500	$3,000	
Variance	($300,000)	($50,000)	$150,000	$75,000	($125,000)
Expense Volume Variance					
Budgeted-actual cases	50	50	-100	-25	
Budgeted expense per case	$3,590	$910	$1,031	$1,218	
Variance	$179,500	$45,500	($103,100)	($30,450)	$91,450
Contribution Margin Variance					
Revenue volume variance minus expense volume variance	($120,500)	($4,500)	$46,900	$44,550	($33,550)

There are several items worth noting in these computations. First, as discussed in Appendix 11-A, in computing a revenue variance, budgeted cases are subtracted from actual cases, whereas in computing an expense variance, the reverse is true. Second, when we disaggregate the contribution margin variance, we see that the hospital lost $125,000 in revenue that it had anticipated receiving, but saved $91,450 in expenses that it had anticipated incurring. These changes were due exclusively to the changes in the volume and mix of cases. Third, when the unfavorable $33,550 contribution margin variance is added to the original budget of $77,000, the result is $43,450, the same amount as the flexible budget.

Finally, note that the actual number of cases was 675 compared to 650 in the original budget. The fact that volume has increased but the surplus under the flexible budget declined by $33,550 indicates that there was a fairly significant shift in case mix. Indeed, the reason for the decline is that the mix shifted from high-margin to low-margin cases. Had the mix (the proportion of each case type) remained the same as budgeted, the flexible budget surplus would have increased with the increase in volume.

Exhibit 11-3 shows the actual results for the 675 cases treated during the accounting period. As it indicates, although revenue per case remained as budgeted, there were several changes in expenses between the original and flexible budgets.

Exhibit 11-3 Actual Results

	Acute MI	Influenza	Pneumonia	Phlebitis	Total
Actual number of cases	250	150	200	75	675
Revenue per case	$6,000	$1,000	$1,500	$3,000	
Total revenue	1,500,000	150,000	300,000	225,000	$2,175,000
Variable expenses per case	3,491	1,126	991	1,252	
Total variable expenses	872,750	168,900	198,200	93,900	1,333,750
Contribution	$627,250	($18,900)	$101,800	$131,100	$841,250
Total fixed expenses					800,000
Surplus					$41,250
Variable expense detail					
Routine Care					
Average number of days per case	19	6	5	7	
Expense per day	$160	$160	$160	$160	
Total expense per case	$3,040	$960	$800	$1,120	
Radiology					
Average number of films per case	4	2	2	0	
Expense per film	$23	$23	$23	$23	
Total expense per case	$92	$46	$46	$0	
Laboratory					
Average number of tests per case	10	3	5	3	
Expense per test	$20	$20	$20	$20	
Total expense per case	$200	$60	$100	$60	
Pharmacy					
Average number of units per case	53	20	15	24	
Expense per unit	$3	$3	$3	$3	
Total expense per case	$159	$60	$45	$72	
Total variable expense per case	$3,491	$1,126	$991	$1,252	

As the exhibit shows, the average length of stay (i.e., the number of patient days) was different for three of the four diagnoses, and the average variable expense per day was $10 more than budgeted; the average number of radiology films was different for three of the four diagnoses, and the average expense per film was $2 less than budgeted; the average number of laboratory tests differed and the average expense per test was $5 more than budgeted; the average number of pharmacy units was different, although the average expense per unit remained as budgeted.

The result is an actual average variable expense per case that differs from the budgeted average one. This total is multiplied by the actual number of cases served to give total variable expenses per case. As is shown in the totals at the top of Exhibit 11-3, the resulting actual surplus is $41,250, which is $2,200 below the $43,450 surplus in the flexible budget.

Exhibit 11-4 shows the calculation of the variances resulting from changes in the use of resources per case (e.g., length of stay, number of radiology films). By multiplying the change in resource units per case by the budgeted unit expense figure, we can isolate the impact on the budget of changes in the use of each resource. The total dollar effect for each case type is the sum of the use variances multiplied by the actual number of cases, and is shown at the bottom of the exhibit. Acute MI cases, with a total of $82,750 had the biggest reduction in resource use, while influenza had somewhat higher resource use (an unfavorable variance of $21,750). Overall, the hospital saved a total of $87,025 from reduced resource use.

Exhibit 11-4 Resource Use Variance

	Acute MI	Influenza	Pneumonia	Phlebitis	Total
Routine care					
Budgeted-actual days per case	2	-1	1	0	
Budgeted expense per day	$150	$150	$150	$150	
Use variance	$300	($150)	$150	$0	
Radiology					
Budgeted-actual films per case	1	-1	0	0	
Budgeted expense per film	$25	$25	$25	$25	
Use variance	$25	($25)	$0	$0	
Laboratory					
Budgeted-actual tests per case	0	2	(2)	4	
Budgeted expense per test	$15	$15	$15	$15	
Use variance	$0	$30	($30)	$60	
Pharmacy					
Budgeted-actual units per case	2	0	-3	-3	
Budgeted expense per unit	$3	$3	$3	$3	
Use variance	$6	$0	($9)	($9)	
Total resource use variances per case	$331	($145)	$111	$51	
Actual number of cases	250	150	200	75	
Total resource use variances	$82,750	($21,750)	$22,200	$3,825	$87,025

Exhibit 11-5 isolates the effect of the changes in expense per unit,—a combination of *rate* and *efficiency variances*. It is called a *rate/efficiency* variance because the expense per resource unit (e.g., a lab test) actually is the result of two separate elements: the rate paid for each input unit (e.g., the laboratory technician wage rate) and the efficiency with which the input was provided (e.g., the number of tests the technician completed in an hour). Thus, in a laboratory, a change in expense per test could come from a change in the wage rate of the lab technicians performing tests, a change in their efficiency in conducting the tests, or some combination of the two.

Exhibit 11-5 Rate/Efficiency Variances

	Acute MI	Influenza	Pneumonia	Phlebitis	Total
Actual number of cases	250	150	200	75	675
Routine care					
Budgeted-actual expense per day	($10)	($10)	($10)	($10)	
Actual average days per case	19	6	5	7	
Rate/efficiency variance per case	($190)	($60)	($50)	($70)	
Total rate/efficiency variance	($47,500)	($9,000)	($10,000)	($5,250)	($71,750)
Radiology					
Budgeted-actual expense per film	$2	$2	$2	$2	
Actual average number of films	4	2	2	0	
Rate/efficiency variance per case	$8	$4	$4	$0	
Total rate/efficiency variance	$2,000	$600	$800	$0	$3,400
Laboratory					
Budgeted-actual expense per test	($5)	($5)	($5)	($5)	
Actual average number of tests per case	10	3	5	3	
Rate/efficiency variance per case	($50)	($15)	($25)	($15)	
Total rate/efficiency variance	($12,500)	($2,250)	($5,000)	($1,125)	($20,875)
Pharmacy					
Budgeted-actual expense per unit	$0	$0	$0	$0	
Actual average number of units per case	53	20	15	24	
Rate/efficiency variance per case	$0	$0	$0	$0	
Total rate/efficiency variance	$0	$0	$0	$0	$0
Total Rate/Efficiency Variances	($58,000)	($10,650)	($14,200)	($6,375)	($89,225)

The rate/efficiency variance per case is multiplied by the actual number of cases served of each type to give a total rate/efficiency variance for each resource type. This figure consists of variable expenses only. Thus, given the *actual* number and mix of cases served, and the number of resource units *actually* ordered, the rate/efficiency variance shows how well each service-providing department performed in meeting its budget. As can be seen, routine care, with an unfavorable variance of $71,750, performed considerably worse than budgeted; the laboratory also had an unfavorable variance ($20,875). The radiology department performed slightly better than budgeted, and pharmacy was right on target.

The rate and efficiency effects are combined in this illustration. However, managers of routine care, the laboratory, and the other service departments might wish to undertake a more detailed variance analysis to isolate the individual effects of rate and efficiency. The approach to doing this would be similar to that for calculating all other variances; that is, the effect of each item would be determined by holding everything else constant and calculating the impact of that item alone.

To illustrate, assume that the following data are available for the laboratory:

	Time per Test (Minutes)	Wage Rate ($ per minute)	Total Expense per Test
Budget	75	$0.20	$15.00
Actual	80	0.25	20.00

To perform the calculations, we look first at the change in efficiency:

(Budgeted time - Actual time) x Budgeted wage = Efficiency variance

or

(75 minutes - 80 minutes) x $0.20 = $1.00 unfavorable

Next we look at the change in wage rate:

(Budgeted rate - Actual rate) x Actual efficiency = Wage rate variance

or

($0.20 - $0.25) x 80 minutes = $4.00 unfavorable

These per-test variances can be applied to the total number of tests to obtain the total variance. The computations are as follows:

Case Type	Actual Number of Cases	Tests per Case	Total Tests	Wage Rate Variance ($4.00)/test)	Efficiency Variance ($1.00)/test	Total
Acute MI	250	10	2,500	($10,000)	($2,500)	
Influenza	150	3	450	(1,800)	(450)	
Pneumonia	200	5	1000	(4,000)	(1,000)	
Phlebitis	75	3	225	(900)	(225)	
Total			4,175	($16,700)	($4,175)	($20,875)

Note that the total variance for the laboratory shown here is the same as the total shown on Exhibit 11-5. With this additional information, however, the laboratory manager can now see that the total is divided between $16,700 that is due to a change in the average wage rate of technicians, and $4,175 that results from a lower than expected technician efficiency (minutes per test).

Managerial Uses of Variances

An important feature of variance analysis is the ability it gives senior management to link changes in revenues and expenses to managerial responsibility. In the case of Nucio Hospital, for example, management might decide that the $33,550 unfavorable contribution margin variance was due largely to factors outside the control of the hospital, namely, a reduction in acute MI and influenza cases. (Some might argue that this variance is senior management's responsibility since senior management is charged with improving the hospital's competitive position vis-à-vis other hospitals in the area.)

The $33,550 negative contribution margin variance reduces the originally budgeted surplus of $77,000 to a flexible budget surplus of $43,450. However, as discussed above, the actual surplus was $41,250, or $2,200 less. This rather small difference is somewhat misleading, since it is due to the combination of a favorable variance of $87,025 in resources per case and an unfavorable variance of $89,225 in the rate/efficiency of the delivery of those resources.

Physicians, who control the resources per case, would appear to be responsible for the former variance. By contrast, cost center or department managers, who are responsible for the efficient delivery of physician-ordered resources, would appear to be responsible for the latter variance. It is for this reason that department managers most likely would want to compute the separate rate and efficiency variances associated with their activities. Most people would argue that they have greater control over efficiency than wage rates.

More generally, with this information, senior management can discuss the reasons underlying each variance with the managers involved, who can take corrective action, if appropriate. As mentioned earlier, a variance is not designed to be used as a club, but rather as a tool to assist in understanding why actual costs diverged from budget, and for exploring these reasons with the appropriate managers so that, if possible, actions can be taken to bring costs (and perhaps revenues) back in line with the budget.

Variances in General. By way of summary, Exhibit 11-6 lists each variance, and identifies in a general sense the department or responsibility center manager who controls it. As it suggests, operating managers ordinarily do not control the volume or mix of services supplied, nor do they usually set wage rates for employees or control the prices paid for raw materials and other input items. Consequently, variance analysis permits management to focus attention on each individual item and the manager who controls it.

Exhibit 11-6 Types of Variances and Controlling Agents

Variance	Controlling Agent
Volume Variance	Marketing department, senior management, and/or the environment (depending on the organization)
Output Mix Variances	Marketing department, senior management, and/or the environment (depending on the organization)
Selling Price Variances	Senior management, marketing department, or responsibility center managers (depending on who in the organization sets prices)
Raw Material Price Variances	Purchasing department/responsibility center managers
Wage Rate Variances	Senior management (who negotiate union contracts; responsibility center managers (who make job offers)
Raw Material Usage Variances	Responsibility center managers
Labor Efficiency Variances	Responsibility center managers
Input Mix Variances	Responsibility center managers

Limitations of Variance Analysis. It is important to remember that while variance analysis can highlight the reasons for a deviation between budgeted and actual performance, and can do so in terms of volume, rate, use, and mix, it cannot explain *why* a particular organizational unit was more or less efficient than budgeted, or *why* volume was higher or lower than anticipated. As a result, variance analysis can be a useful tool to assist managers in asking the right questions and in identifying lower-level managers to whom those questions might be addressed. As with many other accounting techniques, however, it should be considered only as a means to assist managers to learn more about the activities of their organizations. Moreover, in using variance analysis for managerial action, it is important to recognize that few variances can be interpreted independently from all the others. A negative material use variance, for example, may have arisen because the purchasing department bought some raw materials of lower-than-anticipated quality. Thus, what appears as a positive purchase price variance for the purchasing department, may have negative "downstream" consequences in other departments.

In sum, used properly, a negative expense variance (volume, mix, price, rate, or use) can be extremely valuable: it can help to identify areas where operating improvements can take place and can allow managers to see the financial consequences of their corrective actions. Used in a club-like way, however, it can be quite threatening, and may even lead to unproductive conflict or reduced cooperation between managers and their subordinates.

SUMMARY

This chapter has discussed two important accounting techniques that can help managers to understand why actual costs and revenues deviated from budgeted ones. A flexible budget isolates the impact of changes in volume and mix on both revenue and expenses. Once those changes have been identified, variance analysis allows managers to see how other factors affected the organization's overall surplus. In particular, variance analysis identifies the impact of changes in the usage of resources and the efficiency with which those resources were provided.

Suggested Cases for Classroom Use with this Chapter

See the Appendix at the end of the book for a more complete description of each case and ordering information.

Huntington Beach	Creating a flexible budget and computing variances for a road project
Clinique Nosral	Computing variances in a primary care clinic in Africa
La Salle Hospital (B)	Computing variances in a department of pathology
Pacific Park School	Creating a flexible budget and computing variances for a summer camp
Spruce Street Shelter	Preparing a flexible budget and variance analysis for the laundry department in a homeless shelter
Town of Bellington	Preparing a flexible budget for snow removal
Los Reyes Hospital (B)	Preparing a flexible budget and variance analysis in a department of medicine in a hospital
Bandon Medical Associates (B)	Preparing a flexible budget and variance analysis in a physician group practice

Appendix 11-A
Calculating Variances

The accounting technique used to calculate a variance follows two relatively simple rules with slight differences depending on whether a revenue or expense variance is desired:

Expense Variances. With expense variances, when actual expenses exceed budgeted expenses, the organization's financial condition is worsened, i.e., its income is reduced from what it otherwise would have been. Similarly, when actual expenses are below budgeted expenses, the organization's financial condition is improved. Since we wish a negative variance to be a negative number and a positive variance to be a positive number, we use the following rules:

1. For an expense variance related to **use**, subtract the *actual use* from the *budgeted use* and multiply the result by *budgeted rate*. If actual use exceeds budgeted use, the result will be a negative number; if actual use is below budgeted use, the result will be positive.

2. For an expense variance related to **rate**, subtract the *actual rate* from the *budgeted rate* and multiply the result by *actual use*. If the actual rate exceeds the budgeted rate, the result will be a negative number; if the actual rate is below the budgeted rate, the result will be positive.

We can express these rules with formulas:

1. **Use**: $(U_b - U_a) \times R_b$
2. **Rate**: $(R_b - R_a) \times U_a$

Where 'U' stands for *use,* 'R' stands for *rate,* and the subscripts 'a' and 'b' stand for *actual* and *budgeted* respectively.

Revenue Variances. With revenue variances, when actual revenue exceeds budgeted revenue, the organization's financial condition has improved, i.e., its income is greater than it otherwise would have been. Therefore:

1. For a revenue variance related to **volume**, subtract *budgeted volume* from *actual volume* and multiply the result by *budgeted selling price*. If actual volume exceeds budgeted volume, the result is a positive number; if actual volume is below budgeted volume, the result is negative.

2. For a revenue variance related to **selling price**, subtract *budgeted selling price* from *actual selling price* and multiply the result by *actual volume*. If the actual selling price exceeds the budgeted selling price, the result is a positive number; if the actual selling price is below the budgeted selling price, the result is negative.

We also can express these rules as formulas:

1. **Volume**: $(V_a - V_b) \times P_b$
2. **Selling Price**: $(P_a - P_b) \times V_a$

Where 'V' stands for *volume*, 'P' stands for *selling price*, and the subscripts 'a' and 'b' stand for *actual* and *budget*.

Making the Computations. Let's use the information from the graphic example given in the chapter, and perform the calculations according to the above rules and formulas. Since there are no revenue variances, we need not concern ourselves with them; we just need to calculate the expense variances. Recall that the budget was for 100 hours of labor at $40 per hour, and the actual was 120 hours of at $50 per hour. The computations are as follows:

Use (Efficiency) variance	(Budgeted hours)	-	(Actual hours)	x	(Budgeted wage rate)		
	$(U_b$	-	$U_a)$	x	R_b		
	(100	-	120)	x	$40.00	=	(800)
Rate (Wage) variance	(Budgeted- wage rate)	-	(Actual wage rate)	x	(Actual hours)		
	$(R_b$	-	$R_a)$	x	U_a		
	($40.00	-	$50.00)	x	120	=	($1,200)

Graphically, the calculations look as follows (compare this to the graph for the same example in the text):

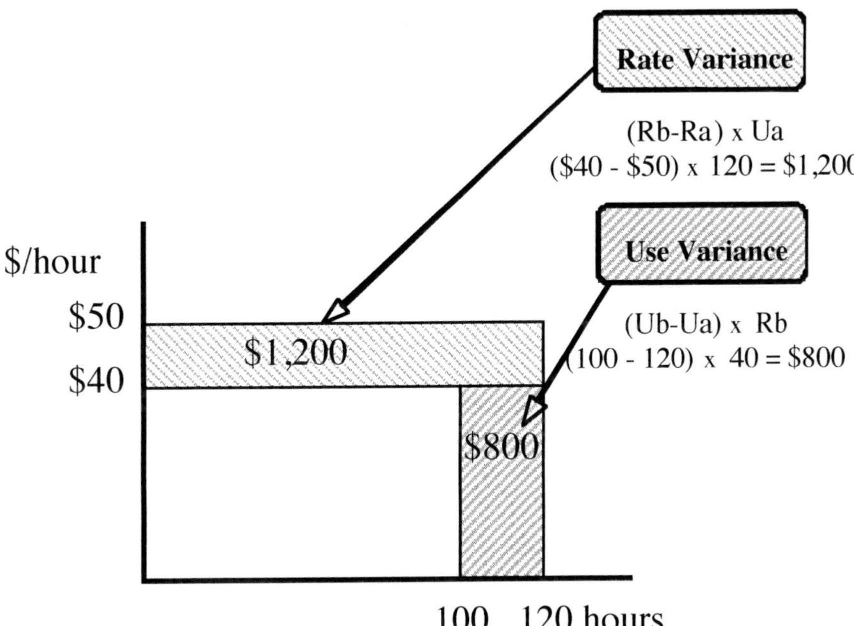

Multiple Variances. Note that this technique was performed in a situation where only two items were involved. It also could be performed where several items have a variance. When volume is involved, for example, a flexible budget can be prepared first, and the remaining variances can be calculated using the actual level of volume. Let's look at this more complicated situation with another example, this time using materials instead of labor.

Example The Haskell Prosthesis Company has budgeted and actual material for one department as follows:

	Number of Units of Output	Material per Unit	Direct Material Cost/Unit	Total Cost
Budget	7,000	10 pounds	$0.20/pound	$14,000
Actual	6,000	12 pounds	$0.25/pound	$18,000

The manager is interested in obtaining a better understanding of the reasons behind the budget overrun. To do so, we begin by preparing a flexible budget for the department—changing the volume from its budgeted to its actual level while holding everything else constant at budgeted levels. We then can determine what the budget *would have been had we known volume in advance*. This budget then can be compared to actual results, as follows:

	Number of Units of Output	Material per Unit	Direct Material Cost/Unit	Total Cost	Variances
Original Budget	7,000	10 pounds	$0.20/pounds	$14,000	
Flexible Budget	6,000	10 pounds	$0.20/pounds	$12,000	$2,000
Actual	6,000	12 pounds	$0.25/pounds	$18,000	($6,000)
Total					($4,000)

Note that the volume variance (original budget - flexible budget) is a favorable $2,000 ($14,000 - $12,000). That is, if we had known our volume in advance, we would have budgeted $12,000 rather than $14,000. Since, to calculate the flexible budget, we held all other factors at the levels in the original budget (10 pounds per unit and $0.20 per pound), this $2,000 positive variance is due *exclusively* to the lower volume. It is favorable since it reduces expenses which, other things equal, improves our income. (Of course, we have excluded revenue variances from the analysis. Assuming we are paid on a per-unit basis, the fall in volume would have led to a negative revenue variance, indicating a reduction in our income.)

In this example, as in many variance calculations, an unfavorable variance (i.e., one that lowers the income of the organization) is shown in parentheses; it is sometimes called a *negative* variance. A favorable (positive) variance does not have parentheses. Sometimes, unfavorable variances are designated as "UF" and favorable variances as "F".

The spending variance (flexible budget - actual) is an unfavorable $6,000 ($12,000 - $18,000), caused, as we can see, by using two additional pounds per unit and paying $0.05 more per pound. The combined result of the volume and spending variances is a total unfavorable variance of $4,000.

We now can calculate the reasons for the spending variance. As indicated, above, a portion of this variance is due to higher use (12 pounds versus 10 pounds), and a portion is due to higher rate ($0.25 per pound versus $.20 per pound). Thus, the expense variances can be calculated as follows:

$$\textbf{Use} = (U_b - U_a) \times R_b = (10 - 12) \times (\$0.20) = (\$0.40)$$
$$\textbf{Rate} = (R_b - R_a) \times U_a = (\$0.20 - \$0.25) \times 12 = (\$0.60)$$

Note that these are variances per unit of output. To obtain the *total* variance, we need to multiply these unit variances by the actual volume of output, i.e., the volume used in calculating the flexible budget, as follows:

	Variance per Unit of Output	x	Actual Volume of Output	=	Total Variance
Use Variance	($0.40)	x	6,000	=	($2,400)
Rate Variance	($0.60)	x	6,000	=	($3,600)
Total					($6,000)

Alternatively, the calculations could be made in one step, as follows:

Variance	(Budget - Actual)	x	Other[1]	x	Actual Volume	=	Total Variance
Use (pounds)	(10 - 12)	x	$0.20	x	6,000	=	($2,400)
Rate ($/pound)	($0.20 - $0.25)	x	12	x	6,000	=	($3,600)
Total							($6,000)

Note 1. "Other" in the case of the use variance, is the *budgeted* rate per pound; in the case of the rate variance, it is the *actual* use of pounds per unit.

As this example demonstrates, variance analysis can help explain the reasons why actual expenses deviated from budget. In the case of Haskell Prosthesis Company, we now can see that the company saved $2,000 in expenses as a result of producing fewer units, but its expenses increased by $3,600 because of higher prices for its raw materials and $2,400 because of a greater use of raw materials per unit of output (most likely because of spoilage or waste, rather than because the labor force made a heavier device!).

Mix Variances. The volume variance computed in the above problem assumed that every unit of volume had the same variable expense associated with it. In many organizations, different types of products and services have different unit variable expense amounts. When this is the case, the volume variances are calculated using weighted averages of the variable expense amounts. If there is a change in the budgeted proportions of the different product or service types, an *output mix variance* develops.

Input mix variances also arise with items such as raw materials and labor. This can happen if, for example, a responsibility center manager uses a different mix of raw materials than budgeted, or if the actual skill mix of labor differs from budget. Techniques for calculating input mix variances are shown in most cost accounting textbooks.

Many organizations do not calculate mix variances. In these organizations, the output mix variance is automatically a part of the volume variance and the input mix variance typically is a part of the rate variance (assuming the different types of raw materials or different skill levels for labor have different rates).

Example In a hospital, an output mix variance results from a change in the hospital's case types (e.g., relatively more coronary artery bypass surgery cases than influenza cases). An input mix variance comes about when there is a change in the mix of services used to treat a given case type (e.g., more or different radiological procedures ordered for each patient undergoing coronary artery bypass surgery). A second type of input mix variance also could take place if the manager of, say, the radiology department used a mix of technicians to take the x-rays that was different from the budget.

Practice Case: El Conejo Family Planning Clinic

Rosa Ruiz, the Director of Finance of El Conejo Family Planning Clinic, recently had received a memorandum from the Chairman of the Finance Committee of the clinic's Board of Trustees. The memorandum had been sent to all department heads, and had expressed concern that the results of the year's operations were considerably worse than budgeted. One reason for this problem was that third-party payers had lowered their rate for one of the clinic's most significant visit types, but there appeared to be some other explanations as well. Ms. Ruiz had been asked to analyze the reasons for the poor performance, meet with the relevant department heads, and make a presentation at the next board meeting concerning the clinic's performance.

In reviewing the budgeted and actual results, Ms. Ruiz discovered that almost all of the clinic's variation from its budget could be attributed to four visit types and four services. For reasons of simplicity, she decided to base her presentation on these only.

DATA

Exhibit 1 contains the original budget for these four visit types: IUD, first visit; oral contraceptive, first visit; special follow-up visits (when problems existed with the contraceptive or contraceptive method); and routine follow-up. It also shows the budgeted variable expenses per visit for the four services: physician care, nursing care, medical supplies, and laboratory tests.

The clinic was paid on a per-visit basis. Its anticipated revenue for each visit type is shown in Exhibit 1, as is the anticipated utilization of services and the variable expense per unit for each service for each visit type. Using these estimates, the total variable expense per visit for each visit type had been calculated. The revenue and total variable expense per visit then had been multiplied by the anticipated number of visits to give total revenue and total variable expenses by visit type. The latter had been deducted from total revenue to give the contribution to fixed expenses from each visit type. The fixed expenses then had been deducted from the total contribution to give a total budgeted surplus of $85,000 for the accounting period.

Ms. Ruiz asked her staff assistant, Anthony Hourihan, to use the actual data for the period as the basis for a report on results for the year. This report was to contain a complete breakdown of the reasons why the clinic's actual surplus diverged from the budget. The report would be submitted to the clinic's chief executive officer, and would be used by Ms. Ruiz for her presentation to the Board of Trustees.

Mr. Hourihan began by computing the actual financial results for the period (Exhibit 2), which showed that, instead of earning a surplus, the clinic actually had incurred a deficit of $218,300. Then, reasoning that the clinic had essentially no control over the number or type of visits, he also prepared a flexible budget (Exhibit 3), which showed that $750 of the difference was due exclusively to the change in the number of visits. Using similar reasoning, he prepared an analysis of the variance due to the changes in the third-party reimbursement rates (shown at the bottom of Exhibit 3), which showed that $17,000 of the difference was a result of these rate changes.

Having analyzed and explained only $17,750 of the $303,300 total difference between budgeted and actual performance, Mr. Hourihan was concerned. He met with Ms. Ruiz to show her the results of his work, and to ask for some guidance. Ms. Ruiz explained to him that he needed to look into matters such as physician and nursing productivity and wage rates, medical supply costs, and laboratory costs. She asked Mr. Hourihan to assess these other reasons why actual results might have diverged from the budget, and to prepare a variance analysis that would explain each of them.

Assignment

1. Be sure you understand how Exhibit 3 was prepared. Do you agree with Mr. Hourihan's analysis so far?

2. Besides changes in the number of visits and the reimbursement rate per visit, what other factors might cause actual results to diverge from budget?

3. Calculate the variance associated with each of the reasons you gave in Question 2. How, if at all, might this information be used in managing the clinic?

EL CONEJO FAMILY PLANNING CLINIC
Exhibit 1. Original Budget

	IUD 1st Visit	Oral Conc 1st Visit	Special Follow-Up	Routine Follow-Up	Total
Number of visits	3,000	2,000	1,000	500	6,500
Price per visit	$200	$100	$125	$40	
Total revenue	600,000	200,000	125,000	20,000	$945,000
Variable expenses per visit	165	75	110	10	
Total variable expenses	495,000	150,000	110,000	5,000	760,000
Contribution	$105,000	$50,000	$15,000	15,000	$185,000
Total fixed expenses					100,000
Surplus					$85,000
Variable expense detail:					
Physician care					
Average #minutes per visit	30	10	15	5	
Average wage per minute	$1.00	$1.00	$1.00	$1.00	
Total expense per visit	$30.00	$10.00	$15.00	$5.00	
Nursing care					
Average #minutes per visit	30	20	30	10	
Average wage per minute	$0.50	$0.50	$0.50	$0.50	
Total expense per visit	$15.00	$10.00	$15.00	$5.00	
Medical supplies					
Average # units per visit	3	1	2	0	
Average expense per unit	$25.00	$25.00	$25.00	$25.00	
Total expense per visit	$75.00	$25.00	$50.00	$0.00	
Laboratory					
Average # tests per visit	3	2	2	0	
Average expense per test	$15.00	$15.00	$15.00	$15.00	
Total expense per visit	$45.00	$30.00	$30.00	$0.00	
Total average variable expense per visit	$165.00	$75.00	$110.00	$10.00	

EL CONEJO FAMILY PLANNING CLINIC
Exhibit 2 Actual Results

	IUD 1st Visit	Oral Conc 1st Visit	Special Follow-Up	Routine Follow-Up	Total
Actual number of visits	2,750	2,200	1,000	600	6,550
Actual price per visit	$200	$90	$130	$40	
Total revenue	550,000	198,000	130,000	24,000	$902,000
Actual variable expenses per visit	218	114	161	15	
Total variable expenses	599,500	250,800	161,000	9,000	1,020,300
Contribution	($49,500)	($52,800)	($31,000)	$15,000	($118,300)
Total fixed expenses					100,000
Surplus					($218,300)
Variable expense detail:					
Physician care					
Average #minutes per visit	25	5	20	10	
Average wage per minute	$1.20	$1.20	$1.20	$1.20	
Total expense per visit	$30.00	$6.00	$24.00	$12.00	
Nursing care					
Average #minutes per visit	40	30	25	5	
Average wage per minute	$0.60	$0.60	$0.60	$0.60	
Total expense per visit	$24.00	$18.00	$15.00	$3.00	
Medical supplies					
Average # units per visit	4	2	2	0	
Average expense per unit	$21.00	$21.00	$21.00	$21.00	
Total expense per visit	$84.00	$42.00	$42.00	$0.00	
Laboratory					
Average # tests per visit	5	3	5	0	
Average expense per test	$16.00	$16.00	$16.00	$16.00	
Total expense per visit	$80.00	$48.00	$80.00	$0.00	
Total average variable expense per visit	$218.00	$114.00	$161.00	$15.00	

EL CONEJO FAMILY PLANNING CLINIC
Exhibit 3 Flexible Budget and Related Variances

	IUD 1st Visit	Oral Conc 1st Visit	Special Follow-Up	Routine Follow-Up	Total
Actual number of visits	2,750	2,200	1,000	600	6,550
Budgeted price per visit	$200	$100	$125	$40	
Total revenue	550,000	220,000	125,000	24,000	$919,000
Budgeted variable expenses per visit	165	75	110	10	
Total variable expenses	453,750	165,000	110,000	6,000	734,750
Contribution	$96,250	$55,000	$15,000	$18,000	$184,250
Total fixed expenses					100,000
Surplus					$84,250
Revenue volume variance					
Actual-budgeted visits	-250	200	0	100	
Budgeted price per visit	$200	$100	$125	$40	
Variance	($50,000)	$20,000	$0	$4,000	($26,000)
Expense volume variance					
Budgeted-actual visits	250	-200	0	-100	
Budgeted expense per visit	$165	$75	$110	$10	
Variance	$41,250	($15,000)	$0	($1,000)	$25,250
Contribution margin variance					
Revenue volume variance plus expense volume variance	($8,750)	$5,000	$0	$3,000	($750)
Revenue price variances					
Actual-budgeted price per visit	$0	($10)	$5	$0	
Actual number visits	2,750	2,200	1,000	600	
Revenue price variance	$0	($22,000)	$5,000	$0	($17,000)

Solution to Practice Case

This case lends itself to the use of a rather simple spreadsheet, which can be used to compute the variances. Once one variance has been computed accurately, the formula used in that cell can be copied and pasted into the remaining cells of a like kind.

Question 1

Exhibit 3 is in the same format as Exhibit 1 but uses the actual volume and mix of visits. It is the same as the flexible budget described in the text, i.e., it holds price, resource use, and so forth at budget, and changes only volume and mix. As it indicates, although the number of visits increased by 50 from the budget, the mix changed in such a way that the surplus should have been $750 lower than the budget.

Exhibit 3 also computes revenue price variances using the formulas described in Appendix 11-A. So far the analysis is sound, although the difference between the flexed surplus of $84,250 and the deficit of $218,300 clearly suggests that there is much more to be uncovered.

Question 2

Some of the other reasons for the large total variance might be the following:

- More or fewer physician minutes, nursing minutes, medical supply units, or laboratory tests per visit, on average, than at budget
- Higher or lower average wage per minute for physicians and/or nurses, or higher or lower expenses per medical supply unit or laboratory test than budgeted
- Higher or lower fixed expenses

Question 3

The computations are shown in Exhibits A, B, and C. The data show the following:

- *Exhibit A*. Productivity and usage variances (the first set of reasons above) accounted for a negative $288,250 variance. Looking along the type-of-service dimension, we can see that over half of the total ($160,500) was for laboratory tests. Looking along the visit-type dimension, we can see that over half ($151,250) was for an IUD first visit. The highest single item was laboratory tests for an IUD first visit.
- *Exhibit B*. Wage, price, and efficiency variances (the second set of reasons) actually summed to a positive variance of $2,700. The $2,700 masked some more significant variances, however, but none was as substantial as the productivity and usage variances.
- Actual fixed expenses did not differ from budget.
- *Exhibit C*. Summary of variances indicates that the total variance was $303,300 (from a budget of a positive $85,000 to a deficit of $218,300). In terms of responsible groups, the area where there was the largest problem in meeting budget was in use of the laboratory, but use of medical supplies also was quite substantial.

In terms of using this information to manage the clinic, Ms. Ruiz might start by examining why more lab tests were ordered for every visit type except a routine follow-up. She also might ask the nurses why they are spending 10 minutes more for first visits, on average, than budgeted. Is it possible, for example, that physicians are saving 5 minutes per visit by giving the nurses more work? If so, perhaps that is appropriate, but there may be quality of care issues that need to be examined. Moreover, there is no savings if it takes a nurse (at half the per-minute wage of a physician) twice as long to do the same task (10 minutes versus 5 minutes).

EL CONEJO FAMILY PLANNING CLINIC
Exhibit A. Productivity/Usage Variances

Type of Service	IUD 1st Visit	Oral Conc 1st Visit	Special Follow-Up	Routine Follow-Up	Total
Physician Care					
Budgeted-Actual minutes per visit	5	5	-5	-5	
Budgeted wage per minute	$1.00	$1.00	$1.00	$1.00	
Productivity variance per visit	$5.00	$5.00	($5.00)	($5.00)	
Total productivity variances	$13,750	$11,000	($5,000)	($3,000)	$16,750
Nursing Care					
Budgeted-Actual minutes per visit	-10	-10	5	5	
Budgeted wage per minute	$0.50	$0.50	$0.50	$0.50	
Productivity variance per visit	($5.00)	($5.00)	$2.50	$2.50	
Total productivity variances	($13,750)	($11,000)	$2,500	$1,500	($20,750)
Medical Supplies					
Budgeted-Actual # units per visit	-1	-1	0	0	
Budgeted expense per unit	$25.00	$25.00	$25.00	$25.00	
Usage variance per visit	($25.00)	($25.00)	$0.00	$0.00	
Total usage variances	($68,750)	($55,000)	$0	$0	($123,750)
Laboratory					
Budgeted-Actual tests per visit	-2	-1	-3	0	
Budgeted expense per test	$15.00	$15.00	$15.00	$15.00	
Usage variance per visit	($30.00)	($15.00)	($45.00)	$0.00	
Total usage variances	($82,500)	($33,000)	($45,000)	$0	($160,500)
Total Productivity/usage per visit	($55.00)	($40.00)	($47.50)	($2.50)	
Actual number of visits	2,750	2,200	1,000	600	
Total productivity/usage variances	($151,250)	($88,000)	($47,500)	($1,500)	($288,250)

EL CONEJO FAMILY PLANNING CLINIC
Exhibit B. Wage/Price/Efficiency Variances

	IUD 1st Visit	Oral Conc 1st Visit	Special Follow-Up	Routine Follow-Up	Total
Actual number of visits	2,750	2,200	1,000	600	
Type of Service					
Physician care					
Budgeted-Actual wage per minute	($0.20)	($0.20)	($0.20)	($0.20)	
Actual # minutes per visit	25	5	20	10	
Wage rate variance per visit	($5.00)	($1.00)	($4.00)	($2.00)	
Total wage rate variance	($13,750)	($2,200)	($4,000)	($1,200)	($21,150)
Nursing care					
Budgeted-actual wage per minute	($0.10)	($0.10)	($0.10)	($0.10)	
Actual number of minutes per visit	40	30	25	5	
Wage rate variance per visit	($4.00)	($3.00)	($2.50)	($0.50)	
Total wage rate variance	($11,000)	($6,600)	($2,500)	($300)	($20,400)
Medical supplies					
Budgeted-actual expense per unit	$4.00	$4.00	$4.00	$4.00	
Actual # units per visit	4	2	2	0	
Rate/efficiency variance per visit	$16.00	$8.00	$8.00	$0.00	
Total rate/efficiency variance	$44,000	$17,600	$8,000	$0	$69,600
Laboratory					
Budgeted-actual expense per test	($1.00)	($1.00)	($1.00)	($1.00)	
Actual # tests per visit	5	3	5	0	
Rate/efficiency variance per visit	($5.00)	($3.00)	($5.00)	$0.00	
Total rate/efficiency variance	($13,750)	($6,600)	($5,000)	$0	($25,350)
Total Wage/Rate/Efficiency Variances	$5,500	$2,200	($3,500)	($1,500)	$2,700

EL CONEJO FAMILY PLANNING CLINIC
Exhibit C. Summary of Variances

	IUD 1st Visit	Oral Conc 1st Visit	Special Follow-Up	Routine Follow-Up	Total
Contribution margin variances	($8,750)	$5,000	$ 0	$3,000	($750)
Revenue price variances	0	(22,000)	5,000	0	(17,000)
Subtotal	($8,750)	($17,000)	$5,000	$3,000	($17,750)
Productivity/usage variances					
Physician care	$13,750	$11,000	($5,000)	($3,000)	$16,750
Nursing care	(13,750)	(11,000)	2,500	1,500	(20,750)
Medical supplies	(68,750)	(55,000)	0	0	(123,750)
Laboratory	(82,500)	(33,000)	(45,000)	0	(160,500)
Subtotal	($151,250)	($88,000)	($47,500)	($1,500)	($288,250)
Wage, rate, and efficiency variances					
Physician care	($13,750)	($2,200)	($4,000)	($1,200)	($21,150)
Nursing care	(11,000)	(6,600)	(2,500)	(300)	(20,400)
Medical supplies	44,000	17,600	8,000	0	69,600
Laboratory	(13,750)	(6,600)	(5,000)	0	(25,350)
Subtotal	$5,500	$2,200	($3,500)	($1,500)	$2,700
Total variances	($154,500)	($102,800)	($46,000)	$ 0	($303,300)
Variances by responsible group					
Physicians	$ 0	$8,800	($9,000)	($4,200)	($4,400)
Nurses	(24,750)	(17,600)	0	1,200	(41,150)
Medical supply department	(24,750)	(37,400)	8,000	0	(54,150)
Laboratory	(96,250)	(39,600)	(50,000)	0	(185,850)
Senior management	(8,750)	(17,000)	5,000	3,000	(17,750)
Total	($154,500)	($102,800)	($46,000)	$ 0	($303,300)

Chapter 12

Reporting on Performance: The Management Control Reports

As Chapter 6 indicated, responsibility accounting systems have both structure and process. Of particular importance in the latter area is the rhythmic flow of activities, consisting of four separate but closely related phases: programming, budgeting, operating and measuring, and reporting and evaluating. Chapters 7 and 8 discussed programming and budgeting, respectively, Chapter 9 discussed operating activities, and Chapters 10 and 11 discussed non-financial and financial measurement. The purpose of this chapter is to build on the concepts discussed in the latter two chapters, and to focus on the *reporting* phase of the management control process.

In all organizations—nonprofit and for-profit—managers need an ongoing flow of information to assist them in carrying out the management control function. Much of this information comes from talking with people and observing performance directly, but much also comes from formal reports. The main focus of this chapter is on the types of formal reports that can be used by nonprofit organizations, including some issues that managers face in using them.

TYPES OF REPORTS

There are essentially two types of formal reports: information reports and performance reports. The primary focus of this chapter is on performance reports, but to understand the distinction, let's examine information reports briefly.

Information Reports

Information reports are designed to tell management "what's going on." As such, they do not always lead to action. A reader studies these reports to detect whether or not something has happened that requires investigation. If nothing of significance is noted in an information report, which is often the case, the report is put aside, forwarded, or filed without action. If something strikes the reader's attention, an inquiry or other action may be initiated.

The information contained in such reports may come from the accounting system or from a variety of other sources. Information reports derived from the accounting system include income statements, balance sheets, cash flow statements, and details on such items as cash balances, the status of accounts receivable and inventories, and a list of accounts payable that are coming due.

An enumeration of non-accounting information reports could easily be quite long. Such reports might include *internal* information such as the number of new clients or patients, or the position titles of an association's members who did not renew their memberships. Information reports using *external* information, might include general news summaries, legislative updates, new regulatory requirements or constraints, information on the industry from trade associations, and general economic information from a variety of publications.

Performance Reports

Performance reports look at three general areas: economic performance, programmatic performance, and management performance. When a conventional income statement is prepared for a program or a profit center, for example, the surplus shown on the statement is a basic measure of the unit's *economic performance*.

Programmatic performance issues were discussed in Chapter 10. In general, they relate to the non-financial results or outcomes that the organization attained during some period of time. Some ways to report on programmatic performance are discussed later in the chapter.

A *management performance* report focuses mainly on the financial performance of a responsibility center's manager. This report, sometimes called a *control report,* may show that the manager is doing an excellent job. If, however, an economic performance report shows that his or her responsibility center is operating at a loss, or is not producing a satisfactory surplus, action may be required despite his or her good performance.

Example An economic performance report showed that the nursing school in a private university was operating at a loss. The loss was explained by the fact that a state university nearby had opened a nursing school and was charging much lower tuition rates. The dean of the nursing school in the private university was not responsible for this environmental change, and, indeed, the control reports showed that her performance was quite good. Nevertheless, a thorough analysis revealed that there was no way to eliminate the school's ongoing loss. Because the school no longer could function as a sound economic entity, the university's provost decided to close it and devote the university's resources to other activities.

In sum, apart from programmatic results, there are two quite different ways to judge the performance of a responsibility center. First, as an economic entity, in which economic considerations are dominant, and second, in terms of the financial performance of the responsibility center's manager compared to commitments made during the budgeting phase. The role of the management control reports is to assist in this latter effort.

CONTENTS OF THE MANAGEMENT CONTROL REPORTS

Each responsibility center is expected to do its part to help the organization achieve its objectives. To the extent that at least some of the expectations consist of achieving targeted revenues, controlling costs, or both, they are set forth in the responsibility center's budget. The purpose of the control reports is to communicate how well the responsibility center managers performed in comparison with the budget (as well, occasionally, with other standards of performance).

If the budget is a valid statement of expected performance, the control report simply calculates the difference between it and actual performance. Positive differences represent good performance, and negative differences represent poor performance. However, such labels are valid only if there has been no change in the circumstances that were assumed when the budget was prepared. This rarely is the case. It also usually is necessary to examine the reasons why actual performance differed from the budget.

The purpose of a control report, then, is to compare actual performance with what performance should have been considering the actual circumstances. If inflation was greater than expected, if volume was down for uncontrollable reasons, or if any of a number of other circumstances altered the original assumptions, a negative variance does not necessarily represent poor performance.

Key Characteristics

Good control reports have three essential characteristics: (1) they are related to personal responsibility, (2) they compare actual performance to the best available standard, and (3) they focus on significant information. Let's examine these characteristics in light of the sample set of reports shown in Exhibit 12-1, which is an example of the way information might be structured in a state human service agency. (There are more programs than the three shown here, but these are sufficient for illustrative purposes.)

Exhibit 12-1 Reporting Hierarchy for a State Human Service Agency (in Thousands of Dollars)

FIRST-LEVEL REPORT: PROGRAM SUMMARY (For Agency Director)

	Actual Results		Under (Over) Budget	
Direct Costs	June	Year to Date	June	Year to Date
Senior citizen services	$ 21,110	$ 120,030	$ (315)	$ 35
Maternal and infant nutrition	*24,525*	*147,280*	*(710)*	*(2,590)*
Early childhood screening	11,235	70,570	(125)	(210)
Total	$56,870	$337,880	$(1,150)	$(2,765)
Controllable overhead	27,120	161,970	320	1,130
Total expenses	$83,990	$499,850	$ (830)	$(1,635)

SECOND-LEVEL REPORT: MATERNAL AND INFANT NUTRITION PROGRAM: Direct Cost Summary (For Program Manager)

	Actual Results		Under (Over) Budget	
Direct Labor	June	Year to Date	June	Year to Date
Counselors	$ 5,340	$ 35,845	$ (625)	$(1,380)
Nutritionists	*3,310*	*19,605*	*(30)*	*(620)*
Physicians	3,115	18,085	90	(135)
Supplies and materials				
Food and beverages	5,740	33,635	(65)	(640)
Stationery	1,865	9,795	(175)	825
Contract services				
Computer expense	3,195	18,015	210	35
Housekeeping	1,960	12,300	(115)	(675)
Total expenses	$24,525	$147,280	$ (710)	$(2,590)

To next page

THIRD-LEVEL REPORT: NUTRITIONISTS (For Nutrition Supervisor)

	Actual Results		Under (Over) Budget	
	June	Year to Date	June	Year to Date
Direct contact time cost	*$ 2,187*	*$ 12,524*	*$ (265)*	*$ 90*
Efficiency variance			(115)	515
Rate variance			(150)	(425)
Non-contact time cost				
Meetings	420	1,916	180	91
Community/collateral work	284	1,748	(75)	(530)
Professional development	115	808	(121)	(384)
Administrative activities	60	721	160	(82)
Sick and vacation time	244	1,888	91	195
Total non-contact time cost	$1,123	$7,081	$235	($ 710)
Total direct labor cost	$ 3,310	$ 19,605	$ (30)	$ (620)

FOURTH-LEVEL REPORT: REGIONAL SUMMARY OF NUTRITIONISTS DIRECT CONTACT TIME (For Regional Manager)

	Actual Results		Under (Over) Budget	
	June	Year to Date	June	Year to Date
Direct contact time cost				
Region 1	$ 750	$ 4,140	($ 85)	$ 27
Region 2	795	3,890	(70)	30
Region 3	642	4,494	(110)	33
Total	$ 2,187	$ 12,524	$ (265)	$ 90
Efficiency variances				
Region 1			($ 15)	$ 120
Region 2			(25)	155
Region 3			(75)	240
Total			$ (115)	$ 515
Rate variances				
Region 1			($ 70)	$ (93)
Region 2			(65)	(120)
Region 3			(15)	(212)
Total			(150)	($425)

Relationship to Personal Responsibility

Because responsibility accounting classifies the costs assigned to each responsibility center according to whether they are controllable or non-controllable, many control reports show only controllable costs. (Some also show non-controllable costs, but as a separate category for information purposes only.) To facilitate analysis and appropriate action, the controllable costs in this human service agency are classified by program, as shown in the first-level report. On this report, controllable overhead is reported separately from direct costs, but non-controllable costs are excluded.

In the second level report, direct costs for each program are broken down by line item (or cost element). Direct costs include both direct labor, and supplies, materials, and contract services.

On the third-level report, the direct labor cost for each job category, such as nutritionists, is divided into direct-contact time and non-contact time in order to facilitate the analysis of the activities of employees and the associated costs. Efficiency and rate variances are calculated for direct-contact time. Non-contact time is divided into categories that are meaningful for the supervisor.

Finally, on the fourth-level report, the costs and variances for direct-contact time are broken down by region. This allows responsibility to be decentralized to a very low level in the organization—in this instance, a regional supervisor of nutritionists.

Note, as the arrows indicate, that each report shows the total of the report above it in the hierarchy, but breaks the total down into items that are useful for the designated report reader. The line item of $24,525 for June for maternal and infant nutrition in the first-level report, for example, is the total in the second-level report, but in this report, it is divided into its separate elements, one of which is $3,310 for nutritionists. This $3,310 is the same as the total in the third-level report, but this report divides it into meaningful line items, one of which is $2,187 of direct contact time. Finally, the fourth-level report divides the $2,187 among the three regions.

Variation in Levels. Not all organizations will structure their report levels in the same way. The design depends on the users and their information needs. Exhibit 12-2 is an example of a set of reports for an integrated delivery system (IDS). It focuses on the Inpatient Division for the more detailed examples.

Exhibit 12-2 Reporting Hierarchy for an Integrated Delivery System (Surplus Amounts in Thousands of Dollars)

FIRST-LEVEL REPORT: DIVISION SUMMARY (For Senior Management)

	Actual Results		Over (Under) Budget	
Division	June	Year to Date	June	Year to Date
Division 1	$ 21,110	$ 120,030	$ (315)	$ 35
Division 2-Inpatient Care	24,525	147,280	(710)	(2,590)
Division 3	11,235	70,570	(125)	(210)
TOTAL	$56,870	$337,880	$(1,150)	$(2,765)
Controllable overhead	27,120	161,970	320	1,130
Total Surplus (Deficit)	$29,750	$175,910	$ (830)	$(1,635)

SECOND-LEVEL REPORT: DIVISION 2-INPATIENT CARE PRODUCT LINE SUMMARY (For Division Vice President)

	Actual Results		Over (Under) Budget	
Product line	June	Year to Date	June	Year to Date
Oncology	$ 5,340	$ 35,845	$ (625)	$(1,380)
Cardiology	3,310	19,605	(30)	(620)
Women's Health	3,115	18,085	90	(135)
Orthopedics	5,740	33,635	(65)	(640)
Pediatrics	7,020	40,110	(80)	185
Total Surplus (Deficit)	$24,525	$147,280	$ (710)	$(2,590)

To next page

THIRD-LEVEL REPORT: CARDIOLOGY REGIONAL BREAKDOWN (For Product Line Manager)

	Actual Results		Over (Under) Budget	
Region	June	Year to Date	June	Year to Date
Region 1	$ 895	$ 5,400	$ 119	$ 75
Region 2	1,030	7,000	176	(50)
Region 3	760	4,500	(160)	(350)
Region n	625	2,705	(165)	(295)
Total Surplus (Deficit)	$ 3,310	$ 19,605	$ (30)	$ (620)

FOURTH-LEVEL REPORT: CARDIOLOGY REGION 1, FACILITY BREAKDOWN (For Regional Manager)

	Actual Results		Over (Under) Budget	
Facility	June	Year to Date	June	Year to Date
Facility 1	$ 245	$ 1,300	$ (35)	$ (65)
Facility 2	300	1,775	20	120
Facility 3	150	780	35	165
Facility n	200	1,545	99	(145)
Total Surplus (Deficit)	$ 895	$ 5,400	$ 119	$ 75

FIFTH-LEVEL REPORT: CARDIOLOGY PRODUCT BREAKDOWN (For Facility Managers)

	Actual Results		Over (Under) Budget	
Facility 1	June	Year to Date	June	Year to Date
Procedure A	$ 90	$ 560	$ (25)	$ (50)
Procedure B	75	350	(20)	(80)
Procedure C	45	280	15	95
Procedure D	35	110	(5)	(30)
Total Surplus (Deficit)	$ 245	$ 1,300	$ (35)	$ (65)

This exhibit contains five levels of information, each of which disaggregates the information above it in the same way as Exhibit 12-1 did, but with a different focus. For example, the Inpatient Care Division is shown as a single line on the first-level report, a report designed for senior management. On the second-level report, the product lines of the division are broken out, such as Oncology, Cardiology, and Women's Health.

Each product line is broken into regions on the third-level report, and regions into facilities in the fourth-level report. The fifth-level report breaks each facility into its individual products.

In reviewing this report, note that there once again is a "drill down" capability. The first-level report shows that the Inpatient Care Division had a year-to-date negative variance (in its surplus) of $2,590 (far right column). This amount is broken down by product lines in the second-level report, which shows that Cardiology had a $620 negative year-to-date variance. This $620 negative variance is broken down into regions in the third-level report, which shows that Region 1 had a $75 *positive* variance. The $75 positive variance is broken down by facilities in the fourth-level report, which shows that Facility 1 had a $65 negative variance, which is divided among the various tests and procedures (called "products") in the firth-level report.

With this set of reports, senior management and line managers have the capability to examine in detail the causes of a variance between the overall budgeted and actual surplus. A division's surplus or deficit can be traced down through the organizational hierarchy to locate its source(s) in product lines, regions, facilities, and individual tests and procedures (called "products").

In summary, reporting on management performance requires that (1) costs (and sometimes revenues) be classified by responsibility center (e.g., Maternal and Infant Nutrition Program, Inpatient Care), (2) costs (and revenues) within each center be classified as to whether they are controllable or non-controllable, and (3) controllable costs be broken down into sufficient detail to provide a useful basis for analysis and action. If it is not possible to give a positive answer to the question "Is there any conceivable action that the responsibility center manager could take on the basis of this report?" the report is a candidate for either revision or elimination.

CRITERIA FOR AN ACTION ORIENTATION

Once appropriate data have been collected and the necessary variances calculated, the results must be structured and presented so that managers receive information they can use as a basis for action. If the reporting phase of the management control process is to provide responsibility center managers with the information they need for taking action, it must meet several criteria.

Timeliness

As discussed previously, timely does not necessarily mean that the information must arrive quickly, but rather appropriately with respect to the managerial action that may be necessary. In some instances, monthly reports that arrive within a few days of the end of each month may be necessary; in others, it may be acceptable for the monthly reports to arrive within a week or two after the end of the month. Similarly, daily, weekly, quarterly, or annual reports may be necessary, and each will have an appropriate time lag between the effective date of the information it contains and the date managers need to receive it in order to take action.

Hierarchy of Information

Information must be available in various levels of aggregation, from summarized to detailed. Generally, not all managers at all levels in the organization will need to have the same level of detail. The manager of a hospital's laboratories, for example, most likely will not want detailed efficiency information for each technician in each laboratory. However, he or she might want to have information about the efficiency of different sections within the labs. Generally the information on the lab sections would appear at a lower level in the hierarchy, so that it does not impede the reading of more summarized information. As a result, as Exhibits 12-1 and 12-2 illustrate, a good reporting system has several levels of detail:

- *A highly summarized level,* used by senior management only, generally to review divisional or departmental performance
- *A breakdown by sections or sub-departments within a division or department,* used primarily by division or department managers but available to senior management for reference

- *A breakdown by activities or products (such as DRGs) within sections or sub-departments,* used primarily by section or sub-department managers, but available to division or department managers for reference

- *A detailed listing of both personnel and supplies,* used for in-depth reference; this level comprises the building blocks for all the previous levels (and also is used for both the financial accounting and full cost accounting systems)

Obviously the levels of detail must be tailored to each organization and its needs. For small organizations, where management is intimately aware of the activities, a highly summarized level and a detail level may be all that are needed. As potential problems are identified, they can be discussed with the individuals involved, using detail information, as necessary, to answer questions. For larger organizations, all four or five (or even more) levels may be needed.

Selection of the Levels. Several factors are central to a decision about the appropriate number of levels and their content: (1) the managerial time associated with using the reports, (2) the kinds of actions that can be taken based on the information, (3) the amount of decision-making latitude given to individuals at different levels of the organization, and (4) the cost of preparing the reports. A careful weighing of these factors is essential to the design of an effective and usable set of reports.

Relevance and Accuracy

A good set of reports is characterized by the presence of relevant and accurate information. Although *accurate* needs no elaboration, *relevant* is more slippery. Many reporting systems offer a great deal of information that is of marginal or no use to managers receiving the reports, and yet certain crucial information is missing entirely. A good example is year-to-date information, which generally is of some use to a manager but often is not included on a set of management reports. By contrast, if an organization has a highly seasonal pattern of operations, year-to-date information may be of little use unless adjusted for seasonality.

Unit cost information also may be of little use. If a manager has no control over volume, then total unit cost information (which includes both fixed and variable costs) is of almost no value, and might be quite misleading. The relevant information is variable cost per unit, which presumably is not affected by volume and therefore includes costs that can be controlled by the manager.

Exhibit 12-3, an abbreviated report for Spenser Rehabilitation Hospital, illustrates one way to achieve relevancy. This report is similar to Exhibits 12-1 and 12-2, but it has a more detailed variance analysis, breaking variances down by several budget drivers. Note that at the senior management- and board-level, the report shows the reasons why a product line has not achieved its targeted surplus. For example, the $710 negative variance for the month for Inpatient Care B is a result of lower prices ($50), a worsened payer mix ($320), a positive contribution margin ($60), worsened utilization ($250), and higher unit costs ($150).

The same drill-down capability as was present in the other exhibits is possible, but is not shown here. At the lowest level, physician chiefs of service and individual physicians can examine their performance for a given DRG (diagnosis-related group). Note, for example, that although Physician 1 came in below the budget in the lab, pharmacy, and physical therapy, he or she had an overall $35 negative variance for the month, due mainly to using more radiology ($50), routine care ($50), and other services ($15) than budgeted. This information can be highly relevant in a discussion between the physician and his or her chief of service about the nature of the physician's patients, and the reasons for overspending the budget.

Exhibit 12-3 Reporting Hierarchy for Spenser Rehabilitation Hospital, Showing Variance Computations for Profit Centers (in Thousands of Dollars)

FIRST-LEVEL REPORT: PRODUCT LINES (For Board and Senior Management)

	------Actual-------		Over or (under) budget		--Revenue--		Contrib. Margin Volume & Mix			Expense	
Surplus (Deficit)	This Month	Year to date	This Month	Year to date	Price	Payer Mix	Rev	Exp	Net	Utiliza-tion	Unit Cost
Inpatient A	$2,110	$12,030	$(315)	$35							
Inpatient B	24,525	147,280	(710)	(2,590)	(50)	(320)	150	(90)	60	(250)	(150)
Outpatient	1,235	7,570	(125)	(210)							
Research	1,180	7,045	95	75				710			
Education	3,590	18,960	(235)	245							
Ambulance	4,120	25,175	160	(320)							
Development	2,245	13,680	180	(160)							
Administration	3,630	22,965	(70)	(730)							
Total	$42,635	$254,705	$(1,020)	$(3,655)							

SIXTH LEVEL REPORT: DRG ANALYSIS BY PHYSICIAN (For Physician Chiefs of Service and Attending Physicians)

DRG Number 1 — In the Spinal Cord Injury Product Line:

	-------Actual------		Over or (under) budget		----------This Month's Variance Analysis----------						
	This Month	Year to date	This Month	Year to date	Lab	Rad	Pharm.	PT	Routine Care	Other	Total
Physician 1	$245	$1,300	$(35)	$(65)	10	(50)	20	50	(50)	(15)	(35)
Physician 2	300	1,775	20	120							
Physician 3	150	780	35	165							
Physician 4	200	1,545	99	(145)							
Total	$895	$5,400	$119	$75							

Comparison with a Standard

The existence of variances in Exhibits 12-1, 12-2, and 12-3 means there must have been a standard against which actual performance was compared. A report that contains information on actual results only is virtually useless for control purposes. To be useful, control reports must compare actual performance with a standard. There are three types of standards that can be used for this purpose: budgeted, historical and external.

Budgeted Standards. If carefully prepared, a budget is the best standard. It takes into account the conditions that are expected to exist in the budget year, and the revenue and expense items show the expected monetary effects of these conditions. Although budgeted amounts are not shown in the Exhibits 12-1, 12-2, and 12-3, it is clear that they exist since there are columns labeled "Under (Over) Budget" when the responsibility center has expenses only, and "Over (Under) Budget" when it is a profit center.

Historical Standards. Some organizations compare current performance with past performance. Results for the second quarter of a given year, for example, could be compared with those for the first quarter of the same year or with the second quarter of the previous year. Ordinarily, an historical standard is not as good as a well-prepared budget for at least two reasons: (1) conditions in the current period are probably different from those in a prior period, and (2) performance in the prior period may not have represented good performance.

Despite these limitations, historical data are better than data in a poorly prepared budged. Since they are drawn directly from the accounting records, they are not influenced by the judgments and persuasive arguments that sometimes affect the budget numbers. Furthermore, if an organization's environment is relatively stable from one year to the next, an historical standard (assuming it represented good performance) may be practically as good as a budget.

External Standards. The standard for analyzing performance in a given responsibility center could be the average performance in similar responsibility centers in the same organization or in similar organizations. The performance of one hospital in a multi-institutional chain can be compared with all other hospitals in the chain, for example. If the conditions in each hospital are similar, a comparison of this sort can provide a reasonable basis for judging the performance of each hospital manager.

In practice, similar conditions may not exist. A hospital's size, demographic and epidemiological environment, labor market, supply market, and other factors all affect its performance in some way. Senior management must decide if these conditions are sufficiently different to invalidate any sort of meaningful comparison.

Many industry associations compile and distribute information about changes in the general environment of their member institutions, and provide current data on average costs and other statistics. Management can use these data for comparative analyses that may provide helpful indicators of whether the organization is drifting out of line with its peers. Of course, senior management must be certain that the comparisons are valid.

Examples

The Healthcare Financial Management Association (HFMA) publishes a variety of hospital financial ratios based on information supplied by hundreds of hospitals. In an effort to make sure the comparisons are valid, the HFMA classifies hospitals by type and bed size, and computes medians, upper quartiles, and lower quartiles for each category.

State governments publish data on cost per mile of highway maintenance. However, some states use "trunkline miles" (i.e. linear miles of main highways), while others adjust the miles for the number of lanes. Still others use "equivalent trunkline miles." Without an agreed-upon set of definitions, managers find it difficult to use data such as these for comparison purposes.

Once definitional difficulties are resolved, comparative measures can be especially useful for control in situations involving a large number of moderately small, discrete and independent entities, with similar clientele, operations, and cost structures. Examples include daycare centers, urban schools, suburban schools, community hospitals, and inner-city job placement programs. In these cases, the indicators measuring similar aspects of performance (such as student-to-teacher ratios, cost of instruction, cost of supervisory personnel, or cost of maintenance) may be valid indicators of *relative performance* even in the absence of an absolute performance measure.

Focus on Significant Information

The problem of designing reports is, in part, one of deciding on the right type of information to give to managers at various levels. Clearly, whenever feasible, managers should be given all the information they request. At the same time, to swamp managers with more information than they can assimilate is not helpful. Indeed, experiments have shown that if *information overload* exists, there is a tendency for a manager to disregard the entire reporting mechanism.

Because of this potential, the controller should assure that line managers are receiving only the information they need. Periodic discussions with them to ascertain what information is being used for what purposes can facilitate this process. Clearly a similar review process should take place at the senior management-level as well.

Definition of Significant. What is significant for one manager may not be significant for another. In general, significant items are those that can make a difference in the way a manager makes decisions. There is no way to specify exactly what such items are, as they vary depending on both the situation and the backgrounds and wishes of the individual managers. Nevertheless, it is possible to make some generalizations:

- The significance of an item is not necessarily proportional to its size. In particular, certain discretionary cost items, such as travel, or dues and subscriptions, may be significant to many individuals, especially professionals, even though the totals are comparatively small.

- Minor items should be aggregated. For example, costs of heating, air conditioning, electricity can be reported as "utilities." Reporting a long list of cost items, many of which are relatively minor, can tend to obscure the few relatively significant items.

- The higher the management level using a report, the more aggregated the information should be. Exhibits 12-1 and 12-2 illustrate this point. In each instance, the report for a given level contains less detail than the level below it.

- Managers ordinarily do not care about the calculations (assuming they are accurate!). As indicated earlier, for example, the reports in the three exhibits do not show the budgeted amounts, but only the difference between actual and budget. Similarly, variances calculations also are omitted.

Key Indicators. In most organizations and their responsibility centers, there are a few factors that must be watched closely. These *key results* or *key success* factors (or, sometimes, *danger signals*) often can signal the possibility of upcoming problems. For example, in many nonprofit organizations, the number of new clients or client inquiries is a key indicator. In a hospital, average length of stay, classified by diagnosis, may play this role.

Examples In a college or university, management needs to be alert to such danger signals as:

- A decrease in the number of inquiries, the number of applications, the quality of applicants, yield, and alumni contributions
- An increase in student aid applications, student attrition rates, or administrative and support personnel

These signals are associated with several different responsibility centers

The director of a mental health clinic stated that, in order to know how well the clinic was doing financially, she only needed to focus on three items: (1) billed hours (i.e., the number of hours spent with clients), (2) accounts receivable as a percent of monthly billings (an indication of how promptly clients were paying their bills), and (3) the ratio of expenses to revenues.

Integration

Ordinarily, control reports should be an integrated package. Reports for lower-level responsibility centers should be consistent with, and easily related to, summary reports prepared for higher-level responsibility centers. The reports shown in Exhibits 12-1 and, 12-2 have this characteristic. As a result, senior and line managers can drill down very deeply into the organization's activities if they wish to do so in order to learn about the underlying reasons for a variance. This, in turn, can help them to plan and implement any needed corrective actions.

Behavioral Factors

For a set of management control reports to be effective, corrective action must be a priority. It is not sufficient to simply prepare and distribute reports. Unless senior management communicates its expectation that the reporting system will be used as a basis for taking action, the system will have little value.

Senior management can take any number of steps to communicate its intent, including holding regular meetings to discuss the reports, requiring follow-up memos from middle managers, or making telephone calls and participating in hallway conversations. Conversely, if senior management ignores the reports, line managers probably will do so also.

MEASURING AND REPORTING NON-FINANCIAL INFORMATION

As discussed in prior chapters, in addition to reporting on financial performance, the management control process in a nonprofit organization must measure and report on non-financial performance. Indeed, managers must constantly bear in mind the fact that the objectives of a nonprofit organization extend beyond the satisfaction of annual surplus targets to encompass a wide variety of non-financial (or programmatic) objectives. These objectives tend to fall into four general categories: (1) improving the quality of an organization's services, (2) avoiding unneeded services, (3) improving client or patient satisfaction, and (4) fostering improved job satisfaction and performance for the organization's professional staff and others. When these sorts of non-financial objectives are important to the organization's strategy, the reporting phase of the management control process must accommodate them.

Example The non-financial measures that a hospital or other healthcare organization might use are shown below:

Area	Positive Measures	Negative Measures
Quality of care	HEDIS [Health Plan Employer Data and Information Set] scores	Hospital-acquired infections
		Post-surgical infection rates
	% of clinical pathways implemented	Patient falls
Prevention	Primary care capacity utilization	Preventable inpatient admissions
	% of children receiving immunizations	Preventable emergency room use

Patient satisfaction	% positive survey results % of HMO re-enrollment	% complaints
Employee satisfaction	% positive survey results % promotions	Absenteeism rate Turnover rate

Managing non-financial (or programmatic) results implies that managers need to receive regular reports concerning the selected measures. To the extent feasible, these reports should be integrated so that managers can determine the resources being consumed in attaining various programmatic results.

Criteria for Good Programmatic Reports

In attempting to develop a useful set of programmatic reports, managers need to consider four interrelated issues. They are illustrated in Exhibit 12-4, which is a programmatic report for an MBA program in a business school.

1. Alignment of Responsibility and Control. The report is divided into several areas of responsibility. Marketing and recruitment, for example, constitute one such area, whereas student performance, program performance, and alumni satisfaction are separate areas. Although it may not be possible to assign a specific person to each area, these nevertheless are areas where different individuals can be expected to take action. The head of the Admissions Office would be expected to take action concerning marketing and recruitment, for example, and the program director would have responsibility for students' satisfaction while they are in the program. The Career Planning and Placement Office and the Development Office presumably would have responsibility for student satisfaction related to job placements and alumni contributions.

2. Relationship Between Outputs and Inputs. Outputs could be related to inputs in several areas. It would be possible, for example, to determine the cost per admitted applicant, the cost per course, or the cost per graduate. In the latter two cases, tuition might be used as a surrogate for cost, and the program's performance per tuition dollar might be calculated.

3. Role of Non-financial Objectives. Most output measures relate directly to non-financial objectives. Presumably the program is interested in attracting well-qualified students. To the extent that its yield is high (assuming it admits only well-qualified students), it is doing its job well.[1] Similarly, it is likely that the program is interested in retaining only well-qualified students, and the two items that help to measure this are: (1) how many well-performing students (A- average or better) leave, and (2) how many poorly performing students (below B- average) leave. Finally, it is likely that the program is interested in placing its students appropriately and having them satisfied with their education. The area of alumni satisfaction addresses this issue.

4. Changes over Time. By setting up a five-year series of comparisons, both the program manager and senior management can see how results are changing over time. The five-year series could be supplemented with a set of budgeted targets so as to measure the program's performance both over time and with respect to the targets.

[1] "Yield" is the percent of accepted applicants who decide to attend.

Exhibit 12-4 Program Performance Report Framework: For an MBA Program in a Business School

Indicator	Year 1	Year 2	Year 3	Year 4	Year 5
Marketing and Recruitment					
1. Number of inquiries					
2. Number of applications sent out					
3. Number of applications received					
4. Application Rate (= 3 ÷ 2)					
5. Number of accepted applicants					
6. Admission Rate (= 5 ÷ 3)					
7. Number of matriculants					
8. Yield (= 7 ÷ 5)					
9. Average GPA for matriculants					
10. Average GMAT for matriculants					
Student Performance in Program					
11. Grade distribution for required courses					
A- or better					
B+ to B-					
Below B-					
12. Grade distribution for elective courses					
A- or better					
B+ to B-					
Below B-					
13. Percent of matriculants with A- average or better leaving program in year 1					
14. Percent of matriculants with average below B- leaving program in year 1					
15. Percent of matriculants graduating from program					
Student Satisfaction/Overall Program Performance					
16. Average instructor rating for required courses					
17. Average instructor rating for elective courses					
18. Percent of graduates attaining job of choice within 3 months of graduation					
19. Average salary of graduates after 5 years					
20. Percent of graduates making annual financial contributions to school					
21. Median gift per graduate					
22. Percent of graduates making a gift of $500 or more					

Presenting the Information

The presentation format for both financial and non-financial information is important to its use. Exhibits 12-1, 12-2, and 12-3 show how this might be done for financial information. However, with the wide variety of feasible measures in each of several areas of concern to senior management, it is possible for the information to become very overwhelming. In response, some organizations have begun to use a "spidergram," such as that shown in Exhibit 12-5.

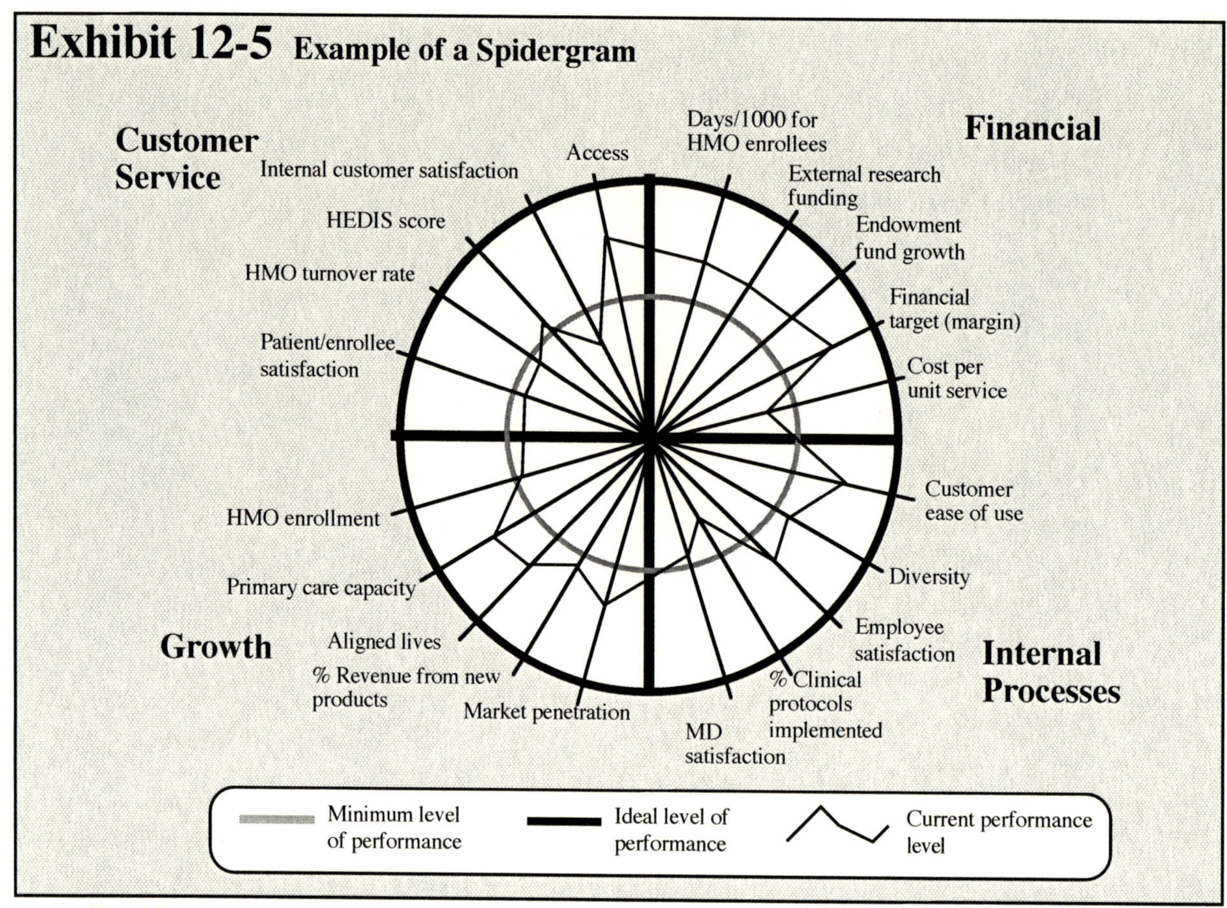

A spidergram can assist senior management to see a variety of measures in several different categories at a glance. To read the spidergram, consider that the inner circle is the minimum acceptable level of performance, the outer circle is the goal, and the jagged line is actual performance for the period in question.

In this report, the organization, a hospital, is looking at four broad areas of performance: customer service, growth, financial results, and internal processes. It has several measures of each, and can use the report to tell at a glance where it is meeting—or failing to meet—its goals.

The hospital prepares a report like this with varying levels of detail depending on the target audience. The report in Exhibit 12-5 is designed for the board of directors, but managers at different levels have modified versions depending on their areas of responsibility. Senior management can focus on those areas where the jagged line is inside the minimum acceptable line and can use the information to discuss specific remedial actions with line managers and others who have responsibility for the different measures.

Whether an organization uses a spidergram or a similar reporting mechanism is less important than recognizing that one consequence of developing and measuring non-financial results is a need to provide reports on these results to the appropriate managers. To the extent feasible, these reports should be integrated so that managers can determine the resources being consumed in the attainment of various non-financial results. And, as with financial reporting, a non-financial reporting system must provide accurate, timely, and useful information to the appropriate managers.

TECHNICAL CRITERIA FOR CONTROL REPORTS

In addition to the basic characteristics discussed above concerning their content, control reports also must satisfy certain technical criteria. While the satisfaction of these criteria is largely the controller's responsibility, senior management needs to be aware of the criteria so it can guide the controller in the design effort, and so that it can recognize problems when they arise.

The Control Period

The period of time covered by a report should be the shortest period in which management can usefully take action and in which significant changes in performance are likely. If a serious situation develops, management needs to know immediately; otherwise, serious difficulties may occur.

Of particular importance is the fact that key indicators usually need to be reported separately from revenues, expenses, and variances. They also need to be distributed more frequently than financial information so as to facilitate timely intervention.

Example The principal of a junior high school received a report that showed the cumulative number of days of absence in the school year for each student. Since there was a strong correlation between attendance and performance, and since 10 days of absences meant that a student needed to repeat a school year, a growing number of absences for any given student was an important danger signal. The only action needed was for the principal to express concern to the student when they saw each other. The fact that the principal knew—and the student knew that the principal knew—provided the proper motivation. To be useful, the report needed to be prepared on a daily basis.

Bases for Comparison

A control report should compare actual amounts with budgeted ones for the same time period. Thus, unless revenues and expenses flow evenly during a fiscal year, the budgeted amounts for, say, a quarterly report should not be obtained by taking one-quarter of the annual budget. Rather, separate quarterly budgets should be constructed by estimating the portion of the annual budget that is applicable to each quarter. Otherwise, the comparison will have little value.

Clarity

A control report is a communication device, and it is not doing its job unless it communicates its intended message clearly. This is much easier said than done, however. Those who design reports need to spend considerable time carefully choosing terminology that conveys the intended meaning, and arranging the numbers in a way that they emphasize the important relationships.

Clarity may also be enhanced if the variances are expressed as percentages of budget as well as absolute amounts. The percentages give a quick impression of the relative importance of the variance. In reports for profit centers, clarity can be enhanced if percentages or ratios are used to call attention to important relationships. Occasionally, depending on the audience, greater clarity can be achieved by using graphs and narrative explanations.

If a narrative explanation is used, it ordinarily needs to go beyond simply restating what a report already says. Rather, it needs to describe the reasons underlying a variance or other items of importance. On the other hand, because many board members of nonprofit organizations are professionals or community leaders, often without a strong background in accounting or finance, narrative explanations, even though restating what the report says, can be helpful in drawing their attention to important items.

Example In a nonprofit community movie theater, each month's financial report began with a brief statement of the month's surplus and the year-to-date surplus, followed by a listing of the revenue that had been derived from each of the films that had been shown that month, and any unusual or unanticipated expenses. The report also computed total revenue and total expenses as percentages of the annual budgeted amounts, and compared those percentages to the percent of the fiscal year that had elapsed. For many of the board members, this allowed them to know what was happening financially without the need to spend a lot of time examining the details. Because there was little seasonality, if the percentages were on track, there was no need to spend a great deal of time discussing the underlying revenue and expense items.

Rounding

To help focus managers' attention on significant information, the accounting staff should round the numbers in control reports, rather than calculate them to the last penny. Most managers care little about cents; some, depending on the magnitude of the budget, may not care about the last thousand dollars. An amount of $433,876 might just as easily be reported for control purposes as $433.9, with the report headed "Dollar Amounts in Thousands," or "$000."

As a rule of thumb, most control reports do not need dollar amounts reported with more than three digits. In general, the amount of rounding depends on the size of the responsibility centers and what makes most sense for their managers.

Benefit/Cost

A reporting system, like anything else, should not cost more than it is worth. Unfortunately, there are great difficulties in applying this obvious statement to practical situations. For one thing, it is difficult to measure the cost of a given report. This is partly because most preparation costs are joint costs for several reports, and partly because the real cost includes not only the preparation cost but also the opportunity cost of the time that managers spend reading reports when they might be doing something else.

Because of the difficulty in assessing the benefit/cost ratio of reports, it is worthwhile to review an organization's management control reports periodically, and eliminate those that no longer are needed. Useless reports are not uncommon, and frequently exist because a problem area, that no longer exists, created a need for a report at some earlier time. A report structure, like a tree, is often healthier if it is pruned regularly.

USE OF CONTROL REPORTS

If control reports are to have any value, they must be used; that is, managers must treat them as an important resource. In this regard, an issue that frequently arises concerns the value of a comparison between expected and actual performance after the performance already has taken place. Since the work has been completed, and the past cannot be changed, of what value is such a report? There are two answers to this question.

First, if managers know their performance is being measured and evaluated, there is some tendency to attempt to influence the results so as to obtain a good report. Assuming the reporting system is fair—i.e., it has been designed so that a good action (one that benefits the organization) on the part of the manager will be reflected accordingly on the control reports—a manager ordinarily will tend to act in ways that benefit both his or her responsibility center and the organization overall.

Second, although the past cannot be changed, analysis of it can be helpful. Among other things, such an analysis can help to identify ways that performance can be improved in the future. Specifically, a good set of control reports can help managers to take whatever corrective action appears to be appropriate. Clearly, an important aspect of this process is the involvement of the managers' superior, who can praise, constructively criticize, or otherwise suggest ways to improve performance.

Review and Identification

A good control report will highlight areas that could benefit from investigation. An investigation sometimes, although not always, may come about because of a significant negative variance between budgeted and actual performance. However, large unfavorable variances are not necessarily a reason for investigation, nor are large favorable variances a reason for complacency. Good managers will interpret the information on a control report in light of their knowledge about conditions in the responsibility center and their intuitive feel for what is right.

Example If a manager has learned from conversations and personal observation that, because of personnel shortages, there was a need for considerable overtime (and therefore payment of premium wage rates) in a particular responsibility center, there is little need to investigate the causes of a large wage rate variance. On the other hand, a large favorable price variance in purchasing for, say, medical supplies for a health center may indicate that low quality supplies were purchased, and problems may arise later on when the supplies are used.

Absence of Surprises. Some managers argue that an essential characteristic of a good management control system is that the reports contain no surprises. These managers expect their subordinates to inform them when significant events occur so that appropriate action can be taken immediately. When the control report subsequently arrives, the manager is not surprised by a particular variance since the factors leading up to it were known, and they are confident that corrective action is underway.

The Exception Principle. Problem identification is facilitated if the control system uses the exception principle. According to this principle, a good control report helps a manager to focus on those limited number of items that if "out of control" will have a negative impact on performance.

Obviously, no control system can make this sort of distinction perfectly. Sometimes, as mentioned above, a large positive variance can be as much of a red flag as a large, negative one. Sometimes a negligible variance masks underlying factors that a manager needs to address. As a result, the exception principle is tricky to apply in practice because it requires a definition of "out of control," which often is a matter of judgment. Nevertheless, a good set of control reports will at least attempt to highlight problem areas so as to save managers as much time as possible in the process of review and problem identification.

Engineered and Discretionary Costs. In reviewing a set of control reports, a manager must distinguish between engineered and discretionary costs. In general, managers are looking for engineered costs to be at or below the standard (consistent, of course, with quality and safety standards). Discretionary costs, on the other hand, are somewhat more complicated, since optimal performance frequently consists of spending the amount agreed upon in the budget. Spending too little may be as problematic as spending too much.

Example To reduce expenses, a manager in a research organization could easily skimp on maintenance or training. The manager of the information services department could turn down requests for special computer runs or new software development. Senior management could cancel an unfunded research project. All of these actions result in lower discretionary costs during the current budget year, but they may not be in the best long-run interest of the organization.

Limitation of the Standard. No standard is perfect. Sometimes, standards are derived in ways that are not methodologically sound. Even if a standard cost is carefully prepared, however, it may not be an accurate estimate of what costs should have been under the particular set of circumstances a manager faced during a given reporting period.

In short, managers should exercise caution in using variances as indicators of performance. A variance may come about because of a combination of causes, some of which were controllable, and some not. At best, a good variance analysis provides the starting point for evaluating performance and discovering the underlying causes of deviations from the budget. Therefore, in deciding what action to take, managers should use not only the control reports, but whatever information they have obtained through other channels, as well as their judgment regarding areas that need attention.

Investigation

Ordinarily, an investigation includes a conversation between a responsibility center manager and his or her superior. The superior typically probes to determine whether corrective action of some sort is needed. Frequently, it turns out that special circumstances gave rise to the variance; that is, the assumptions that underlay the budget did not hold. If these changes were not controllable by the subordinate, there is little that can be done. Certainly there is no cause to criticize the subordinate. This does not mean that no corrective action cannot be taken, however, but rather that corrective action may need to be taken at some level above the subordinate's.

It also is possible that the variance resulted from a random occurrence that is unlikely to be repeated, such as an equipment breakdown or a strike. In this case, about all that can be done is to accept the variance and assume that it will not recur.

Finally, it is possible that the variance came about from performance that needs to be modified. In this case, the superior needs to determine the underlying causes of the deviation from budget, and assist the subordinate to take corrective action to reverse the trend.

Action

Usually, if a meeting between a superior and a subordinate revolves around one or more specific variances, the result is a planned course of action. If a variance is negative, the two individuals may agree on the steps that must be taken to remedy the situation. If a favorable variance is the result of good performance, praise is appropriate.

In all respects, it is important for superiors to weigh the tradeoffs between current performance and the long-run interests of the organization. An inherent weakness of management control systems is that they tend to focus on short- rather than long-run performance. They measure current revenues and expenses, for example, rather than the effect current actions will have on the organization's future financial health, or the quality of its services. Thus, if too much emphasis is placed on financial results as they are depicted in the current management control reports, long-run performance may be affected.

SUMMARY

Performance reports, as distinct from information reports, typically address three types of performance: economic, programmatic, and management. Most of this chapter has focused on management performance, which is the subject of the management control reports.

Good control reports have three essential characteristics: (1) they are related to personal responsibility, which typically calls for several levels of detail; (2) they compare actual performance to a standard, usually the budget; and (3) they focus on significant information, which frequently includes key indicators (many of which are non-financial in nature). By focusing on key indicators, managers may see a problem developing, and can take action to avert it before it becomes serious.

Good control reports also must satisfy certain technical criteria. They must (1) cover a period of time that facilitates management action; (2) be timely enough to allow management's actions to have an effect; (3) clarify important relationships, which frequently requires using graphs and narrative explanations, and rounding numbers; (4) consist of an integrated package in which the reports of lower-level responsibility centers are consistent with and easily relatable to the reports for higher-level responsibility centers; and (5) be worth more than they cost.

A good set of control reports functions as a feedback mechanism that guides managers in identifying and investigating areas for possible action. To do this, the reports should function on the exception principle, which can help managers to focus their attention on a few areas where investigation, and perhaps action, is required. In so doing, managers need to bear in mind that a standard, no matter how carefully prepared, may not be an accurate depiction of what the costs or revenues should have been under actual circumstances. Therefore, variances should be used with caution—they are a means to guide a manager's investigation and subsequent action, but not necessarily a reason for criticism.

Suggested Cases for Classroom Use with this Chapter

See the Appendix at the end of the book for a more complete description of each case and ordering information.

Franklin Health Associates (B)	Computing variances and designing a report to present them
United Medical Center	Assessing reports with variance computations already made
Burinam Health Services Division	Assessing the reports needed for a manager in a ministry of health in a developing country
University Daycare Center	Calculating a flexible budget and preparing reports with some tricky variances
Water Authority Daycare Center	Calculating a flexible budget and preparing reports with some tricky variances

Chapter 13

Program Evaluation

Chapters 11 and 12 described the regular, recurring process of monitoring the current activities of an organization. This chapter describes a process—called *program evaluation*—that is used to analyze and assess the effectiveness of an organization's programs. The objective is to recommend whether a program should be expanded, contracted, redirected, or discontinued.

The program evaluation process described in this chapter differs from the monitoring processes described in Chapters 11 and 12 in several respects. It usually: (1) is made at irregular intervals, perhaps every five years or so, rather than on a monthly or quarterly basis; (2) is much more thorough and time-consuming than routine performance monitoring; (3) is conducted by an outside individual or team, or by a headquarters' staff unit, rather than by an operating manager; and (4) uses different techniques than routine performance monitoring.

A program evaluation asks whether the goals of a program are appropriate, and whether the program is attaining them in the most effective and efficient way possible.

Example A program evaluation of a job training program would attempt to determine whether the program's graduates have acquired the desired skills, whether the benefits exceed the costs, and perhaps whether society needs persons with these skills.

As this example suggests, a program evaluation can be somewhat vague in nature. The vagueness starts with the objectives of the program and continues through each step in the process. For this reason, program evaluators usually prepare a careful plan and obtain the assent of the parties to this plan before undertaking the evaluation.

In addition, because of this vagueness, a program evaluator must be knowledgeable about the type of program being evaluated. An expert in education, for example, is not likely to make a sound assessment of a healthcare program. Moreover, at least one member of the evaluation team should be an expert in statistical and experimental methods if the evaluation method involves them.

RATIONALE FOR PROGRAM EVALUATION

Programs tend to go on forever unless they are subject to periodic, hardheaded reexamination.[1] Consequently, there is a need to ascertain whether the benefits of each program continue to exceed their cost and/or whether there are ways to improve their effectiveness. Although opportunities for improvement exist in every organization, there is a general feeling that these opportunities are especially significant in nonprofit organizations, primarily because the semiautomatic measure of effectiveness and efficiency provided by the bottom line on a business income statement does not exist in nonprofit organizations.

Evaluations of some type have been going on ever since there have been programs. It has been said that a moderately large metropolitan hospital is periodically evaluated by 100 or more agencies, ranging from fire inspection to the Joint Commission (on Accreditation), without whose certificate the hospital cannot continue to operate. The concern in this chapter is not with evaluation of specific

---

1 For a discussion of this issue, see Larry B. Hill, "Is American Bureaucracy an Immobilized Gulliver or a Regenerative Phoenix?" *Administration and Society*, November 1995.

aspects of an organization, however, but rather with the broad assessment of a single program, particularly one whose continued existence is optional.

The Impetus for Program Evaluation

The legislative or other governing body that initially authorized and funded a program ordinarily wants to find out how well it is working, generally as a basis for continuing, changing, or ending it. The public and the media also are interested in certain programs, particularly those that they believe to be ineffective. Users or potential users of a program, such as prospective students of a university's MBA program, or physicians considering the referral of patients to a hospital's substance-abuse program, want information about the program's quality. Donors or other fund providers to arts organizations, charities, museums, and the like, want to know how well the funds were spent.

The federal government funds (and often carries out) many thousands of programs. Legislation requiring regular review of these programs was first enacted in the early 1970s when the federal government delegated to the states the task of providing many social services, and required, as a condition of funding these programs, that a formal means of evaluating them be established. At about the same time, there was widespread interest in sunset legislation-laws that provided for the automatic discontinuance of a program unless it was evaluated every six to eight years and found to be effective. The majority of states now have such sunset laws.

An evaluation of a government-funded program usually is conducted under the direction of a committee of the legislature. At the federal level, evaluations are performed by the United States Government Accountability Office (GAO). The GAO is the largest and most sophisticated evaluation organization in the country. Its professional staff includes economists, social scientists, accountants, public policy analysts, attorneys, and computer experts, as well as specialists in fields ranging from foreign policy to health care. It conducts hundreds of evaluations every year.[2]

Many more evaluations are conducted annually at state levels, and also within some government agencies or departments, such as the Centers for Disease Control. Professional journals, such as *Evaluation Quarterly, Evaluation and Program Planning,* and the *American Journal of Evaluation* are now well established, along with a professional organization, the American Evaluation Association. Indeed, according to Eleanor Chelimsky, who, at one time, was the Assistant Comptroller General for Program Evaluation and Methodology of the U.S. General Accounting Office (the former name for the U.S. Government Accountability Office):

> Today, program evaluations are a familiar adjunct of congressional policy-making; they now figure notably in program reauthorizations, legislative decisions and markups, oversight, and an informed public debate. One PEMD [Program Evaluation and Methodology Division] evaluation caused working mothers leaving AFDC to receive Medicaid health insurance for their children over longer periods; another set of studies held up production of the inadequately tested Bigeye bomb; another evaluation led to doubled funding for the high-quality Runaway and Homeless Youth program, whose appropriations the relevant executive agency had proposed halving; another (on employee stock ownership plans) was responsible for a reduction of nearly $2 billion in tax expenditures; still another—showing that an increase in the drinking age from 18 to 21 unambiguously reduces traffic fatalities—spurred legislation to this effect in 16 states, resulting in the estimated saving of 1,000 young lives.[3]

---

[2] To learn more, go to http://www.gao.gov/about/index.html

[3] Eleanor Chelimsky, "Expanding GAO's Capabilities in Program Evaluation," *The GAO Journal,* Winter/Spring 1990.

PROBLEMS IN PROGRAM EVALUATION

A program evaluation seeks to answer several broad, fundamental questions: Is the program being carried out according to the intent of those who authorized it? If not, why not? What would have happened if there had been no program? Answering these questions is an extraordinarily difficult task. Among the more important problems are these:

- Objectives are often difficult to define
- Results are often difficult to measure
- The relationship between cause and effect is often obscure
- The effort required to make a valid judgment may cost more than it is worth
- Appropriate follow-up action may not be forthcoming

These problems are discussed below.

Problems in Defining Objectives

In general, those who initially approved a program had in mind one or more objectives that they hoped the program would accomplish. In a program enacted by legislation, these objectives are supposed to be stated in the authorizing act. The fact is, however, that various supporters of a program may differ in their ideas about the program's objectives. Additionally, the stated objectives may be worded ambiguously to accommodate various points of view. Moreover, these objectives—either stated or unstated—may be numerous and possibly contradictory.

Example Some people viewed the purpose of the Comprehensive Employment and Training Act (CETA) as primarily to remove people from the unemployment rolls, others as a way of training unskilled persons so that they would qualify for better jobs, others as a device for channeling federal funds to reduce the tax burden of hard-pressed municipalities, others as a way of providing welfare payments, and still others as a device for reducing crime by taking youths off the street. Most of the program's advocates had more than one of these objectives in mind, but they differed as to the relative importance of each.

For some programs the objectives may be murky. Scholars have made many attempts to define the objectives of a liberal arts college in a way that permits evaluation, but with no success. A charitable organization may start out with a well-defined objective, such as providing a shelter for homeless people, but the objective may change over the years into providing other types of support. Sometimes this happens without an explicit decision by the governing body.

The evaluators must make every attempt to discern the real objectives and the relative importance of each. If they begin with the wrong objectives, the whole evaluation may be discredited on the grounds that it is based on a false premise.

Problems with Results Measures

Chapter 10 discussed problems in measuring a program's output and the limitations of various output measures. For many programs, there are no valid techniques for measuring what actually happened as a consequence of undertaking the program. In educational programs, for example, there are no reliable ways to measure how much additional education a given program produced, except in the case of certain basic skills such as reading and arithmetic. Therefore, a comparison of some new educational effort, such as computer-assisted instruction, team teaching, or programmed learning, is unlikely to reveal any significant difference between those who learned in the new way and those who learned by conventional methods. Indeed, it is said, with considerable truth, that the best way to kill an educational experiment is to evaluate it. One can be almost certain in advance that the measurable results will not show a significant improvement.

Example The U.S. GAO reported that despite increased attention to removing the barriers that prevented the full involvement of persons with disabilities in work and other activities, the Department of Education had not evaluated the effectiveness of its $1.8 billion-per-year program of vocational rehabilitation. The GAO's evaluation showed only modest gains in earned income, in contrast to the dramatic short-term employment effects often cited by the program.[4]

Problems with Cause-and-Effect Relationships

If the results of a program are favorable, there is a tendency to conclude that the program's efforts caused this result, but this conclusion may be erroneous. In education, reference is often made to the *Coleman Effect,* a term derived from a report by James S. Coleman and his colleagues, which gave an impressive body of evidence to support the conclusion that no important quantifiable correlation exists between the cost of education and its quality, and specifically between student learning and such variables as class size, teachers' salaries and/or experience, age of plant, or type of plant. The effects of these variables were swamped by the influence of the student's family environment.[5]

Although there is considerable disagreement with Coleman's conclusions, most people concur that it is very difficult to devise experiments that demonstrate quantitatively that one teaching tool or technique is more effective than another. However, even if the evaluation team recognizes that extraneous variables may have an effect, their importance in explaining program results may not be measurable.

Example The U.S. GAO compiled information on the effectiveness of three federal agencies whose programs provided economic development assistance: the Appalachian Regional Commission (ARC), the Department of Commerce's Economic Development Administration (EDA), and the Tennessee Valley Authority (TVA). The GAO was unable to find any study that established a strong causal linkage between a positive economic effect and an agency's economic development assistance. In the case of the ARC, for example, it was impossible to say with certainty whether Appalachia's economy grew because of the ARC or whether much of the measured growth was caused by the rising price of coal.[6]

A similarly difficult problem is that of measuring the *impact* of a program as contrasted with its output. For example, the Clean Air Act limits the amount of pollutants that industrial plants may release into the air, and the results of the Environmental Protection Agency's programs can be assessed by measuring the pollutants in the atmosphere. However, if the objective of these limitations is to reduce to tolerable limits the amount of acid rain that is damaging forests and water supplies, it

[4] United States General Accounting Office, *Program Evaluation Issues* (Washington, D.C., December 1992).

[5] James S. Coleman et al., *Equality of Educational Opportunity,* OE-38001, Washington, DC, U.S. Department of HEW, 1966.

[6] Judy A. England-Joseph, *Economic Development-Limited Information Exists on the Impact of Assistance Provided by Three Agencies,* Washington, D.C., U.S. General Accounting Office, April, 1996.

is much more difficult to determine whether this objective has been achieved. In particular, the impact of such programs may not be measurable for many years after the presumed corrective action has occurred.

Example The Head Start Program, which was begun in the 1960s, was based on the assumption that a brief intervention in the formative years could raise children's IQs. This was considered important, since IQ correlates with school achievement, persistence, motivation, social skills, and self confidence. A 1969 report on Head Start performed by the Westinghouse Learning Corporation revealed that the IQ gains by children in preschool programs dissipated by the time they reached the third grade. Many years later, the Head Start Program still existed, not because it raised IQs, but because it enhanced school readiness, improved health services for young children, educated parents about community services, and got some parents involved in their children's education. In addition, it produced several important side effects, including employment for many low-income people.[7]

Problems with the Scope and Cost of the Analysis

As is the case with any activity, the results of an evaluation should be worth more than the cost of obtaining them. Analyses range in complexity, cost, and time required; and they can vary from a simple observation to an elaborate experiment involving thousands of people and lasting several years. Before an evaluation is undertaken, the agency that authorizes it should give considerable thought to the likelihood of obtaining useful results within the available time and cost constraints.

Example In a statement before the House Education and Work Force Committee on the subject of Federal Compensatory Education Programs, Professor Maris A. Vinovskis of the University of Michigan concluded that while there have been some useful national assessments of the overall impact of Head Start and Title I, usually these evaluations have not even attempted to ascertain in a rigorous and systemic manner which components of their programs have been successful. He gave four major reasons for this: (1) the limited funds available for educational research and development, (2) the misallocation of research and development funds to small, short-term projects that often had limited scientific validity and little practical usefulness, (3) constraints established by the Department of Education on the ability of its agencies to design and monitor high-quality research and development, and (4) the relatively low priority that had been assigned over the years by educators and policy makers to the design and rigorous testing of educational interventions to find out which were most effective with at-risk populations in different settings.[8]

Problems in Obtaining Action

Some groups that evaluate programs view the evaluation as a challenging research effort and lose interest when the research has been completed. They do not plan for, nor care about, using the results as a basis for action. In other cases, the evaluation effort is undertaken by a program's manager to prove that the program is beneficial; if the evaluation comes to a contrary conclusion, it is buried.

---

[7] Constance Holden, "Head Start Enters Adulthood," *Science* 247, no. 22 (March 23, 1990), pp. 1400-1402. For more recent information on Head Start, go to: http://www.acf.hhs.gov/programs/ohs/

[8] Maris A. Vinovskis, "Prepared Statement Before the House Education and Work Force Committee," *Federal News Service,* July 31, 1997.

Furthermore, the conclusion that a program is worthwhile is a necessary but not sufficient reason for continuing it. In a world of finite resources, worthwhile programs must compete with other programs that may be even more worthwhile. The legislative body or other group that decides how best to use limited resources has a more complicated task than does the team that evaluates a single program—it must decide which of many worthwhile programs should continue to be supported and at what level.

Example A survey of 91 human service agencies in the Dallas Metropolitan area, found that although 96 percent of the agencies indicated that they planned to use the results of an evaluation to make improvements in a program's operations, only 16 percent indicated that they planned to use the results to shift funding *toward* successful programs. No respondents planned to shift funding *away from* an unsuccessful program. Most planned to use the results to advocate for increased funding.[9]

TYPES OF PROGRAM EVALUATIONS

Before a full-scale evaluation is undertaken, the evaluators ordinarily make a preliminary analysis to settle on the type(s) of evaluation to be used, and work out a plan for the evaluation effort. This section lists the principal types of evaluations and briefly describes the advantages and limitations of each. A more thorough description of different types of evaluation can be found on the GAO's Website.[10]

Subjective Evaluations

The majority of program evaluations are subjective; that is, they are characterized by judgments arrived at by personal observations by an individual or a small team. The validity of such evaluations depends heavily on the expertise of those involved. Judgments also are influenced by the situations that the evaluators happen to observe. They may be unduly impressed by what might appear to be either excellent or poor results in particular cases.

Because support for the conclusions from such an evaluation is based on unsubstantiated evidence, decision makers may be unconvinced. For this reason, the evaluators may develop statistical or other data as a means for adding credence to their opinion.

In some situations, the evaluation is subjective simply because a more elaborate approach is not warranted. If a team visits a vocational education school and observes that only half the students regularly attend class and that those who do attend are taught by incompetent teachers using ineffective methods, there is little need to collect data on the effectiveness of the school.

Peer Review Evaluations

Colleges, universities, and hospitals are regularly evaluated by accrediting organizations. The evaluation is conducted by a team of peers, who work at similar organizations. The team is guided in part by specified minimum standards (e.g., for a college, the number of books in the library, the proportion of faculty with advanced degrees) and, in part, by observation and discussion. This is a relatively inexpensive approach. A favorable conclusion means that the institution meets certain minimum requirements, but there is no attempt to rank the institution on a scale of excellence.

---

[9] Richard Hoefer, "Accountability in Action? Program Evaluation in Nonprofit Human Service Agencies," *Nonprofit Management and Leadership*, Winter 2000.

[10] www.gao.gov/about/index.html

Case Study Evaluations

In a case study, the evaluation team identifies a few situations that it believes to be typical and examines each in depth. Although statistically valid conclusions cannot be based on such an approach, the results may be informative. This approach is often used as a preliminary step in an evaluation, since it it gives the evaluators a feel for the situation. Based on what they uncover, the evaluators may decide not to proceed further. If they decide to proceed, the case studies can help them select the appropriate research design.

Statistical Evaluations

An evaluation may be based, at least in part, on data about the program that have been collected routinely, or on data that have been collected for another purpose but can be recast to provide information relevant to the evaluation. There are four possible approaches, each of which has merit. The one or ones chosen will depend to a great extent upon the kinds of data available and the needs of the agency sponsoring the evaluation.

1. Compare Current Results with Performance Data Gathered Some Time Prior to the Initiation of the Program. Assuming there are no other significant intervening variables, this approach allows the sponsoring agency to determine if the program has had some impact over a baseline situation.

Example After two sociology professors published the results of a rigorous study, concluding that exposure to the Drug Abuse Resistance Education (DARE) Program did not produce any long-term effects on adolescent drug use rates, DARE officials continued to claim that an earlier study showed that kids who went through the program accepted drugs less often than kids who had not gone through the program. The earlier study did not ring true to many researchers, however, because it had no pretest. In other words, students were only surveyed after graduating from DARE. Without measuring drug use before DARE, it was difficult to know if the students' behavior had changed.[11]

2. Compare Current Results with Historical Trends. This approach allows the sponsoring agency to observe how well the program is performing over time.

Example If a job training program placed 25 percent of its graduates during its first year, 30 percent during its second year, 40 percent during its third year, and 50 percent during its fourth year, there is a good indication that the program is improving. Clearly, however, the evaluators would need to look for other factors, such as a change in the program's selection criteria.

3. Compare Current Results of the Program with the Results of Similar Programs. Using this approach assumes that a sufficiently similar program can be found, and that the available data will be comparable to those for the program being evaluated.

Example A federally funded program to increase the quantity of low- or moderate-income housing in one city can be compared with a similar program in another city. If the two cities are reasonably comparable in terms of the difficulty of constructing new housing, the comparative results should allow the sponsoring agency to determine which is the more successful.

---

[11] Stephen Glass, "Don't You D.A.R.E.: An Anti-Drug Program Strong-Arms Its Critics," *The New Republic*, March 3, 1997.

4. Compare Current Results with the Results that were Anticipated When the Program was Initiated. The validity of this comparison obviously depends on the soundness of the original estimates of results.

Example A program to provide literacy training projected that 3,000 people a year would become literate as a result of its training activities. This number can be compared with the actual number. If the actual is less than anticipated, the program's manager can be asked to explain why. The results can be used to set an objective for the subsequent year, or to estimate the output of similar programs in other locales.

Problems with Statistical Evaluations. Many problems are encountered in statistical evaluations. For example, it may be difficult to: (1) define the measures to be used, (2) assure that data from different data bases are comparable, (3) determine that the data are reliable, (4) allow for extraneous factors, and (5) decide whether trends or comparisons are significant.

Evaluators need to determine in advance whether these problems are sufficiently manageable to make the results of the statistical analysis worth the considerable cost that may be involved in gathering and analyzing the data.

Sample Survey Evaluations

A survey of a sample of the target group (i.e., the individuals the program is intended to benefit) or of others who may be knowledgeable about the program may provide highly useful information. The survey may be either in the form of a written questionnaire or an interview. The latter technique is much more expensive, but permits more probing than is possible with a questionnaire. Occasionally, some combination of the two may be feasible. To assure valid results, evaluators must word survey questions so that respondents' answers are unambiguous. They must also take care to select a sample so that the responses approximate those that would be given if the whole population were surveyed, and they must take steps to avoid biases in administering the survey. Sampling theory is a complex topic, and, unless proper techniques are used, the results are likely to be questionable.

Field Experiments

In evaluating the efficacy of a new drug or a new medical or surgical procedure, medical researchers have a well-developed protocol. Two groups of subjects (animals or humans) are created: an experimental group and a control group. Individual subjects are assigned to one of these groups either randomly or in such a way that the factors that may affect the outcome of the experiment (e.g., age, sex, weight, health) are similar for each group. The experimental treatment is administered to the experimental group. (In a double-blind experiment, the experimenter does not know to which group an individual subject belongs nor whether the chemical administered is the test drug or a placebo.)

Factors other than the experimental treatment that might affect the outcome are either insulated from the experiment or observed and allowed for when results are analyzed. After results are measured, statistical tests are applied to determine if there is a significant difference (associated with the treatment) between the experimental group and the control group. If there is, and the results are beneficial, the treatment is judged to be successful.

Much of the literature on program evaluation discusses ways to apply analogous experimental methods to social programs. Success with these *social experiments* has been minimal, however. In many cases, the analysis did not show a significant difference between the two groups. Moreover, in most cases with a statistically significant difference, critics maintained that the experiment did not satisfactorily answer the key question: Were the results caused by the treatments or something else?

Example Some of the largest social experiments have been related to income maintenance. Most experiments were designed to find out whether cash payments to low-income people (the negative income tax) were preferable to welfare programs. The first effort was in New Jersey, begun in the late 1960s, followed by experiments in six other states, with those in Denver and Seattle being the most comprehensive. These experiments involved 8,500 families at a cost of $112 million. Despite the abundance of data, there was no consensus on whether a negative income tax worked better than a traditional welfare program.

Problems with Social Experiments. Social experiments carry special problems that do not exist for medical experiments. For one thing, most people do not like to be subjects. Laboratory rats can't object, and medical patients usually do not object because they see possible benefits to themselves. But subjects of social experiments often see no benefit in being treated like lab rats. In particular, control groups usually know from the beginning that they are not going to benefit, and their dropout rates consequently are high. This compromises the statistical database. Furthermore, to measure results, the experimenters usually must ask personal questions of the subjects, and despite pledges of confidentiality, these are often regarded as an invasion of privacy. It therefore is difficult to determine whether the answers are honest. Even if they are honest, many answers depend on memory, which can be fallible.

Although field experiments have these limitations and although they are expensive, they can, if properly done, provide extremely good information on the results attributable to *the program;* that is, the relationship between cause and effect.

STEPS IN MAKING AN EVALUATION

There is no clear consensus among evaluators on the exact procedure an evaluation team should follow. Nevertheless, the following eight steps seem to take place in most evaluations.

1. Decide on the Purpose of the Evaluation

Is it to appraise the success of the program as a basis for deciding its future? Is it to provide recommendations for improvement? Is it political in nature with, perhaps, a hidden agenda to eliminate the program?

Presumably, the body that requested the evaluation should answer these questions. As a practical matter, however, the charge from that body may be vague, and the evaluation team may need to identify the most useful questions to address. These questions must be carefully thought out and specifically stated; otherwise, the evaluation may proceed down the wrong road, with a waste of time and resources. The questions are subject to change, of course, if the team finds that the answers cannot feasibly be obtained, or if it uncovers better questions.

2. Examine the Available Information

In some cases, information that is already available, either within the organization or from other sources, may provide an adequate basis for evaluation. Alternatively, such information may provide a useful starting point, but more data will be needed.

3. Select a Tentative Strategy

Which of the various types of evaluations is the most appropriate, considering the limitations of time, expertise, and money available for the study? What research design best suits the approach selected? If the evaluation involves the use of quantitative data, a model should be constructed that shows how these data are to be analyzed. The model should be examined for feasibility and relevance to the evaluation questions. The team also should develop a project plan, showing personnel assigned to the project, their tasks, and a timetable.

The evaluation strategy should be presented to the body requesting the study, and that body should sign off on the strategy. If the resources initially available are inadequate, or if the completion time originally expected is too short, additional money or time should be negotiated with the requesting body. If additional money or time is not forthcoming, the scope of the project should be narrowed or, in the extreme case, discontinued. All of these decisions need to be agreed upon by the requesting body before the evaluation commences.

4. Test the Proposed Design

Some sort of testing usually is desirable, and tests should be made before major resources are committed to the project. A pretest of questionnaires or interview questions, collection and tabulation of a sample of statistical data, or (if the evaluation is to be conducted at many sites) a complete test at one site may lead to a revision of the evaluation design. The result frequently can lead to significant cost savings.

5. Carry Out the Evaluation

In carrying out the evaluation, the evaluation team should pay attention to both the agreed-upon timetable and the allowed budget. Exceeding either without prior approval, and usually without sound justification, can cost the team some of its credibility, even though the loss of credibility may have nothing to do with the quality of the evaluation itself. Indeed, as Eleanor Chelimsky noted:

> Evaluators working for the legislative branch much be extremely concerned about the timing of the final product and how it dovetails with congressional policy cycles and plans for use. We've learned that what is most important sometimes is not having the best design, but having an adequate design that will bring the findings in at the time they were promised.[12]

6. Draft a Tentative Report

In undertaking this task, the evaluation team should think about the best way to "sell" the results to those who are expected to act on them. Does the audience prefer a written report? An oral presentation? Both? Are there different audiences with different desires? Initial responses to the tentative report may, for example, lead the team to issue a "watered down" formal report with wide circulation, and an oral report that discuses the more sensitive findings.

7. Obtain Informal Feedback

Within the organization conducting the evaluation, someone other than a member of the evaluation team should carefully examine the draft report. This quality control check should range from

[12] Eleanor Chelimsky, "What Have We Learned about the Politics of Program Evaluation?" *Evaluation Practice* 8, No. 1, February 1987.

such details as arithmetic accuracy and proper grammar to the broad question of whether the conclusions are substantiated by the underlying data.

The draft also should be submitted for comment to the agency being evaluated. The resulting comments may lead to changes in the report. Even if the evaluating team disagrees with these comments, they should note them in the report, together with the reasons for disagreement. It is much better to find out about errors or disagreements before the final report is submitted than to have it discredited after it has been formally submitted.

Example A study of 140 nonprofit organizations that had completed at least one program evaluation in the prior three years found that stakeholder involvement in an evaluation increased the likelihood that the evaluation results would be used, and that the evaluation processes would continue. In particular, in those evaluations with high stakeholder involvement, 58 percent led to changes in resource allocation within the organization, compared to only 22 percent of the evaluations with low stakeholder involvement.[13]

8. Sell the Findings

By the time it has completed its final report, the evaluation team frequently has considerably more knowledge about the program than perhaps even the program's managers. When this is the case, there is a tendency to present too much information without appropriate summaries. The team must think about a reader with limited time, and present the information in such a way that it is both succinct and compelling. Key points should be highlighted in an executive summary, and most of the statistical computations should be relegated to appendices, no matter how elegant the team thinks they are. As Chelimsky put it:

> We have learned that telling all is tantamount to telling nothing. The important thing is to answer the policy question as clearly and simply as possible, to emphasize a few critical and striking numbers, and to do all that in such a way as to highlight those findings that give rise to policy action.[14]

In sum, the program evaluation process is as much political as it is scientific. The recommendations will not be implemented unless those who have the authority to do so are convinced that implementation is desirable. The decision maker is often influenced by factors other than those set forth in the report, no matter how scientifically sound the analysis may be. The evaluation team should attempt to identify and deal with these political factors, even though they may be regarded as illogical.

SUMMARY

In conducting a program evaluation, the evaluation team needs to: (1) obtain a mandate from a body that is prepared to act on its recommendations, (2) identify objectives, (3) determine a strategy for conducting the evaluation, (4) carry out the evaluation, and (5) make and sell recommendations.

A program evaluation's objectives frequently are difficult to define. Moreover, output often is tricky to measure, and cause-and-effect relationships can be elusive. The choice of the most appropriate type of program evaluation frequently is highly debatable. Subjective, peer review, case study, statistical, sample survey, and field experiments are all candidates, and it frequently is not clear

[13] Allison H. Fine, Colette E. Thayer, and Anne I. Coghlan, "Program Evaluation Practice in the Nonprofit Sector," *Nonprofit Management and Leadership,* Spring 2000.

[14] Chelimsky, "What Have We Learned?"

which will provide the best information for assessing whether a program should continue as is, be modified, or be discontinued.

Despite these difficulties, governing bodies need to undertake program evaluations. In a world of scarce resources, they provide essential information for the difficult task of making tradeoffs among a variety of possible programmatic endeavors. Indeed, without undertaking program evaluations, a governing body cannot be certain that it is using resources in the most appropriate way to achieve the organization's goals.

Suggested Cases for Classroom Use with this Chapter

See the Appendix at the end of the book for a more complete description of each case and ordering information.

Bureau of Child Welfare	Evaluating the performance of an adoption program
Timilty Middle School	Evaluating the performance of a new program in a public school
Housing Finance Agency	Evaluating a project selection system in a state housing assistance agency

Chapter 14

Management Control Systems in Context

Chapter 1 positioned management control between strategy formulation and task control, and briefly discussed the structure and process of a management control system. Later chapters fleshed out the details of both structure and process. Those chapters were preceded with a discussion of several of the building blocks needed to understand the accounting information that lies at the heart of a management control system: the nature of nonprofit organizations (Chapter 2), full and differential cost accounting (Chapters 3 and 4), and pricing (Chapter 5).

The value of these building blocks, and the concepts of structure and process that form the basis of a management control system is in their applicability to real-world situations and problems. The ultimate goal is to develop a management control system that facilitates improved organizational performance. Doing so requires assessing how the management control system fits into its broader organizational context.

The chapter begins with a brief summary of the key characteristics of a good management control system. The management control system is then positioned as part of seven interrelated organizational activities, a perspective that is consistent with much of the shift in many organizations toward cross-functional management. Finally, the chapter looks at some of the issues involved in implementing a new management control system, or making changes to an existing one.

CHARACTERISTICS OF A GOOD MANAGEMENT CONTROL SYSTEM

Most of the chapters had in mind an organization of at least moderate size, one with, say, a hundred or more employees and several million dollars of annual operating expenses. Smaller organizations can operate successfully with a less sophisticated management control system than the chapters have described, although they no doubt will find some of the basic concepts helpful. More generally, an organization that is performing in accordance with the concepts and approaches of good management control displays several characteristics:

1. It has a strong governing body. Some members of this body spend considerable time examining program and budget proposals before they are submitted to the full board. Members of the governing body also analyze formal reports on performance, as well as communications from clients and others on how well the organization is performing.

2. In performing its functions, the governing body is careful not to infringe on the prerogatives of management. The governing body ensures that the chief executive has full authority to execute policies, and it supports his or her decisions. The governing body also ensures that the CEO's compensation is appropriate.

3. Line managers have the authority to use their judgment in running their responsibility centers and in accomplishing results. However, they may be required to operate within somewhat closer budgetary and other constraints than is customary in for-profit organizations.

4. The management control system contains two principal account classifications, one structured in terms of programs and the other in terms of organizational responsibility. This frequently results in a matrix-like structure.

5. The management control accounts are part of the organization's overall accounting system, which, when appropriate, includes a full-cost accounting system. However, while the full-cost accounting system and the management control system draw information from the same sources, the two are not co-mingled.

6. Except in unusual circumstances, such as with public goods, the organization charges its clients for the services they receive, sometimes through third-party payers. In this way, the organization generates a monetary measure of the quantity of its outputs, and motivates its managers to be concerned about the cost and quality of the services they provide.

7. The pricing unit is as specific as feasible so as to provide a good measure of the quantity of services rendered, and a good basis for decisions on the allocation of resources.

8. Senior management's selection of responsibility centers is based on its assessment of the resources a manager controls. The goal is to hold each manager responsible only for those resources over which he or she exerts a reasonable amount of control. In abiding by this *fairness* criterion, senior management does not allow the accounting staff to allocate overhead costs into responsibility centers.

9. Profit centers are used whenever feasible, even though the idea of a profit center in a nonprofit organization seems contradictory. However, in all instances, senior management is seeking *goal congruence,* such that a decision that is "good" for a given responsibility center also is good for the organization overall. This may mean using other types of responsibility centers for some activities.

10. Where feasible, support centers that provide intra-company services are set up as (zero-surplus) profit centers. Under these circumstances, senior management makes sure that there is an appropriate set of transfer prices to facilitate the control process. The transfer prices, along with shared agreements (for service departments without an output unit), are used in lieu of allocations for determining a responsibility center's costs.

11. Unless the organization continues with the same activities year after year, it has a programming phase in the management control process that is used for generating ideas for new programs, analyzing these ideas, reaching decisions on them, and incorporating new programs into ongoing operations. Capital investment decisions also are made in this phase.

12. Programming decisions include a financial analysis that considers the time value of money, with future cash flows discounted using a rate that is based in part on the organization's weighted cost of capital. This analysis does not dominate the decision-making process, but is an important ingredient therein.

13. Budgeting is viewed as an important part of the management control process. The annual operating budget is derived from the approved programs, and responsibility for carrying out the programs is assigned to individual responsibility centers.

14. The measurement and reporting phase of the management control process helps to assure that actual spending is kept within budgetary limits. At the same time, the organization has a procedure for revising the budget, or allowing deviations from it, should circumstances require doing so.

15. Senior management devotes considerable attention to developing satisfactory output measures. It recognizes that although many output measures are of limited validity, they are better than nothing. As a result, there is a constant search for new, more valid measures.

16. Despite the fact that many people, especially professionals, dislike the idea of accountability, which is associated with the measurement of outputs, senior management proceeds with such measurements. All levels of management, including senior management, are involved in performance monitoring.

17. Responsibility center managers receive reports containing both financial and non-financial information. These reports are (a) made available in a timely way, (b) designed so as to highlight significant information, and (c) structured so that managers can "drill down" to increasingly detailed information. Where appropriate, variances between planned and actual spending are isolated by cause: volume, mix, rate, and efficiency.

18. Senior management holds meetings with immediate subordinates to discuss results, variances, and planned corrective actions. It expects these individuals to hold similar meetings with their subordinates, and so on down the line.

19. Senior management undertakes systematic evaluations of the effectiveness of the organization's programs. These evaluations are conducted at infrequent intervals, perhaps every five years or so for each program, but each program receives such an evaluation periodically.

20. Senior management assures itself that the management control system fits with, supports, and is supported by a variety of other organizational activities, including its own management style, the organization's culture, and a motivation system that rewards responsibility managers for good performance.

THE MANAGEMENT CONTROL CONTEXT

Given these criteria, the management control system can now be put into a somewhat expanded context. Specifically, the management control system, by necessity, is part of—and is influenced by—an organization's broader set of managerial activities.[1] One such activity is strategy formulation, since an organization's strategy influences its financial and programmatic goals. Other activities include conflict management, since it occasionally is the case that organizational (as distinct from interpersonal) conflict can arise concerning matters such as the best programs to adopt, the best approach to client management, or the best programmatic objectives to pursue. Still other activities relate to the ways that an organization's senior management uses compensation packages and other mechanisms to motivate its employees in an attempt to encourage good performance.

[1] For a discussion of these activities in the context of integrated delivery systems in health care, see David W. Young and Sheila McCarthy, *Managing Integrated Delivery Systems: A Framework for Action*, Chicago, Health Administration Press, 1999. For a more general discussion, see David W. Young, "The Six Levers for Managing Organizational Culture," *Business Horizons*, September-October 2000.

Beyond these activities, senior management uses recruitment, training, and severance in an effort to maintain the organization's culture. It also gives considerable thought to how authority and influence flow within the organization, and to how that affects the way that clients are "managed."

Overall, there is a need to attain a *fit* among these various activities. To attain this fit, senior management must address a wide variety of matters. It must, for example, assure itself that the programming phase of the management control process process is leading to programs that support the full range of services needed to achieve the organization's strategy.

Other managerial activities tend to flow from these two, but, in many instances, also can influence them. For example, some of the decisions that senior management makes in strategy formulation will depend on the kind of information it receives from the reporting phase of the management control process. Similarly, depending on its design, the motivation process can encourage professionals to propose new programmatic endeavors, or, more generally, to act in the best interest of the organization overall. Or it can discourage them from doing so.

These activities are shown in Exhibit 14-1. As the exhibit indicates, beyond assuring that the organization has a well-designed management control process, senior management needs to make sure that there is:

Exhibit 14-1 Cross-Functional Processes in an Organization

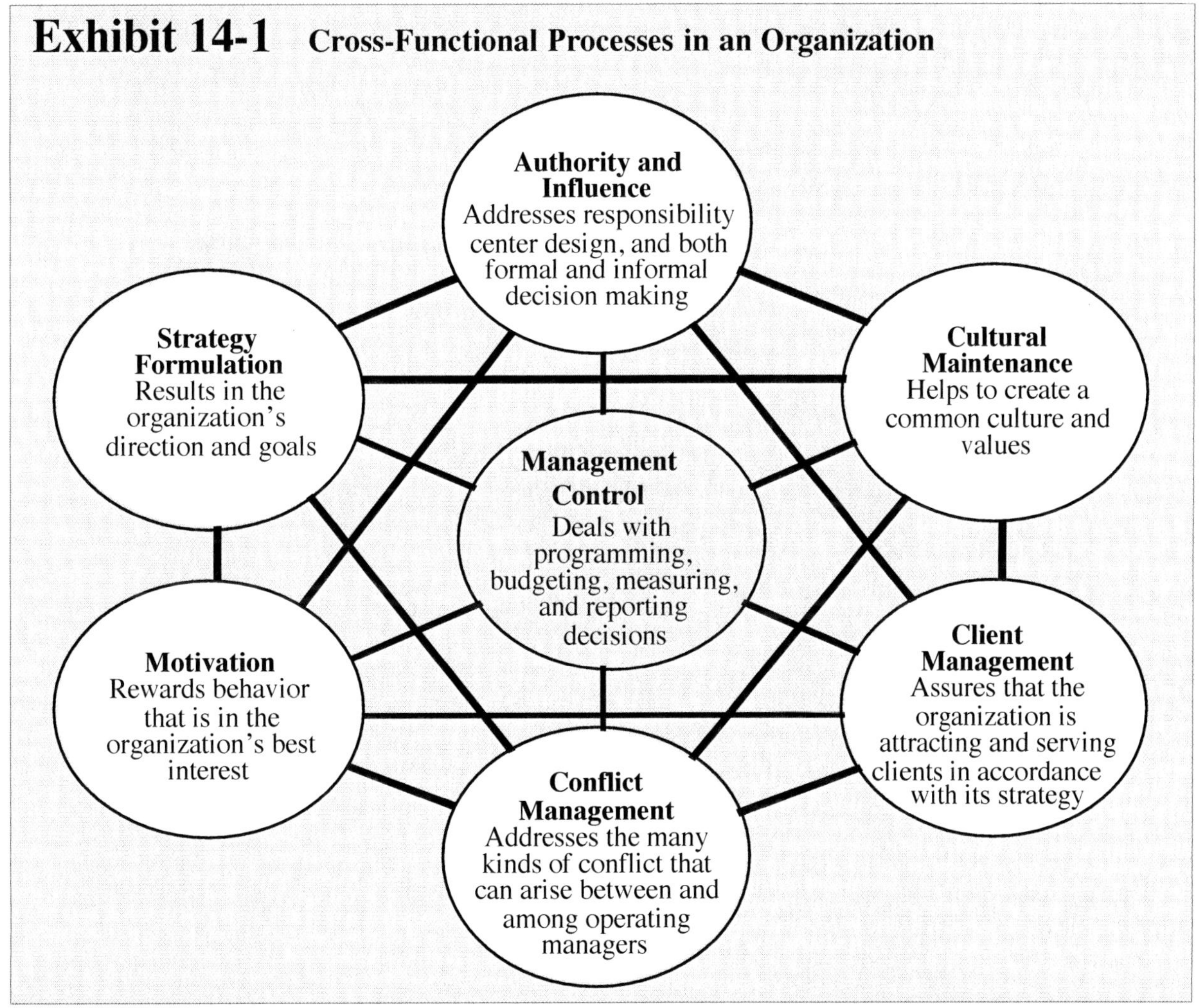

- A strategy-formulation process that addresses the organization's environment, including regulatory and competitive forces, and decides on an appropriate set of goals

- An *authority and influence* process that has an appropriate network of responsibility centers, and that fosters collaborative decision making when necessary

- A *motivation* process that provides appropriate signals, and rewards people for behavior that is in the best interest of the organization

- A set of *conflict management* processes that addresses the many kinds of conflict that can arise in the course of attempting to achieve the organization's strategy

- A *client management* process that helps the organization to attract clients who are consistent with its strategy, and that provides them with appropriate services at appropriate times, in appropriate sites

- A set of *cultural maintenance* processes that helps to create common values in the organization

A list of the kinds of questions senior management needs to ask itself in conjunction with each of these cross-functional processes is contained in Exhibit 14-2. As this list indicates, senior management must continually take action on several related fronts: planning, organizational, and informational. Not only is each of these fronts important in an of itself, but, perhaps most importantly, as the lines in Exhibit 14-1 indicate, the various activities must reinforce one another. As such, they collectively help to assure the organization that its clients are receiving appropriate, timely, coordinated, and cost-effective services.

MANAGING THE CHANGE EFFORT

It's one thing to want it, but quite another to get it. If senior management wishes to make some changes to its management control system, how does it go about the change effort? Harvard's John Kotter, a leading authority on change management, has described eight steps that a manager or management team must take:[2]

1. Establish a Sense of Urgency
2. Form a Powerful Guiding Coalition
3. Create a Vision
4. Communicate the Vision
5. Empower Others to Act on the Vision
6. Plan and Create Short-term Wins
7. Consolidate Improvements and Produce Still More Change
8. Institutionalize New Approaches

Although these steps may seem evident and intuitive, Kotter's article discussing them contains the ominous subtitle "why transformation efforts fail," suggesting that change efforts are frequently unsuccessful. His article is required reading for any senior management team considering modifications to its management control system.

[2] John P. Kotter, "Leading Change: Why Transformation Efforts Fail," *Harvard Business Review*, March-April 1995

Exhibit 14-2 Questions Concerning Cross-Functional Processes

Strategy-Formulation

- What sorts of analyses are carried out, by whom?
- Are decisions well-formulated, with significant senior management involvement, or are they a result of individual groups acting independently?
- Does the organization's strategy reflect its values?

Client Management

- How do clients flow through the organization?
  - > How does a client initially come into contact with the organization?
  - > What decisions are made about how that person will (or will not) be served? Who makes those decisions?
  - > What decisions are made concerning a client leaving the organization? By whom?
- Are services delivered at the best site and by the most appropriate person?

Cultural Maintenance

- What are the principal values of the organization? That is, what does the organization see as its relatively unchanging decision-making criteria?
- How do the organization's programs fit with these values?
- How are the values reinforced and maintained through activities such as recruitment, training, promotion, and severance?

Authority and Influence

- What kinds of responsibility centers have been overlaid on the organizational structure? Do they satisfy the fairness and goal congruence criteria?
- Does the flow of authority and influence foster collaborative decision-making where appropriate?
- What formal mechanisms exist for professionals to influence decision-making in the organization? Do these help the organization move toward its strategy?

Motivation

- How are people rewarded for doing good work?
- Is there is an incentive compensation system? If so, is it part of the budget formulation process?
- How deeply into the organization does the incentive-compensation system extend? Does it cover the professional staff, for example?

Conflict Management

- Where are the potential sources of conflict within the organization? Who typically is involved?
- How is the conflict managed? That is, what sorts of formal mechanisms are in place (such as permanent or ad hoc committees) to manage the conflict?

Management Control

Programming

- How and by whom are decisions made to begin new programs? To change or drop existing programs?
- Does the process lead to programs that reflect and reinforce the organization's strategy?
- How are requests for new capital addressed?
- Do accepted requests move the organization toward its strategy?

Budgeting

- Who participates in formulating the organization's annual budget? What is the timetable?
- How does the budget relate to programs?
- What kinds of "drivers" are used to build the budget?
- If there is cross-subsidization among programs and responsibility centers, how are subsidies determined?
- Have transfer prices been established? If so, are responsibility center managers allowed to purchase from outside the system if they think a transfer price is too high? If not, how is the problem addressed?

Financial Measuring and Reporting

- How is information reported to key managers? How are people held responsible for the resources they control?
- Are fixed and variable costs measured for different mixes of clients in different programs, and are the relevant variances computed?
- Do the resulting reports help managers to assess their financial performance against the budget?

Programmatic Measuring and Reporting

- How are programmatic results measured (such as for quality, client satisfaction, etc.)?
- How do programmatic and financial measurement and reporting relate to each other?
- What are the organization's key success factors, and how are these incorporated into the reports? Are these results linked to the motivation process?

Resistance to the Change Effort

It is highly likely that some (perhaps many) people in an organization will resist senior management's efforts to implement a change in the management control system. How senior management deals with these individuals is partially style-based. For example, some CEOs will embrace the resistors and attempt to work with them, while others will attempt to ride roughshod over them. Regardless of its style, however, the senior management team must recognize that line managers' and others' commitment to the change effort can be classified into one of four categories identified by BU's Professor Martin Charns, and shown in Exhibit 14-3.

Exhibit 14-3 **Categories of Commitment to Change**

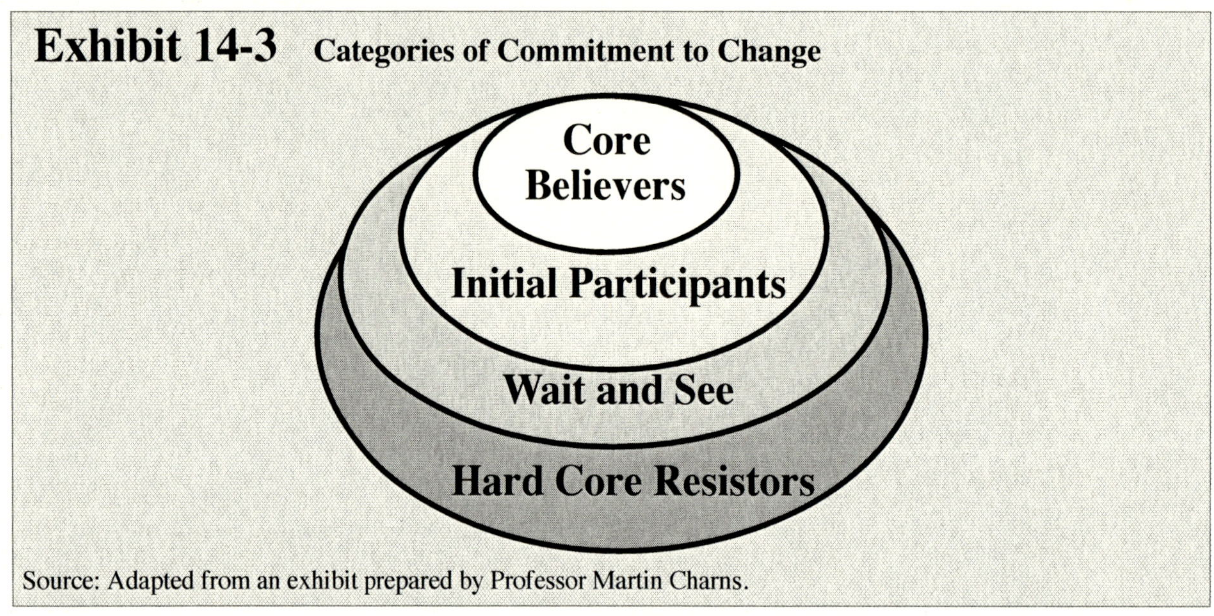

Source: Adapted from an exhibit prepared by Professor Martin Charns.

Generally, when senior management selects a "powerful guiding coalition" (Step 2 of Kotter's 8 Steps), it chooses the coalition's membership from among the core believers and perhaps the initial participants. That is, the change effort begins with the inner circle and moves to the outer one.

There is no clear consensus on how to deal with hard core resistors. On the one hand, they may fear that the changes, once implemented, will have a negative impact on their careers, income, power in the organization, or something else of a personal nature. Under those circumstances, any attempt to involve them may be futile, and the best course of action might be to encourage them to seek employment elsewhere.

On the other hand, hard core resistors may be resisting the change for good reasons, and their views might be important, perhaps even constructive, contributions to the change effort. When this appears to be the case, a manager may try to bring them into the effort early on, either as members of task forces focused on specific issues, or as sources of concern.

There are basically six methods to deal with resistance to change, each of which is appropriate under certain circumstances, and each of which has some advantages and disadvantages.[3] Sometimes, education and communication can be effective in making people aware of why the change is underway. At other times, asking people to participate or become involved in the effort can be useful. Sometimes, people simply need to be supported in "embracing" the change, and sometimes negotiation may be needed to secure their support. At the extreme, there may need to be a much

[3] For a discussion of these methods, and their advantages and disadvantages, see John P. Kotter and Leonard A. Schlesinger, "Choosing Strategies for Change," *Harvard Business Review,* March-April, 1979

heavier hand, that might involve co-optation or coercion. In general, senior management must attempt to fit the method to the need in light of its advantages and disadvantages.

Short-Term Wins

Again, it is easy to say that senior management should plan and create some short-term wins (Kotter's Step 6), but it is much more difficult to determine in advance what those might be. To assist with this selection effort, BU's Charns has developed the 2x2 matrix shown in Exhibit 14-4.

Exhibit 14-4 **Impact Versus Difficulty**

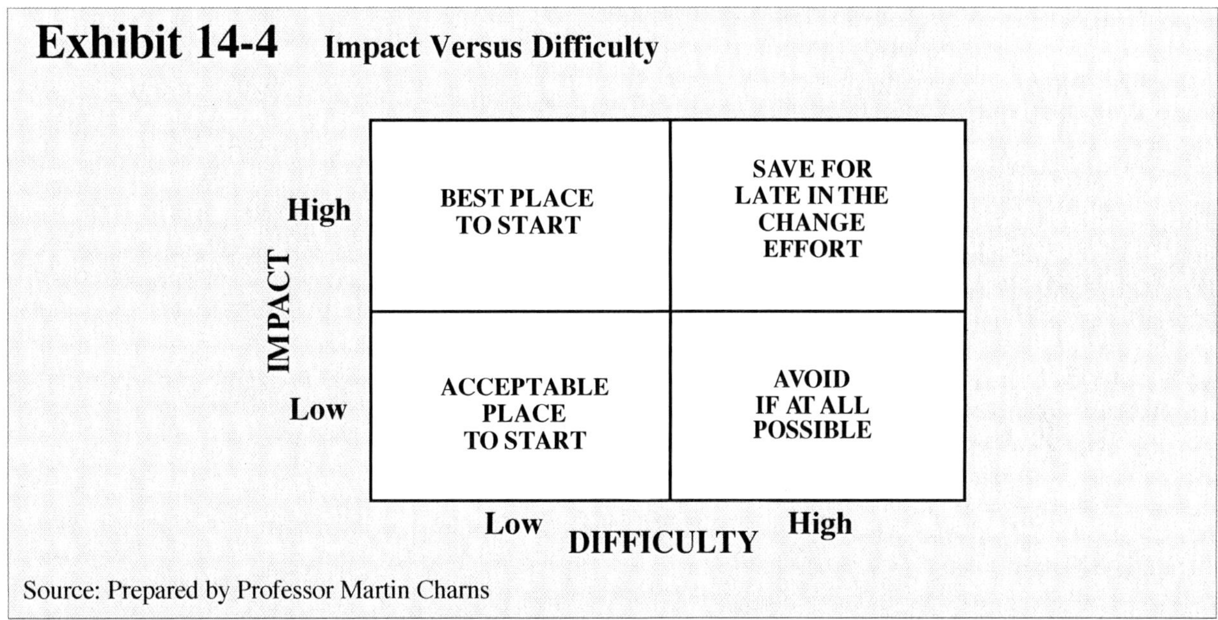

Source: Prepared by Professor Martin Charns

Clearly, to create some short-term wins, senior management should start in the column of low difficulty, preferably in the high-impact quadrant. For example, in one successful change effort, senior management chose as its first task the goal of making sure that all the clocks in the facility were running on time, an easy and seemingly low impact item. Yet, because unreliable clocks were a source of considerable employee dissatisfaction, the task actually had a high impact on morale. Subsequent tasks were much easier as a result.

Despite how obvious this seems, it is amazing how many change efforts begin in the lower right quadrant! In a school of management, for example, where a new dean was attempting to strengthen the school's reputation in the business and academic communities, one of his first efforts was to attempt to substitute 10-year contracts for tenure. Well over a year of time, scores of meetings, two faculty votes, and many reams of paper were consumed in the effort, while the school continued to languish in the bottom 50 of the top 100 schools given ratings.

Consolidating and Moving Forward

In most organizations, the hard-core resistors cannot be left out of the effort indefinitely. Sooner or later they either must be brought into the effort or encouraged to leave the organization. Assuming the former is to take place, one or more of the methods discussed above can be used by senior management as it consolidates and moves forward (Step 7 in the Kotter Model).

SUMMARY

Designing and implementing a new management control system is a complex undertaking. Revising an existing system may be even more difficult, as people have grown accustomed to it, including all of its flaws. In both instances, there is bound to be resistance, due in part to the uncertainty about the consequences of the change, and in part to the fact that, other than a salary increase, few people like change.

The design or redesign effort is further complicated by the fact that the management control system does not exist in isolation—it is part of a much larger organizational whole, and senior management needs to see it in that context. The management control system cannot be divorced from strategy formulation, for example, as it both helps to provide relevant information to senior management as it thinks about strategy, and must, at the same time, be designed so that it reports on movement toward the strategy. Nor can it be divorced from the organization's motivation processes; if people are not rewarded for good performance, they likely will have little incentive to worry about accomplishing the organization's goals. The management control process is similarly linked to authority, conflict and culture, and ultimately to an organization's success (or lack thereof) in attracting and serving clients in accordance with its strategy.

This is true in all organizations, but especially so in nonprofit organizations, where adequate financial performance is a necessary, but not sufficient condition for success. Indeed, the purpose of a nonprofit is to achieve its goals within the constraints imposed on it by funders and other resource providers. Thus, a well-functioning management control system—linked to the organization's several other cross-functional process—is an essential ingredient in meeting client and other constituent needs as effectively and efficiently as possible.

Suggested Cases for Classroom Use with this Chapter

See the Appendix at the end of the book for a more complete description of each case and ordering information.

Laverne Hospital: The Orthopedic Center	Assessing the issues involved in managing operating rooms
Apogee Health Care	Assessing the issues involved in a new incentive system for a physician group practice
Omega Research Institute	Assessing the MCS implications of a change in strategy
Penn State-Geisinger Health System	Dealing with some tricky design issues in a merged organization
Easter Seal Foundation of New Hampshire & Vermont	Assessing the issues involved in a transition in leadership
Fletcher Allen Health Care	Determining why an integrated care system is having difficulties in implementing a new management control system

APPENDIX. Potential Cases by Chapter and Supplemental Materials on Financial Accounting and Management

		Course		Sector Focus				
		Beg	Adv	Govt	Hlth	Edu	Other	Brief Description
CASES BY CHAPTER		**Part I. Introduction**						
Chapter 1	***The Management Control Function***							
	Hamilton Hospital	*	*		*			Distinguishing among strategic planning, management control and task control in a physician group practice
	Boulder Public Schools	*	*			*		Assessing structure and process issues in a highly bureaucratic context, and the appropriate balance between centralization and decentralization in a management control system.
	South Kingston Health Center		*		*			Determining a viable strategy in a neighborhood health center
	Commonwealth Business School	*	*			*		Attaining a balance between departments and programs
Chapter 2	***Characteristics of Nonprofit Organizations***							
	Granville Symphony Orchestra	*	*				*	Uncovering some misleading results in the financial reports in an annual report
	New England Trust	*	*	*	*		*	Using ratios and some minimal other information to figure out which nonprofit is which.
	South Central Mental Health Association	*	*		*			Resolving some organizational issues in a mental health agency
	Office of Community Development		*	*				Resolving some organizational issues in a anti-poverty agency
	Usuluteca (A)		*		*			Formulating a national drug policy in a developing country
	Usuluteca (B)		*		*			Assessing further issues and tradeoffs in the national drug policy
CASES BY CHAPTER		**Part II. Management Control Principles**						
Chapter 3	***Full Cost Accounting***							
	Croswell University Hospital	*			*			Determining the cost of different procedures in a department of Ob-Gyn
	Jefferson High School	*				*		Determining the cost of different students in a high school
	Harbor City Community Center	*	*				*	Preparing a stepdown analysis to compute full cost
	Lincoln Dietary Department		*		*			Assessing the potential for ABC in a dietary department
	Owen Hospital (A)	*			*			Making a simple full cost computation
	Owen Hospital (B)	*			*			Using ABC to improve upon the simple cost computation
	Neighborhood Servings		*				*	Using ABC for costing meals to the homebound
	South Bristol Hospital		*		*			Determining DRG "winners" and "losers" in a hospital
Chapter 4	***Measurement and Use of Differential Costs***							
	Huntington Hospital	*			*			Developing a cost equation for a dietary department
	Carlsbad Home Care	*			*			Conducting a breakeven analysis for a home health agency
	Springfield Handyman Program	*					*	Performing a tricky breakeven analysis
	Abbington Youth Center	*					*	Computing breakeven with multiple programs
	Abbington Health Center	*			*			Computing breakeven with multiple departments
	Energy Associates (C)	*					*	Computing breakeven with multiple products, and budgeting.
	Opportunities Unlimited, Inc.	*					*	Computing breakeven with multiple programs for job retraining
	Jiao Tong Hospital	*			*			Breakeven with multiple departments in a Chinese hospital
	Museo de la Casa	*					*	Analyzing a keep/drop decision in a small museum
	Lowalos General Hospital	*			*			Doing a contribution analysis for two different DRGs
	Lakeside Hospital		*		*			Analyzing a keep/drop decision in a hospital
	Cittá di Forenna		*	*				Outsourcing risks and management in two Italian municipalities
	Town of Rovereto		*	*				Making an alternative choice decision concerning snow removal
Chapter 5	***Pricing Decisions***							
	Harlan Foundation	*					*	Analyzing breakeven for a camp, and computing the price for a seminar
	Town of Levinton		*	*				Pricing water and sewer services
	B.U.. Medical Center Hospital		*		*			Pricing DRGs in a competitive environment
	Central Valley Primary Care Associates	*			*			Devising a methodology to compute a sub-capitation rate
	Massachusetts Eye and Ear Infirmary		*		*			Pricing based on three different pricing unit
	Sonsonala (A)	*			*			Determining the appropriate markup for drugs for community pharmacies in a developing country
	Boise Park Health Care Foundation (B)		*		*			Deciding whether cash or accrual should be used to measure a request for a rate increase.
	The Meredith Center		*				*	Analyzing a tricky pricing problem in a center for the blind
	University of Miami Medical Center		*		*			Determining the cost of graduate medical education
	Atherton Medical Education Programs		*		*			Determining the cost of graduate medical education
CASES BY CHAPTER		**Part III. Management Control Systems**						
Chapter 6	***The Management Control Environment***							
	Franklin Health Associates (A)	*	*		*			Determining the link between strategy and programs, and analyzing responsibility centers in a small group practice
	Piedmont University	*	*			*		Considering the potential for profit centers in a university
	Southern Seattle University Health System ()A)		*		*			Assessing responsibility centers in a faculty practice plan
	Commonwealth University	*				*		Resolving a relatively simple transfer pricing situation
	Milan Sanitation Department	*	*	*				Using shadow prices to create a profit center in a municipality
	White Hills Children's Museum	*					*	Resolving a transfer pricing dispute
	National Youth Association		*				*	Resolving a transfer pricing dispute
	Converse Health System		*		*			Resolving a tricky transfer pricing problem in an integrated delivery system

APPENDIX. Potential Cases by Chapter and Supplemental Materials on Financial Accounting and Management

		Course		Sector Focus				
		Beg	Adv	Govt	Hlth	Edu	Other	Brief Description
Chapter 7	*Programming*							
	Yoland Research Institute	*					*	Assessing a capital investment decision when behavioral factors are involved
	Dovetown Parking Authority		*	*				Making a tricky present value computation, with an unusual twist
	Green Valley Medical Center		*		*			Including non-financial considerations in an investment decisions
	The Heartbreak of DRGs		*		*			Analyzing a tricky programming computation for treating psoriasis
	Stonehill Family Practice		*		*			Valuing a family practice for purposes of acquisition
	Disease Control Programs		*	*				Making programmatic tradeoffs that require valuing a life
Chapter 8	*Operations Budgeting*							
	Moray Junior High School	*				*		Making budget tradeoffs
	Los Reyes Hospital (A)	*			*			Building a budget using cost drivers
	Southern State University Health System		*		*			Assessing responsibility centers and a line item budget. Combinates Southern Seattle (A) and (B)
	Southern Seattle University Health System (B)		*		*			Building an activity-based budget in a faculty practice plan
	Urban Arts Institute (A)		*			*		Building a budget in a small college
	Urban Arts Institute (B)		*			*		Assessing additional budgetary issues in a small college
	La Salle Hospital (A)		*		*			Assessing the budgetary process for a department of pathology
	Centro Italiano Sviluppo		*		*			Creating "decision packages" in a ZBB system
	North Lake Medical Center		*		*			Building a budget using cost drivers
	Rush-Presbyterian-St. Luke's Medical Center		*		*			Dealing with some tricky issues in building a budget
	North Lincoln		*	*				Preparing a budget in a state government with a great deal of game playing going on
Chapter 9	*Control of Operations*							
	Hospital San Pedro	*			*			Creating a patient flow chart in a developing country
	WIC Program			*	*			Analyzing the flow of food vouchers and detecting fraud
	Cittá di Forenna		*	*				Assessing a municipality's outsourcing strategy for trash collection
	The Robert Wood Johnson Medical School		*		*			Assessing the role of an incentive system in controlling operations
	Haas School of Business	*	*			*		Considering some ethical issues associated with supplemental payments to faculty in a business school
Chapter 10	*Measurement of Output*							
	Charlottesville Fire Department		*	*				Evaluating non-financial measures of performance in a fire department
	Barrington High School	*				*		Creating a balanced scorecard for a public school
Chapter 11	*Reporting on Performance: Technical Aspects*							
	Huntington Beach	*		*				Creating a flexible budget and computing variances for a road project
	Clinique Nosral	*			*			Computing variances in a primary care clinic in Africa
	La Salle Hospital (B)	*			*			Computing variances in a department of pathology
	Pacific Park School	*				*		Creating a flexible budget and computing variances for a summer camp
	Spruce Street Shelter	*					*	Preparing a flexible budget and variance analysis
	Town of Bellington	*		*				Preparing a flexible budget for snow removal
	Los Reyes Hospital (B)	*	*		*			Preparing a flexible budget and variance analysis
	Bandon Medical Associates (B)		*		*			Preparing a flexible budget and variance analysis
Chapter 12	*Reporting on Performance: The Management Control Reports*							
	Franklin Health Associates (B)		*		*			Computing variances and designing a report to present them
	United Medical Center	*	*		*			Assessing a set of reports with variance computations already made
	Burinam Health Services Division		*		*			Assessing the reports needed for a manager in a ministry of health in a developing country
	University Daycare Center		*			*		Calculating a flexible budget and some tricky variances
	Water Authority Day Care Center		*				*	Calculating a flexible budget and some tricky variances
Chapter 13	*Evaluation*							
	Bureau of Child Welfare		*	*				Evaluating the performance of an adoption program
	Timilty Middle School	*	*			*		Evaluating the performance of a new program in a public school
	Housing Finance Agency		*	*				Evaluating a project selection system
Chapter 14	*Management Control Systems in Context*							
	Laverne Hospital: The Orthopedic Center		*		*			Assessing the issues involved in managing operating rooms
	Apogee Health Care		*		*			Assessing the issues involved in a new incentive system for a physician group practice
	Omega Research Institute		*				*	Assessing the MCS implications of a change in strategy
	Penn State-Geisinger Health System		*		*			Dealing with some tricky design issues in a merged organization
	Boston Health Care for the Homeless Program, Inc.		*		*			Dealing with some tricky management issues in measuring performance and providing health care to the homeless
	Easter Seal Foundation of NH and Vt.		*				*	Assessing the issues involved in a transition in leadership
	Fletcher Allen Health Care		*		*			Determining why an integrated care system is having difficulties

APPENDIX. Potential Cases by Chapter and Supplemental Materials on Financial Accounting and Management

		Course		Sector Focus				
		Beg	Adv	Govt	Hlth	Edu	Other	Brief Description
SUPPLEMENTAL MATERIALS ON FINANCIAL ACCOUNTING AND MANAGEMENT								
Topic:	***Basics of Financial Accounting***							
Note:	*Financial Accounting in Nonprofit Organizations*							
Cases:	Brookstone Ob-Gyn Associates (A)							Computing a simple set of financial statements
	Carson Housing Authority (A)	*					*	Doing some basic financial accounting for a housing authority
	Oceanside Nursing Home	*			*			Revising a set of incorrect financial statements
	Los Nachos Day Care Center	*					*	Preparing a relatively simple financial accounting situation
	The Opera Workshop	*					*	Basic financial accounting in a small arts organization
	Mangpu Central Hospital (A)	*			*			Preparing financial statements for a Chinese hospital
	National Association of Accountants	*					*	Revising a set of incorrect financial statements
	The Athenaeum School	*	*			*		Assessing the impact of SFAS 116 and 117 on a nonprofits financial statement
	Pi Kappa Phi, Inc.		*				*	Assessing some tricky financial accounting issues in a fraternity
	Merced College		*			*		Assessing a college's approach to spending policy for its endowment
	Boise Park Health Care Foundation (A)		*		*			Assessing some tricky financial accounting issues in an HMO
	City of Douglas		*	*				Revising a set of municipal financial statement to more closely reflect GAAP
Topic:	***Financial Analysis and Management***							
Notes:	*Note on Financial Management*							
	Note on Financial Surpluses in Nonprofit Organizations							
	Note on Ratio Analysis							
Cases:	Coolidge Corner Theatre Foundation	*	*				*	Computing the appropriate size of a surplus in a nonprofit arts organization
	Energy Associates (A)							Preparing a statement of cash flows
	Long-Term Care Division	*			*			Undertaking ratio analysis with a twist
	Gotham Meals on Wheels	*					*	Assessing the impact of growth on cash
	Brookstone Ob-Gyn Associates (B)	*	*		*			Assessing the impact of growth on cash
	Mangpu Central Hospital (B)	*			*			Assessing cash versus accrual for a Chinese hospital
	Menotomy Home Health Services	*	*		*			Determining why a profitable organization is running out of cash
	Sonsonala (B)	*			*			Determining the working capital needed for an essential drug program in a developing country
	Boise Park Health Care Foundation (B)		*		*			Question of whether cash or accrual should be used to measure a request for a rate increase.
	Westbrook Community Housing, Inc.		*				*	Assessing problems in some audited financial statements
	Van Buren Community Hospital		*		*			Analyzing the financial viability of a hospital
	Transitional Employment Enterprises, Inc.		*				*	Analyzing the causes of poor financial performance
	Caregroup, Inc.		*		*			Assessing the reasons why an organization is in financial difficulty
	Northridge		*	*			*	Computing the appropriate size of a surplus in a retirement community

GLOSSARY

Selected Terms and Concepts Related to Management Control in Nonprofit Organizations[1]

Absorption costing. A costing system that treats fixed manufacturing costs as a product cost and hence holds these costs in inventory until the product is sold. See variable costing and activity-based costing.

Activity-based costing (ABC). A costing system that uses multiple cost pools and cost drivers to attach manufacturing overhead to products. Considered to be more accurate than a method that uses a single absorption rate, or even several absorption rates if they are all related to the number of units produced. ABC is especially useful when there is product or volume diversity. See absorption costing, product diversity, volume diversity, facility-sustaining activities, product-sustaining activities, batch-related activities, and unit-level activities.

Allocated overhead. The fixed and variable overhead, usually pertaining to a central office or general administration, that is distributed to individual responsibility centers, departments, and programs according to pre-established formulas. Usually a basis of allocation is chosen such that each organizational unit receives its "fair share" of the overhead based on its use of the basis. For example, in a hospital the overhead cost of laundry usually is allocated on the basis of pounds processed, and housekeeping might be allocated on the basis of square feet.

Balanced Scorecard. A technique that measures both non-financial as well as financial performance. The typical non-financial measures are clustered into three categories: customer satisfaction, internal process improvement, and employee growth and development.

Batch-related activities. One of four general categories of activities that influence the use of manufacturing overhead. These are activities that are performed each time a batch of products is manufactured, such as setups for machines, material movements, and inspections. See product-sustaining activities, facility-sustaining activities, unit-level activities, and activity-based costing.

Budget driver. An activity or measure that can be managed and that can cause an organization's net income to increase or decrease.

Business Risk. Refers to the predictability or certainty of an organization's cash flows. Organizations that have a high degree of *uncertainty* about their cash flows have a relatively high business risk. Organizations with a high degree of *certainty* about their cash flows have a relatively low business risk. Compare to *financial risk.*

---

[1] This Glossary contains some terms not used in the text that nevertheless may be useful to readers

Cash-Related Cycles. The operating cycle and financing cycles. The former is concerned with day-to-day operations; the latter with longer-term financing. They must be managed to be certain that the organization does not run out of cash.

Contribution. Usually the difference between revenue and variable costs but sometimes the difference between revenue and the sum of variable costs and direct fixed costs of, say, a department or a program. An example of the former is the contribution of a dialysis procedure to the dialysis unit's fixed costs. An example of the latter is the contribution of the dialysis unit to the organization's overhead costs.

Cost driver. An activity that can be directly linked to an increase or decrease in costs. Cost drivers are frequently relatively easy to identify but sometimes difficult to measure. Thinking in terms of cost drivers allows managers to shift their focus away from the traditional departmental structure of an organization and toward the activities that cause the existence of costs and, perhaps most important, toward the managerial actions that can influence and control costs.

Cross-Functional Processes. A set of seven process that must be coordinated for an organization to be successful: strategy formulation, authority and influence, motivation, conflict management, cultural maintenance, patient (or client) management, and management control.

Debt Structure. The mixture of short- and long-term liabilities on an organization's balance sheet. By matching the term of the debt to the life of the asset, a company's principal payments on the debt will be equal to the asset's depreciation, and, other things equal, its cash flows will be the same as its income before taxes on an accrual basis.

Differential cost. A cost that will change depending on a choice made by management. Differential costs are calculated for make-or-buy, keep-or-discontinue, special-price, and obsolete asset alternative choice decision making. They include the variable costs of any products involved and may include both step-function and fixed costs, depending on the circumstances. If a cost will be the same regardless of the alternative chosen (as depreciation will be, for example), it is not a differential cost.

Direct cost. A cost that can be attributed unambiguously to either a product or an organizational unit. If the former, it is classified as either direct material or direct labor. If the latter, it can be somewhat complicated. For example, depreciation of machines in a plant is a direct cost of the plant; however, it is generally considered an indirect cost of the products produced in the plant.

Direct labor. Labor that is unambiguously associated with a unit of finished product: for example, a worker on an assembly line or a lab technician working on a specific test. See indirect labor.

Direct material. Material that is unambiguously associated with a unit of finished product: for example, film for an X ray. See indirect material.

Discount rate. The interest rate used to compute the present value of a future stream of cash flows.

Discretionary expense center. A responsibility center whose manager's financial performance is measured in terms of the total expenses incurred by the center regardless of how much output the center produces. See standard expense center.

Dual aspect concept. The accounting concept that is represented by the fundamental accounting equation: Assets = Liabilities + equity. Assets are what an organization owns or has claim to, liabilities are funds owed to outsiders, and equity represents the combination of contributions from owners (or donors) and retained earnings.

Effectiveness. Accomplishing what the organization wants to do. The more of an organization's objectives a responsibility center accomplishes, the greater its effectiveness. See efficiency.

Efficiency. Accomplishing an something at a low cost. It can be measured by a ratio of outputs to inputs-that is, amount of output achieved per unit of input. Measures of efficiency do not consider whether the output was in support of the organization's objectives. See effectiveness.

Facility-sustaining activities. One of four general categories of activities that tend to influence the use of manufacturing overhead. Facility-sustaining activities are the highest-order activity and include work such as plant management, building repair and maintenance, security, and grounds maintenance. See product-sustaining activities, batch-related activities, and unit-level activities, and also activity-based costing.

Fairness. (in a responsibility accounting system) When a manager makes a good financial decision from the standpoint of achieving the goals of his or her responsibility center, the measurement and reporting system shows improved financial results. A lack of such fairness ordinarily means that the measurement system needs to be revised to distinguish between controllable and non-controllable items and that the manager's performance needs to be measured with regard to those items over which he or she exerts a reasonable amount of control.

Financial Risk. Synonymous with leverage are synonymous. Other things equal, the higher an organization's leverage, the higher its debt service obligation, and the greater the risk that it will be unable to meet this obligation, i.e., the greater its financial risk. Compare to *business risk*.

Financing Cycle. See Cash-Related Cycles

Fixed cost. A cost that remains unchanged over a wide range of volume. The classic example is rent. Fixed costs ordinarily have a relevant range, that is, a certain number of units or volume of activity over which they remain fixed. Rent, for example, would increase if an organization's volume of activity increased to such an extent that it needed to move into larger and more expensive facilities. See variable cost and step-function cost.

Flexible Budget. A technique that recalculates a budget based on the actual volume and mix of output. It is used as a first step in computing variances, and isolates the impact of volume and mix on a responsibility center, allowing the manager to isolate labor, and material variances. It is especially important for a standard expense center where the manager has limited or no ability to control volume and mix. See Standard expense center.

Goal congruence. Alignment between the goals of managers of individual responsibility centers and the goals of the organization as a whole. The term is borrowed from social psychology. Goal congruence is an important consideration in designing a management control system, and a lack of it ordinarily results in behavior on the part of responsibility center managers that is not in the best interests of the organization as a whole. It ordinarily means that some changes are needed in the nature of the organization's responsibility centers or its transfer pricing structure. See transfer price.

Gross present value. The value in today's terms of a future stream of cash flows. Because money has time value, cash flows received one or more years from today are not worth as much today as their dollar amount in the future. They are thus "discounted" using a discount rate.

Indirect labor. Labor that cannot be identified directly with a unit of finished product: for example, supervisors or maintenance people. The costs of indirect labor become part of manufacturing overhead. See direct labor and manufacturing overhead.

Indirect material. Material that cannot be identified directly with a unit of finished product: for example, solvents used to lubricate machines in a department. The costs of indirect material become part of manufacturing overhead. See direct material and manufacturing overhead.

Internal rate of return. The discount rate that will result in a net present value of zero. See Net present value.

Investment center. A responsibility center whose manager's financial performance is measured in terms of the total revenues minus the expenses of the center, computed as a percentage of the assets used by the center-that is, the center's return on assets. See profit center, standard expense center, revenue center, and discretionary expense center.

Leverage. Defined at Assets ÷ equity, is a measure of the amount of debt relative to equity on an organization's balance sheet. Allows an organization to own more assets than would be possible if it relied only on its own equity. In effect, the organization is using debt as a "lever" to expand its asset base. This, in turn, allows it to deliver more services or to produce more goods than otherwise would be possible, and therefore to earn more revenue.

Line manager. A person responsible for the day-to-day operations of an organizational program or responsibility center. This is a person whose judgments are incorporated into the organization's plans, who must see to it that those plans are implemented, and whose performance is measured by the responsibility accounting system. Line managers are sometimes called operating managers. See senior management and staff.

Manufacturing overhead. Costs other than direct material and direct labor. Includes indirect material, indirect labor, and other costs that are associated with the manufacturing effort but that are neither material or labor: for example, utilities, depreciation, and taxes. See variable manufacturing overhead, indirect labor, and indirect material.

Net present value. Gross present value less the amount of the investment needed to achieve it.

Operating Cycle. See Cash-Related Cycles

Operating managers. See line managers.

Payback period. The number of years needed to recover an investment. It is equal to the amount of the investment divided by the incremental annual cash flows resulting from the investment.

Period cost. A cost that is not assigned to a product. Period costs generally include marketing and general administration costs. They are expensed each accounting period, whether or not any products are actually sold. See product cost.

Product cost. A cost that is assigned to a product: for example, direct material, direct labor, and manufacturing overhead. These costs are assets and are held in a finished goods inventory until the products are sold, at which point they become part of cost of goods sold. See period cost.

Product diversity. The condition that exists when different products use overhead-related services in different proportions: for example, when one product requires considerably more inspection time than another. Product diversity is important only when the costs of the different activities are significantly different. See relative-cost factor, volume diversity, and activity-based costing.

Product-sustaining activities. One of four general categories of activities that tend to influence the use of manufacturing overhead. Product-sustaining activities are needed to ensure that products are produced according to specifications. They include process engineering, product specifications, engineering change notices, and product enhancements. See facility-sustaining activities, batch-related activities, and unit-level activities.

Profit center. A responsibility center whose manager's financial performance is measured in terms of the total revenues of the center minus its total expenses. See investment center, standard expense center, revenue center, and discretionary expense center.

Relative cost factor. A significant difference in the costs of the different activities related to the use of overhead. See product diversity, volume diversity, and activity-based costing.

Responsibility center. An organizational unit headed by a manager charged with achieving certain agreed-upon results. Usually the unit comprises a group of individuals who work together to accomplish one or more of the organization's objectives. The unit's manager has overall responsibility for its performance. From a responsibility accounting perspective, the number of people in the group is relatively unimportant. The key issue is determining how senior management will measure the group's financial performance. Senior management's goal is to design responsibility centers in such a way that individuals are responsible for those activities over which they exercise a reasonable amount of control. See investment center, profit center, standard expense center, revenue center, and discretionary expense center.

Revenue center. A responsibility center whose manager's financial performance is measured in terms of the amount of revenue earned by the center: for example, a development office in a university or a sales office in a company. See profit center, standard expense center, investment center, and discretionary expense center.

Revenue driver. An activity that can influence an organization's revenue. In most organizations, revenue drivers are price, volume, and mix. For example, in a company selling personal computers, operating revenue for each type of computer is the company's price for that type multiplied by the number sold of that type. Summing this revenue across all types of computer gives total revenue.

Senior management. Collectively, the individuals at the top of the organization's hierarchy. They are responsible for seeing that the organization accomplishes its objectives. They generally formulate the organization's overall strategic directions, sometimes with assistance from line management. See line manager and staff.

Staff. The individuals who collect, summarize, and present information that is useful in the responsibility accounting process. Although staff members may be numerous, they do not make significant decisions for the organization. See senior management and line manager.

Standard expense center. A responsibility center whose manager's financial performance is measured in terms of the expense incurred per unit of output but not in terms of the total expenses incurred by the center. For example, in a hospital the laundry department is budgeted for a certain level of fixed costs and a certain variable cost per pound washed. For each reporting period, the budget is flexed by multiplying the variable cost per pound by the actual number of pounds washed and then adding the fixed costs. The result is a performance budget, against which the manager's actual expenses are compared for the purpose of measuring his or her financial performance. Sometimes the unit of output is adjusted by type. In a laboratory in a hospital, for example, the budget is influenced by both the volume and the mix of tests performed. See discretionary expense center.

Statement of Cash Flows. One of the three basic financial statements (the other two are the income statement and the balance sheet). It explains, in an organized way, the changes in cash that took place between two balance sheets. It classifies the changes into operating, financing and investing activities.

Step-function cost. A cost that is essentially fixed but for which the relevant range is relatively small. A good example of a step-function cost is supervision. When the number of employees increases to a certain level, a new supervisor must be hired. Supervision salaries thus increase or decrease in a step-like fashion rather than smoothly. See fixed cost and variable cost.

Structure (of the responsibility accounting system). An organization's network of responsibility centers. See responsibility center.

Sunk cost. A cost that is associated with a past decision. It either has been committed (like the rent payments on a lease, for example) or has actually been spent (like the depreciation on a machine, for example). Sunk costs are not relevant for alternative choice decision making as they will remain the same regardless of the option that is selected.

Transfer price. The price at which an intra-organizational transaction takes place. For example, in a hospital, the Department of Surgery purchases lab tests from the Clinical Pathology Department. Because both are departments of the same hospital, their transaction is intra-organizational. The transfer price for such transactions can range from market price to variable cost. Transfer prices frequently are important elements of an organization's responsibility accounting system.

Unit-level activities. One of four general categories of activities that tend to influence the use of manufacturing overhead. Unit-level activities are tied directly to the number of units produced: for example, they might include utility usage and machine hours. Unit-level activities also include direct manufacturing costs; the three other activity categories include only manufacturing overhead. See product-sustaining activities, facility-sustaining activities, batch-related activities, and activity-based costing.

Variable manufacturing overhead. Costs that are not directly associated with any given product but that vary with the activity level in the department where the product is produced. For example, a copy center's toner usage would not normally be considered part of the direct material cost of a particular copying job but would increase with the volume of copying in the department. See manufacturing overhead, indirect labor, and indirect material.

Variable cost. A cost that increases in an almost linear fashion with volume. For example, as the number of visits in an outpatient department increases, the cost of medical supplies increases at about the same rate. See fixed cost and step-function cost.

Variance. A difference between an actual revenue or expense item and the budgeted one. Variances are usually due to one or more of the following: volume, mix, use, and rate.

Volume diversity. The condition that exists when products are manufactured in batches of different sizes. See product diversity, relative cost factor, and activity-based costing.

Weighted cost of capital. The weighted interest rate of all the sources used to finance an organization's assets. It uses the interest rate paid for each liability (such as a mortgage or bond) as well as the rate assigned to the organization's equity.

Subject Index

D

E

F

ABOUT THE AUTHOR
www.davidyoung.org

David W. Young is Professor of Management, *Emeritus,* at Boston University's School of Management, where he was nominated four times for BU's prestigious Metcalf Award for teaching excellence. During each of his last two years at BU, he was voted best professor by Cohort C of the School's MBA students. While at BU, he taught courses in for-profit, nonprofit, and healthcare contexts. During each of his last four years, he also taught the capstone course on competition, innovation, and strategy in the school's MBA Program.

Professor Young has been a core faculty member for the past 35 years at Harvard University's School of Public Health, where he teaches in the Programs for Chiefs of Clinical Service and Leadership Development in Health Care. He has been the lead faculty member for the past 10 years in the AAIM [Alliance for Academic Internal Medicine] Executive Leadership Program for physicians in departments of internal medicine.

Professor Young has been a visiting professor in the International MBA Programs at the University of Bologna and the University of Pisa. He also has taught at the China Europe International Business School in Shanghai, the University of Reykjavik, the Clinical Effectiveness Program in Buenos Aires, IESE and ESADE Business Schools in Barcelona, and the Summer School on Public Management at the Forlí campus of the University of Bologna. He has lectured throughout Europe, Latin America, Asia, and the Middle East on a variety of management and strategy topics.

In the late 1990s, Professor Young was appointed by the Governor of Massachusetts to serve a 3-year term as commissioner and chair of the Massachusetts Hospital Payment System Advisory Commission. This was a 7-member body charged with monitoring access, quality, and fair-market standards as the state shifted to a more market-oriented healthcare system. In 2006, he received the Special Recognition Award from the Association of Professors of Medicine, an award presented annually to a nonmember who has contributed the most to helping the association meet its mission of providing leadership and direction to academic internal medicine.

In addition to his teaching and service awards, Professor Young has received several research awards, including "best article of the year" from both the American College of Healthcare Executives and (twice) the Healthcare Financial Management Association.

In 2008, Professor Young published the 2nd edition of *Management Accounting for Health Care Organizations,* and in 2012, he published the 9th edition of *Management Control in Nonprofit Organizations* (earlier editions of this text were translated into Italian and Japanese). Also, in 2012, he co-authored (with Emanuele Padovani) *Managing Local Governments: Designing Management Control Systems that Deliver Value,* a book that focuses on improving the way local governments are managed.

Professor Young earned a B.A. from Occidental College, an M.A. in economics from the University of California at Los Angeles, and a doctorate from the Harvard Business School. He was selected to be a Milton Fund Fellow at Harvard Medical School, and was elected to Beta Gamma Sigma (the national honor society for accredited business programs).